S0-BVP-327

HO-PING: Food for Everyone

by Medard Gabel
with the
World Game Laboratory

Anchor Books
Anchor Press/Doubleday
Garden City, New York
1979

HO-PING: Food for Everyone

Strategies to Eliminate Hunger on Spaceship Earth

by Medard Gabel with the World Game Laboratory

Library of Congress Cataloging in Publication Data

Gabel, Medard
    Ho-ping: Food for Everyone
    "A companion volume to Energy, Earth and Everyone."
    "An outgrowth of World Games Workshops."
    Includes bibliographical references.
    1. Food supply. 2. Agriculture. 3. Food.
I. World Game Workshop, University of Pennsylvania, 1975.
II. Title. III. Title: Food for Everyone.
HD9000.6.G3   338.1'9
ISBN: 0-385-14082-7
Library of Congress Catalog Card Number 77-92214

The Anchor Books edition is the first publication of *Ho-ping: Food for Everyone.*

Anchor Books edition: 1979

Designed by Hal Hershey and Brenton Beck, Fifth Street Design Associates, Berkeley, with Jane Bernard, Jake Belsky, Barbara Silverman, Bob Cooney and Carol Egenolf.
Illustrations by Pedro Gonzalez.
Typesetting by Polycarp Press, San Francisco.

Illustrations on page 155 from *The Book of the New Alchemists,* edited by Nancy Jack Todd. Copyright © 1977 by The New Alchemy Institute, Inc. Reprinted by permission of the publisher, Elsevier-Dutton.

Illustrations on pages 216 and 217 from *Radical Agriculture,* edited by Richard Merrill, courtesy of The New Alchemy Institute, Inc. Copyright © 1976. Reprinted by permission of Harper Colophon.

Photos on pages 24 and 34 used courtesy of the United Nations Photo Library.

Photo of the earth courtesy of the National Aeronautics and Space Administration. Other cover photos courtesy of the United Nations Photo Library, Brenton Beck, Medard Gabel and Michael Wiese.

for M. C.

The author gratefully acknowledges the following for their various contributions to this document:

Buckminster Fuller, whose work in design science formulated the perspective for this document, and whose insights and friendship nourished and made possible this book; Howard Brown and his group of researchers, especially Carol Harlow, at Yale University, who did preliminary work on the global food problem in preparation for the 1975 World Game Workshop; the participants of the 1975 World Game Workshop, who executed the initial framework of this document: Diana Acevedo, Doreen Anderson, John Attaway, Larry Barrows, Jeffrey Christiansen, Robert Hayes, David Heeney, Ken Holder, Jim Knighton, Jon MacPhail, Joe Pattin, Jim Phelan, Sr. Anne Pierotti, Judy Simon, Alexandra Snyder, Mary Styron, and Dane Winberg; especially Jeff Christiansen, Jon MacPhail, David Heeney, and Judy Simon, who stayed on and helped with this document after the workshop was over; the participants of the 1974 World Game Workshop who did similar work in the energy area and who helped develop some of the methods used in this study; the participants in the Design Science Laboratory of the Department of Design, Southern Illinois University, who in the fall of 1971, did initial research on the global food systems; Edward Higbee, who lectured on the world food problem at the 1975 World Game Workshop: Russell Ackoff, Ervin Lazlo, Nicholas Georgescu-Roegan, Tom Robinson, Gene Youngblood, and especially Ed Schlossberg, whose feedback and consultation throughout the entire World Game Workshop was pivotal in shaping this document; the staff at Buckminster Fuller's office, especially Janet Bregman-Taney, whose invaluable assistance added enormously to this book; John Joline, the cartographer for the world food maps; Shirley Sharkey, Kiyoshi Kuromiya, and Dan Daniel, who patiently typed the manuscript; Bill Strachan, my editor at Doubleday, who had the patience and strength ; Brenton Beck and Hal Hershey whose care and skill in design have made this book immeasurably more readable; and last but not least, to the Jesse Noyes Foundation and the Rockefeller Brothers Fund, whose support of the 1975 World Game Workshop helped make this book possible.

Preface

Without food you die. Very simple. Without adequate nutrition you're malnourished. Not very simple. Without adequate global food production, storage, processing, packaging, wholesaling, retailing, pricing, quality control, standardization, branding, regulating, testing, exchange of ownership, delivery, preparation, and waste disposal some people eat well, some people eat too well, others eat hardly at all. Very complicated. And, to those who don't eat too well (and to some who do), very outrageous.

When you read this the world may be facing famine or it may be unconcerned about its food supplies. Food may be scarce or it may be abundant. Depending on the weather, our variable food supplies are looked on as either a commodity or the staff of life whose distribution becomes a highly charged emotional issue. Our changing weather guarantees changing harvests which guarantee to keep us on an emotional roller coaster. One thing is certain right now: the condition we are in will change.

Is it possible for everyone on Earth to be fed? Well fed? How? This document attempts to prove beyond the shadows of anyone's doubt that there are enough resources on Earth for everyone—those who are alive today as well as those who will be alive in the future—to have all the food we all need to be optimally nourished.

There is plenty of food for everyone on Earth to have a nutritionally sound diet. There is, in fact, so much food and potential food on Earth that if presently known and readily available techniques were utilized, everyone on Earth could have the ignominious distinction of dying of obesity if they so choose. Everyone who graces this planet with their presence deserves all the food their body needs to function optimally. Food for life should be a birthright, not an earned right. Billions of humans should not have to work their lives away for food and suffer the consequences if they are not successful.

The entire resources of Spaceship Earth are for and can meet, if used and reused wisely, the regenerative life support needs of 100% of humanity on board. The world's total production of cereals, roots, pulses, fruits, nuts, vegetables, meats, fish, milk, and eggs is enough to supply every child, woman and man with over 2.3 kilograms (5 pounds) of food per day (Chart 3). A well nourished human being can be taken care of with under .6 kilograms dry weight (Chart 5) of the right combinations of the above foods plus water. The present state of human know-how is such that this condition can not only be improved, but maintained on a continually sustainable basis for all generations to come if we husband and midwife our resources as well as we know how.

This document attempts to destroy the suicidal complacency, the "why try" or triage "ethic" of those who would have us believe that there is no way the world can feed itself; that some of us are doomed to starvation while others are doomed to watch that starvation on color television. It points out that starvation is not the inevitable given condition of a segment of humanity; that hunger need not be experienced by anyone against his will; that there is no scarcity of food; that there are plenty of viable solutions for eliminating starvation and hunger; that the end to hunger is just around the corner from the realization that hunger need not exist; and that you can make a difference. The cure for smallpox had been available for one hundred and fifty years, but it was not until the 1970's that it was decided to totally rid the Earth of the scourge of this disease. The "cure" for the more insidious disease of starvation is also available to humanity; what is needed is the widespread knowledge that cures for starvation exist and the commitment to bring them about. This document takes a design science approach to global food problems,

"We have, over the course of time, made discoveries in compassion as well as discoveries in technology. Many problems that had been judged insoluble in the past are no longer tolerable."[1]

shows how everyone on Earth could not only be fed, but well fed, and issues a challenge to all of us to bring this desired goal to fruition.

The book also attempts to deal with the very real problems of food surpluses and the problems that arise, for instance in the United States, from such a situation. What do we do when we have all the food we need? What happens with the "surplus" food and manpower if food production in the future is even more mechanized than it is in the present, as the trends indicate it will be? What are the next priorities—ones that won't negate the progress already made in the food system? And finally and most importantly, the book attempts to deal with the whole of global economic and social development, not just food. The focus, the frame of reference is food and the globe, but food can no more be separated from energy, health, education, transportation, or economics than can the human digestive system be separated from its nervous or circulatory systems. Nor can the individual nation-states be separated from their inter-dependence and integration with each other, the planet as a whole, and their common heritages of humanity, compassion, and the desire for an improved life. Global problems have to be viewed globally. The sum of local solutions will never equal or even come close to adequately dealing with a global problem. Conversely, the synergies of global solutions can mitigate or eliminate local problems.

Clearly not a doomsaying document, this book, nevertheless, readily acknowledges the precarious position of our global food system and its life and death balance with both the changing global climatic conditions and the possible impending shortfalls in world grain production some researchers anticipate in the 1980's. Strategies for insuring our survival and eliminating the threat of famine even in the face of the worst possible weather changes are presented.

The title of this book needs some explanation. "Ho-ping" is a Chinese word for peace. Its etymological roots, when translated literally, mean "food for everyone." Ho-ping is written in Chinese as 咊平; 口 is a symbol for mouth, 禾 represents grain, and in particular corn (note tasseled top and roots). When all people, 口, have enough to eat, 禾, there will be peace. Another interpretation of the etymology of the character is that the blowing of grain, 禾, in a field is like the harmony of people singing.[4] 禾 refers to harmony and physical contentment, while 平 refers more to security and safety.[5]

Everyone in China is at present adequately nourished. With over 800 million people (20% of the world's population) in an area about the size of the U.S.A. (which has 220 million people),[6] with only a fraction of her farmland naturally endowed with the combination of smooth topography, fertile soil, and favorable climate necessary for high crop yields (about one-third less cultivated land than the U.S.A.),[6] and with an extended and recent history of periodic famine (1,830 famines between 108 B.C. and 1929 A.D.)[7] this is no meager accomplishment.

In twenty years China has increased her grain production by over 100%. In 1949 grain output was 100 million metric tons, in 1977 it was 242 million metric tons.[6] Since 1966 she has been nearly self-sufficient in cereal grain and has built up reserves by 1975 of some 80 million tons. China is the world's largest exporter of rice; in each of the years 1974, 1975, and 1976, more than 2.2 million tons were exported (the U.S.A. exported an average of 1.9 million tons during each of those years). In 1974, 1975, and 1976, there was improvement on the record grain harvest of 1973. Most areas in China now reap two crops a year and triple-cropping is increasing in the south. Ninety thousand acres of former desert in Sinkiang have been reclaimed utilizing the waters of the Tarin River.[8] More area is under irrigation in China, (85 million hectares) than in any other country of the world[6] (the U.S.A. has 16 million hectares of irrigated land).

"Only the whole big system works."[3]

One of the reasons for this success is that agriculture has received strong emphasis in China, given priority over industry in planning and expenditure. For example, in recent years water conservation and utilization projects have led to the end of the centuries-old succession of drought and flood which characterized the drainage basins of the three great rivers of China—the Haar, Yellow, and Haiko. The immense importance of this is readily apparent when one sees that one-third of China's population and over one-third of her arable land are in these basins. China's agricultural success is the result of a unique blend of vast, decentralized—yet centrally coordinated—manpower utilization programs and a progressive modernization program. China, while engaged in extremely labor-intensive agriculture, has increased her use of power machinery, fertilizers, and new high-yield seeds. The post-Mao "four modernizations" intend to accelerate this development. The state purchase of grain has kept the China market stable while the price to the producer has increased and that to the consumer has been kept constant. Taxation is structured to encourage output, not to discourage it, and is adjusted to production so that it is virtually a fixed receipt to the government but a declining one to the communities paying it, if they improve output. The annual agricultural tax in 1953 was 12% of the gross production value of agriculture; today it is only slightly above 5%.[8]

China has only one-fifth of the world's population, but given the tragic condition of China thirty years ago—which was in as poor or worse shape than any region today—and where she is today and seems to be heading—with population stabilizing, extensive health and child care services now operating, major communicable diseases controlled, relatively little crime, logistical stability, social equity, resource-use efficiency standards for industry, and the necessary all-pervasive ethic of doing "more with less"[9]—China's accomplishments and the possibilities of accomplishing similar things elsewhere can be viewed as one of the great lessons and hopes of humanity. With 8.6% of the world's arable land, China feeds 20% of the world's people. Applying China's

---

"We can, for the first time in history, afford a collective conscience."[2] Not only afford; we need a collective conscience to survive.

---

techniques world-around, the planet could today feed over nine billion people.

We do not mean to imply that China or China's food system is perfect; it isn't. For example, there is little attempt to collect and preserve the rich genetic diversity of China's crops, a trend that if continued would result in the loss of irreplaceable genetic resources. Also, China is the world's largest producer of tobacco, a phenomenon that contradicts the avowed commitment to preventive medicine and wastes valuable land that could be used to grow food crops. It is also important to realize that China's agricultural success did not just happen overnight or come about through a set, preconceived theory; rather, it evolved pragmatically. During the first fifteen years, the most outstanding feature of agricultural organization was rapid and frequent transformation; in the first ten years alone, there were five radical changes.[10] Clearly, decision-makers were fearless enough to change policies if things didn't work as well as hoped. Further, almost anyone from the Western world would have serious qualms or objections to some of the methods employed to achieve the successes of China's food system. Like everyone else, China has made mistakes and will continue to make them. Long term or large scale weather reversals, new crop diseases, or internal strife could possibly bring the specter of hunger or famine back. While what is suitable

for China may not be suitable for Africa, India, South America, or the United States, we have learned from the Chinese experience that it is possible to feed a large population on relatively little land with a lot of hard work, organization, and diligence.

In Chinese, Ho-ping means peace, and food for everyone. In English, hoping is the expectation of a desired event, and, surely, nothing is more desirable than food for everyone and peace on Earth.

Contents

Preface 3
Introduction: Design Science 9

FOOD, EARTH AND EVERYONE

Overview
1. Perspective..................................... 15
2. Beginnings 16

Food Problems, Prospects and Present State
3. Food on Earth................................. 23
4. Definitions.................................... 25
5. History....................................... 27
6. Scare City: The Absence of Food 30
7. The Starvation Diseases....................... 34
8. The Vicious Circle 34
9. Preferred State............................... 35
10. Problem State................................ 36
11. Decision-Making Criteria 76
    References................................... 79

FOOD SOURCES/ PRODUCTION TECHNIQUES

Introduction 83
1. Aboriginal Agriculture......................... 84
2. Modern Agriculture 89
   Energy and Mechanization.................... 90
   Agribusiness................................ 98
   Irrigation/Drainage 100
   Fertilizers 113
   Pesticides 123
   Land Use/Soil 128
3. Organic Agriculture 135
4. Animal Husbandry 136
5. Fishing...................................... 147
6. Aquaculture 152
7. Controlled Environments/Greenhouses.......... 161
8. Hydroponics 164
9. Insects...................................... 167
10. Leaf Protein 170
11. Non-Photosynthetic Single Cell Protein 172
12. Photosynthetic Single Cell Protein 173
13. Sprouting.................................... 175

14. Synthetic Nutriments 176
15. Decentralized Food Production/Home Gardens 177
16. New Foods 178
17. Alternative Animal Feed....................... 181
18. Exotic Food Sources.......................... 183
19. All the Food Needed to Feed the World:
    Food and Plenitude 185
    References................................... 186

FOOD DISTRIBUTION: PROCESSING, STORAGE, PACKAGING, PREPARATION AND DELIVERY

Food Processing 190
References.. 201

STRATEGIES FOR A REGENERATIVE FOOD SYSTEM

Making the World Work 204
1. The Chinese/American Alternative............... 206
2. Dare to be Ethical: People First................ 209
3. Blueprints for Cornucopia 231

Strategies for a Regenerative Food System

4. The Long Ranger 251
5. Design Initiative and What Needs to be Done 253
6. References 254

APPENDIX

Organizations 256
Weights, Measures and Conversion Factors 267
Afterword—A Personal Note 272

Maps

Note: The maps appearing in this book are based on R. Buckminster Fuller's Dymaxion Sky-Ocean World Map. This map projection was chosen to display world resources because of its unique properties; namely, it has a minimum amount of distortion and it is possible to see all the world's land masses and resources as one, almost interconnected, island. The base maps and their component parts and methods of projection are fully protected by international copyright convention and can not be reproduced without permission of R. Buckminster Fuller. Cartographers: R. B. Fuller and Shoji Sadao. Patent Number: 2,393,676. Copyright 1967.

World Population 1979 and Major Famines of the
    Last 100 Years 32
Food Priority Areas 33
World Cereal Production 45
World Vegetable/Melon Production 46
World Root/Tuber Production 47
Wheat 48
Rice 49
Barley 50
Millet and Grain Sorghum 51
Oats 52
Corn 53
Sugar 54
Soybeans 55
Potatoes 56
Sunflower Seed 57
Groundnuts 58
Rapeseed 59
Citrus Fruits 60
Bananas 61
Casava 62
Apples 63
Grapes or Wine 64
Tobacco 65
Tea 66
Coffee 67
Cocoa 68
Rubber 69
Cotton 70
Jute 71
Flax 72
Hemp 73

Silk 74
Hunting, Gathering, Fishing and Primitive Cultivation 85
Subsistence Agriculture 85
Nomadic Herding 86
World Agricultural Tractors in Use 1976 92
World Irrigated Land 101
Irrigated Land: Locations 102
Normal Mean Annual Precipitation 106
Drought 1976–1977 107
Arid Land 108
Risk of Desertification 109
Coastal Deserts Which Could Be Irrigated with
    Desalinated Water from the Sea 110
Fertilizer Consumption 115
Cumulative Effects of Erosion in the United States 128
World Arable Land 130
Cultivated Cropland 131
Potentially Arable 132
Forests 133
World Meat Production 137
Extensive Grazing or Stock Raising 139
Cattle 140
Dairy Farming 141
Pigs 142
Sheep 143
Major Fisheries 149
Tidal Sites 158
Occurrence of Kelp in Quantities Sufficient for
    Harvesting 159

Charts and Illustrations

Hierarchy of Systems 17
Earth's Energy Balance 18
Photosynthetic Energy Conversion 19
Number of Organisms on Earth 21
Recommended Intake of Nutrients 26
Energy Requirements for Various Activities 27
Two Hundred Years of Famines 31
World Agricultural Production 37
World Sugar Consumption 39
Daily Metabolic Turnover for One Person 40
Approximate Daily Metabolic Turnover for All of
    Humanity 40
Present Food System: Qualitative Inputs
    and Outputs 41

Present Food System: Levels, Constraints and Forcing Functions 42
Present Food System: From External Metabolics to Internal Metabolics 43
Present Food System: World Overview 44
Present Food System: U.S. Overview 44
Development of Agriculture, Food Processing and Food Preservation 87
Farm Output as a Function of Energy Input to the U.S. Food System............................ 91
Energy Subsidy for Different Foods 91
Technology Hierarchy 93
Human Directed Energy Use in Typical North American Farming System 95
The Hydrosphere................................... 103
Desalting Plants by Size............................ 103
Desalting Plants by Geographic Location 103
Irrigated Land in World............................. 104
World Hydrologic Cycle 104
Two Types of Water Flow 111
Export Prices for Some Major Fertilizer Materials....... 116
The Cost of Scarcity 116
World Fertilizer Consumption 1800–1976............. 117
Fertilizer Consumption per Acre of Arable Land 117
Crop Yields with Fertilizer 117
Corn-Yield Gains from Successive Fertilizer Applications 117
Typical Fertilizer Response Curve 118
Nitrogen and Phosphorus Cycles 118
Nitrogen Fixing on Earth............................ 120
Feedstocks Used in World Ammonia Production, 1971 120
Percentage of Production on Primary Synthetic Ammonia..................................... 120
World Potash Resources 120
World Phosphate Rock Resources.................... 120
Persistence of Pesticides in Soils 124
Examples of Biological Control in the U.S. 125
Cultivatable Land.................................. 134
Some African Animals Suitable for Harvesting.......... 138
Livestock Protein Conversion Efficiency 138
Materials Balance for Livestock 144
Composition of Various Meats 145
Ocean Food Chain.................................. 148
World Fish Catch................................... 149
Peruvian Anchovy Catch 149

Chinese Carp Culture 153
Acres of Catfish Ponds in the U.S. 153
Yields from Catfish Ponds 153
Profile in Integrated Aquaculture-Agriculture System Used in Singapore 154
Biological Relationships in the Backyard Fish Farm 155
New Alchemy's Backyard Fish Farm.................. 155
Estimated Production of Fin Fish in Aquaculture 155
Production of Shrimps and Prawns in Aquaculture 156
Production of Mollusks in Aquaculture 156
Nutrient Composition of Nori........................ 156
Bamboo Tube Rafts Used for Kelp Culture in China 156
Selected Examples of Aquaculture Yields............. 157
Some Common Commercial Preparations of Seaweeds 157
Vertical Greenhouse Designs 162
Gross Yields per Acre per Year...................... 165
Comparative Yields for a Single Crop................. 165
Insects as Food 168
The Insect Orders 169
Typical Protein Yields 171
Average Composition of Single Cell Proteins 172
Time for One Doubling in Mass 172
Protein Percentage of Algae 174
Protein Production Per Acre Per Year in Kilograms 174
Protein Content of Some Animal Wastes.............. 182
Processed and Fresh Fruit and Vegetable Consumption in the United States 191
Food Processing Methods 192
Unit Operations in Food Processing.................. 192
Functional Use of Food Additives.................... 193
Raspberry Flavor Formulation 193
Types of Food Packages 194
Food Distribution Mediums, Industries or Organizations 194
Allocation of U.S. Food Dollar Budget 195
Allocation of U.S. Food Energy Budget 195
Food Storages 195
Common Food Preparation Techniques 196
Common Food Utensils 196
Global Poverty: Unmet Basic Human Needs 205
China/USA Agricultural Portrait 207
Global Food Service 211
Average and Record Yields, 1975 214
An Idealized Polyculture Farm and Research Center 216
The Ark 217

Cutaway of the Ark Showing the Interior 217
Ocean-Based Solar/Wind/Algae/Fish/Power and Food Plant 218
Aboveground, Dry Biomass Yields of Selected Plant Species or Complexes......................... 223
The Birthrate and Energy Production................. 230
Strategy Outlines
    Level 1 234
    Level 2 234
    Level 3 235
    Level 4—Global Food Service.................... 236
    Aboriginal Agriculture.......................... 236
    Energy Use 237
    Agribusiness................................... 238
    Water Supply/Irrigation/Drainage................. 238
    Fertilizer 239
    Seed Development 239
    Land Use...................................... 240
    Pesticides 240
    Animal Husbandry 241
    Hydroponics 241
    Fishing 242
    Greenhouses 242
    Aquaculture 243
    Insects.. 243
    Leaf Protein, Sprouting, Single Cell Protein...... 244
    New Foods 244
    Exotic, Synthetic Nutriments.................... 245
    Decentralized Food Production 245
    Nutrition 246
    Population 246
    Africa 247
    Far East....................................... 248
    Near East 249
    Europe and USSR 249
    North America 250
    Latin America.................................. 250

Introduction: Design Science

Ho-Ping: Food for Everyone is a companion volume to *Energy, Earth and Everyone* (first published in November, 1975, and reissued with extensive updating in 1979) that deals with global energy development and strategies that could be pursued to achieve a regenerative energy supply for 100% of humanity in ten years. Briefly, *Energy, Earth and Everyone* shows that using current know-how and technology, the world could, within ten years, harness about three times the amount of energy (in the form of the non-depletable energy sources—sun, wind, tides, geothermal, etc.) than it presently consumes in the form of our rapidly diminishing fossil and nuclear fuels. It presents a comprehensive plan for the transition from a fossil and nuclear fueled economy to a regeneratively powered economy. Clearly, energy and food are intimately related. When viewed from far enough away, they are, in fact, the same phenomenon. Food is energy for our individual internal metabolics, energy is food for our collective external life-support metabolics. Of the two, food is of necessity the priority, but one cannot be developed without the other. Food and energy development go hand in hand.

Both this book and *Energy, Earth and Everyone* are outgrowths of World Game Workshops sponsored by R. Buckminster Fuller and the research, planning, and educational organization, Earth Metabolic Design. The "World Game" is a method for dealing with crucial problems in holistic, environmentally sound, and resource efficient ways.

In contra-distinction to the "War Games" that are played by the generals and admirals of the Pentagon, Kremlin, and all other nation states and their alliances to figure out the best strategic and tactical military moves and countermoves and counter-counter moves in hot and cold war situations, the World Game concerns itself with strategic and tactical moves that will make 100% of humanity successful. War Games concern themselves with allocating and deploying world resources and weaponry to beat the other side: "we win, they lose." For example, more than $400 billion are spent each year by the nation states of the world on weaponry. Fifty million people are engaged directly or indirectly for military purposes throughout the world: 23–24 million are in the armed forces, and one quarter to one half of all the world's scientists and technical community engaged in research and development are employed on military work. The U.S. has 30,000 deliverable nuclear warheads[1]; there is enough explosive force in the world for each person on Earth to have the equivalent of at least 15,000 tons of T.N.T. The World Game deals with the whole world's resources and "livingry" technology in ways that attempt to make everyone a winner. The World Game asks and answers the questions: "How can the world's resources and know-how be used and reused so that everyone on Earth is better off? How can the world be made to work for 100% of humanity in environmentally sound and resource efficient ways?" War Games ask and seek to answer questions such as: "How many B-1 bombers and Minuteman missiles need to be deployed to cripple the enemy's retaliatory capabilites?, or, can tactical nuclear warheads stop a Russian invasion of Western Europe?"

The military and multinational corporations are the predominant groups that deal with the globe as one unit. In War Games the whole Earth is the playing field. National boundaries are ignored in time of war. What needs to be done to "win" is done, no matter how much it costs. In the World Game, the whole Earth is also the playing field and whatever is possible, effective, efficient, and considerate can be utilized to improve the world. The players in War Games are an elite few who—as self-appointed representatives for all life on Earth—toy with various permutations of cataclysm, catastrophe, desolation, annihilation, and extinction. Players in the World Game can be any person concerned with life on Earth and interested in developing new alternatives and opportunities for humanity. Players compete to improve mutual advantage; self-interest is understood to be collective interest because the fragile world environment is shared by all. In the World Game, political dogma, nation-state self-interest at the expense of everyone else, and warfare are obsolete, contrary to all rules, and thus pro-hibited; weaponry is converted to "livingry." Any resort to armed conflict immediately disqualifies players. "Winning" in the playing of the World Game is determined by the move or moves that 1) makes the world work (that is, satisfies human needs for food, energy, shelter, etc.), 2) for the most people, 3) using the least amount of resources, 4) with the least environmental im-pact, 5) in the quickest amount of time, and 6) with the most degrees of freedom or alternatives afforded to humanity. War Games are based on the now fallacious premise that there is not enough to go around, that sooner or later there will be an eventual Armageddon showdown over the use of a dwindling supply of resources. The World Game is based on the premise that there are enough resources and know-how for everyone on Earth to be better off than anyone is right now, and that war is obsolete. In the World Game, individuals expand their own and society's wealth by finding ways of doing more with less. The World Game provides a context for scientists, researchers, policy-makers, and concerned citizens to participate in solving global problems in such areas as food, energy, shelter, health care, education, transportation, communication, and economics. One of the goals of the World Game is to involve as many people as possible in the research, design, and development of strategies for solving world-wide problems in the most peaceful and effective manner.

The World Game and both the energy and food books attempt to illustrate and use a new paradigm for viewing our world and its problems. The approach is comprehensive in that it deals with the whole Earth, 100% of humanity, and all the relevant variables of a problem that have been ascertained; e.g., not just food production, but processing, storing, distributing, and utilizing food as well as the food system's role and relation to such things as energy, health, population, culture, transportation, etc. The approach is anticipatory in that it does not seek to deal with problems just in their crucial state but also before they reach a crisis. And perhaps more importantly it is a design approach, that is, it attempts to deal with the whole Earth and all of humanity with a long range evolutionary perspective, paying attention not to just what is wrong or what shouldn't be, but with what *is* and what *should be,* and how to get from here to there as well. We have to ask ourselves, "What is needed?" not only, "What is wrong?"

Design science is a new paradigm for viewing

The elements of Section I—Food, Earth and Everyone—are all in one way or another introductions to the world food problem: each deals with the global food situation from a different perspective. Each is necessary for a full understanding of the many dimensions of our food problem.

our world. Simply put, design science can be seen both as a process of recognizing, defining, and solving problems, and of formulating a goal and the systematic path of reaching that goal. It is not a new specialized discipline, but rather an integration of all disciplines. Its practice is not a further winnowing of the secrets of the universe, such as the frontiers of physics or biology, but an integrative discipline wherein the findings of all sciences and humanities are brought to bear to solve humanity's problems.

One way of viewing the purpose of design science is that it, like traditional science, tries to discover more about the universe through the formulation and testing of various hypotheses. In design science, the researcher may wish to find the answer to a question such as "can current resources and know-how meet the regenerative food needs of the world by 1985 (or 1990, etc.)?" or, more specifically, "can current methods of food storage eliminate enough spoiled food to feed those who are now hungry?" or, more specifically yet, "will this fiberglass and bamboo grain bin keep out bugs, rodents, and moisture?" Design science is vitally interested in all these levels of the problem—from the recognition of symptoms to a solution's reduction to practice. If the evidence—the answer to the question— indicates a positive position, the design scientist can pursue this new option of humanity and reduce it to practice; he or she can also

communicate the information to those who can evaluate this new evidence and offer feedback. If the response is negative, then the design scientist examines the situation to see what he/she can do to change this condition through the development of new artifacts or organizational structures. ("Artifacts" are physical structures rather than political ones; a telephone, windmill, or airplane rather than propaganda or a law.) As in the previous example, perhaps one artifact would be new structures for storing food in developing countries where losses are heaviest and food needs the highest.

Design science sees the environment and the human condition as being ever improvable through the application of new information and understanding. It takes the demonstrable point of view that it is possible to continually do more with less; to increase a given amount of work done by energy, or functions performed by a given amount of materials, with less energy and materials. There is no magic in this, it is merely the substitution of new information and organization for existing energy and materials.The new breakthrough that was uncovered in physics that made the transistor possible did much more with less than its predecessor, the vacuum tube. The vacuum tube, in turn, could do not only more, but new things that its predecessor, the crystal, could not do. Continuing more with less leads eventually to new functions as well as more functions that can be performed by a given artifact. The latest electronic advances in large-scale integration now do so much more with so much less than the original transistors that they are making possible desk-top computers whose equivalents twenty years ago would have taken up a whole room.

The design science approach involves understanding the critical interrelated nature of our problems and their global scope; the inability of present, locally focused planning methods to deal effectively with these problems; and new systematic alternative approaches for recognizing, resolving, and preventing our present and anticipated problems through the development of artifacts.

[The primary emphasis] in design science is committed to new forms rather than political reform; that is, to possible inanimate artifact development versus negative propaganda, legal and other restraints. It does not try to stop other people but tries to start itself. The strategy is to make that which is socially objectionable obsolete by developing superior inanimate means of solving economic and other problems. One way of looking at all problems is that they are physical. What is challenging us— creating our problem—is physical. To solve a problem something is needed that is not present. What is needed can always be translated into something physical, an artifact. The design scientist asks the question, "What artifacts do I develop in the environment that will solve the problem?" The procedure is to identify the problem and then the artifacts.[2]

The idea is not to ignore politics but to develop the artifacts that will make it obsolete. New artifacts create a demand for institutional changes by opening up productive opportunities unrealizable without such change.[3] Instead of seeking to have a law passed outlawing the use of inefficient energy consumers, design science seeks instead to develop an artifact that performs the same function (or more functions) as the inefficient design but uses fewer resources and less energy. This is in no way intended to mean or imply that the design scientist would be opposed to sensible, considerate legislative efforts (there are a number of "social design" strategies later in this book), but merely that the priority is on the development of new physical artifacts and alternatives that the decision-makers as yet do not have.

A design scientist, like many research scientists, does not wait to be hired by a patron or employer to do their bidding, but rather takes the personal initiative to solve the problems that his/her experience has taught are important to solve for the betterment of humanity. Unlike "pure" science which sometimes claims to be value-free, design science is value-laden. Design is the development or structuring of environments in preferred directions. Our preferred directions, "where we want to go," are determined by our values. Our future, the part we have control over in the present, is determined by the values we have today.

One of the underlying tenets of design science is that we are all in "this" together; "this" being the Earth, humanity, and our innumerable problems. Problems are all interconnected just as is our ecology. Problems are parts; design science seeks to deal with wholes, with systems. The method of design science is one of always starting with the whole and working toward the particular. In the specific effort documented in this book, food energy is dealt with within the context of the energy flows of the universe; the unique food problems of humanity on board Spaceship Earth are dealt with within the context of 100% of humanity, its total history, cultural inheritance, and needs of the whole planet. A major objective of the World Game workshops is to formulate design science strategies for eliminating human privations and to identify artifacts that could be developed that would lead to this state.

One of the more crucial dilemmas humanity is imbedded within is the fact that all of our critical problems are global problems, and global problems cannot be solved with a local solution. Decision-makers—be they local, regional, national, international, or just "plain" planetary citizens in general—need handles for recognizing global phenomena and solving world problems. Both *Energy, Earth and Everyone* and *Ho-Ping* are intended to illustrate one way of getting a handle on a global problem. The type of research study presented in both books is the first stage of design science planning. These books contain frames of reference for recognizing what is wrong and where we want to be going as well as pointing out the specific steps that need to be taken along the way. In addition, they identify numerous artifacts that a design scientist could take the initiative with and develop. These two books attempt to deal with the most pressing, fundamental systems of problems confronting humanity at this time, and in so doing to present a paradigm and methodology for viewing all the systems of problems confronting humanity. It is hoped that other invididuals and groups will be able to tackle our energy and food problems, as well as those in transportation, shelter, communication, education, health care, materials, economics, etc. with the same or similar methods, thereby furnishing themselves and all decision-makers with new perspectives and new alternatives for resolving our predicaments.[4]

Food, Earth and Everyone

Perspective

Change your perspective for a moment:

You are on a spaceship. You are captain of that spaceship. The spaceship is in trouble. Something, or many things have gone wrong. Your food systems are malfunctioning; some people are starving, many are malnourished. You don't know what is happening, where it is happening, when it happened, how it happened or whom it affected or affects. You don't know where you are or where you are going.

What information do you need in order to make a rational decision about your survival?

Well, for a start, you might like to know:

What is food? What is nutrition? What is proper nutrition?

How critical is the need for food? How much time do I have to act?

What does one human need? What do all the spaceship inhabitants need? For one day? For a year? For a lifetime?

What is hunger?

Where is all the food right now?

Who needs it the most? And where are they?

Is one kind of food as good as another?

What is the relationship between malnourishment in infancy and intelligence?

How much food is there? How much per person?

How is food produced? How much food is lost? Where does food come from?

How many steps are there from the Sun to my plate to my stomach?

How is food stored? Processed? Packaged? Delivered? Prepared? Disposed of?

What resources are needed for the food system? How much energy is needed? To feed one person? To feed humanity?

What effects will there be if the food problems are not solved?

What are all the alternatives for meeting the food needs of humanity?

How would a strategy for solving the food problems be implemented?

Has the food problem occurred before? What was done? Why and how? What's different today?

How could the food problem be prevented from recurring?

How much of the food problem is the result of our economic accounting system?

What are the limits to our solutions?

What resources are available to solve the food problem?

How could everyone on Earth be nutritionally fed on a regenerative basis?

How can the food system be continuously improved?

Is there a finite number of questions that need to be asked and answered to make a rational decision about survival?

What have I forgotten?

When should I stop asking questions and act?

These questions outline a perspective on the resolution of the world food problem that this document uses. As we all know by now we are on such a spaceship and need to ask some very fundamental questions and expose our assumptions.

Some of the questions asked could strike some as naive, but it is time, as Buckminster Fuller has said, for us to "dare to be naive." When it comes to recognizing, defining, and resolving our global problems, when it comes to being conscious, responsible citizens of a spaceship, we are all amateurs. The best we can hope and strive for is to be intelligent amateurs.

2 Beginnings

"Humanity on Earth teeters on the threshold of revolution. If it is a bloody revolution where the top is pulled down as in all previous political revolutions, it is oblivion for all. The alternative to the bloody revolution is the design revolution."[3]

In design science problem solving it is important to have as large a context for any specific problem as is possible so that you will be able to recognize the true systemic dysfunctions rather than just the problems or imagined problems' symptoms. Symptoms are what "show-up"; what are visible. Problems are never solved by dealing with just symptoms. Symptoms are "parts"; to recognize and solve problems you need to deal with the whole. The way of seeing, of getting a handle on the whole is by defining a larger system of which it is a part. Because we are dealing with the global food system, the magnitude and complexity of that system demands that we begin our problem solving by defining an even larger or "meta" system or systems that the human food system fits into. One such meta-system is the Sun/Earth/Moon system and the general processes of life that are nurtured in the synergetic synthesis of these elements. Another, even larger meta-system is the ephemeral "set of rules," "generalized principles," or "laws of nature" as they are variously called, that govern the behavior of all systems, whether they be cosmological or biological. Given the eventual subject matter or problem that is to be tackled, there is one set of generalized principles formulated by western science under the general heading of "thermodynamics" that are especially relevant. Thermodynamics refers to a set of rules that govern all energy flows and the possible behaviors of complexity in the universe. Food is a form of energy and complexity; the food system could be viewed through the window or context of the general laws that govern all energy and complex systems. Thermodynamics states that entropy, the tendency for the randomness of systems to increase, is present in all subsystems of the Universe. Co-existent with this tendency is an opposite force called anti-entropy or syntropy that produces order, interrelatedness, and organization within a system. The syntropic development of greater degrees of complexity/order requires the input of energy, whereas the entropic development of greater degrees of randomness occurs spontaneously and gives off energy. The entropic energy release can be used or "consumed" by syntropic processes, as for instance, the entropic radiation from the Sun being used by the syntropic photosynthetic processes on Earth. From the constant interaction of these two forces on Earth life is produced.

A constant stream of entropic energy flows from a hot source, the Sun, through the Earth's biosphere and then into a sink, that is, cooler parts of the Universe. As this energy flows away from the Sun, randomness increases. Along the way, though, some of this energy is impounded and stored by syntropic processes in our biosphere; it maintains what we refer to as life. Life is a syntropic force that takes energy and processes it into greater degrees of complexity and order. It does so against the ever-present forces of entropy so that the efficiency of this conversion is never 100%.

The volume of our biosphere is roughly a thousandth of that of the Earth around which it exists in the form of a delicate shell. If the Earth were reduced to a globe one foot in diameter, the thickness of the biosphere would be no thicker than the ink printed on that globe and the water vapor condensation from your breath would be deeper than the oceans. Within the system of the biosphere there exist two general subsystems that define the parameters within which the global food system resides. These two subsystems are 1) the ecological context, and 2) the external metabolics of humanity (see Chart 1). External metabolics is the life-support technology that human intellect has developed over the eons. It processes energy to organize complexity as does its analogue, internal metabolics. External metabolics can be seen as the life-support system of humanity while internal metabolics is the life-support system of the individual human. These two systems, the ecological context and the external metabolics of humanity, must remain in relative harmony if the larger system is to include humanity in its continued operations. Within these two accommodative systems is located the subsystem with which this document deals—the human food system. Before dealing specifically with this system we need to take a further look at the evolution of the biospheric system.

Compared to the major activities in the Universe, the natural fluctuations in the biosphere

Chart 1. Hierarchy of Systems.

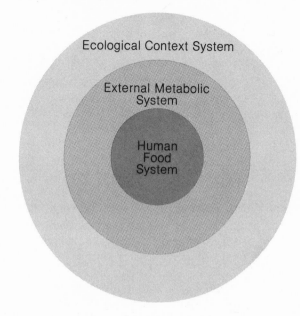

Ecological Context System

External Metabolic System

Human Food System

are very small. They are not small enough, though, for the optimum control of crop processes within the human food system because plants appear to have an obstinate nostalgia for the climates of long ago. Plants, particularly those with carbon biochemical pathways, thrive better in artificial environments having low oxygen or high carbon dioxide concentrations. During the 4.5 billion year history of the planet, its atmosphere has changed from a probably hydrogen-rich one to one that is now rich in oxygen, and life has probably evolved from chemosynthetic anaerobic bacteria to the present photosynthetic plants and human life. This evolution was made possible by the early synthesis of a syntropic trap for the Sun's entropic radiation: chlorophyll.

One-billionth (2×10^{17} watts) of the Sun's total radiation is intercepted by the Earth. Of this, less than one-tenth of one percent is used by the Earth's plants' chlorophyll in photosynthesis. Because all life is based on the products of photosynthesis there would be no animal life, including humanity, without chlorophyll and green plants.

Another way of viewing plants and the processes going on within them that is different than the entropic/syntropic interactions is as manifestations of electromagnetic interactions. An "interaction" in this sense is a coupling, attractive or repulsive, between two or more simple entities or particles that have well-defined positions, energies, and momenta. The life forms or biomass of our biosphere are temporary traps for the low energy quanta that are associated with the weak bindings between electrons and atomic nuclei. Molecules and plants are examples of bound matter in which the attractive electromagnetic forces dominate the repulsive forces. The binding strength and energy levels of bound matter are determined by certain universal laws of nature which are incorporated into the fudamental physical theory known as quantum mechanics. The energy activity within our biosphere is many orders of magnitude less than that at the center of the sun or in nuclear reactors where changes to nuclear processes dominate the scene, and even these hotter environments are many orders of magnitude less active energetically than the hot spots of the Universe such as the quasars, pulsars, neutron stars and black holes associated with the birth and death of stars. Nevertheless, in our relatively cold biosphere, life forms are probably the most complex kind of matter that exists in the Universe, since hot

Time to take a plunge; in this section, we get into some areas that at first do not seem to have much to do with hungry people, but do in fact, have everything to do with recognizing the realities every empty stomach is embedded within and resolving those outrages.

environments dissociate all weakly bound matter.[1]

"Complexity and organization distinguish one form of bound matter from the other. Uranium differs from hydrogen through its complexity and organization, not through a difference in the kinds of fundamental subatomic particles. A small bacterial cell can be regarded as the least complex form of life. One way a living cell differs from the same chemical constituents of that cell just mixed without the organizing force of 'life' is by the amount of energy that binds these chemicals together. The cell can be said to have an 'energy enrichment' over that of the equilibrium state of its constituent elements which would have existed if the sun had not shone upon the Earth. This energy enrichment is so large that the probability that it could have occurred by a spontaneous fluctuation in an equilibrium ensemble of these atoms is one in one trillion ($1:10^{12}$). This probability is so extremely small that even if we were to sample a larger ensemble containing all the atoms of the Universe as frequently as 10^{16} times per second throughout the Universe's history of about 10^{18} seconds, the probability of finding a cell is not significantly higher."[1]

All forms of life in our biosphere are so energy-rich that a continual flow of energy must pass through them to create and sustain them against entropic degradation. Nevertheless,

17

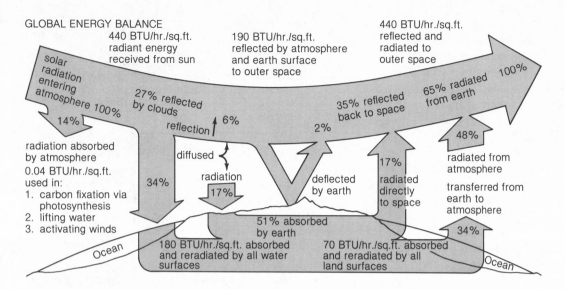

GLOBAL ENERGY BALANCE

440 BTU/hr./sq.ft. radiant energy received from sun

190 BTU/hr./sq.ft. reflected by atmosphere and earth surface to outer space

440 BTU/hr./sq.ft. reflected and radiated to outer space

solar radiation entering atmosphere 100%

27% reflected by clouds

6% reflection

35% reflected back to space

65% radiated from earth

100%

14%

2%

48%

radiation absorbed by atmosphere 0.04 BTU/hr./sq.ft. used in:
1. carbon fixation via photosynthesis
2. lifting water
3. activating winds

diffused

radiation

17%

34%

17%

deflected by earth

17% radiated directly to space

radiated from atmosphere

transferred from earth to atmosphere

34%

Ocean

180 BTU/hr./sq.ft. absorbed and reradiated by all water surfaces

51% absorbed by earth

70 BTU/hr./sq.ft. absorbed and reradiated by all land surfaces

Ocean

GENERALIZED BIO-ENERGY FLOW IN THE BIOMASS FOOD CHAIN

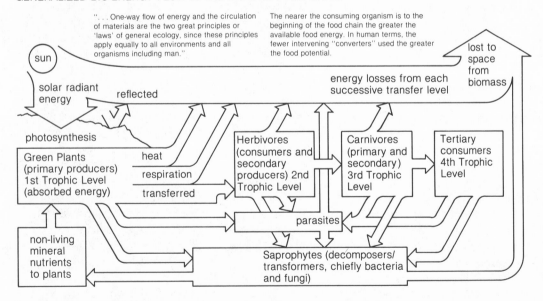

". . . One-way flow of energy and the circulation of materials are the two great principles or 'laws' of general ecology, since these principles apply equally to all environments and all organisms including man."

The nearer the consuming organism is to the beginning of the food chain the greater the available food energy. In human terms, the fewer intervening "converters" used the greater the food potential.

sun

solar radiant energy

reflected

energy losses from each successive transfer level

lost to space from biomass

photosynthesis

Green Plants (primary producers) 1st Trophic Level (absorbed energy)

heat

respiration

transferred

Herbivores (consumers and secondary producers) 2nd Trophic Level

Carnivores (primary and secondary) 3rd Trophic Level

Tertiary consumers 4th Trophic Level

parasites

non-living mineral nutrients to plants

Saprophytes (decomposers/ transformers, chiefly bacteria and fungi)

The transfer of food energy from the source in plants through a series of organisms with repeated eating and being eaten is referred to as the *food chain*. At each transfer a large proportion of the potential energy is lost as heat. The number of steps or "links" in a sequence is limited, usually to four or five. The shorter the food chain (or the nearer the organism to the beginning of the chain) the greater the available energy which can be converted into *biomass* (= living weight, including stored food) and/or dissipated by respiration. Food chains are of three types: the *predator* chain, which, starting from a plant base, goes from smaller to larger animals; the *parasite* chain, which goes from larger to small organisms; and the *saprophytic* chain, which goes from dead matter into microorganisms. Food chains are not isolated sequences, but are interconnected with one another. The interlocking pattern is often spoken of as the *food web.* In complex natural communities, organisms whose food is obtained from plants by the same number of steps are said to belong to the same *trophic* level. Thus, green plants occupy the first trophic level, plant-eaters, the second level, carnivores which eat the herbivores the third level, etc. . . . A given species population may occupy one, or more than one, trophic level according to the energy actually assimilated. The *energy flow* through a trophic level equals the total assimilation at the level which, in turn, equals the production of biomass plus respiration.

E. P. Odum.

Sources: 1. "Solar Radiation Power," POWER, September 1957. p. 24. 2. *Fundamentals of Ecology,* Eugene P. Odum, (Pennsylvania: W. B. Saunders Co.), Second Edition, 1962. pp. 46–47. 3. "Energy Resources," M. K. Hubbert, National Academy of Sciences.

Photosynthetic Energy Conversion[4]

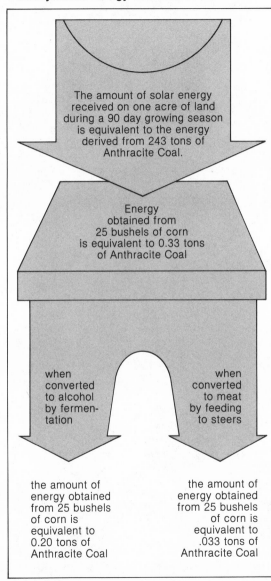

The amount of solar energy received on one acre of land during a 90 day growing season is equivalent to the energy derived from 243 tons of Anthracite Coal.

Energy obtained from 25 bushels of corn is equivalent to 0.33 tons of Anthracite Coal

when converted to alcohol by fermentation

when converted to meat by feeding to steers

the amount of energy obtained from 25 bushels of corn is equivalent to 0.20 tons of Anthracite Coal

the amount of energy obtained from 25 bushels of corn is equivalent to .033 tons of Anthracite Coal

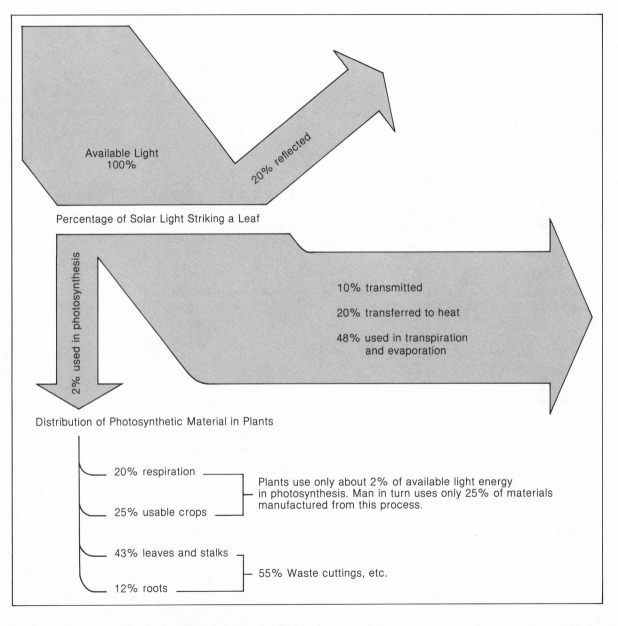

Available Light 100%

20% reflected

Percentage of Solar Light Striking a Leaf

2% used in photosynthesis

10% transmitted

20% transferred to heat

48% used in transpiration and evaporation

Distribution of Photosynthetic Material in Plants

20% respiration

25% usable crops

Plants use only about 2% of available light energy in photosynthesis. Man in turn uses only 25% of materials manufactured from this process.

43% leaves and stalks

55% Waste cuttings, etc.

12% roots

Sources:

1. "Food for the World," Howard W. Mattson, *International Science and Technology,* December 1965. p. 34.

2. "Photosynthesis," H. A. Spoehr, (Chemical Catalog Com. Inc.), 1926. pp. 31–40.

3. "Direct Use of the Sun's Energy," Farrington Daniels, *American Scientist,* Vol. 55, January 1967. p. 16.

degradation, loss of complexity, or death does occur; physical life forms are only temporary traps or storages of the flow of energy from the sun.

"The annual syntropic yield of dry biomass in our biosphere is about 1×10^{41} atoms, (150 billion tons of organic matter; 150 pounds per day for each person on Earth) and the total energy trapped or stored per year is about 3×10^{40} electron volts (1.135×10^{15} kwh), about 18% of the total energy incident on the Earth's surface.

"The really distinctive thing about living processes is that they manifest programmed activities. There exist instructions of the form, "if, then" which control a plant's response to environmental changes, and there also exist instructions whereby a plant is organized temporally and spatially from its germination to its reproductive phase. These self-realization instructions act through cell differentiation."[1]

These incredible plants are responsible for and to our presence on this planet. Plants do for humanity what we cannot do for ourselves; that is, entrap, capture, bind, and store solar energy. The Earth's biomass processes the Sun's random radiation into complexity. The food we eat is nothing less than sunlight made edible, made into a form suitable for use in maintaining life. The action of sunlight on human skin does produce Vitamin D, but we do not have the wondrous capacity that green plants have of fixing carbon through the action of sunlight and chlorophyll. There are at least 100 steps in the

"The remarkable thing about photosynthesis is that the plant achieves something a chemist finds hard to accomplish with 5400 degrees of heat: it splits a water molecule."[1]

photosynthetic process linking the absorption of light to the formation of stable end products. The rate of photosynthesis is determined by three environmental factors: light intensity, temperature, and CO_2 concentration.[3] For every 10°C. increase in temperature, the rate of biological activity doubles. This is where, either directly or indirectly, our food comes from. Without organisms capable of capturing sunlight and building it up into more complex forms, there would be no life on Earth, much less the possibility of higher forms of life. Besides providing the basis for our food supply, green plants in natural eco-systems form self-sustaining and regulating communities that require no energy subsidy either directly or indirectly by humanity. Besides being our food, plants are the basis and context for all life and civilization. As far as we can tell, they do not need us; we do need them.

Within the human food system, life forms which can take in energy and process it into higher degrees of complexity are made use of by humanity. In terms of human usage this complexity can be thought of as nutrition. It is only because they are living that organisms are able to develop nutritional complexity; as soon as the organism stops working syntropically, the omnipresent force of entropy takes over and decay sets in, diminishing the nutritional complexity of the food.

The progressive subdivision of systems we are engaged in here—from the meta-systems of Sun/Moon/Earth to the biosphere system to the ecological context and external metabolic systems to the human food system—can continue by dividing the human food system into the productive system (all that happens before harvest) and the distribution system (all that happens after harvest). The rationale for this seemingly arbitrary division is that we have divided the food system into its syntropic and entropic parts. Food production entails the increasing of complexity. Once the flow of energy from the Sun is shut off, i.e., the plant is harvested, the built-up complexity begins to decrease. In thermodynamic terms, the system goes from an open to a closed system. Entropy/disorder can only increase in a closed system. Viewed in this way, food distribution is the attempt to preserve the complexity (which is the same as nutritional quality) of the raw food stock as much as possible. This view is extremely useful because it helps to clarify the major forces at work within the food system and its major subsystems that the designer/problem solver has to deal with. For instance, in the delivery system the syntropic effect formerly supplied by the Sun/organism interaction now has to be supplied by humanity. In the food production system the major problems are concerned with optimizing the syntropic flow of energy and the building of complexity; in the distribution system the major problems are concerned with retarding the spontaneous entropic loss of complexity of the nutritional content of the harvested food.

Another major problem that the food system has to contend with is the fact that food production (as it now exists) is altered by changes in the ecological context and is therefore subject to huge fluctuations in its total amount produced each year. Adding to this problem is the fact that these changes are largely unpredictable and that the ecological context is affected by the food and other subsystems of humanity's external metabolic system. Meanwhile, the demand for food that is

Chart 2. Number of Organisms on Earth.[5]

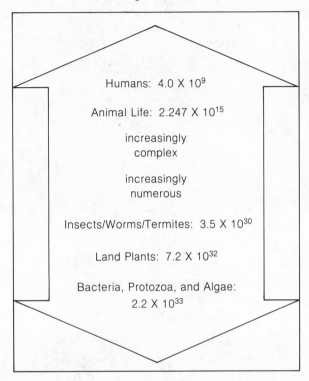

Humans: 4.0×10^9

Animal Life: 2.247×10^{15}

increasingly
complex

increasingly
numerous

Insects/Worms/Termites: 3.5×10^{30}

Land Plants: 7.2×10^{32}

Bacteria, Protozoa, and Algae: 2.2×10^{33}

generated by human nutritional needs remains relatively constant. On the aggregate level of the systems we are dealing with here, the food production system is one unit while the distribution system is composed of three main subsystems: processing, storage, and delivery. Processing is the attempt to stop or retard as much as possible the entropic decay of nutrition. It involves the human directed input of energy into the food product so as to cut it off or to isolate it from the entropic process. As will be seen in the processing section of this document, this energy input can take a wide variety of forms.

Storage, in entropic/syntropic terms, can be seen as part of a syntropic process. In order for syntropic organisms to survive, in order for complexity to survive in the presence of entropy, there needs to be a steady flow of energy into that complexity. Because of the always occuring unpredictable variations in the environment of organisms there is no such thing as an absolutely steady flow of energy. In fact, most flows of energy are interrupted quite frequently, and, on occasion, drastically, as in the case of a prolonged drought. Storage performs the function of maintaining a steady flow of inputs in order to maintain the complexity of the system in the face of environmental fluctuations and entropy. A system will store energy or complexity so that when the outside supply diminishes or ceases, the organism can draw upon its reserves to tide it over until the outside supply resumes.

Evolution seems to progress in the direction of increasing complexity and decreasing number of units (see Chart 2). Each level exhibits a greater capacity for storage. The overall function of storage capabilities is to allow ever greater degrees of freedom from dependence upon the unpredictable fluctuations of the environment. One way of viewing storage in the human food system is merely as a slow-down in the rate of delivery.

The delivery system of the human food system functions as the link between the harvest and the plate. In terms of entropy, the shorter the route between the harvest and the plate the less time will the nutritional content of food have to degrade.

If the function of life is to maintain and increase complexity, then the function of the human food system should be to maintain and increase the nutritional content of food. Viewed in this way all aspects of the human food system—including preparation—should be designed to get the optimum amount of nutrition into individual human systems. As mentioned earlier, entropy makes the conversion of 100% of the nutrition in food impossible so the waste from all aspects of the food system—production, processing, storage, delivery, preparation, and internal metabolic waste—all need to be recycled back into the food production system.[2]

Food Problems,
Prospects,
and Present State

Food on Earth

Without adequate food supplies available to all the people of the world, peace on Earth will continue to be an elusive pie in the sky. Shortages of food or the resources that are necessary for food have caused more human misery and deprivation than any other factor in world history. The reasons for this are as obvious as our own stomachs: without a steady supply of food we relatively quickly experience hunger pains; without any supply of food, we die. Because food is dependent on the natural ecosystem and that system is subject to periodic fluctuations of droughts, floods, frosts, insect populations, etc., our supply of food also fluctuates.

A world which can produce "two ton automobiles, color television sets, and electric tooth-brushes at a greater speed than the increase in world population, but is simultaneously menaced by mass starvation is disturbing."[2] It is paradoxical, to say the least, for people to speak of food which does not reach the millions of humans who can use it, who need it, as "excess" or "surplus." Similarly, when subsistence farmers in the developing regions of the world are forced to sell food to acquire a bare minimum of cash to maintain their place in the economic system, we call this produce "marketable surplus," even

"The struggle—the ceaseless war against hunger—is as old as man himself, and never across the face of our planet has the outcome been more in doubt."[1]

though these farmers often do not have enough food for themselves. When the livestock of the rich world are in direct competition with the humans of the poor world and the market for animal feed generates more interest in financial circles than the market in food for hundreds of millions of children, women, and men, more is wrong than just the farmers not growing enough food.[3]

The world food situation is more difficult now (1972) than at any time since the years immediately following the devastation of the second world war.

With shattering suddenness, a cross fire of forces converged in 1972 to disrupt the world's food supplies. With about 75 million more people to feed in 1972 than 1971, world food production *declined.* World output of cereals (wheat, grains, and rice) fell by 33 million tons. Drought and frost reduced grain yields in eastern Europe and the Soviet Union; dry weather withered crops in India, Australia, Argentina and Africa. Typhoons and drought

slashed harvests in the Philippines, and excessive rains bogged down U.S. corn and soybean crops. Peru's fish catch, traditionally the world's largest, drastically declined—and with it a major source of poultry and livestock feed. Ominously, the world's need for fertilizer, increasing each year by leaps and bounds, shot past manufacturing capacity.

Meanwhile the grain short U.S.S.R., reversing a practice of belt tightening during times of poor harvests, quietly entered world markets and bought up a staggering 28 million tons of grain, most of it from the U.S. The U.S. surpluses had cushioned the world against food shortages and price fluctuations for two decades. With these all but gone, needy nations scrambled for what was left. Prices soared, and food switched roles from an anchor against inflation to a leader in the spiral. During 1972 and 1973, corn, wheat, rice, and soybeans all more than doubled their 1971 prices. A year later the energy crises struck, hitting hardest the poor nations lacking both oil and fertilizer, and the money to buy them.

The threat of food shortages has already become a harsh fact in the Sahelian zone of west Africa, where because of prolonged drought, more than 6 million people came

close to famine. Even where the situation is less dramatic, many millions have been added to the large number of people already inadequately fed. Food prices have risen almost universally, bringing additional hardship to the poorer consumers who have to spend most of their income on food. While food prices rose higher and higher, food aid dwindled.

It is intolerable that, on the threshold of the last quarter of the twentieth century, the world should find itself almost entirely dependent on a single season's weather for its basic food supplies.[1,3,4]

It becomes readily apparent that something, or many things, are dreadfully wrong with our system of producing and distributing food. As long as this situation exists, there can be no peace or constructive stability in the world. As long as malnutrition and starvation exist, potential intelligence which could contribute to the improvement of human welfare will be wasted and lost, and energy and time which could otherwise be employed in the betterment of all humanity will be drained to support those handicapped by malnourishment in infancy. Global, comprehensive, and anticipatory long range strategic planning, coupled with a decentralized, activist participation in the local evolution and implementation of appropriate tactics, is needed to get all of humanity adequate nutrition and to insure the highest intellectual potential of our collective and individual human potentials in as short a time as is possible.

Definitions

Food is a material—either a solid or liquid—that is taken or absorbed into the body in order to sustain growth, repair, and all vital processes, as well as to furnish energy for all activity of the organism. More colloquially, "food is what we eat," and "we eat what is edible (or, if we're lucky, what tastes good)." Food is eaten to satisfy an inborn hunger condition; no one needs to tell us that we are hungry. But food is also eaten to satisfy other needs, social and psychological.

Food is a human being's first experience of consumption, and first experience as a consumer. A culture's attitude toward food shapes his entire attitude towards everything else it consumes. China's attitudes toward food (as well as energy consumption and consumption in general)—reflected in her mores and customs of food use, and formed over centuries of food scarcity—are distinct from the attitudes held in the U.S. The U.S. has never had a widespread famine. This attitude of bounty that the U.S. has in relation to the food it consumes has fostered an attitude that has led to its overconsumption and wasteful use of almost all the items it consumes. Because the U.S. has never been hungry, we use (and waste) energy as if it were as plentiful as our experience of food has been. The average American is up in arms about the high cost of food (and energy), but his argument strikes the rest of the world as ludicrous because they pay a much higher proportion of their income on food and energy than do Americans. For example, steak costs one third more and gasoline two to three times as much in Europe as it does in the U.S. In developing countries, even a higher proportion of income goes to purchase food than it does in America or Europe.

Because of the human organism's never-ending dependence on food and its historical periodicities of plenty and scarcity, it is also used by some as an economic commodity, a source of influence, a diplomatic tool, a form of reparation, or as a political weapon. As Earl Butz said, "Food is power."

Food is an energy source and storage which connects its consumer's metabolism with the environment of which it is a part. Food comes into the human organism from the surrounding environment as a product of that environment's life, energy flows, and material cycles; it leaves the human organism as waste by-products and heat discharged into the environment. Food—as proper nutritional requirement (see Table 1)—maintains the optimal health of the human organism and allows it to be an effective participant in its environment (see Table 2). As the World Health Organization defines it, health is "a state of complete physical, mental, and social wellbeing and not merely the absence of disease or infirmity." Proper nutrition leads to and insures good health.

Table 1 lists what the family of human beings needs to be adequately nourished over time.

The above needs to be viewed from another perspective as well—that of palatableness. Our perception of what food is, and what foods taste good is determined by our environment and culture. Food can be many different things to many people, but one thing is common: without it, we die.

Table 1. Recommended Intake of Nutrients

Age	Body weight	Energy (1)		Protein (1,2)	Vitamin A (3,4)	Vitamin D (5,6)	Thiamine (3)	Ribo-flavin (3)	Niacin (3)	Folic acid (5)	Vitamin B_{12} (5)	Ascorbic acid (5)	Calcium (7)	Iron (5,8)
	kilo-grams	kilo-calories	mega-joules	grams	micro-grams	micro-grams	milli-grams	milli-grams	milli-grams	micro-grams	micro-grams	milli-grams	grams	milli-grams
Children														
1	7.3	820	3.4	14	300	10.0	0.3	0.5	5.4	60	0.3	20	0.5–0.6	5–10
1–3	13.4	1,360	5.7	16	250	10.0	0.5	0.8	9.0	100	0.9	20	0.4–0.5	5–10
4–6	20.2	1,830	7.6	20	300	10.0	0.7	1.1	12.1	100	1.5	20	0.4–0.5	5–10
7–9	28.1	2,190	9.2	25	400	2.5	0.9	1.3	14.5	100	1.5	20	0.4–0.5	5–10
Male adolescents														
10–12	36.9	2,600	10.9	30	575	2.5	1.0	1.6	17.2	100	2.0	20	0.6–0.7	5–10
13–15	51.3	2,900	12.1	37	725	2.5	1.2	1.7	19.1	200	2.0	30	0.6–0.7	9–18
16–19	62.9	3,070	12.8	38	750	2.5	1.2	1.8	20.3	200	2.0	30	0.5–0.6	5–9
Female adolescents														
10–12	38.0	2,350	9.8	29	575	2.5	0.9	1.4	15.5	100	2.0	20	0.6–0.7	5–10
13–15	49.9	2,490	10.4	31	725	2.5	1.0	1.5	16.4	200	2.0	30	0.6–0.7	12–24
16–19	54.4	2,310	9.7	30	750	2.5	0.9	1.4	15.2	200	2.0	30	0.5–0.6	14–28
Adult man														
(moderately active)	65.0	3,000	12.6	37	750	2.5	1.2	1.8	19.8	200	2.0	30	0.4–0.5	5–9
Adult woman														
(moderately active)	55.0	2,200	9.2	29	750	2.5	0.9	1.3	14.5	200	2.0	30	0.4–0.5	14–28
Pregnancy														
(later half)		+350	+1.5	38	750	10.0	+0.1	+0.2	+2.3	400	3.0	30	1.0–1.2	(9)
Lactation														
(first 6 months)		+550	−2.3	46	1,200	10.0	+0.2	+0.4	+3.7	300	2.5	30	1.0–1.2	(9)

[1] Energy and Protein Requirements. Report of a Joint FAO/WHO Expert Group, FAO, Rome, 1972. — [2] As egg or milk protein. — [3] Requirements of Vitamin A, Thiamine, Riboflavin and Niacin. Report of a Joint FAO/WHO Expert Group, FAO, Rome, 1965. — [4] As retinol. — [5] Requirements of Ascorbic Acid, Vitamin D, Vitamin B_{12}, Folate and Iron. Report of a Joint FAO/WHO Expert Group, FAO, Rome, 1970. — [6] As cholecalciferol. — [7] Calcium Requirements. Report of a FAO/WHO Expert Group, FAO, Rome, 1961. — [8] On each line the lower value applies when over 25 percent of calories in the diet come from animal foods, and the higher value when animal foods represent less than 10 percent of calories. — [9] For women whose iron intake throughout life has been at the level recommended in this table, the daily intake of iron during pregnancy and lactation should be the same as that recommended for nonpregnant, nonlactating women of childbearing age. For women whose iron status is not satisfactory at the beginning of pregnancy, the requirement is increased, and in the extreme situation of women with no iron stores, the requirement can probably not be met without supplementation.

History

5

Table 2: Energy requirements for various activities (kilocalories/hour)

Light work		Hard work	
Sitting	19	Polishing	175
Writing	20	Joiner work	195
Standing relaxed	20	Blacksmithing	275–350
Typing	16–40	Riveting	275
Typing quickly	55	Marching	280–400
Sewing	30–90	Cycling	180–600
Dressing and undressing	33	Rowing	120–600
Drawing	40–50	Swimming	200–700
Lithography	40–50		
Violin playing	40–50	**Very hard work**	
Tailoring	50–85	Stonemasonry	350
Washing dishes	60	Sawing wood	420
Ironing	60	Coal mining (average for shift)	320
Bookbinding	45–90	Running	800–1000
		Climbing	400–900
Moderate work		Walking very quckily	570
Shoemaking	80–115	Rowing very quickly	1240
Sweeping	85–110	Running very quickly	1240
Dusting	110	Skiing	500–950
Washing	125–215	Wrestling	1000
Charring	80–160	Walking upstairs	1000
Metal working	120–140		
Carpentering	150–180		
House painting	145–160		
Walking	130–240		

Food production is the base of civilization. Food is not only needed to keep the human population of any given region alive and healthy, but agricultural products are needed to supply the surrounding towns and also to supply raw materials for the many industries that use agricultural products such as tobacco, beverages (alcoholic beverages, tea, coffee, and cocoa), industrial alcohol, other fermentation products, organic chemicals, pharmaceuticals, plastics, paper, wood, textiles, clothing, ropes, sacks and other containers, footwear, rubber, and timber. As a region develops, agricultural products are exported and used as foreign exchange; in addition, agriculture provides widespread employment and through taxation and private commercial initiatives it provides a substantial part of the capital used for general development. Houses, stores, schools and other public buildings, roads, dams, irrigation canals, drains, storage facilities, and processing plants all need to be built, thus providing increased life support services, employment, and income for people. From this perspective, it is clear that agriculture and food production are not merely growing food but also intimately tied in with the general economic and social development of the entire region. The food problem in developing regions where poverty is widespread and usually synonymous with malnourishment is not just one of how to grow more food, but really a constellation of problems concerned with social and economic development. In rich, developed regions the food problem could be looked at as just the need to increase production, but not so in the poverty-stricken developing regions where three quarters of the world's population resides. There, because of the basic role agriculture plays in comprehensive social and economic development and vice versa, the food problem is also an energy problem, transportation problem, education problem, materials problem, logistical problem, health problem, demographic problem, shelter problem, communications problem, and ecological problem.

There are only four ways of obtaining food: growing your own food, or at least part of it, for those who have land; purchasing food, for those who have money; and receiving food as a gift, or stealing it, for those who don't have either land or money. Producing more food will not necessarily increase the nutritional standards of those who most need it, the poor. If there is no way for the poor to obtain food from distribution networks and then prepare and eat it, then the poor will be as bad off as before. Worse in fact, because if the food is there but out of reach, people will be more frustrated or angry than before.

Agriculture is concerned with the deliberate use and control of resources and processes in biological systems for the purpose of food production. Over the centuries four basic approaches to cropping have developed. These are perennial tree or vine crops, represented by such agricultural enterprises as orchards, vineyards, and rubber plantations; cultivated annual crops such as corn, wheat, and rice; grazing of animals on permanent grasslands; and the alternation of cultivated crops with grass or some other forage crop.[1] Historically, agriculture is the principal means by which our species, as a social organism, uses its environment. It first appeared around 10,000 years ago in both the new and old worlds and has since then transformed the face of the Earth. Before that, archeological evidence tells us that we and our predecessors subsisted for eons by hunting and gathering and these activities did not have more than small, local effects upon our ecosystems.

Today agriculture and the global food system shapes everyone's everyday lives. About 3 billion people (2.5 billion in the developing regions of the world, ½ billion in the developed) depend directly upon agriculture for their livelihood. The other billion of us on the planet are all indirectly dependent upon agriculture for our life and livelihood. Because of advances in food production and distribution and health care the human population on Earth has increased to its present level of 4 billion individuals and will increase still further. By 1985 there will be about 4.5 billion and by 2000 the population could perhaps reach 6 billion.

As explosive as population growth has been in all parts of the world, but especially in the poorer, developing regions, food production has been more spectacular. Food output has increased to such an extent that, except in certain parts of Africa, estimated average food supply per person is higher today than ever before. If the index for the average per person supply in 1952–56 is taken as 100, then the figure for all the developing regions in 1970 is 106; with India at 110, South America at 104, and tropical Africa just over 100.[1] In 1960 grain production per person on Earth was under 600 pounds; in 1972–73 it was 632 pounds[3] and in 1977 it was 782 pounds.[4] Food production grew at a rate of 2.8% annually. This is substantially larger than the 2% annual growth in world population. On the average, the 3.8 billion people alive in 1973 ate 21% more food per person than was consumed by the 2.7 billion living in 1954.[6] The reasons for these increases in agricultural productivity can be traced to the conscious application of new knowledge to our age-old food problems. New high-yield seeds as well as the means for producing the most from these seeds, such as irrigation, fertilizer use, and pest and disease control were developed at various research centers and from there have spread throughout the world. Labeled the "green revolution," these new high yield grain seeds, and the techniques for their optimal productive output, offer great potential for further improving food production, especially in developing regions where more food is needed.

Rice yields per acre in Bangladesh, for instance, are only about half those of the world average, only a quarter of those harvested in America, and only 15% of those obtained on experimental stations in Bangladesh. By raising her yields to just the world average, Bangladesh's per capita production would be over 530 pounds, higher than Japan's at the beginning of the 1960's.[3] By 1972 the joint wheat harvest of India and Pakistan was more than double what it had been in 1965. But as dramatic as this widespread "revolution" has been and could be, it is not free of its own problems. To effectively realize the potentials of the green revolution has necessitated national and international tactics to produce, store, and distribute certified seed of the new high-yield varieties on a massive scale; the production of chemical fertilizer factories; the production of other manufacturing plants to produce the crop protecting pesticides and the equipment for applying both these and the fertilizers; networks of distribution for these various products that will insure that the seeds, fertilizers, pesticides, and equipment are all available to the farmer at the right place, time, and cost. All this is by and large impossible without the essential infrastructure of roads, railways, ports, transport vehicles, and communication facilities, which

many countries or regions, usually those who are in greatest need of food, do not have. The advances of the green revolution are so far most widely available to the farmer who has the resources to invest in the new equipment that is needed to most effectively harness the fruits of modern agricultural research. It is not as yet ideally suited to the marginal subsistance farmer, though progress is being made in this direction. What is needed to make the green revolution as effective as possible with the least amount of negative impacts on both the long term productivity of the soil and the social well being of the farmers who use or are victimized by the products of the green revolution is to approach the world's food problems holistically. We need to combine the possibilities of the green revolution with the perspective of the design revolution.

Scare City: The Absence of Food

What happens when a human being starves to death? A 150 pound man in a northern country needs approximately 3000 calories a day; a 125 pound woman or a six-year-old child each need about 2000 calories per day. In the tropics where body heat is easier to maintain, these requirements are less. When food intake drops below energy expenditure, the body must draw on its own tissues for energy. If this energy drain continues too long, the person starves. The body burns up its own fats, muscles, and tissues; kidneys, liver, and endocrine systems often cease to function properly; the heart shows a "brown atrophy" characteristic of starvation, blood pressure and pulse fall drastically, edema usually occurs, skin acquires the consistency of paper, abnormal "lanugo" hair grows on the forearms and backs of children; lassitude and confusion set in so that starvation victims often seem unaware of their plight; "the individual becomes obsessed with food, mentally restless physically apathetic, and self-centered to varying degrees, the extremes being murder and cannibalism"[1]; and the body's immunological defenses drop. Large scale panic, separation of families, adolescent gangs, banditry, looting, the spread of epidemics, and the loss of farm animals and seeds for future crops all add to the impact of

> *"Hunger is a curious thing: at first it is with you all the time, working and sleeping and in your dreams and your belly cries out insistently, and there is a gnawing and a pain as if your very vitals were being devoured, and you must stop it at any cost ... Then the pain is no longer sharp but dull, and this too is with you always."*
> —*Kamela Markandaya*

famine. Most famine victims die from infectious disease before they actually starve to death: children afflicted with malnourishment die from diseases such as tuberculosis, measles (fatality rates from measles are often 200 times higher in poor developing countries than in industrialized countries), smallpox, chicken pox, and gastro-intestinal infections. Once more than forty percent of body weight is lost, death is virtually inevitable.

The World Health Organization estimates that there are 10 million severely malnourished children under five years of age in the world. There are about 70 million people whose lives dangle by a thin thread above the stinking pit of starvation. The Food and Agriculture Organization of the United Nations estimates that undernutrition affects about 460 million people in the world. The World Bank estimates that 930 million people do not have an adequate

basic diet and that some 1.2 billion people lack clean drinking water. "These are not just cold statistics among statistics; they describe the daily physical privation of fellow human beings adversely affecting health and physical growth and seriously reducing the capacity of children to learn and adults to work, as well as provoking high infant and child mortality rates."[1]

For seventy million people to be threatened with death through starvation in a world as rich as ours is so shocking and outrageous that it may tend to obscure the fact that this is less than 2 percent of the world's population—a lower proportion, in all likelihood, than ever before.[4]

Adults can recover from near-starvation; children are permanently damaged. No amount of vitamin D can straighten bones damaged by rickets. Eighty percent of human brain growth occurs between conception and the age of two. Brain development cannot take place in the fetus if the mother is malnourished, nor can it take place if the infant is starving. Brain development that does not occur when it is supposed to will never take place. The child is permanently damaged by physical deformity and mental retardation with no hope of recovery. Six to seven percent of the children under four years of age in developing regions are probably seriously retarded because of inadequate diet.[4] More than 100 thousand children go blind in the Far East alone each year due to vitamin A deficiency.[7]

The major causes of famine include the indeterminacies of weather, such as drought, flood, wind, and snow; diseases which affect plants, animals, and humanity; and civil disturbances such as wars, riots, and strikes. Most of the major famines of the last two centuries have resulted from weather problems. There are three major exceptions—that in Russia, 1932–33, which was caused by collectivization; in Holland, 1944–45, caused by Nazi Germany cutting off all food supplies to Western Holland; and in Biafra, 1968–69, due to civil war. Other famines of the last two hundred years include:

1769	France	Five percent of population said to have died.
1769–70	India, Bengal	Caused by drought. Estimates of deaths range from 3,000,000 (a tenth of population) to 10,000,000 (a third of population).
1770	Eastern Europe	Famine and pestilence caused 168,000 deaths in Bohemia and 20,000 in Russia and Poland.
1775	Cape Verde Islands	Great famine—16,000 people died.
1790–92	India, Bombay, Hyderabad, Orissa, Madras, Gujurat	The Doji Bara or skull famine, so-called because the dead were too numerous to be buried. Cannibalism.
1803–04	Western India	Caused by drought, locusts, war, and migration of starving people. Thousands died.
1837–38	Northwest India	Drought. 800,000 died.
1846–51	Ireland	Great potato famines. A million died from starvation and disease; even more emigrated.
1866	India, Bengal, and Orissa	Poor distribution of rainfall. 1,500,000 deaths.
1868–70	India, Rajputana, Northwest and Central Provinces, Punjab, Bombay	Drought. Famine followed by fever. Deaths estimated at a fourth to a third of total population of Rajputana. In one district 90% of cattle died. Shortage of water for cooking and drinking.
1874–75	Asia Minor	150,000 deaths.
1876–78	India	Drought. Over 36,000,000 affected; deaths estimated at 5,000,000.
1876–79	North China	Drought for 3 years. Children sold. Cannibalism. Estimated deaths—9,000,000–13,000,000.
1892–94	China	Drought. Deaths estimated at 1,000,000.
1896–97	India	Drought. Widespread disease. Estimates of death range up to 5,000,000. Relief efforts successful in several areas.
1899–1900	India	Drought. Extensive relief efforts, but 1,250,000 starved. Another estimate, including effects of disease, 3,250,000.
1920–21	North China	Drought. Estimated 20,000,000 affected; 500,000 deaths.
1921–22	U.S.S.R., especially Ukraine and Volga region	Drought, U.S. assistance requested by Maksim Gorki. Despite relief efforts 20,000,000–24,000,000 affected, estimates of death 1,250,000 to 5,000,000.
1928–29	China, Shensi, Honan, and Kansu	Comparable in extent and severity to great famine of 1877–78, though because of railroads deaths were probably less. In Shensi alone an estimated 3,000,000 died.
1932–34	U.S.S.R.	Caused by collectivization, forced procurements, destruction of livestock by peasants. Estimated 5,000,000 died.
1941–43	Greece	War. Losses because of increased mortality and reduced births estimated at 450,000.
1941–42	Warsaw	War. Starvation, directly or indirectly, estimated to have taken 43,000 lives.
1943	Ruanda-Urundi	35,000 to 50,000 deaths.
1943–44	India, Bengal	Drought. Burmese rice cut off by war. 1,500,000 died.
1947	U.S.S.R.	Reported by Khrushchev in 1963. Referring to Stalin and Molotov: "Their method was like this: they sold grain abroad, while in some regions people were swollen with hunger and even dying for lack of bread." (*Pravda*, Dec. 10, 1963.)
1960–61	Congo, Rep. of the (Kasai)	Caused by civil war.[6]

Major Famines of the Last 100 Years

Sources:
Encyclopedia Britannica, 1971;
and Mayer, J., "Management of
Famine Relief," *Science,*
5-9-75, p. 572.

Africa
Algeria: 1962
Angola: 1971–74
Burundi: 1972
Central African Republic:
  1971–74
Chad: 1971–74
Dahomey: 1971–74
Egypt: 1974
Ethiopia: 1973–75

Ghana: 1971–74
Mali: 1971–74
Mauritania: 1960, 1971–74
Morocco: 1960
Mozambique: 1971–74
Nigeria/Biafra: 1967–70
Nigeria: 1971–74
Niger: 1971–74
Republic of Congo: 1960–61

Ruanda/Urundi: 1943
Sahel: 1968–73
Senegal: 1971–74
Sudan: 1973
Togo: 1971–74
Tunisia: 1958
Upper Volta: 1971–74

Middle East
Iran: 1962
Iraq: 1954
Syria: 1969
Syria/Palestine: 1945–49

Europe
Greece: 1942–43
Holland: 1944–45
Poland: 1941–42

South America
Chile: 1960
Ecuador: 1949
El Salvador: 1951
Haiti: 1954
Nicaragua: 1972
Peru: 1970

USSR
1921–22
1932–34
1947

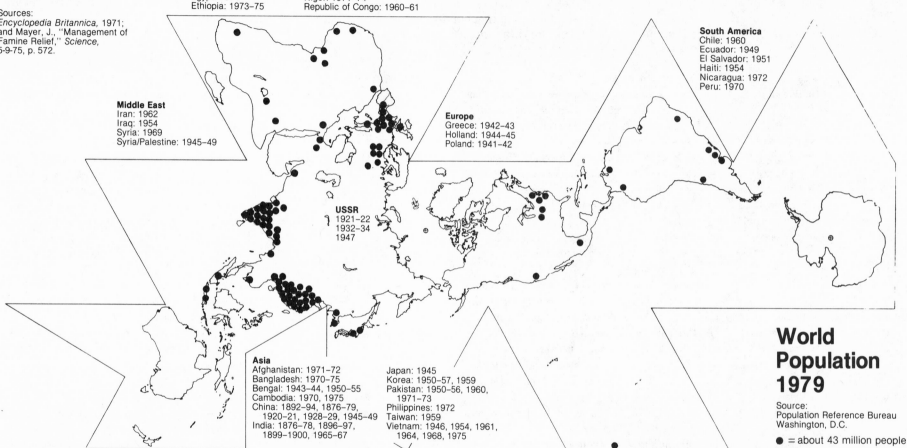

Asia
Afghanistan: 1971–72
Bangladesh: 1970–75
Bengal: 1943–44, 1950–55
Cambodia: 1970, 1975
China: 1892–94, 1876–79,
  1920–21, 1928–29, 1945–49
India: 1876–78, 1896–97,
  1899–1900, 1965–67

Japan: 1945
Korea: 1950–57, 1959
Pakistan: 1950–56, 1960,
  1971–73
Philippines: 1972
Taiwan: 1959
Vietnam: 1946, 1954, 1961,
  1964, 1968, 1975

World Population 1979

Source:
Population Reference Bureau
Washington, D.C.

● = about 43 million people

World Population 1979 (in millions)

World:	4,321	Latin America:	352
Africa:	467	North America:	244
Asia:	2,498	Oceania:	23
Europe:	483	USSR:	264

Food Priority Areas

Source:
Scientific American, September 1976, p. 32

(Low incomes, inadequate diets, and large projected cereal-grain deficits)

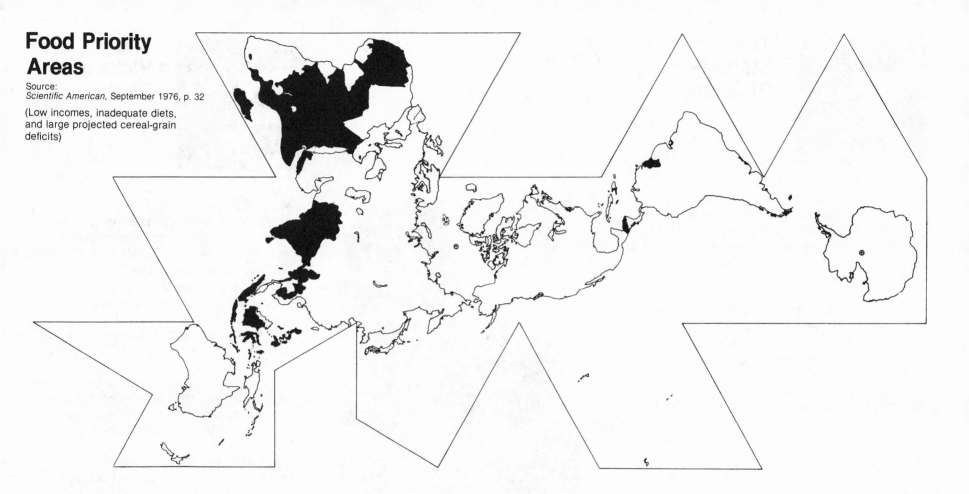

7 The Starvation Diseases

Beriberi is a disease of the peripheral nerves caused by a deficiency of vitamin B. It is characterized by pain in and paralysis of the extremities and severe emaciation or swelling of the body; it affects the heart, circulatory system, and brain.

Kwashiorkor is a nutritional disease of infants or children associated with a lack of protein and characterized by tissues swollen with fluid, liver trouble, loss of appetite, apathy, potbelly, changes in skin pigmentation, a scaly rash, and a change in hair color to a coppery color. It kills tens of thousands of children each year in Africa, India, Southeast Asia, and parts of South America.

Pellagra is a disease caused by a deficiency of niacin and characterized by skin changes, severe nerve dysfunction, and diarrhea.

Rickets is a disease characterized by softening of the bones as a result of malnutrition, ordinarily lack of vitamin D, or of insufficient ingestion of calcium, or both, and often resulting in deformities.

Marasmus is a disease caused by insufficient calories and protein. Victims may weigh only half as much as normal. It is characterized by stick limbs, bloated belly, wide eyes, the stretched skin face of an old person, anemia, diarrhea, dehydration, and a ravenous appetite.

"They that die by famine die by inches."

8 The Vicious Circles

1. Malnutrition leads to higher death rates which in turn motivates large families that in turn increase the need for more food that leads to more malnutrition.
2. Malnourishment makes children more susceptible to diseases such as diarrhea, respiratory infections, malaria, and measles that in turn makes these children less able to make use of whatever food they take in that in turn causes worse malnutrition.
3. A hungry child is in pain, which causes him to cry. A crying child uses twice as many calories as a contented baby that in turn makes him hungrier and causes him more pain.
4. Food-short developing countries seek to increase their agricultural productivity by investing their limited capital in fertilizers, pesticides, new seeds, etc. that in turn increase cash crop output for the wealthy landowner because he is the only one who can afford these products but decreases actual food for the poor who are often kicked off their now profitable land and left without resources to even purchase the food that is available from the landowner (who now exports his crops which benefits

the government's balance of payments) which causes the government to invest even more in fertilizer, etc. to increase crop productivity which makes the rich richer and poor hungrier.

5. Increasing numbers of people graze more animals on the limited grasslands that they have access to which results in a deterioration of the range that results in less meat per animal that causes more animals to be raised which destroys the range still further.

6. Locally available trees and bushes are chopped down in developing regions for use as firewood to cook food that leads to soil erosion and floods that lead to more difficulties with growing food and the exploitation of trees and bushes for firewood in ever increasing distances from home that leads to people needing more food because of the increased energy expenditures in getting firewood and more soil erosion and flooding.

7. Scarcity or rising prices of one commodity generate scarcity or rising prices of others thereby contributing to inflation (and possibly to unemployment) and increasing prices or unavailability of original commodity.

8. "Massive diversion of investment capital and technical resources to meet the crisis of the moment—attempting to compensate for lack of foresight with brute force applied too late—weakens a system elsewhere and thus promotes crises in other sectors later."[8]

9. Rising food prices force up OPEC oil prices which make the energy used directly by the

---

"Malnutrition has clearly emerged as the major public health problem of the world today."
—W.H.O.

---

food system, along with the energy used indirectly in the form of fertilizer and other energy dependent items, more expensive, which in turn forces up energy prices.

10. The U.S. and other highly developed countries sell weaponry to developing countries to obtain the foreign exchange they need to pay for raw materials they import from developing countries which leads to a spiraling arms race between the developing countries and diverts crucial funds and resources that are needed for raising the standard of living thereby causing unrest, interruptions in the flow of raw materials, and destabilization of world peace, which leads to further arms purchases by both developed and developing countries.

11. A well-fed person who knows about the world's food problems does nothing about the world food problems because he thinks someone else is doing what needs to be done that in turn encourages someone else to do nothing.

The insidiously vicious part of a vicious circle is that it often cannot be broken by dealing with just one part. A vicious circle must be dealt with comprehensively. Unfortunately, this is not the way bureaucracies are set up to deal with them. Wholes rarely fit into bureaucratic slots of responsibility or vision.

Preferred State

9

2074094

A design science orientation to problems does not involve complaining about symptoms or merely analyzing in ever more regressive or debilitating detail a problem's wide ranging difficulties, effects, or implications. A design science approach to the world's food problems would *begin* with a description of how things should be functioning. "What is needed?" and not, "What is wrong?" Given the present, what is the preferred state? Defining a preferred state involves the articulation of a set of values as well as possibilities. The limits of a preferred state are ecological compatibility and technological feasibility.

Given the present global food problems, a preferred state would be one which satisfied the following:

1. Sufficient, nutritionally sound food for 100% of humanity's healthful survival and evolution.

2. A global food system should allow for maximum individual flexibility in choosing food types so as to allow for as much cultural diversity as possible.

3. Food should be a birthright, not an economic weapon of exploitation.

4. The food system, as well as food, should be safe; for example, farm workers should not

be exposed to dangerous pesticides, nor should the consumer of the food product.

5. There should be as little coerced human labor involved in the food system as possible.
6. The global food system should be regenerative; that is, it should not be based on resources or practices which are inherently short lived—such as the fossil fuels or poor soil management.
7. It should not only have the least possible negative environmental impact, but as much of a positive impact as possible; as for example, in the development of poor soils into rich soils.
8. There should be an optimum diversity of food crops and a diversity of different strains within each crop. There should be an overall "genetic bank" increase.
9. There should be a minimal dependence on adverse fluctuations in natural cycles.
10. The global food system should operate efficiently in terms of energy, materials, land, and human time use in all stages of the food system. It should continuously strive to do more with less.
11. There should be a built-in flexibility to the system; there should be back-up storage systems to insure the maximum amount of nutritionally sound "forward days" for all of humanity. The fear of an inadequate food supply should be vanquished. Planning and management of the global food system should be as comprehensive and anticipatory as possible to insure a regenerative supply of food for everyone.
12. A global food system should have a high amount of monitoring and feedback for quality and quantity control. Such things as satellite sensing of all farm areas and

cataloging the diversity of all species and plants should be carried out.
13. Access to all accurate food information should be made as widespread as possible.
14. There should be a maximum amount of research and development related to improving the food system.
15. There should be a maximum amount of participation in the making of decisions that affect the food system.

These aspects of a preferred state outline how one group of people addressing themselves to the global food situation think the system should function. There are undoubtedly other general qualities that should be incorporated into a preferred state. Each locale may also have unique preferences that are desirable to just it.

The inverse of this preferred state is, in fact, a description of the current global food state.

Problem State

The problem state of the world food situation is characterized by the following:

1. One-hundred percent of humanity does not have enough nutritionally sound food to achieve or insure their maximum health or potential. Approximately 45% of humanity is not serviced optimally; that is, they suffer from some form of malnourishment (predominantly under nourishment, but obesity is also a problem), and up to 70 million (2% of humanity) are endangered by starvation and famine.
2. Unsafe and non-nutritious foods are consumed, and there are unsafe practices in the food system which endanger the workers in the system.
3. Food is not a birthright, but rather, people and their food needs are exploited through inequitable distribution and consumption. Often a developing country's best land is used for non-food, or cash crops for export. Poverty often stops or impedes people from obtaining the food they need even when it is available because they do not have the money to purchase food.
4. There is a great deal of coerced human labor within the food system as well as unemployment; there is both employment and unemployment without compensation.
5. The present food system is non-

regenerative, that is, it is primarily based on the fossil fuels, it lacks wide diversity in food types and crops (monoculture), and it is over-specialized.

6. It has an adverse ecological impact—soil depletion, erosion, genetic bank decrease, pollution, and over-cultivation all occur.
7. It is energy and materials intensive.
8. It is inefficient in all stages of its operation; for example, there are production losses, storage losses, loss of nutrients in processing and preparing, overconsumption, overcultivation, and misuse of good land for non-food crops.
9. There is a large dependency on the fluctuations of the natural eco-cycles; crops are wiped out by floods, droughts, locusts, etc.
10. There are no efficient global back-up systems; global food reserves were down to the shocking level of about twenty-six days in 1975. There is a pervading fear of inadequate food supply, both on the social and personal level in many parts of the world.
11. There is inadequate monitoring and feedback for food quality and quantity control; there is little or no coordinated global food system planning; there is inaccurate and misleading information propagated, for example in advertising, lack of access to accurate nutritional data on foodstuffs, and a lack of adequate labeling on foodstuffs.
12. Large, centrally controlled agri-business is non-responsive to changing needs and situations.
13. There is not near enough research and development going on related to all stages of the food system, but especially in regards to small-scale production and processing.
14. There is relatively little participatory decision-making in the food system by those who are affected by the food system.

The major problems facing the world food system are a result of:

—the lack of effective storage and distribution of food;

—the increase in population;

—the dependence upon fossil fuels;

—the dependence upon monoculture;

—high use of chemical pesticides and fertilizers;

—increased use of meat and other items high on the food chain;

—the maximization of the profit motive in the food system to the detriment of nutritional quality.

The present state of the world food system is outlined in the following tables, charts, and maps. The first chart lists total world agricultural production in order of tonnage produced. The maps indicate where the major crops are grown. Maps of livestock and fish production will be found in the following section that deals specifically with these topics. Most of the world's four billion people live on only fifteen staple crops: rice, wheat, maize, sorghum, millet, rye, barley, cassava, sweet potatoes, potatoes, coconuts, bananas, common beans, soybeans, and peanuts. These crops furnish about 90% of the world's food and occupy about three-fourths of the total tilled hectares of the world. The maps indicate these and other crops that are cultivated and the quantities produced from each.

Chart 3. 1977 World Agricultural Production[1]

	Million Metric Tons
Sugar Cane	737.48
Cow Milk	409.09
Wheat	386.60
Rice	366.51
Maize	349.68
Potatoes	292.94
Sugar Beets	290.12
Barley	173.09
Sweet Potatoes	138.09
Cassava	110.17
Soybeans	77.50
Fish	73.50
Grapes	57.01
Sorghum	55.41
Oats	52.47
Pulses	47.96
Beef and Veal	46.24
Tomatoes	45.02
Pig Meat	43.81
Millet	42.89
Seed Cotton	41.76*
Bananas	36.87
Oranges	32.85
Coconuts	32.42
Wine	28.80
Buffalo Milk	27.44
Cotton Seed	26.69*
All Eggs	25.08
Poultry Meat	24.39
Rye	23.77
Watermelons	22.61
Cabbages	22.25
Apples	21.35
Plantains	19.62
Dry Onions	17.61
Groundnuts	17.46
Cotton	14.29*

	Million Metric Tons			Million Metric Tons			Million Metric Tons
Mangoes	13.35	Green Beans	2.35	The Earth	5.9×10^{21}
Dry Beans	12.91	Dates	2.25	The Hydrosphere	1.4×10^{18}
Dry Peas	12.43	Sesame Seeds	1.95	The Atmosphere	6×10^{15}
Sunflower Seeds	11.75	Tea	1.76	The Biosphere	2×10^{13}
All Cheeses	10.18	Goat Meat	1.72	Higher plants	3×10^{12}
Olives	8.15	Olive Oil	1.60	Terrestrial animals	1.5×10^{12}
Cucumbers and Gherkins	7.80	Garlic	1.53	Man	2×10^{3}
Rapeseed	7.65	Palm Kernels	1.51		
Sheep Milk	7.27	Cacao Beans	1.41		
Tangerines	7.25	Strawberries	1.316		
Chick-Peas	6.92	Buffalo Meat	1.309		
Carrots	6.85	Artichokes	1.28		
Pears	6.813	Lentils	1.27		
Butter and Ghee	6.810	Apricots	1.25		
Goat Milk	6.55	Papayas	1.24		
Peaches and Nectarines	6.20	Avocados	1.22		
Pineapples	6.11	Safflower Seeds	1.02		
Dry Broad Beans	6.10	Honey	.95		
Pumpkins, Squash, Gourds	5.95	Dry Whey	.93		
Chiles and Green Peppers	5.70	Raisins	.91		
Tobacco Leaves	5.65*	Walnuts	.88		
Mutton and Lamb	5.59	Almonds	.76		
Cantaloupes and Other Melons	5.57	Flax	.694*		
Lemons and Limes	5.05	Castor Beans	690		
Copra	4.77	Cashew Nuts	.54		
Green Peas	4.58	Chestnuts	.51		
Evaporated and Condensed Milk	4.57	Horse Meat	.471		
Plums	4.47	Sisal	.471*		
Green Coffee	4.34	Hazelnuts	.43		
Jute and Substitutes	4.31*	Currants	.29		
Grapefruit and Pomelo	4.25	Hemp	.23*		
Wool	4.10*	Raspberries	.15		
Cauliflower	4.05	Hops	.12		
Eggplants	3.90	Tung Oil	.10*		
Palm Oil	3.75	Pistachios	.07		
Rubber	3.61*	Silk	.05*		
Linseed	2.90	Hempseed	.03*		

* non-food crop

Source: *Encyclopedie Francaise,* in reference #2.

Chart 3. Summary. 1977 World Agricultural Production[1]

	Million Metric Tons	Total Kilograms per Person per Year	Kilograms per Person per Day
1. TOTAL CEREALS:	1,459	365	1.
2. TOTAL SUGAR CANE & BEET PRODUCTION:	1,028	257	.70
3. TOTAL SUGAR PRODUCTION:	105	26	.07
4. TOTAL ROOTS & TUBERS:	570	142	.39
5. TOTAL MILK:	450	112	.30
6. TOTAL VEGETABLES & MELONS:	318	79	.22
7. TOTAL FRUITS & BERRIES:	257	64	.17
8. TOTAL MEAT & FISH:	200	50	.13 (130 grams)
9. TOTAL NUT PRODUCTION:	3.5	.87	.002
10. TOTAL NON-EDIBLE PRODUCTION:	102	25	.07
11. TOTAL PRODUCTION:	4,492	1,123	3.07
12. TOTAL FOOD PRODUCTION:	3,362	840	2.3

Chart 4. World Sugar Consumption[1]

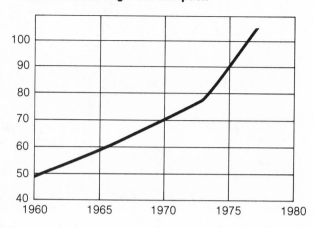

Total food production is 2.3. kg. (5 pounds) per person per day. The fact that a human being requires less than 0.6 kg. per day of food plus water (see Chart 5) dramatically points out the need for better food distribution, storage, and conservation strategies. The world food system currently produces enough food for over 15 billion people! Where does all this food go? A rough estimate would be that animals eat enough for 2–8 billion people, 20–40% is lost, about 2 billion humans eat enough for 3–4 billion, one billion humans eat enough for one billion, and another billion eat enough for three-quarters of a billion people.

"Since passage of the 1971 Cancer Act, we have determined that 80% to 90% of cancers are apparently environmentally caused. More striking is the discovery that 40% of the cancers in men and 60% in women are nutrition-related."

—George McGovern

An interesting and perhaps shocking item in the above chart is the huge quantity of sugar cane and sugar beet produced. Except for relatively small amounts that are used for animal food, seed, or the manufacture of alcohol, this agricultural product is turned into sugar for the sweet tooths of the world. About

105 million metric tons of sugar were produced in 1977, almost twice the amount produced in 1940 (see Chart 4). The average person in the world now eats about 20 kg. (44 pounds) per year, with over 45 kg. (100 pounds) per year being eaten by each American, Cuban, Costa Rican, Australian, and Israeli. The land area devoted to growing the world's largest crop (in terms of raw tonnage—ninth in terms of processed product) is only 21.4 million hectares: small when compared to the 744 million hectares devoted to our cereal crops, but large in terms of the questionable nutritional content of sugar.

Chart 5. Daily Metabolic Turnover for One Person.

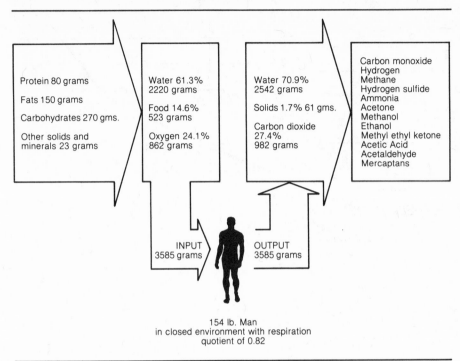

Protein 80 grams

Fats 150 grams

Carbohydrates 270 gms.

Other solids and minerals 23 grams

Water 61.3% 2220 grams

Food 14.6% 523 grams

Oxygen 24.1% 862 grams

Water 70.9% 2542 grams

Solids 1.7% 61 gms.

Carbon dioxide 27.4% 982 grams

Carbon monoxide
Hydrogen
Methane
Hydrogen sulfide
Ammonia
Acetone
Methanol
Ethanol
Methyl ethyl ketone
Acetic Acid
Acetaldehyde
Mercaptans

INPUT 3585 grams

OUTPUT 3585 grams

154 lb. Man
in closed environment with respiration
quotient of 0.82

Chart 6. Approximate Daily Metabolic Turnover for All of Humanity.

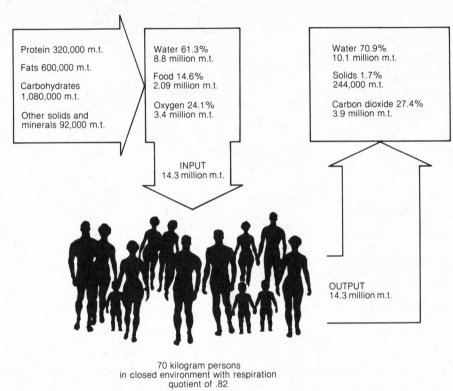

Protein 320,000 m.t.

Fats 600,000 m.t.

Carbohydrates 1,080,000 m.t.

Other solids and minerals 92,000 m.t.

Water 61.3% 8.8 million m.t.

Food 14.6% 2.09 million m.t.

Oxygen 24.1% 3.4 million m.t.

Water 70.9% 10.1 million m.t.

Solids 1.7% 244,000 m.t.

Carbon dioxide 27.4% 3.9 million m.t.

INPUT 14.3 million m.t.

OUTPUT 14.3 million m.t.

70 kilogram persons
in closed environment with respiration
quotient of .82

The world produced 3362 million metric tons of cereals, fish, meat, vegetables, milk, roots and tubers, fruit and berries, and nuts in 1977. Assuming a 50% water content, this amounts to 1681 million metric tons of dry weight, which is still over twice the amount (763 million metric tons) needed to feed the world's population of 4 billion people.

Chart 7. Present World Food System—Qualitative Inputs and Outputs.

Inputs needed for the production/delivery of food by the world food system:	Food system:	Outputs from the food system:
1. Know-how	Organizes materials with energy through know-how to produce food (forward survival for humans).	1. Increased know-how
2. Energy —sun —human labor —animal labor —fossil fuels		2. Energy —spent human labor (tired humans) —returns to environmental energy processes: a) heat b) molecular transformation (i.e., gasoline, CO, CO_2, etc.) c) spatial relocations —caloric content of foods produced
3. Materials —soil —seeds —fertilizers —water —CO_2 —pesticides —packaging		3. Materials —fertilizer, pesticides, soil runoff —seeds —food —organic waste—corn stalks, manure, etc. —fossil fuel wastes—CO, CO_2, NO_2, etc. —containers, wrappings, etc.
4. Tools		4. Tools —obsolete and worn out tools
5. Ecological Context —climate, weather —gravity, time, etc. —moon —photosynthesis —crop diseases, pests —beneficial insects		5. Ecological Context —changed environment —ecological imbalance —weather modifications
6. Cultural Context —values —needs, demands —taste		6. Food, Nutriments —health and mental abilities —reinvestable time

Chart 8. Present Food System—Levels, Constraints, and Forcing Functions.

	Agricultural System	Technological System		Human System		Modern Agriculture
Level 1	PRODUCTION	PREPARATION		Satisfaction of human nutritional needs		Small scale traditional agriculture, home garden
		STORAGE 1	**STORAGE 2**	**STORAGE 3**		
Level 2	PRODUCTION	PROCESSING PACKAGING	DELIVERY	PREPARATION	Satisfaction of HUMAN NUTRITIONAL NEEDS	
	Ecological Constraints	Energetic & Logistical Constraints		Nutritional & Palatability Constraints		

The world food system can be divided into the three realms shown in this flow chart: food production or the agricultural realm, with ecological constraints on performance; the technological realm, with energetic and logistical constraints; and the human realm, with nutritional and palatability constraints.

Level 1: Production is from local gathering, hunting, fishing, or garden; food is picked, harvested, etc. and eaten shortly thereafter.

Level 2: Food is produced in large quantities and stored in grain bins and other types of large storage facilities before processing. After processing, food is again stored before delivery to the consumer. Consumer will then store food again in refrigerator, pantry, cellar, etc. before preparation and consumption of food. Besides the individual or family, "consumer" includes restaurants, caterers, and vending machines.

Constraints on food system:
a) nutrition
b) palatability
c) values
d) technology
e) ecology; environmental impact, climate, weather
f) resources
g) economics
h) socio-political
i) time
j) geography
k) safety

Forcing functions:
a) hunger
b) increasing population
c) increasing demand per capita; rising expectations
d) new know-how; i.e., increased performance per function (increased economy)
e) evolution

Present Food System: From External Metabolics to Internal Metabolics

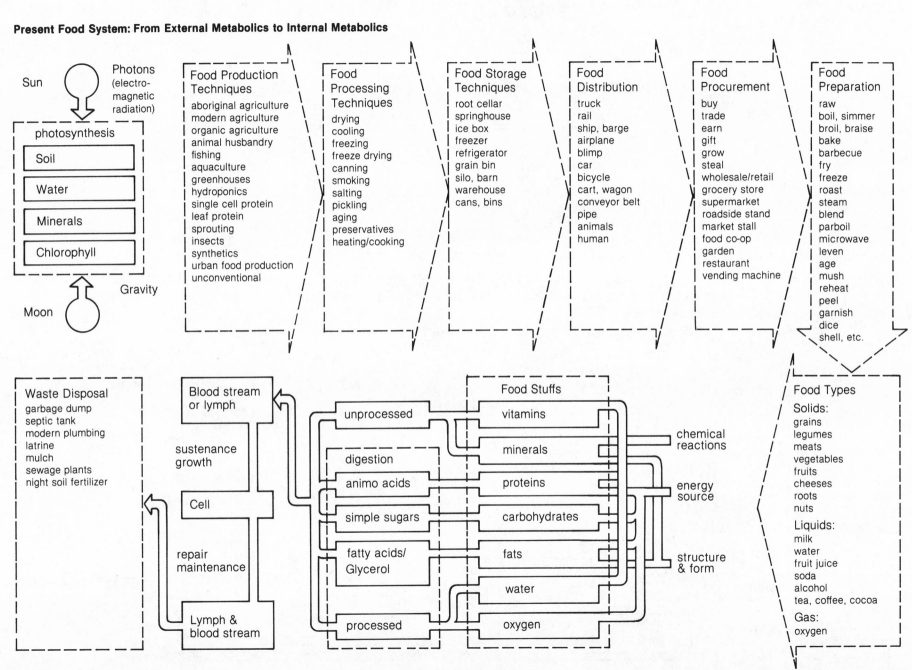

Sun

Photons (electro-magnetic radiation)

photosynthesis
- Soil
- Water
- Minerals
- Chlorophyll

Moon

Gravity

Food Production Techniques
aboriginal agriculture
modern agriculture
organic agriculture
animal husbandry
fishing
aquaculture
greenhouses
hydroponics
single cell protein
leaf protein
sprouting
insects
synthetics
urban food production
unconventional

Food Processing Techniques
drying
cooling
freezing
freeze drying
canning
smoking
salting
pickling
aging
preservatives
heating/cooking

Food Storage Techniques
root cellar
springhouse
ice box
freezer
refrigerator
grain bin
silo, barn
warehouse
cans, bins

Food Distribution
truck
rail
ship, barge
airplane
blimp
car
bicycle
cart, wagon
conveyor belt
pipe
animals
human

Food Procurement
buy
trade
earn
gift
grow
steal
wholesale/retail
grocery store
supermarket
roadside stand
market stall
food co-op
garden
restaurant
vending machine

Food Preparation
raw
boil, simmer
broil, braise
bake
barbecue
fry
freeze
roast
steam
blend
parboil
microwave
leven
age
mush
reheat
peel
garnish
dice
shell, etc.

Waste Disposal
garbage dump
septic tank
modern plumbing
latrine
mulch
sewage plants
night soil fertilizer

Blood stream or lymph

sustenance growth

Cell

repair maintenance

Lymph & blood stream

unprocessed

digestion

animo acids

simple sugars

fatty acids/ Glycerol

processed

Food Stuffs
vitamins
minerals
proteins
carbohydrates
fats
water
oxygen

chemical reactions

energy source

structure & form

Food Types

Solids:
grains
legumes
meats
vegetables
fruits
cheeses
roots
nuts

Liquids:
milk
water
fruit juice
soda
alcohol
tea, coffee, cocoa

Gas:
oxygen

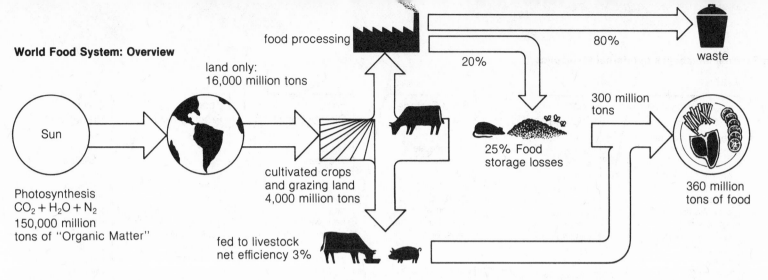

World Food System: Overview

Sun

Photosynthesis
$CO_2 + H_2O + N_2$
150,000 million
tons of "Organic Matter"

land only:
16,000 million tons

cultivated crops
and grazing land
4,000 million tons

fed to livestock
net efficiency 3%

food processing

20%

80%

waste

25% Food
storage losses

300 million
tons

360 million
tons of food

*Man uses his stock of
potential food
wastefully: He feeds
grain to inefficient
animals, eats only parts
of plants, and lets
various vermin nibble at
his stores.*

U.S. Food System: Overview. (All figures refer to million tons of dry organic matter.)

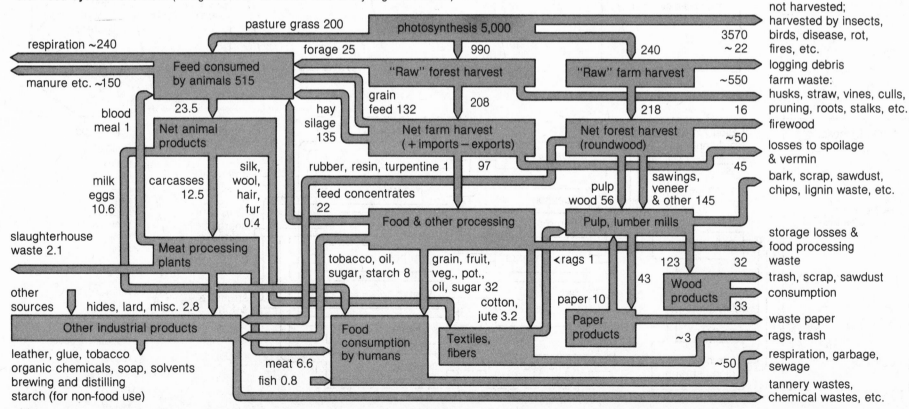

pasture grass 200

photosynthesis 5,000

respiration ~240

forage 25

990

240

3570
~ 22

not harvested;
harvested by insects,
birds, disease, rot,
fires, etc.

Feed consumed
by animals 515

"Raw" forest harvest

"Raw" farm harvest

logging debris
farm waste:

manure etc. ~150

grain
feed 132

208

218

16

~550

husks, straw, vines, culls,
pruning, roots, stalks, etc.

blood
meal 1

23.5

hay
silage
135

Net farm harvest
(+ imports – exports)

Net forest harvest
(roundwood)

~50

firewood

losses to spoilage
& vermin

Net animal
products

rubber, resin, turpentine 1

97

milk
eggs
10.6

carcasses
12.5

silk,
wool,
hair,
fur
0.4

feed concentrates
22

Food & other processing

pulp
wood 56

sawings,
veneer
& other 145

45

Pulp, lumber mills

bark, scrap, sawdust,
chips, lignin waste, etc.

slaughterhouse
waste 2.1

Meat processing
plants

tobacco, oil,
sugar, starch 8

grain, fruit,
veg., pot.,
oil, sugar 32

<rags 1

123

32

storage losses &
food processing
waste

other
sources

hides, lard, misc. 2.8

cotton,
jute 3.2

paper 10

43

Wood
products

33

trash, scrap, sawdust
consumption

Other industrial products

Food
consumption
by humans

Textiles,
fibers

Paper
products

~3

waste paper

rags, trash

leather, glue, tobacco
organic chemicals, soap, solvents
brewing and distilling
starch (for non-food use)

meat 6.6
fish 0.8

~50

respiration, garbage,
sewage

tannery wastes,
chemical wastes, etc.

44

World Cereal Production 1977

Source:
1977 FAO Production Yearbook,
Vol. 31 (United Nations, 1978)

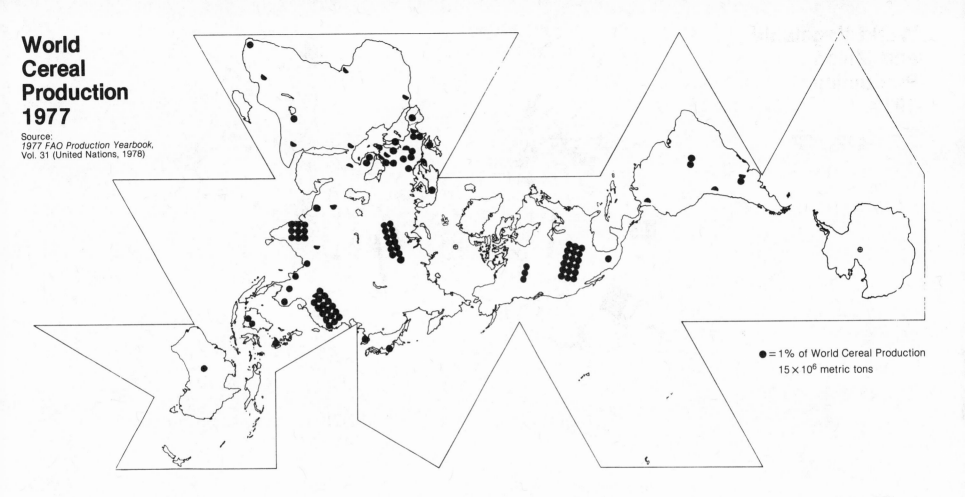

● = 1% of World Cereal Production
15 × 10⁶ metric tons

Grains provide

70% of the food supply in Asia

45% of the food supply in Africa

50% of the food supply in South
America

Slightly more than one-half of
the harvested land of the world
is used to grow grains.

World Vegetable and Melon Production 1977

Source:
1977 FAO Production Yearbook,
Vol. 31 (United Nations, 1978)

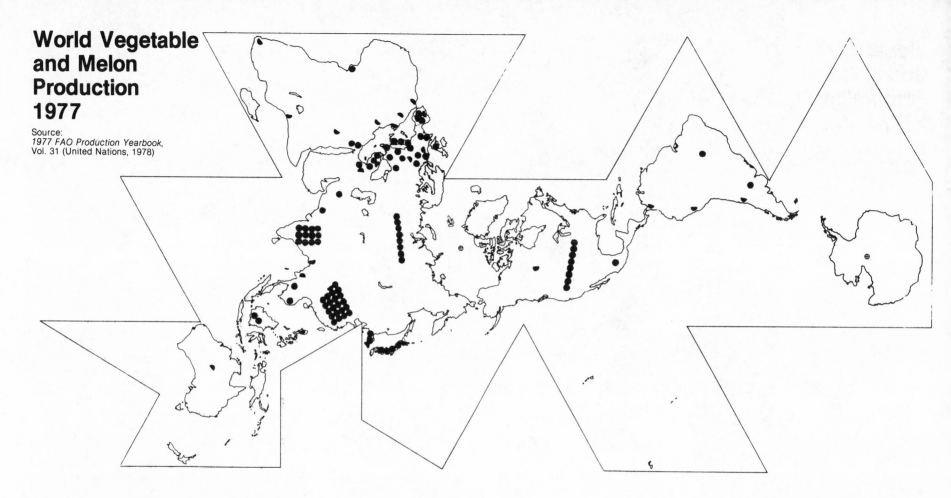

● = 1% of World Vegetable and Melon Production
3.2 × 10⁶ metric tons

World Root and Tuber Production 1977

Source:
1977 FAO Production Yearbook,
Vol. 31 (United Nations, 1978)

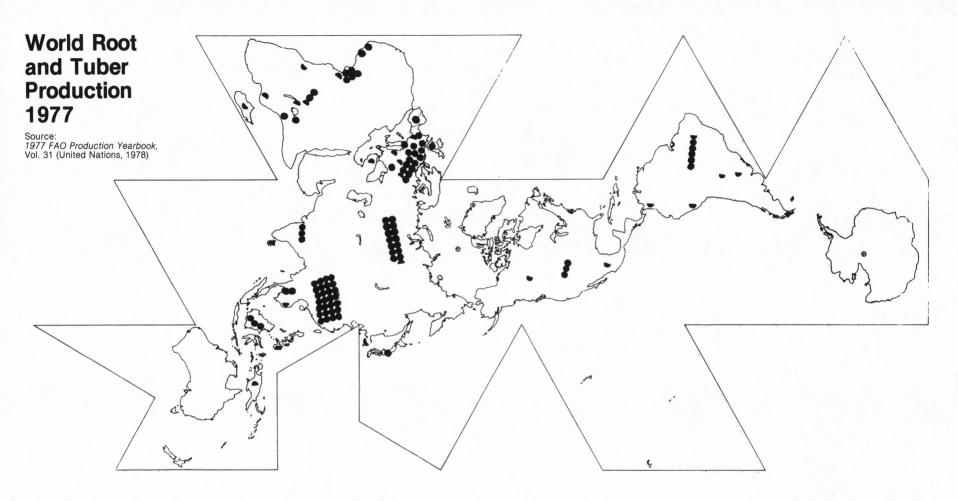

● = 1% of World Root and Tuber Production
    5.7 × 10⁶ metric tons

Wheat

One dot represents 1,000,000 bushels
Source:
Goode's World Atlas, 1975

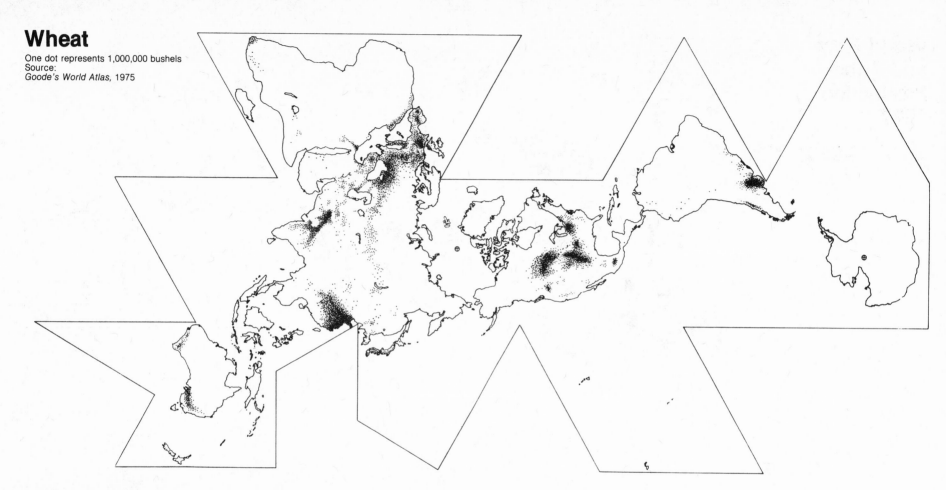

Wheat is a grain that is not only the most widely grown food crop, but the main staple in the diet of one third of the world's population. Valued as a high energy food and important protein source, its principal use is in its milled form as flour to produce bread (leavened and unleavened) and noodle products. The growth of wheat has spread from the Near East (in about 7000 B.C.) to other grasslands of the temperate zone. Since the 1940's, extensive research programs have been carried out to produce wheat varieties that resist diseases that limit their production, that have an improved amino acid balance for higher quality protein, and that produce higher yields.

1975 Yields (kg/ha):   1,295 (developing countries average)
2,085 (U.S. average)
14,526 (world record)

Wheat research: International Maize and Wheat Improvement Center, El Batan, Mexico; also International Center for Agricultural Research in Dry Areas, Lebanon

Wheat—1977 World Production:	387
Africa:	8.2
North and Central America:	77
South America:	9
Asia:	108
Europe:	82
Oceania:	9.7
USSR:	92

All units in million metric tons

Rice

Major Areas of Production
Source:
Oxford Economic Atlas, 1972

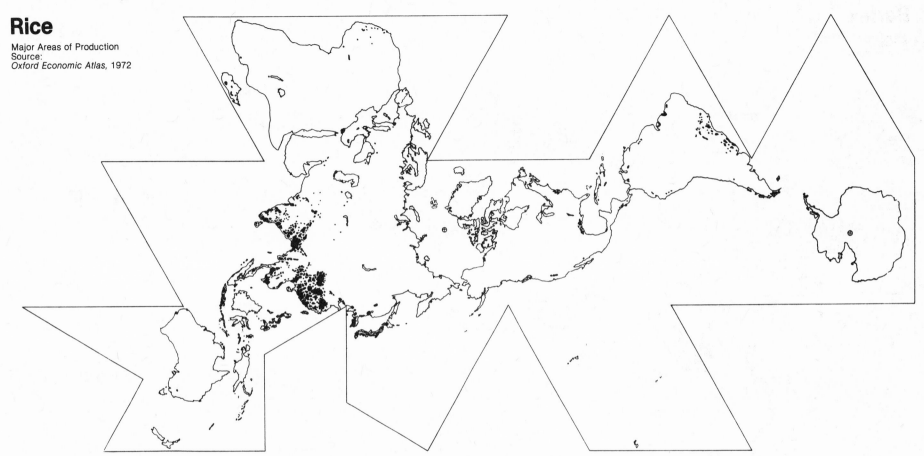

Rice is a grain utilized by about 90% of the world's low income people for at least one fourth of their diet. Polished white rice is the major source of food (carbohydrates) for nearly one half of the world's people, with per capita consumption reaching 200 to 400 lbs./year in parts of the Orient. With origins in Southeast Asia more than 6,000 years ago, rice has been cultivated and developed into about 30,000 varieties all belonging to one species, *Oryza sativa.* Because most rice is cultivated in fields submerged in 4–6 inches of water, two or more successive crops are grown, thereby achieving much higher yields per hectare per year

than by the growth of wheat. Minor by-products include alcoholic beverages, animal feed, and straw for thatching, mats, and paper.

1975 Yields
(kg/ha/crop/112 days):
2,500 (U.S. average)
14,400 (world record)

Rice research: International Rice Research Institute, Los Banos, Philippines; also International Institute of Tropical Agriculture, Ibadan, Nigeria: International Center of Tropical

Agriculture, Palimra, Colombia; and West African Rice Development Association, Monrovia, Liberia

Rice—1977 World Production:	367
Africa:	7.8
North and Central America:	6.2
South America:	13
Asia:	335
Europe:	1.5
Oceania:	.6
USSR:	2.2

All units in million metric tons

49

Barley

Major Areas of Production
Source:
Goode's World Atlas, 1976

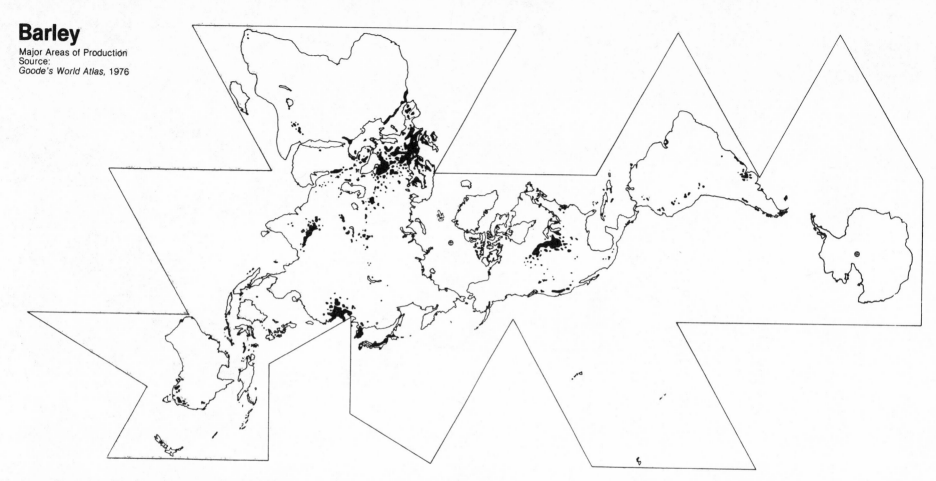

Barley, one of the earliest grains cultivated by man, can be traced to origins in Egypt over 5,000 years ago, and was the chief bread material in Europe as recently as the sixteenth century. Present-day difficulties with barley include the fact that it is subject to many diseases and that it matures earlier than the other small grains, thereby making it difficult to grow in hot and humid climates. As a special-purpose grain with numerous varieties, it is only rarely ground into flour, more often being used in soups, as stock feed, for malting in brewing beer or ale, or in producing industrial alcohol, paper, and textiles.

1975 Yields (kg/ha):
1,154 (developing countries average)
2,367 (U.S. average)
11,405 (world record)

Barley research: International Maize and Wheat Improvement Center, El Batan, Mexico, and International Center for Agricultural Research in Dry Areas, Lebanon (primarily research on beer-making and feed for cattle)

Barley—1977 World Production:	173
Africa:	3.1
North and Central America:	21
South America:	1.1
Asia:	27
Europe:	65
Oceania:	2.9
USSR:	53

All units in million metric tons

Millet and Grain Sorghum

Major Areas of Production
Source:
Goode's World Atlas, 1975

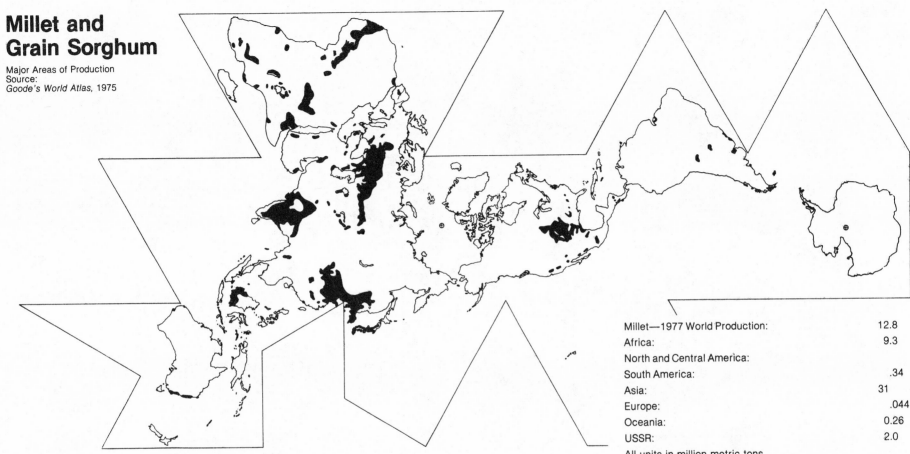

Millet—1977 World Production:	12.8
Africa:	9.3
North and Central America:	
South America:	.34
Asia:	31
Europe:	.044
Oceania:	0.26
USSR:	2.0
All units in million metric tons	

Millet is a cereal grain grown where the rainfall or length of the growing season is inadequate for grain sorghum or maize. In Asia and Africa, it is used like rice, ground into meal or made into cakes. It has a high starchy component (55–65%) and its protein quality varies widely. Like maize, it is generally low in the amino acid lysine so it requires supplementation to furnish complete protein. In North America it is primarily grown as animal feed.

Millet research: International Crops Research Institute for the Semi-Arid Tropics, Hyderabad, India

Cultivated in many varieties and known by various names, sorghum can be divided into two main types: grain sorghum, which is used as a food or animal forage, and sweet sorghum, which is used as a forage or to make syrup or molasses. In use it resembles maize, but it has good drought-resistant properties and its short-stem hybrids are ideal for mechanical harvesting.

1975 Yields (kg/ha):
867 (developing countries average)
3,295 (U.S. average)
21,521 (world record)

Sorghum research: International Crops Research Institute for the Semi-Arid Tropics, Hyderabad, India

Sorghum—1977 World Production:	55.4
Africa:	9.4
North and Central America:	24
South America:	8.1
Asia:	12
Europe:	.65
Oceania:	.96
USSR:	.965
All units in million metric tons	

Oats

Major Areas of Production
Source:
Goode's World Atlas, 1975

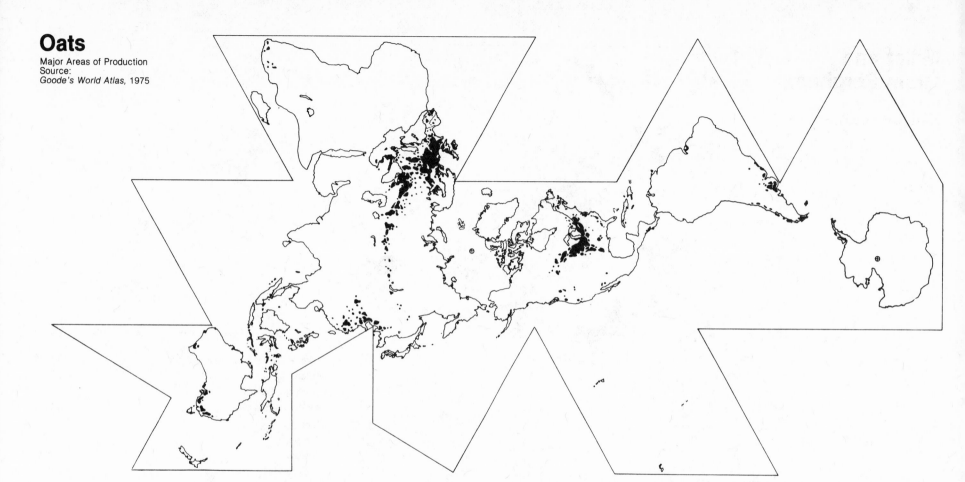

Oats rival corn, rice, and wheat as the leading grain crop. Only 5–10% of oat production is for human consumption, usually as rolled oats or breakfast cereal since it lacks the glutenous protein necessary for bread-making. Its chief value as a pasturage and hay crop primarily for horses dates from the late Bronze Age in Northern Europe. Its relatively recent domestication continues as disease-resistant strains are developed.

1975 Yields (kg/ha):
1,199 (developing countries average)
1,722 (U.S. average)
10,617 (world record)

Oats—1977 World Production	52
Africa:	.17
North and Central America:	15
South America:	.76
Asia:	2.5
Europe:	14.4
Oceania:	1.0
USSR:	18.3

All units in million metric tons

Maize/Corn

Major Areas of Production
Source:
Goode's World Atlas, 1975

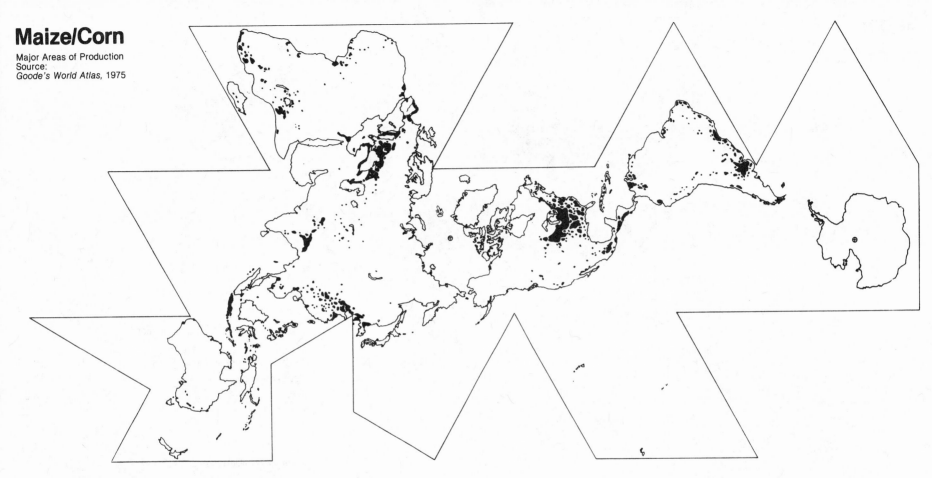

Maize (also called corn) is a grain which has been grown under very diverse soil and climatic conditions throughout the world since prehistoric times. In the U.S., where 60% of the world production is located, most of the corn is grown for livestock feed (80%), but in other parts of the world it is used primarily for human consumption.

1975 Yields (kg/ha):
1,325 (developing countries average)
5,398 (U.S. average)
21,216 (world record)

Maize research: International Maize and Wheat Improvement Center, El Batan, Mexico; also International Institute of Tropical Agriculture, Ibadan Nigeria; International Center of Tropical Agriculture, Palmira, Colombia

Maize—1977 World Production:	350
Africa:	26
North and Central America:	177
South America:	31
Asia:	54
Europe:	50
Oceania:	.40
USSR:	10.9

All units in million metric tons

Sugar

Major Areas of Production
Source:
Oxford Economic Atlas, 1972

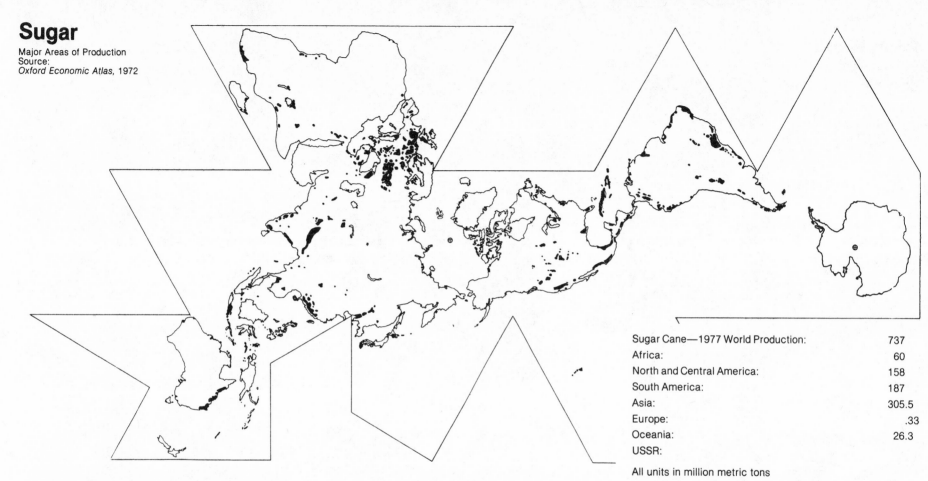

Sugar Cane—1977 World Production:	737
Africa:	60
North and Central America:	158
South America:	187
Asia:	305.5
Europe:	.33
Oceania:	26.3
USSR:	

All units in million metric tons

Sugar Beet—1977 World Production:	290
Africa:	1.06
North and Central America:	23.9
South America:	2.8
Asia:	24.7
Europe:	144
Oceania:	
USSR:	93

All units in million metric tons

Although present in all green plants, sucrose ($C_{12}H_{22}O_{11}$) is obtained commercially from only two plants: sugar cane (56% of world supply) and sugar beet (44%). Sugar cane, a member of the grass family, originated as a crop in New Guinea about 15,000–8000 B.C. and later spread to other tropical areas with plentiful rainfall or irrigation (Polynesia, Asia, South America, and Africa). The stalk of the sugar cane is hand-harvested and then processed in large factories by milling, clarification, and centrifuge (to produce centrifugal sugar) and smaller factories (to produce brown or non-centrifugal sugar). Since Napoleonic times, European and USSR sugar has come from locally-grown sugar beets.

1975 Yields (kg/ha/year):
sugar cane   50,000 (U.S. average)
            150,000 (world record)
sugar beet   50,000 (U.S. average)
            120,000 (world record)

Soybeans

Major Areas of Production
Source:
Oxford Economic Atlas, 1972

Legumes provide about 20% of the world's human protein supply.

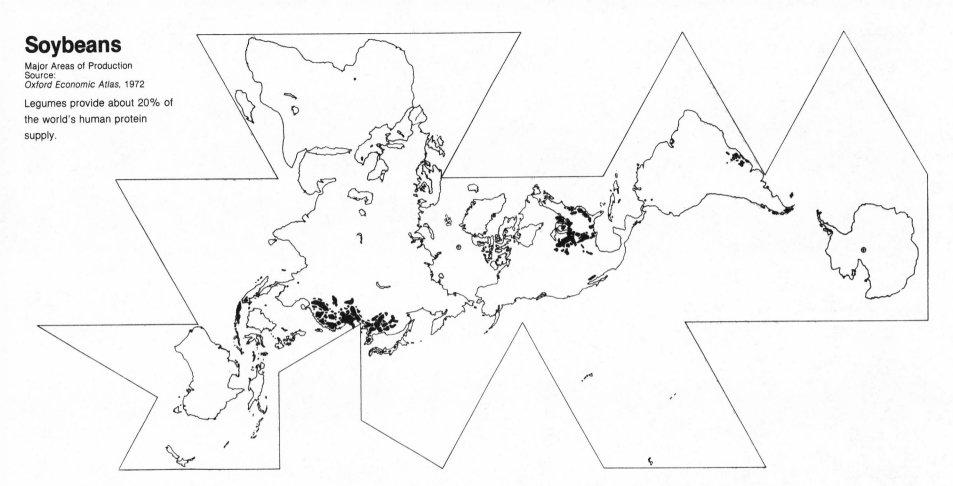

The soybean, a legume of the pulse family, has been a principal crop in the Orient for 5,000 years. It was introduced in the United States (and France) in the 1700's as a curiosity, but now the U.S. is the world's largest producer of this high-protein food commodity—soybeans and maize are the two largest U.S. agricultural exports in monetary value. In the U.S., 98% of the soybean protein is consumed by livestock, but elsewhere it is made into soy sauce, soy flour or grits, vegetable oil, vegetable cheese and milk, curds or cake, textured vegetable protein (meat substitute), and a coffee substitute. It is a rich source not only of protein but B complex vitamins, calcium, phosphorus, potassium, magnesium, and iron.

1975 Yields (kg/ha):
1,544 (developing countries average)
1,883 (U.S. average)
7,398 (world record)

Soybean research: International Center of Tropical Agriculture, Ibadan, Nigeria, and International Soybean Program, Puerto Rico

Soybeans—1977 World Production:	77.5
Africa:	.126
North and Central America:	48
South America:	14
Asia:	14.6
Europe:	.43
Oceania:	.055
USSR:	.5

All units in million metric tons

Potatoes

Major Areas of Production
Sources:
Oxford Economic Atlas, 1972

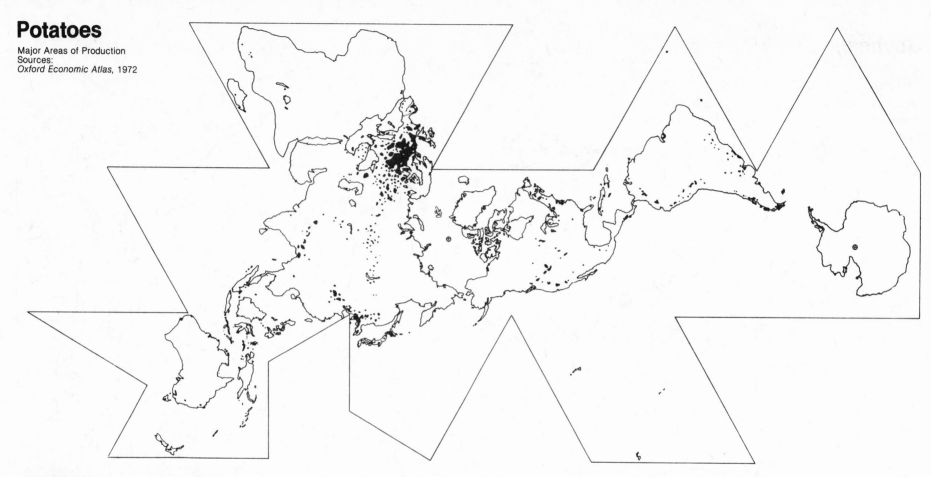

The potato, a root crop, cultivated by the Incas about 3500 B.C. and a staple of the pre-Columbian South American Indian diet, was introduced to Europe in the 1500's where it was first called the potato, and reintroduced to North America in the 1600's. Although starch comprises 65–80% of its dry weight, potato protein contains substantially more of all the essential amino acids, except histidine, than does whole wheat, and potatoes supply more vitamin C to the U.S. food supply than any other major food.

1975 Yield (kg/ha):
9,129 (developing countries average)
26,632 (U.S. average)
94,153 (world record)

Potato research: International Potato Center, Lima, Peru

Potatoes—1977 World Production:	293
Africa:	4.4
North and Central America:	19
South America:	9.3
Asia:	60.9
Europe:	114.5
Oceania:	.99
USSR:	83

All units in million metric tons

Sunflower Seed

Major Areas of Production
Source:
Oxford Economic Atlas, 1972

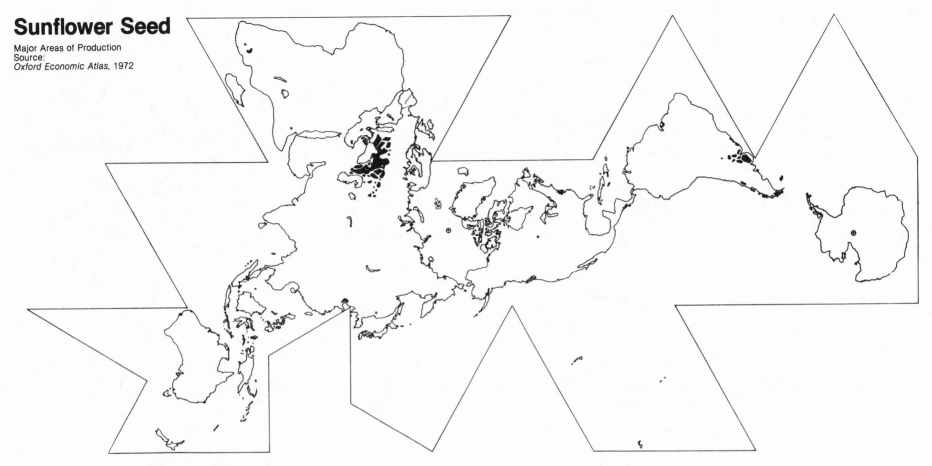

First cultivated by the Plains Indians of North America over 3,000 years ago and then spread by early explorers to Europe (where most of it is grown today), the sunflower seed is an important source of high-quality, edible oil, high in the polyunsaturated fatty linoleic acid, that can be used in cooking, salad dressing, margarine, and soap. The high-protein meal remaining after the extraction of the oil from the seed is used as a food supplement for animals and could be developed into a suitable protein supplement in human diets.

Sunflower Seed—1977 World Production:	11.75
Africa:	.57
North and Central America:	1.3
South America:	.95
Asia:	.59
Europe:	2.4
Oceania:	.074
USSR:	5.9

All units in million metric tons

Groundnuts

Major Areas of Production
Source:
Oxford Economic Atlas, 1972

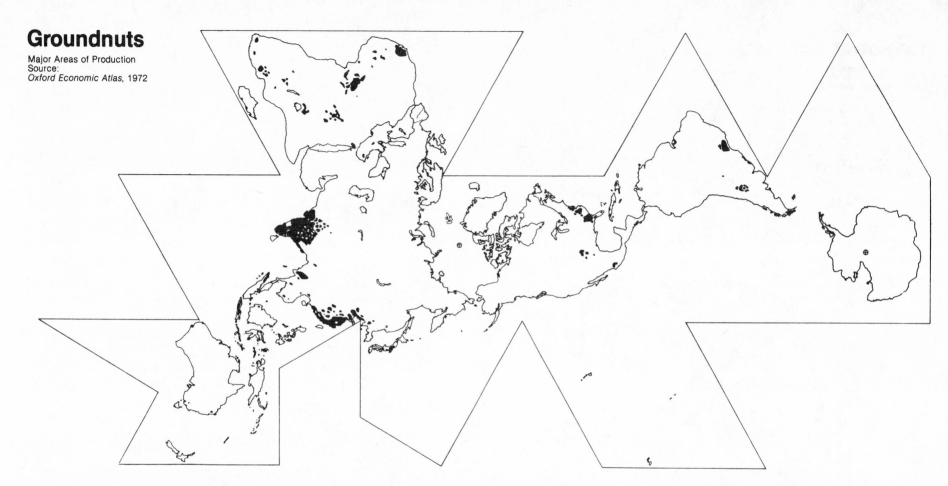

The groundnut (also called peanut or goober) is not a true nut but a legume. It was grown extensively by Bolivian Indians in pre-Columbian times (1,000 B.C.) and carried by merchant ships in the early sixteenth century to the Old World, China, India, and Africa. The groundnut is grown in many places primarily for its high-quality oil, but in the United States the protein-rich meat of the nut is ground into peanut butter (half the crop), and the whole nut is roasted or used in confections and bakery goods.

Groundnut research: International Crops Research Institute for the Semi-Arid Tropics, Hyderabad, India

Groundnuts—1977 World Production:	17
Africa:	4.5
North and Central America:	1.8
South America:	1.7
Asia:	10
Europe:	.023
Oceania:	.033
USSR:	2

All units in million metric tons

Rapeseed

Major Areas of Production
Source:
Oxford Economic Atlas, 1972

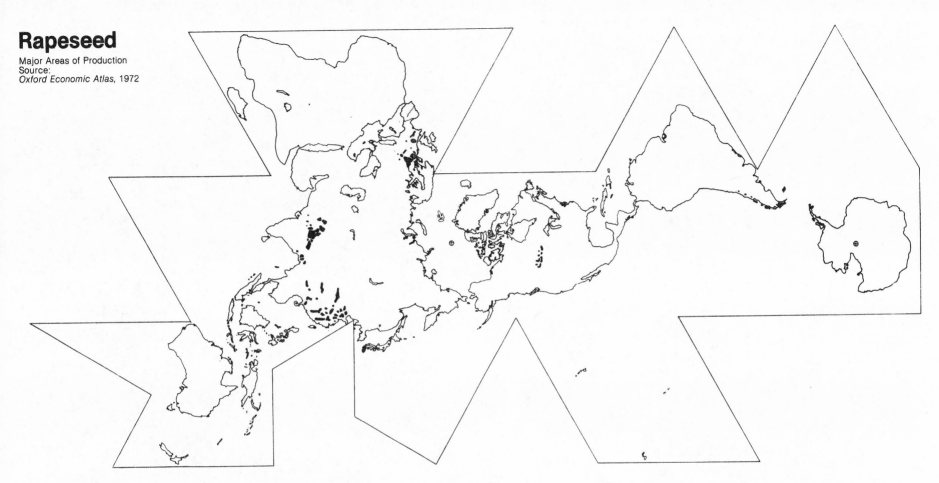

The rape plant (close relative of the turnip and mustard) is highly valued in Europe and Asia for the salad and cooking oil drawn from its tiny, black seeds (100 seeds in 2–5 grams; 40% oil) borne in long, slender pods. The oil (called colza) contributes about 10–12% of the world's edible oil and some forms of the whole plant are used as a leaf vegetable in Asia and as protein-rich forage for cattle, sheep, and swine in other areas of the world.

Rapeseed—1977 World Production:	7.65
Africa:	.02
North and Central America:	1.8
South America:	.083
Asia:	3.2
Europe:	2.5
Oceania:	.015
USSR:	.016

All units in million metric tons

59

Citrus Fruit

Major Areas of Production
Source:
Oxford Economic Atlas, 1972

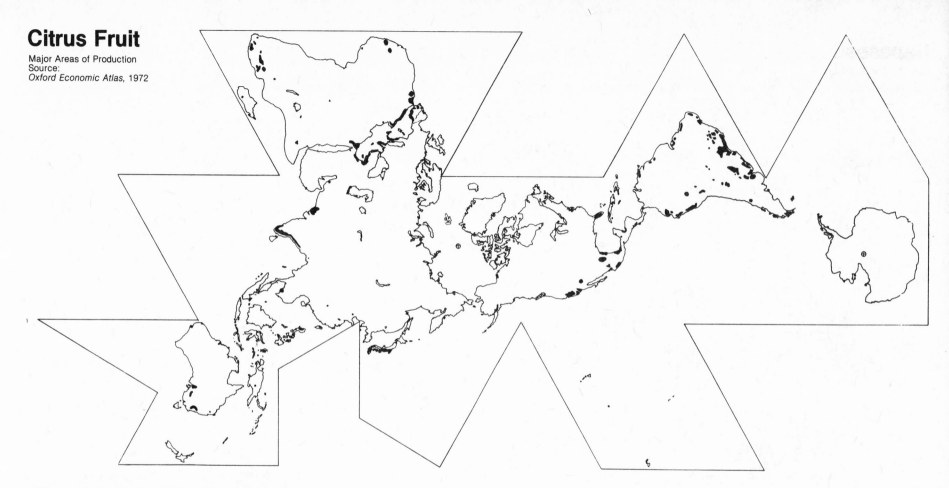

The most important citrus fruits originated in India or
Southeast Asia, with the orange being introduced to the
Mediterranean area about the first century A.D. and the
lemon and lime arriving about a thousand years later. The
grapefruit is believed to be a more recent hybrid first
appearing in the Caribbean area about 1750 A.D. under the
name "Forbidden Fruit." Valued as prime sources for
vitamin C and fruit drinks, these fruits are highly cultivated
in the warm climates of California and Florida, with much of
that output for consumption in the U.S.

Bananas

Major Areas of Production
Source:
Oxford Economic Atlas, 1972

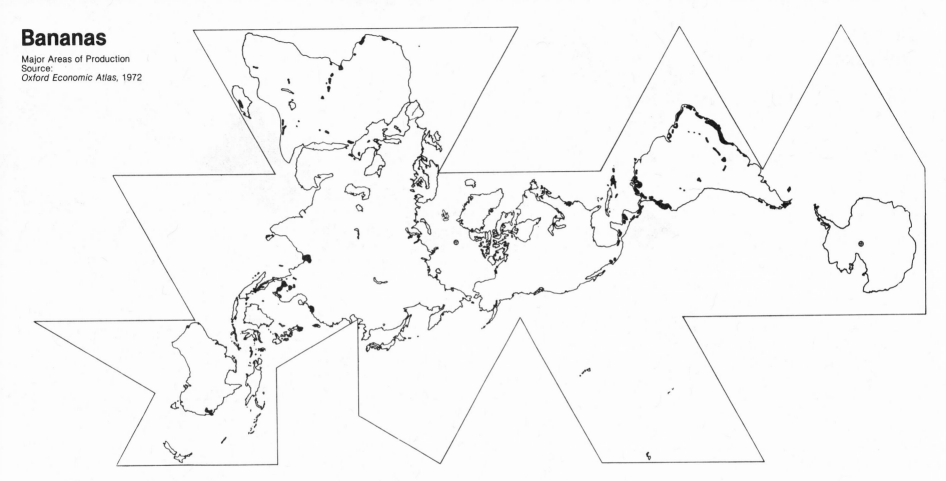

Believed to have originated in the tropics of Southeast Asia, the banana (an African name) is one of the earliest fruits to be cultivated by man (in 1200 B.C.) and remains one of its most important because of its distinctive flavor, food value, and year-round availability. Over three-quarters of the bananas now grown come from the American tropics and most are exported to the United States, Great Britain, and Europe. When ripe, the fruit is 22% carbohydrate (mainly sugar) and is a good source for several vitamins. The cooking varieties (plantains), which are starchy rather than sweet, are used extensively in the tropics.

Bananas—1977 World Production:	36.9
Africa:	4.4
North and Central America:	6.8
South America:	11.8
Asia:	12.4
Europe:	.399
Oceania:	1.02
USSR:	

All units in million metric tons

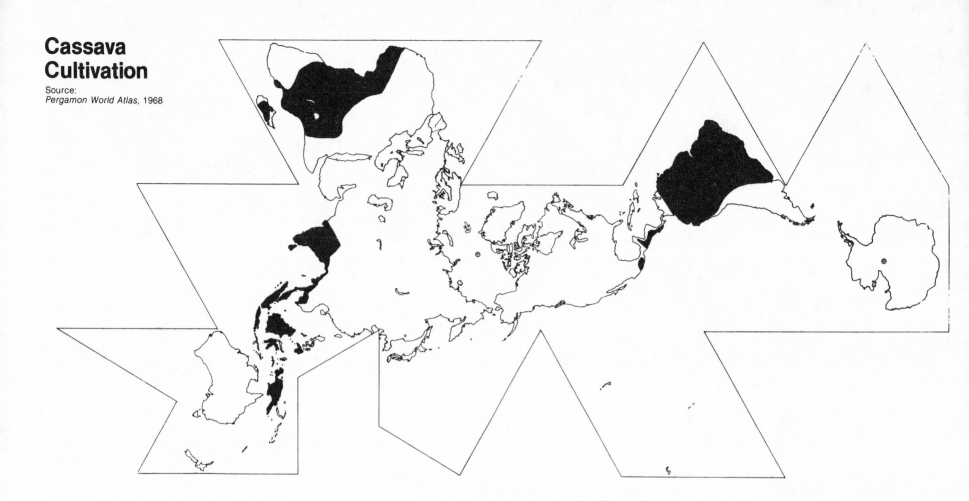

Cassava
Cultivation

Source:
Pergamon World Atlas, 1968

Apples

Major Areas of Production
Source:
Oxford Economic Atlas, 1972

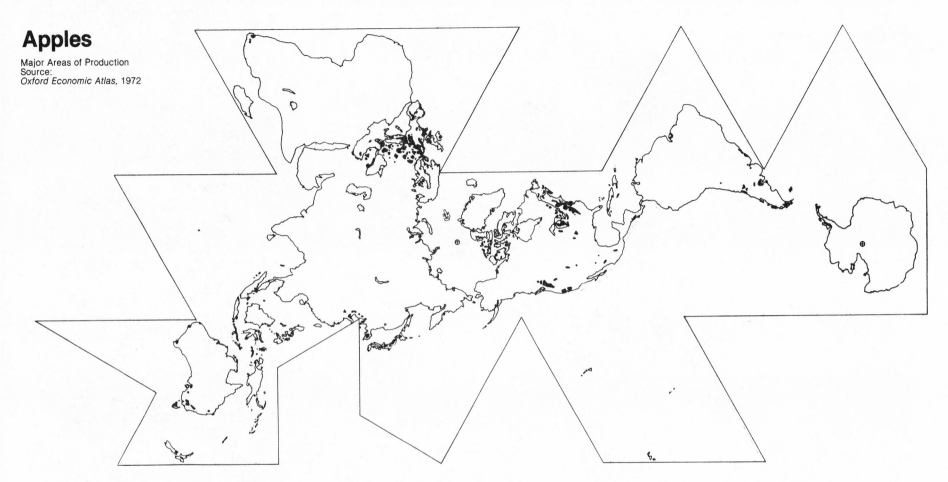

The apple has its origins in the Near East and Europe in the third millenium B.C. and was cultivated by the Greeks as early as the fourth century B.C. It was spread by early settlers to North America and today thrives around the world at latitudes from 30° to 60° north and south of the equator. Sixty-one per cent of the U.S. apple crop is marketed fresh (year-round) and 16% is processed into juice or cider. Although subject to many diseases and insect predators, sophisticated programs of grafting and selecting superior seedlings, along with chemical pesticides, have produced high quality, hardy apples in many varieties.

Apples—1977 World Production:	21
Africa:	.38
North and Central America:	3.7
South America:	`1.1
Asia:	4
Europe:	11.6
Oceania:	.44
USSR:	

All units in million metric tons

Grapes or Wine

Major Areas of Production
Source:
Oxford Economic Atlas, 1972

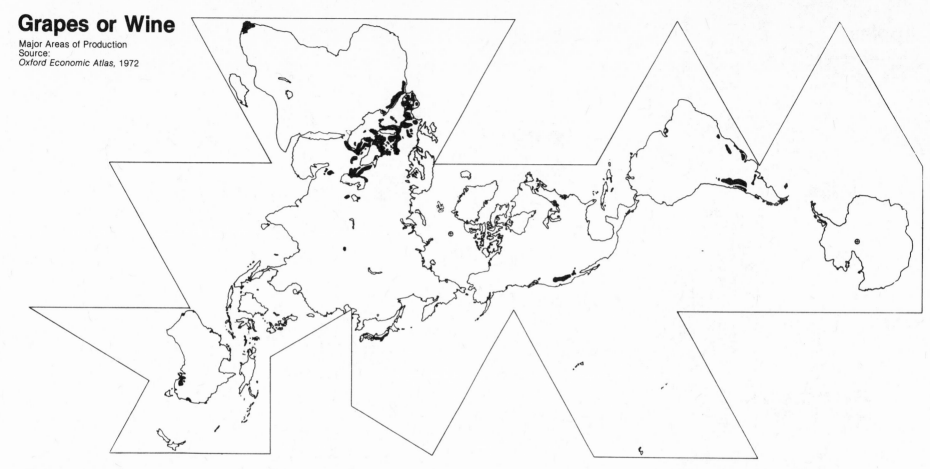

World grape production probably exceeds that of any other fruit. Evidence of viticulture (cultivation of grapes) dates back to Swiss lake dwellings of the Bronze Age and Egypt of 2400 B.C. In the area around Armenia and the Caspian Sea, the earliest cultivation of *V. vinifera* (the most common grape for raisins, wines, and eating) took place about 5000 B.C. Grape vineyards require long, dry summers and cool winters for best development. Europe accounts for over half of the grape production, and of that amount, over half is crushed for use as wine, brandy, or juice.

Wine—1977 World Production:	28.8
Africa:	1.0
North and Central America:	1.5
South America:	3.5
Asia:	.19
Europe:	19
Oceania:	.37
USSR:	3.1

All units in million metric tons

Grapes—1977 World Production:	57
Africa:	2.2
North and Central America:	4.1
South America:	.5
Asia:	6.5
Europe:	32.3
Oceania:	.7
USSR:	5.6

All units in million metric tons

Tobacco

Major Areas of Production
Source:
Oxford Economic Atlas, 1972

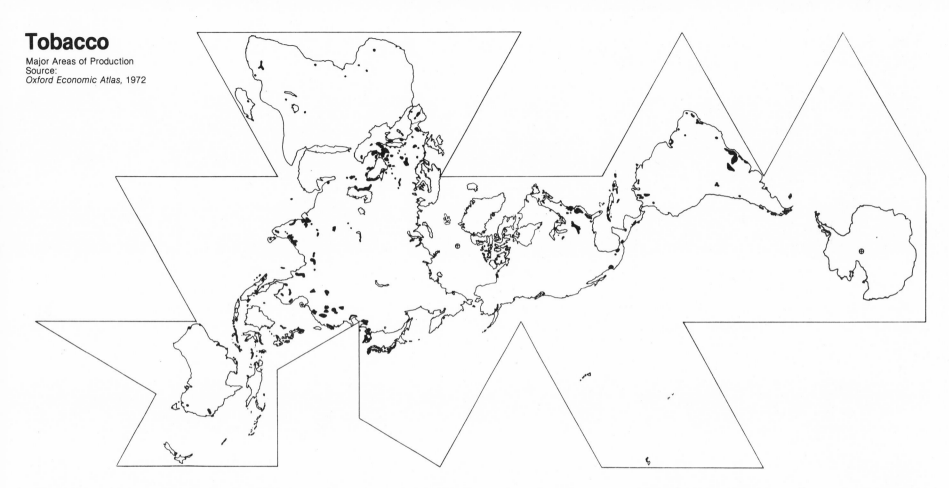

Tobacco, first cultivated by the Indians of North and South America for smoking in peace pipes, was brought to Europe by Columbus and later explorers for its supposed medicinal qualities. The 2–3 foot long leaves of the plant are used after aging and processing for smoking, chewing, and snuffing. The largest producers of cigarettes are, in order, the Chinese government monopoly, the British-American Tobacco Company, the Soviet government monopoly, the Japanese government monopoly, and Phillip Morris, Inc. Despite research linking tobacco smoking with respiratory and coronary disease, three of the top five cigarette producers are public rather than private enterprises that derive much revenue from tobacco-generated taxes for their governments as well as income from related industries.

Tobacco—1977 World Production:	5.6
Africa:	.29
North and Central America:	1.2
South America:	.59
Asia:	2.5
Europe:	.74
Oceania:	.019
USSR:	.31

All units in million metric tons

Tea

Major Areas of Production
Sources:
Goode's World Atlas, 1975
Oxford Economic Atlas, 1972

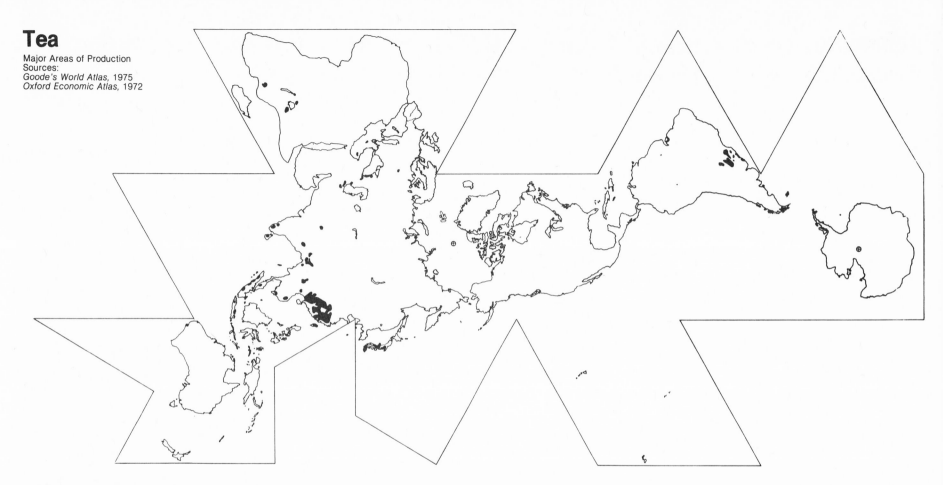

China, where according to legend tea was discovered in 2500 B.C., produces half the world's supply of this beverage that is known for its stimulating properties (caffeine), astringency (tannins), and flavor and aroma (essential oils). Prepared from the dried and cured leaves of small trees (constant pruning keeps them shrubs), tea requires a warm climate where annual rainfall averages 90 to 200 inches, with the highest quality varieties grown more slowly in the higher altitudes of South Asia. A new crop is produced about every forty days. Differences in processing techniques yield the three main varieties: green, semi-fermented (oolongs), and black. Over half the world's tea exports are destined for the United Kingdom.

Tea—1977 World Production:	1.75
Africa:	.19
North and Central America:	
South America:	.045
Asia:	1.41
Europe:	
Oceania:	.006
USSR:	.099

All units in million metric tons

Coffee

Major Areas of Production
Source:
Oxford Economic Atlas, 1972

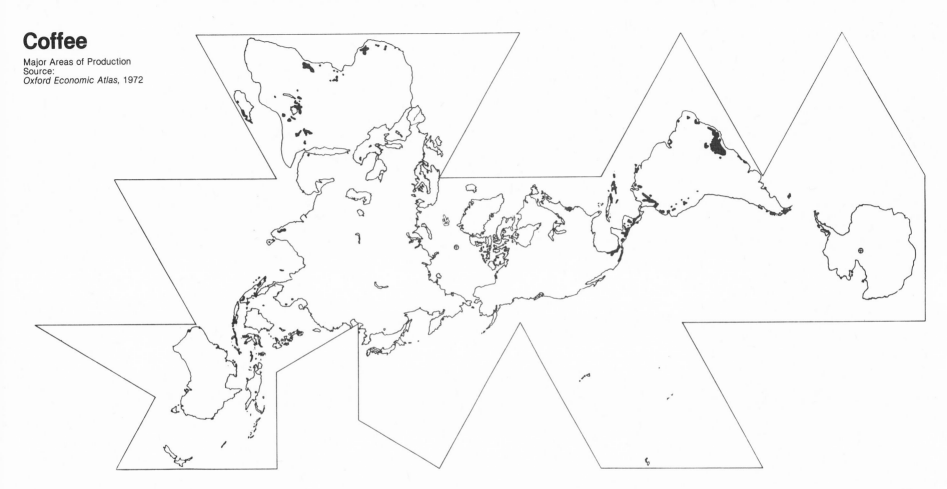

The hot or cold caffeine beverage produced from the roasted bean of the coffee plant is consumed in an amount greater than any other beverage. Its origins are rather obscure, but it was probably discovered in the Near East or Africa about 850 A.D. and has since spread to warm, humid climates and altitudes of 1,500 to 6,000 feet in various parts of the world, especially Central and South America (Brazil grows half the world's supply). Although there are nearly sixty species, only four are of commercial value and of those the Arabian species accounts for nine-tenths of the world's supply. Coffee beans are cleaned, roasted, ground, and packaged, and then shipped to the consumer. The United States consumes nearly half the world's coffee production.

Coffee—1977 World Production:	4.3
Africa:	1.3
North and Central America:	.91
South America:	1.7
Asia:	.39
Europe:	
Oceania:	.047

All units in million metric tons

Cocoa

Major Areas of Production
Source:
Goode's World Atlas, 1975

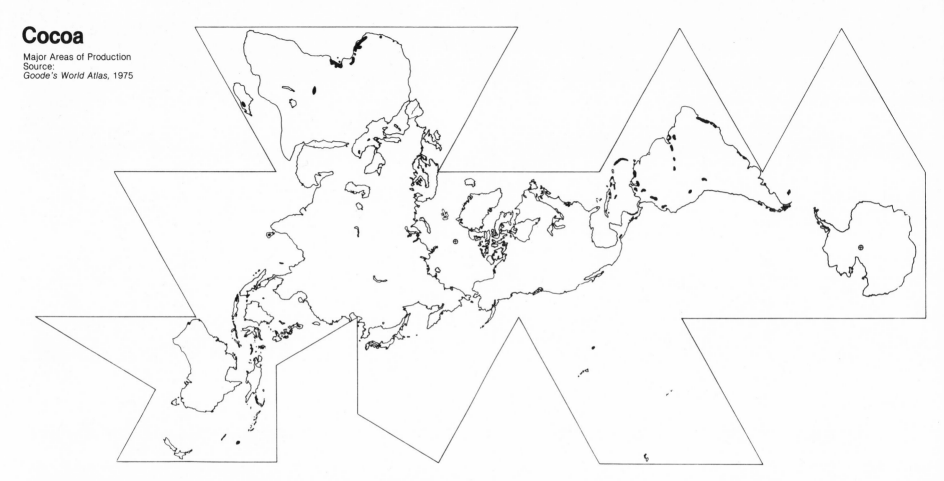

Originally cultivated in the American tropics by the Aztecs, the cocoa bean and its seeds produce an oily paste when fermented and roasted. It is used in producing bitter chocolate, sweet chocolate when sugar is added, or cocoa butter that is used mainly in cosmetics and perfumes.

Cocoa—1977 World Production:	1.4
Africa:	.9
North and Central America:	.095
South America:	.351
Asia:	.025
Europe:	
Oceania:	.031
USSR:	

All units in million metric tons

Rubber

Source:
Oxford Economic Atlas, 1972

One dot

represents 5000

metric tons

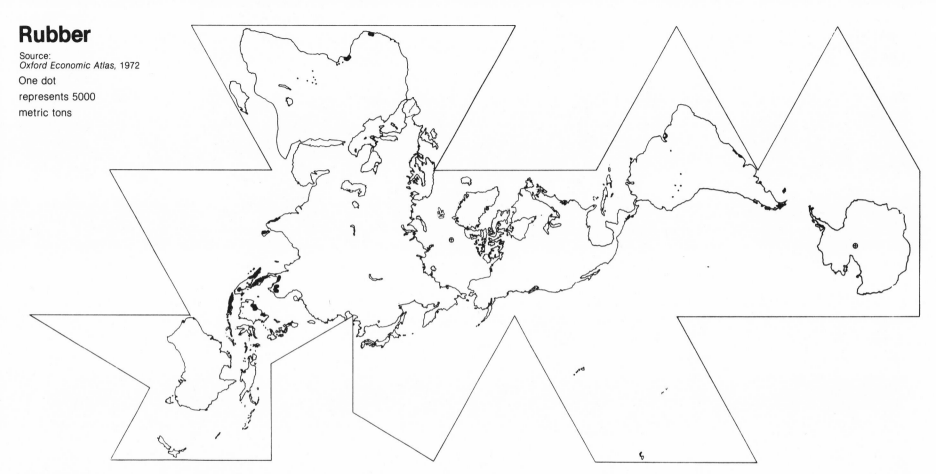

Rubber (caoutchouc—"weeping wood") is produced from the latex that is found in the veins which lie just beneath the bark of rubber-yielding trees of the tropics and sub-tropics. The main American and South Asian source of crude rubber is the *Hevea brasiliensis*, but in the East Indies and Africa vine-like plants yield some of the rubber supply. The earliest references to rubber come from about the time of Columbus's second voyage when the Indians of Haiti were observed bouncing rubber balls. The prime market for today's natural rubber is automobile tire manufacturers.

Rubber—1977 World Production:	3.6
Africa:	.24
North and Central America:	
South America:	.031
Asia:	3.3
Europe:	
Oceania:	.006
USSR:	

All units in million metric tons

Cotton

Source:
Goode's World Atlas, 1975

Areas of Production
■ major
▨ minor

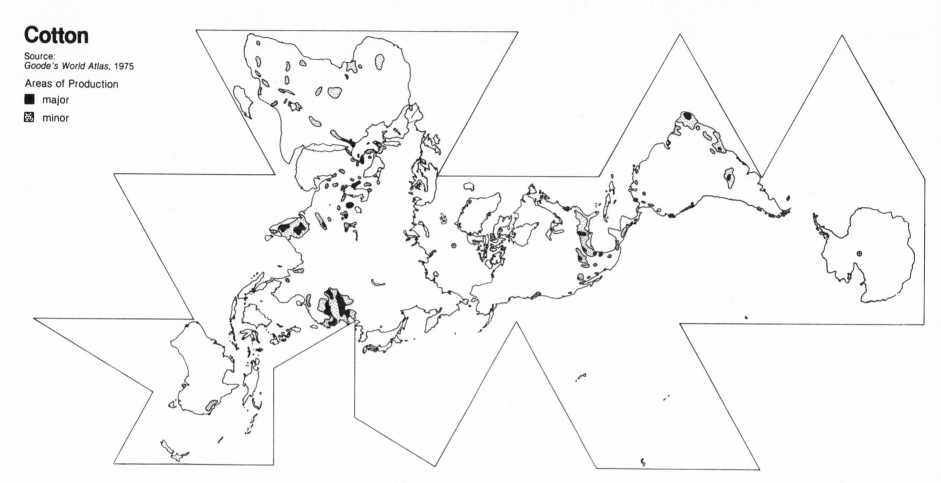

The world's most important vegetable fiber has been known through spun cotton yarn dating from as early as 3000 B.C. in Egypt, China, and India; has been found in prehistoric American pueblo ruins, and was used in grave cloths, fishing nets, and lines in pre-Inca Peru. Cotton fibers develop as elongations of the outer layer of cells of the cotton seed, filling the boll with easily spinnable fiber. In 1794 the modern cotton gin for separating fiber from seed was developed by Whitney, but it wasn't until after World War II that modern machinery for machine-harvesting of cotton has been put to use along with pesticides to control the boll weevil and the 500 other insects that attack cotton. Each pound of fiber production yields two pounds of cottonseed as a by-product, which is refined into oil for use as cooking and salad oil and shortening. The U.S. at one time accounted for most of the world's production, but much of the export production today is from the U.S.S.R. and India.

Cotton research: International Center for Agricultural Research in Dry Areas, Lebanon

Cotton—1977 World Production:	14.3
Africa:	1.2
North and Central America:	3.8
South America:	1
Asia:	5.15
Europe:	.22
Oceania:	.028
USSR:	2.7

All units in million metric tons

Jute

Major Areas of Production
Source:
Oxford Economic Atlas, 1972

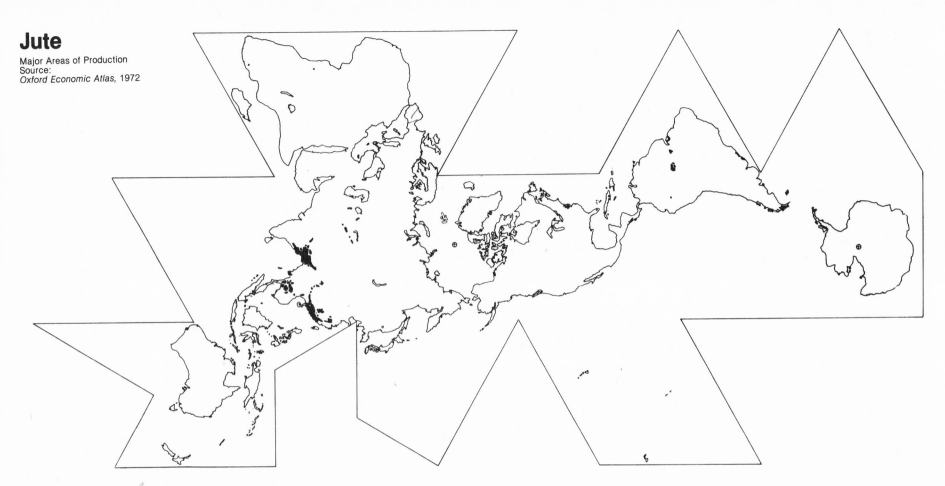

Valued for the six to ten foot long fibers in its bark, jute has been cultivated since remote times in India, and has been used commercially in the West since 1830. Because its cellulose content is rather low and its fiber-strand diameters vary, the cloth spun from jute yarn is rather weak and deteriorates rapidly. However, it is inexpensive to produce and 90% is used for burlap or baling (as in gunny sacks), with the remaining 10% used in twine, rope, carpet, and insulation.

Jute—1977 World Production:	4.3
Africa:	.021
North and Central America:	.009
South America:	.101
Asia:	4.1
Europe:	
Oceania:	
USSR:	.050

All units in million metric tons

Flax (Fiber)

Source:
Goode's World Atlas, 1975

Areas of Production
■ major
▨ minor

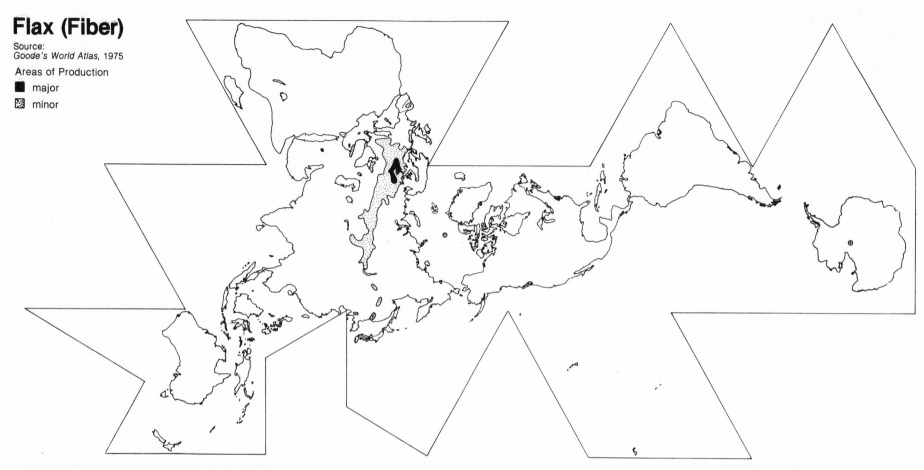

A flowering plant with fiber-filled seed bolls, flax has been cultivated in the Mediterranean area and Near East since prehistoric times, perhaps originally for food, but later for linen cloth in ancient Egypt. Before the cotton gin made cotton inexpensive, the flax plant's fiber was used extensively for cloth-making. Today, it is the source for two products: flaxseed for linseed oil and fiber for linen products (notably fine Irish linen).

Flax—1977 World Production:	.69
Africa:	.017
North and Central America:	
South America:	.004
Asia:	.003
Europe:	.15
Oceania:	.001
USSR:	.52

All units in million metric tons

Hemp

Source:
Goode's World Atlas, 1975

Areas of Production
■ major
▩ minor

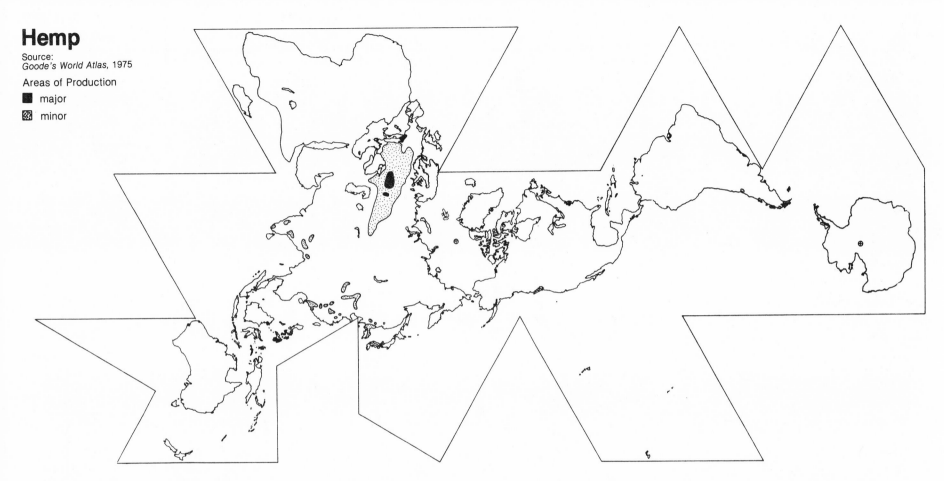

Cannabis sativa (the only true hemp plant, although manila hemp, sisal hemp, and other varieties are also called hemp) has been valued for its long durable fibers for 5,000 years in Central Asia, and its cultivation has spread to Europe and North America. Its fiber is used to make fine fabrics and coarse ropes in countries where people do their own spinning and weaving. Other uses are as a mild narcotic made from its leaves or resin, hempseed oil for paints and soap, and hempseed as feed for caged birds.

Hemp—1977 World Production:	.231
Africa:	
North and Central America:	
South America:	.004
Asia:	.108
Europe:	.066
Oceania:	
USSR:	.054

All units in million metric tons

73

Silk

Major Areas of Production
Source:
Goode's World Atlas, 1975

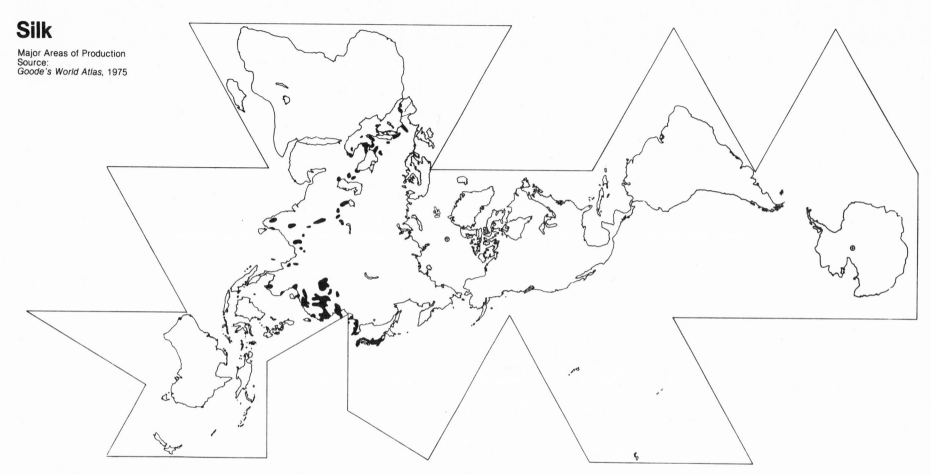

A variety of insects produce silk fiber (for webs or cocoons) but commercial silk comes from the mulberry silkworm (*Bombyx mori*). Sericulture, the breeding and cultivation of the silkworm, has its origins in ancient China. Although development of sericulture has been tried in various places in both hemispheres, Japan has been by far the greatest producer since 1865, and continues to be the greatest consumer by a wide margin. Although inexpensive man-made fibers have been developed recently, silk remains the first choice for luxurious clothing both in the Orient and the West.

Silk—1977 World Production:	.047
Africa:	.000025
North and Central America:	
South America:	.0097
Asia:	.041
Europe:	.0005
Oceania:	
USSR:	.003

All units in million metric tons

The trends of the present global food system assumed most likely to continue through 1985 and probably to 2000 follow:

1. Overall population will continue to increase.
2. Rate of population growth will continue to decrease in developed regions and more and more developed regions will arrive at a net zero population growth.
3. Overall food production, both gross food and per capita food, will continue to increase.
4. Year-round diversity of food types will continue.
5. Yield per acre will continue to increase.
6. Per capita food demand will continue to increase.
7. Malnutrition will continue to be a serious world problem
8. New advances in food production, processing, packaging, storage, distribution, and disposal technologies will continue to be invented and proliferated; diversity will continue to increase.
9. Fossil fuel reserves will continue to decline and their costs continue to rise.
10. Foods produced with a fossil fuel subsidy will continue to increase in cost.
11. Energy will continue to be used by the agricultural system in larger quantities.

12. Lag between invention and implementation of food production, processing, etc. technology will continue to decrease.
13. Food production, processing, etc. will continue to simultaneously decentralize and miniaturize while at the same time centralizing and expanding in capacity.
14. Income energy sources will play an increasingly larger role in powering food system technology.
15. Impact of the food system on the ecological context will continue to increase.
16. World co-operation and globalization of institutions in regards to food will continue to increase.
17. Coordination and standardization of tools and contact (end use) products regarding food will continue to increase.
18. Understanding of nutrition and metabolic processes will continue to increase.
19. Food will continue to have an aesthetic and entertainment value.
20. The emerging ecological and global awareness will continue to expand and proliferate.
21. More and more people will be more healthy, live longer, and have more reinvestable time.

Other assumptions:

1. State-of-the-art food technology will be used wherever possible.
2. Viable alternatives have to be technologically feasible before they are economically feasible.
3. Food surpluses will be increasingly prone to management and planning rather than merely left to chance.

When planning complex systems, the desired effects of one's plan need to be explicitly stated, and stated in a time frame, i.e., what should happen when. These planned—and hoped for—results must be constantly compared with actual developments. Actual developments are monitored through indicators much in the same way a medical doctor monitors the indicators of pulse, blood pressure, and reflexes to measure the health of the individual patient. "Key" indicators are correlated with a set of other variables, thus giving an accurate assessment of the functioning of the entire system. The indicators need to be monitored as a set, not individually—in internal metabolics, pulse might be normal, but the patient might have cancer.

Key indicators for the health of collective humanity from a food system perspective are:

 **Decision-Making Criteria**

1. Incidences of starvation and malnutrition related diseases and life expectancy.
2. Per capita food supply and consumption per area.
3. Amounts of food and nutritional contents of food lost between producer and consumer.
4. Amount of energy needed to produce, process, etc. food.
5. Total population and rates of growth and stabilization.
6. Impact of food system on ecological context.
7. Diversity of crops and sources of production.
8. Choices of food available to consumer.
9. Amount of human labor and resources involved in food system.
10. Amount of integration of entire food system.
11. Food production per agricultural worker.
12. Food production per hectare.
13. Food costs.

Decision-making criteria are the values that formulate a preferred state made explicit, as well as guidelines for decision-makers, success criteria, and, in a way, general performance specifications for the designer of artifacts.

Decision-makers in the food system are many and diverse. Each has his or her own view of the objectives to be pursued, their own formulation of the issues, their own choice of the criteria for decision and the priorities among them, their own selection and analysis of pertinent facts, and their own art of applying the criteria to the issues on the basis of the facts in pursuit of the objectives.

"Who are the decision-makers? In the first instance they are the enterprises—the agri- or food business, private companies, local government agencies, and such national and international organizations as the Food and Drug Administration, Department of Agriculture, and the Food and Agriculture Organization of the United Nations. The initiating enterprises—farmers, food processors, etc.—draw others into the decision-making process, notably their sources of capital and commercial finance (investment and commercial banks for private companies, budget offices and appropriations committees for government agencies) and the state and national regulatory agencies that issue certificates or permits required by law or administer legal measures for safety, health, or environmental protection. Even the courts—state and federal— are drawn into the decision process. Their authority can be invoked through statutory procedures to review the orders of regulatory agencies or through independent proceedings initiated by complainants. Still other decision-makers participate in a more general and diffuse but nonetheless critical way: Congress and the President; the legislatures and governors of the states; scientific, engineering, legal, and other academic or professional organizations or groups; and the general public who are the consumers of the food and the beneficiaries or victims of food policies and services. At times these officials and groups are directly involved in the decision-making process, but even when they are not, they influence the process by modifying the societal medium in which it takes place."[1] In centrally planned economies the decision-making is done not by the commercial enterprises but by the state and bureaucracy.

Food Criteria:

Maximum value placed on feeding 100% of humanity nutritionally sound food.

Maximum value placed on maintaining and encouraging food related cultural diversity and choices.

Maximum value placed on maintaining nutritional content of food.

Maximum value placed on fresh foods, minimum on processed foods.

Maximum value placed on a diverse source of food sources and types.

Maximum value placed on local self-sufficiency and appropriate technology.

Energy Criteria[2]:

Maximum value placed on doing the most with the least amount of energy.

Minimum use of energy-intensive materials.

Maximum use of reusable materials and packaging.

Minimum use of nonreusable materials and packaging.

Minimum energy use in construction, maintenance, and recycling.

Minimum dependence on one source of energy.

Maximum diversification and inter-dependence of energy sources.

Maximum availability and distribution of power.

Maximum concentration of energy-intensive activities.

Maximum interlinkage of energy-intensive activities.

Maximum use of low impact decentralized energy-harnessing artifacts.

Maximum energy conversion and transport efficiency use.

Minimum discharge of heat into the environment.

Ecological Context Criteria:

Maximum value placed on virgin areas of globe.

Minimum topographical, hydrological, physiographical, limnological, meteorological, soil, vegetation, and wildlife disturbance.

Minimum land use, water use, water-space use, air, and airspace use.

Minimum input of solid, liquid, gaseous, and heat waste into ecological context.

User Criteria:

Maximum value placed on 100% of humanity as food user; sufficiency—enough food for everyone; accessibility—enough distribution to everyone.

Maximum quality control of food related artifacts, system, or service.

Maximum reliability of food related artifact, system or service; maximum use of back-up systems.

Maximum durability of food related artifact, system, or service.

Maximum ease, simplicity, and clarity of use of food related artifact, system, or service.

Maximum cultural, esthetic, and individual human option diversity.

Maximum value placed on obtaining "free" or reinvestable time and decreasing coerced time for humans.

Maximum value placed on user's time and energy.

Maximum comprehensive responsibility and responsiveness to the needs of food consumer by food supplier.

Safety Criteria:

Maximum value placed on human life.

Maximum safety in construction, operation, maintenance, and recycling.

Maximum designed-in safety for emergencies and breakdowns.

Maximum safety for future generations.

Adaptability Criteria:

Maximum value placed on adaptive stability.

Maximum responsiveness to short-term food demand changes.

Maximum expandability/contractibility (responsiveness to long-term food demand changes).

Maximum reserves of emergency supplies and facilities.

Maximum flexibility and adaptability to new technology, needs, and know-how.

Efficiency Criteria:

Maximum value placed on doing more with less.

Maximum use of minimum number of food related artifacts, systems, and services.

Maximum food output per invested manhours, materials, and energy input.

Maximum ease, simplicity, and clarity of repair, replacement, and recycling in minimal time.

Maximum use of modularity of construction where applicable.

Organizational Criteria:

Maximum compatibility between parts of the food system.

Maximum compatibility or standardization of all similar parts of the food system.

Maximum compatibility between different food systems, as food production units designed for use by single families, schools, health units, etc.

Maximum decentralization of information and decision flow.

Maximum use of feedback.

Maximum indexing and cataloging of food systems, parts, services, and outputs.

Maximum knowledge about food system interactions with all other systems, especially the ecological context.

Maximum centralization of coordination functions, maximum decentralization of decision-making functions.

References

Preface

1. Mayer, J., "Management of Famine Relief," *Science,* Vol. 188, 5-9-75, p. 577.

2. Polerman, T., "World Food: A Perspective," *Science,* Vol. 188, 5-9-75, p. 510.

3. Fuller, R. B., *Synergetics: Explorations in the Geometry of Thinking,* MacMillan, New York, 1975.

4. Wieger, L., *Chinese Characters,* Dover, New York, 1975. Reprint of study originally published in 1915.

5. Laing, J., Professor, Univ. of Pennsylvania, Chinese Dept., personal communication.

6. *1977 Food and Agriculture Organization Production Yearbook,* Vol. 31, FAO/UN, Rome, 1978.

7. "Famines," *Encyclopaedia Britannica,* 1974 Edition—reporting on study made at Univ. of Nanking.

8. Kung, P., "Farm Crops of China," *World Crops,* Mar./Apr. and May/June, 1975.

9. Orleans, L. A., and Suttmeier, R. P., "The Mao Ethic and Environmental Quality," *Science,* Vol. 170, 12-11-70, pp. 1173-76.

10. Walker, K. R., "Organization of Agricultural Production," *Economic Trends in Communist China,* ed.

Eckstein, et al., Aldine Publishing Co., Chicago IL, p. 397.

11. My thanks to Sandy Primm, who did the research on the word "Ho-ping."

Introduction: Design Science

1. Schneider, B. R., *The Defense Monitor,* Center for Defense Information, excerpted in *The Philadelphia Inquirer,* 4-6-75.

2. Fuller, R. B., Correspondence, 1974.

3. Crosson, P., "Institutional Obstacle to Expansion of World Food Production," *Science,* Vol. 188, 5-9-75, p. 519.

4. For further information on design science, see the *Design Science Primer,* Earth Metabolic Design, Inc., Box 2016 Yale Station, New Haven, CT 06510, 1976.

Beginnings

1. Parts of this section, besides those in quotes, have been adopted from Jarman, P. D., "Crop Processes and Physics," *Crop Process in Controlled Environments,* Academic Press, New York, 1972, pp. 185-94. Proceedings of an International Symposium

held at the Glasshouse Crops Research Institute, Little-hampton, Sussex, England, 12-71. Rees, A. R., et al, eds.

2. Raven, R. H., Berlin, B., Breedlove, D. E., "The Origins of Taxonomy," *Science,* Vol. 174, 12-17-71, p. 1210.

3. Berry, J. A., "Adaptation of Photosynthetic Processes to Stress," *Science,* Vol. 188, 5-9-75, pp. 694-750.

4. McHale, J. *The Ecological Context,* World Resources Inventory, Southern Illinois Univ., Carbondale, IL, 1968.

5. Adapted from Doane, R., *World Balance Sheet,* Harper & Row, New York, 1957.

6. Much of this section owes its insights, but not mistakes, to Jeff Christianson, whose "Food Storage" done at the 1975 World Game Workshop was freely borrowed from here.

Food on Earth

1. Canby, T. Y., "Can the World Feed Its People?," *National Geographic,* 9-75.

2. Georgescu-Roegan, N., *The Entropy Law and the Economic Process,* Harvard Univ. Press, Cambridge MA, 1972.

3. Ganzin, M., "With Food and Justice for All," *UNESCO Courier,* 5-75.

4. "Preliminary Assessment of the World Food Situation: Present and Future," United Nations, 4-74.

History

1. Loomis, R. S., "Agricultural System," *Scientific American,* 9-76, p. 99.

2. Bunting, A. H., "Pests, Population and Poverty in the Developing World," *Journal of the Royal Society of Arts,* 3-19-72, pp. 227-39.

3. Eberstadt, N., "Myths of the Food Crisis," *The New York Review of Books,* 2-19-76, pp. 32-36.

4. *FAO Production Yearbook,* Vol. 31, UN, New York, 1977.

5. Paddock, W., Paddock, P., *Famine 1975!,* Little, Brown & Co., Boston, 1967.

6. Walters, H., "Difficult Issues Underlying Food Problems," *Science,* Vol. 188, 5-9-75, p. 525.

The Absence of Food

1. Mayer, J., "Management of Famine Relief," *Science,* Vol. 188, 9-9-75, p. 572.

2. Brown, L., "Redefining National Security," *Development Forum,* 11-12-77, United Nations.

3. Poleman, T., "World Food: A Perspective," *Science,* Vol. 188, 9-19-75, p. 518.

4. Hellman, H., *Feeding the World of the Future,* M. Evans & Co., Inc., New York, 1972, p. 18.

5. Eberstadt, N., "Myths of the Food Crisis," *The New York Review of Books,* 2-19-76, pp. 32-37.

6. "Famine," *Encyclopaedia Britannica,* 1974 Edition.

7. Pyke, M., *Man and Food,* McGraw-Hill, New York, 1970, p. 127.

8. Ehrlich, P. R., Holdron, J. P., Ehrlich, A. H., *Ecoscience,* W. H. Freeman & Co., 1977.

Food System Charts

1. FAO, *1977 Production Yearbook,* Vol. 31, FAO/UN, New York, 1978.

2. Borgstrom, G., "The Human Biosphere and its Biological and Chemical Limitations," in *Global Impacts of Applied Microbiology,* ed. M. Starr, John Wiley & Sons, Pub., New York, 1964.

3. Based on human consumption of about 219 kg (482 pounds) per year; this is considerably higher than the 118 kg mentioned in Janick, J., Noller, CH., Rhylerd, C. L., "The

Cycle of Plant and Animal Nutrition," *Scientific American,* 9-76, p. 78.

4. *Dietary Goals for the U.S.,* Government Printing Office, Washington, D.C., 1977.

5. McHale, J., *World Facts and Trends,* George Braziller, New York, 1972.

Decision-Making Criteria

1. Adapted from Katz, M., "Decision Making in the Production of Power," *Scientific American,* 9-71, p. 149.

2. The following criteria are from *Energy, Earth and Everyone,* and based on "Working Document on Decision Making Criteria," by Brown, H. J., Carpenter, J., and Gabel, M., Earth Metabolic Design, Inc., New Haven, CT.

Food
Sources/
Production
Techniques

The following section describes food sources or means of increasing food production that are either being used or could be used to feed humanity. Each production technique or food source is described in terms of what it is, its history, advantages, disadvantages, and what needs to be done with the respective techniques/sources to increase their capabilities to feed more people.

It should be kept in mind that, contrary to popular understanding, food *production* is not the major or sole problem facing the world's food systems. The world *already* produces more than enough food for everyone to be adequately nourished, and, as the last page of this section shows, there are a number of alternative production methods that far outstrip current techniques. "Even during the 'scarcity' year of 1972–73, there was 9% more grain per person on Earth than in an 'ample' year like 1960. Inadequate production is clearly not the problem."[1] Distribution is not the sole problem either; nor is land reform, food storage, population control, or insuring that the means of producing food belongs to the rural poor. The world food problem is not a single problem, it is a complex web or constellation of problems; it is a system of problems that includes all the above in an interacting network. The world's food problems need to be dealt with holistically, not reductionistically. In our complex world, we can no longer point the finger in any one direction; to paraphrase a famous saying of Pogo, "We have met the enemy and he is everywhere."

Like all reductionist strategies, focusing on just one facet of a system of problems could cause as many or more problems than are solved. Focusing on food production, for instance, has led to the green revolution which has come to mean high-yield seeds, fertilizer, irrigation, pesticides, and machinery. The whole food system problem is reduced to increasing food production. This is then reduced further to the problem of increasing irrigation, fertilizer, pesticides, and machinery. This reductionist strategy has greatly benefitted the large land holder, but has often harmed those who need food the most—the poor. This is because the techniques offered for increasing food production (i.e., increasing fertilizer, etc. production) are only available to those who already have the resources to utilize them. The poor don't have enough resources to fully utilize fertilizer, irrigation, or machinery. In turn, mechanization enables the large land owner to produce more food with fewer people, thereby compounding the problem of poverty and urban overcrowding.

In this complex web, food production is just one intertwined factor. We *do* need to produce more food to solve our problems, just as we have to deal with the other dimensions of the food problem. It is akin to our energy problem in the sense that we need to increase our supplies of non-depleting energy sources while also conserving the energy now used, distributing it more equitably and decreasing the negative impact of energy use on the environment. Our global food and energy problems need to be tackled in a fashion similar to a military advance along an entire front wherein coordinated strategic and tactical offensive moves—from land, sea, and air—are made to defeat the "enemy." A gain or advance in one area can act to stimulate or support improvements in other areas. To defeat global hunger, all facets of the hunger problem need to be dealt with. In this context, the following pages describe the various food production techniques that could be utilized to produce more food, or to produce food more efficiently, in more locations, and under wider environmental conditions than current production techniques do. Subsequent sections deal with food processing, storage, and distribution, with the last section of the book integrating all the various factors of the world food system into a series of strategic and tactical moves for ending hunger on Earth.

Aboriginal Agriculture

Aboriginal agriculture refers to those methods of food production which have been used from pre-historic times: hunting and gathering, cultivation by the "slash and burn" method, and pastoral husbandry or nomadic herding. All three are still in use throughout the world, usually in marginal survival areas.

Hunting and gathering societies fish, hunt wild animals, and gather wild plants, mostly berries, for their sustenance. Such societies are at the mercy of the natural fluctuations of the environment and are thus usually found in areas of abundant natural food sources, especially areas where fishing is good. Hunting and gathering involve a passive approach to the environment. The culture uses the environment but does not significantly alter it. They "most often lived within one ecosystem, or at most a few closely related ecosystems, and depended entirely on the continued functioning of those ecosystems for their survival . . . their ways of life involved a close and intricate relationship between culture and nature."[1] These communities are usually small, as it takes a large wild area to provide food for each human.

"Slash and burn" cultivation is a highly efficient and complex agricultural technique that is used in forested areas where weed competition is fierce. In this technique, fields are cleared by burning the brush and trees off the land and then a variety of crops is planted. The fields are cultivated for no more than three years in a row before being allowed to lie fallow, whereupon the horticulturalist moves on to another forested area and slashes and burns this area. Meanwhile, the original plot reverts to

Hunting, Gathering, Fishing, and Primitive Cultivation

Predominant Economy
Source:
Oxford Economic Atlas, 1972

Subsistence Agriculture

Predominant Economy
Source:
Oxford Economic Atlas, 1972
Subsistence or traditional agriculture is based upon the kinds of factors of production— land, seed, labor, domestic animals, knowledge, and wisdom—that have been used by farmers for generations.

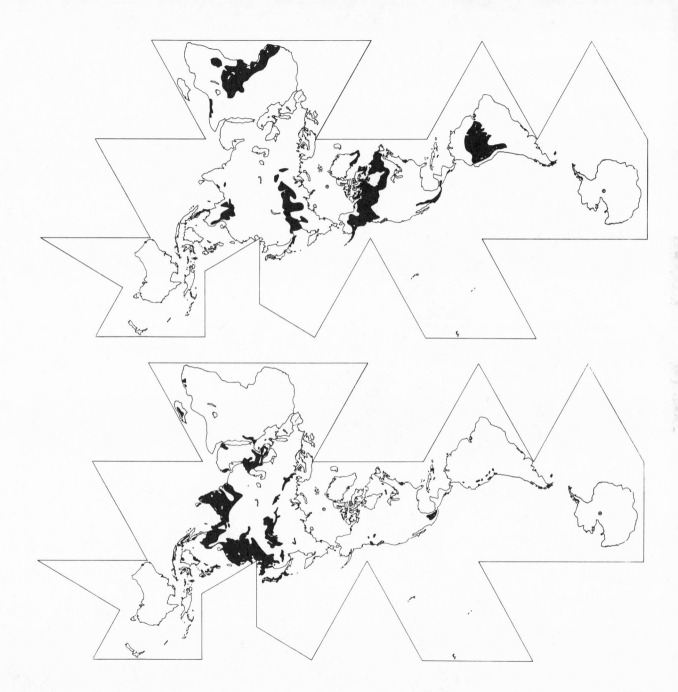

Nomadic Herding

Predominant Economy
Source:
Oxford Economic Atlas, 1972

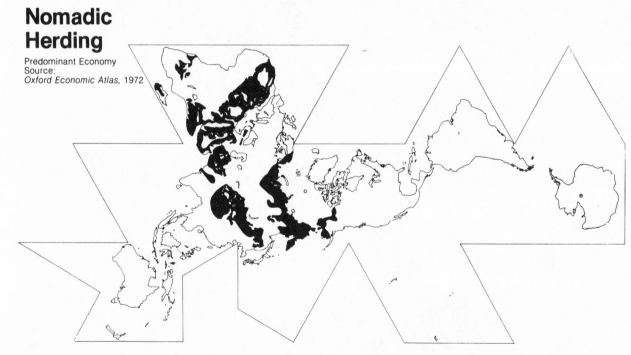

its original forested condition and regenerates its soil. In slash and burn cultivation, fields are rotated instead of crops, with the cultivation period for the plot of land being relatively short and the lying fallow period lengthy.

In today's world, slash and burn cultivation provides a marginal existence. It is not always replaced by intensive modern agriculture because of the ecological limitations of the jungles or tropical soils where these techniques are most often practiced. If the population of the society grows while the land available to it remains stable, the period for soil regeneration allowed a given area between plantings is reduced. In recent years this has happened in areas where slash and burn cultivation is still practiced. The results have been a gradual reduction of soil fertility and the appearance and take-over of a grass which has proved to be almost impossible to remove with traditional implements. Reduced soil fertility results in lower crop yields and organic matter that is returned to the soil to help guard against soil erosion. Low crop yield results in larger clearings and plantings and less fallow time for the land being cultivated. This progressive deterioration of the land gathers momentum as topsoil is washed away.[3]

Pastoral husbandry is a system of food production through the care of herd animals. It is often a cultural adjustment to grasslands in which ruminants can survive but hoe agriculture cannot. Mobile, nomadic, non-territorial cultures such as the Lapps of Scandinavia and the Nuer of Sudan and Ethiopia still practice pastoral husbandry. As with slash and burn cultivation, an increase in the population of the society can have disastrous consequences. With more people, there is a need for more animals. With

Development of Agriculture, Food Processing, and Food Preservation[2]

Period	Dates[a]	Agriculture	Foods	Processing and preservation techniques	Examples of science and technology
Palaeolithic (Old Stone Age)	Before 15,000 B.C.	None	Eggs, fruit, nuts, seeds, roots, insects, fish, honey, small animals[b]	Roasting, pounding, drying	Bags, baskets, clothes, stone and bone implements, "made" fire, painting, sculpture, language
Mesolithic (Middle Stone Age)	15,000 B.C.	None	Greater variety, stored wild fruits and berries	Dried fish, boiling, food storage, smoking? steaming?	Bow and arrow, dog, goat, reindeer and sheep probably domesticated, clay-covered baskets
Neolithic New Stone Age) (villages)	9000 B.C. or earlier	Seasonal culture of cereals, hoe culture, plowing, permanent fields, pruning	Domesticated animals[c], milk, butter, cheese, gruel, dates, olives, grapes, beer, vinegar, wine	Alcoholic fermentation, acetification, salting, baking, bread-making, sieving, primitive pressing, seasoning	Pottery wheel; spinning, weaving; wood, flint and bone sickles; saddle quern; mortar; fishing with hooks and nets
Bronze (cities)	3500 B.C.	Irrigation[d], horse-and-ox-drawn plows, much local and long-distance trade	Soybean, figs, rice, olive oil, vegetables, lentils, cabbage, cucumbers, onions	Filtration, lactic acid fermentation, more types of flavoring, flotation, leavened bread, sausage making, frying, sophisticated and complicated pressing, clarification	Architecture, smelting, wheeled carts, ships, mathematics, bronze tools, rotary millstones, bronze weapons, astronomy, shadufs, medicine, chemistry
Iron	1500 B.C.	Land and sea trade common, heavier plows	Fruits, spices, beans, artichokes, lettuce, sauces	Refinement of flavoring and of cookery	Pulleys, glass, improved and cheaper tools and weapons, currency
Roman	600 B.C.–400 A.D.	Reaping machines, legume rotation, plows on wheels, food trade extensive	Sugar cane in West, apples, asparagus, beets, orange	Food adulteration common	Water mills, donkey mills, wooden cooperage

[a]The dates indicate only the beginnings in the main centers or origin. They appeared much later in other areas, may not have developed at all, or may even have retrogressed. Tasmania was discovered in 1642 and the evidence up to Cook's visit in 1777 was that the people of Tasmania had retrogressed from the Neolithic to Palaeolithic period. Stone implements continued to be used long after the Old Stone Age. It is important to remember that a food processing operation may have originated in one region long before another. Also, Bronze Age implements continued to be used for a long time into the Iron Age.

[b]Big-game hunts occurred in areas of cliffs about 400,000 B.C. when fire and axes and spears were used. Pit-hunting and use of knives appeared about 75,000 B.C.

[c]The order of domestication is unknown but goats, yak, buffalo, pig, and cattle were domesticated early in this period but not the horse or camel. The horse, camel, ass, elephant, and poultry were domesticated toward the end of this period.

[d]Irrigation existed prior to 3500 B.C. but its widespread use about this time is believed to account for the spectacular increase in the population of Mesopotamia.

more and more animals, the amount of land available to each animal decreases. If this trend continues, overgrazing results and the soil cover for the land is completely eaten away. When this happens, soil erosion is rapid and deserts will either form or existing deserts will expand (as in the case of the Sahara expanding into the area of the Nuer of Sudan and Ethiopia).

Advantages:

1. Aboriginal agricultural methods (except slash and burn cultivation) have less of an ecological impact than modern agricultural methods if they are practiced in moderation.
2. The people practicing aboriginal agricultural methods are often more in touch with their environment than today's food consumers.

Disadvantages:

1. Aboriginal agricultural methods are inefficient for producing large amounts of food.
2. Aboriginal agriculture is often victimized by the natural fluctuations of the environment.
3. Aboriginal methods are not suitable for raising enough food to feed 4–6 billion people.
4. Aboriginal methods—such as overgrazing or forest stripping—can have disastrous consequences if misused, or used in excess.

What Needs to be Done

1. Set up a Global Aboriginal Agriculture Research Institute to collect, correlate, and research appropriate agricultural techniques usable by aboriginal people, and disseminate in a format assessable by them.
2. Set up local food reserves to act as a cushion in case of failures in aboriginal food production.
3. Inventory and study aboriginal agricultural techniques for possible adaptation and use by modern agriculture. Study energy use and efficiency of aboriginal agriculture.
4. Develop appropriate techniques and tools for use by aboriginal people to increase their food production.
5. Develop improved artifacts for preparing (cooking) food appropriate to aboriginal peoples.
6. Develop improved artifacts for preserving and storing food appropriate to aboriginal peoples.

Modern Agriculture

Modern agriculture is characterized by large productivity and the heavy use of fertilizers, pesticides, irrigation, energy, and machines. It is global in scale rather than local, and compared to aboriginal agriculture it is a prodigious user of energy, predominantly the fossil fuels. It is free of the restraints of any one particular ecosystem since it can draw upon the energy and resources from a technological network that extends throughout the Earth's biosphere. Unlike aboriginal agriculture, failure in any one ecosystem does not necessarily threaten its survival because it can draw more heavily on other ecosystems. This "freedom" permits the overriding of the ecological controls in any one system and hence the ability to do far greater damage than could be accomplished by a group that was totally dependent on just one ecosystem.[1]

Most of the food eaten on Earth comes by way of modern agriculture. This large productivity of modern agriculture was made possible through numerous advances in the previously mentioned areas over the last two hundred years and the specialization of production units into producing a limited number of products very efficiently. These developments have permitted, for example, a three to fourfold increase in food production in the United States. The following six sections deal with the major components of modern agriculture.

Energy and Mechanization

Food abundance can be achieved and maintained almost anywhere if adequate sources of low-cost energy are available. As pointed out earlier, from the larger perspective food and energy are the same phenomena. One fuels the human being, the other our life support facilities. Both can be measured by their relative heat values—calories or BTUs. Just as it takes food to get energy—to feed the people working on the oil rigs, for example—it takes energy to get food—to power tractors, harvesters, and grain dryers as well as to produce the tractors, fertilizers, and pesticides we now use. Each step in the global food system relies on some form of energy: from preparing the ground before planting, clearing, leveling where needed, installation of pipelines, pumps, and drainage ditches if irrigation is needed, plowing, planting, fertilizing, cultivating, spraying, harvesting, transporting the crop to market, storage or processing—drying, canning, freezing, freeze drying, baking—then packaging, transporting to market, display, consumer transportation to and from the store, food storage and preparation in the home, and disposal of the waste. A simple rule is that the more steps from field to plate, the more energy is used. A can of corn embodies more energy consumption than corn from your back yard.

The history of agriculture is not the history of increased energy applied in the field, but of the increased organization of that energy. This increased organization has raised the carrying capacity of a hectare of arable land from 0.004 humans in hunting/gathering systems to 2.5 humans through simple farming to 46 humans with industrialized agriculture.

As a system becomes more highly tuned to performance or output, more of its internal maintenance and repair needs must be supplied by the next larger system. In the case of agriculture, this means that concentrated energy forms must be supplied by man, so that more of the high-grade energy which the plants produce from diffuse solar energy can be employed for increased production. The maintenance needs which man supplies are insect resistance, through pesticides, weed resistance, through herbicides and mechanical cultivation, and starvation resistance, through fertilizers. He has also devised hybrid plants which are amenable to channelling larger portions of their energy into growth.

In one sense, the system has simply expanded, with man now consciously performing many of the functions which the plants themselves used to do, and with the energy for increased crop yield coming from elsewhere in the technologised ecosystem.[1]

Another way of viewing energy use in the food system is as a substitute for essential resources that are currently in shorter supply or more "expensive" than energy. For example, energy is substituted for land in the form of fertilizers that permit crop quantities to be harvested from one acre that would have taken several acres if fertilizers were not used; the amount of land needed to provide a bushel of corn has been reduced 60% since 1945, thereby releasing large tracts of land for the production of additional crops.[2] Energy is substituted for human and animal labor in the form of mechanical power that enables a single human being to do the work of many or to do it more quickly. For example, "if all the bullocks in Raipur District in India were put to work preparing the unirrigated paddy land with the country plow, it would take them about fifty days. If the mouldboard plow were substituted, it would take twenty-seven days. These unirrigated fields cannot be tilled until some rain falls at the start of the monsoon season and the time available from the beginning of the rains is fifteen days."[3] In other words, the unassisted Raipur farmer can only prepare one quarter to one half his land. With an added energy subsidy in the form of a small tractor, he would be able to plant nearly twice the amount of crops. Energy is also substituted for rain in the form of irrigation, and, for a complex ecosystem with numerous checks and balances of pests, in the form of pesticides to keep down crop predators.

As food production and consumption has grown from a local, self-sufficient activity to a global interdependent endeavor, the energy input into the food system has enlarged enormously. Food is now grown in many parts of the world on a near mass production basis, mass processed, and then shipped long distances. The infrastructure needed to process, store, and distribute these large quantities of perishable foods is enormous both in its extent and in its energy use.

It has always taken vast quantities of energy

to obtain our food, but until relatively recently that energy was almost exclusively in the form of nondepleting solar energy. The sun, via photosynthetic plant growth, furnished us with almost all the necessary energy for producing our food, the rest being supplied by animals and human labor. The relatively miniscule amount (one ten-thousandth or less of the sun's input) of animal and human energy (plus human know-how) is what keeps an agricultural system viable. Without these human directed energy inputs, an agricultural system would proceed toward its natural state, as in the case of weeds taking over a garden or an abandoned farm reverting to a forest.[4] The human-directed energy is focused primarily on those aspects of the natural system that limit agricultural growth.

From the industrial revolution on, in the mid-1800's, this energy flow from the sun to our stomachs has been supplemented by machines that were powered by fossil fuels. There are upward limits of ecological compatibility and economic and biological possibility when it comes to energy input. Figure 1 illustrates how farm output tends to level off no matter how much supplementary energy is put into it. For many modern cropping systems a ten to fifty-fold increase in energy input has only doubled or tripled the digestible energy yield. Figure 2 shows the amount of human directed energy

Chart 1. Farm Output as a Function of Energy Input to the U.S. Food System, 1920 through 1970.[5]

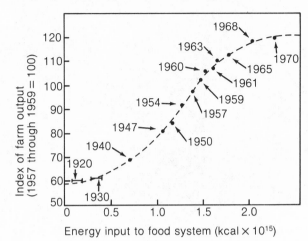

subsidy that it takes to obtain one calorie of food energy. The most efficient in terms of only energy input are the most human labor-intensive, like the Philippine and Thailand rice cultures. Unfortunately, the same agricultural systems are also the least productive in terms of digestible energy per acre. Industrialized food systems are the most productive in per acre production and per man-hour production, but the least efficient in terms of energy use per food calorie output.

Machines can be looked upon as inanimate "energy slaves." They do work that humans or animals would have to do if the machines did not exist, and they consume food/fuel that people or animals would have to consume if they were the ones doing the work. In many instances the specialized energy slave put the human slave out of business or work because it could work longer, harder, under worse

Figure 2. Energy Subsidy for Different Foods.

Food Type	Human-Directed Energy Subsidy (in calories)
Feedlot beef	10–15
Distant fishing	10–15
Grass fed beef	3–4
Modern milk	1
Coastal fishing	1
Eggs	.5
Range fed beef	.5
Corn	.5
Soybeans	.5
Rice	.16
Hunting and gathering	.15
Wet rice agriculture	.02–.1
Shifting agricultures	.03

To feed all the world with a North American type food system would take up to 60% of the total amount of commercial energy in use throughout the world.[6] Present-day agriculture uses about 3.5% of the world's commercially available energy.[7]

conditions, and more cheaply than could its general purpose human counterpart. If these energy slaves consumed human food instead of non-edible fossil fuels, there would have been widespread famine, very few machines, or both. As it turned out, our energy slaves were powered by a convenient, noncompeting energy source primarily in the form of fossil fuels, with water-powered mills for grinding grain and wind-powered water pumps also in widespread use in the very early days of industrialization. These

World Agricultural Tractors in Use 1976

Source:
1977 FAO Production Yearbook,
Vol. 31 (United Nations, 1978)

● = 1% of World Agricultural Tractors in Use

● = 183,031 tractors

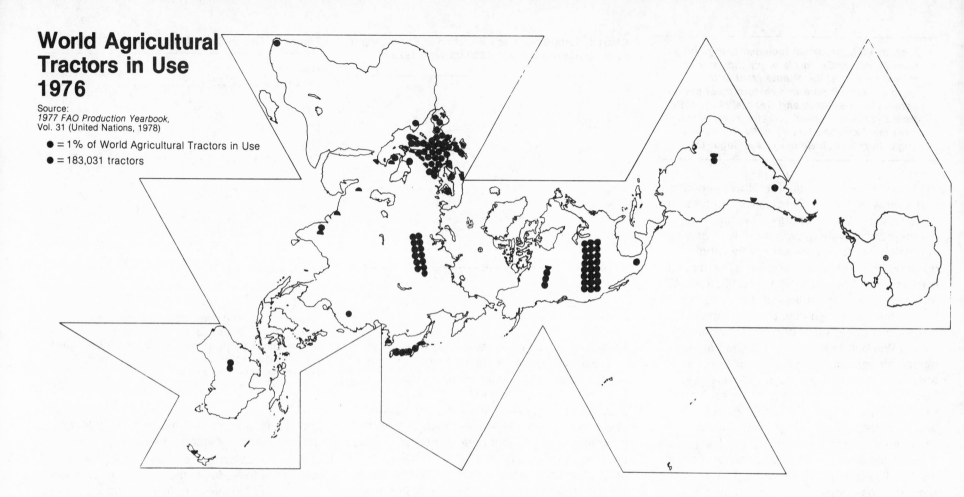

energy sources were not competitive with human food. If the farmer of yesteryear wanted to produce the same amount of food that is produced today by the modern farmer with his inanimate energy slaves, he would need hundreds of thousands of human slaves to plow, plant, weed, fertilize, control pests, irrigate, harvest, process, and distribute food. A hard working human being consumes about 1.27×10^6 kilo calories per year. The U.S. food system consumes about 2.17×10^{15} kilo calories; this is the energy equivalent of 1.7 billion energy slaves (eight times the number of people in the United States).

It is important in this discussion to keep in mind that there are differences between the processes, dynamics, and demands of present day machines and those of ecosystems.

Biological systems are incredibly more complex than human engineered technological systems. Where humans obtain their personal life-support energy, their food, is a more complex system than where humanity's extensions, their machines, obtain their energy. There are many more alternative pathways for energy flows in natural eco-systems than in our comparatively primitive technological systems. In the case of most industries, these differences can be potentially resolved by keeping the two systems—industrial and ecological—separate. This can be accomplished by making the industrial system into a closed, recycling system. Present-day mechanized agriculture, on the other hand, represents an interface between the industrial and the ecological. It is for this reason that many of the general operating principles—like standardization and mass production—that apply so well to specialized industrial systems cannot be applied wholesale to agriculture unless food production becomes a closed system. Food production could be a closed or industrialized system (see Single Cell Protein and Hydroponics sections), but it would take a massive input of energy to replace all the services supplied by non-specialized Nature—e.g., Sun, rain, pollenization, disease, and pest control; or it would take a "massive" input of know-how to make our technological systems in tune with their ecological contexts. Either we transform our environmental ecology into technology with energy by bringing it indoors, or we make technology into or in tune with ecology with information and know-how. As we cannot industrialize Nature, the easier choice is the latter.

Within the industrial system there are

Technology Hierarchy

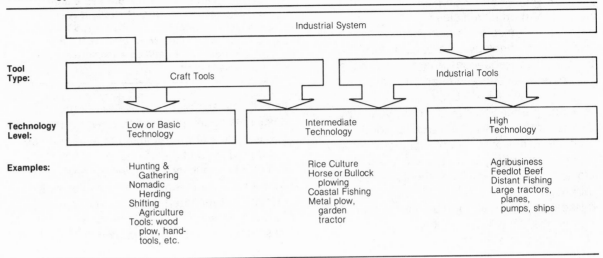

differences between tools and between levels of technology. There are fundamentally two different types of tools—craft tools and industrial tools.[8] Craft tools are those tools that anyone starting alone and ignorant in the wilderness could develop—a stone and stick hoe, for example. Industrial tools are tools that could only be developed by a plurality of individuals—a forged steel rake or ocean liner. There are three levels of technology or industrialization: basic or low, intermediate, and high technology. Low technology is almost always composed of craft tools and characterized by being human and animal labor intensive and with low productivity. Intermediate technology uses craft and small scale industrial tools, is usually human and animal labor intensive, but is much more productive than low technology. High or "advanced" technology

uses industrial tools, both small and large scale, and is energy, machine labor, and capital intensive with high productivity. There are advantages and disadvantages to both high technology and lower technologies. An airplane, for instance, is a high technology that is now enabling some farmers to produce much more than before. "A plane can do more in an hour's time in areas such as seeding, fertilizing, and spraying pesticides than a tractor can do in a day and it does it with about 10% of the fuel."[9] More than 200 million acres in the United States were treated by airplanes in 1975; nearly 90%

of the country's rice crops were seeded by air because seeds can be dropped on land that is too wet for ground vehicles.[9]

Trying to transplant a high technology directly onto a low technology area could have disastrous consequences. Planting all of the Philippine rice culture with an airplane, if it were possible, could put millions of people out of work and perhaps lead to their starvation by eliminating their ability to purchase food. Technology needs to be appropriate to an area; if it is not appropriate, a new technology that is, should be developed. Tools should be adapted, not people or their cultures.

Because of the use of machinery and fossil energy, there has been a massive shift away from human labor on the farm, resulting in increased productivity, but also human displacement and a growing dependence on limited energy sources. There are fewer people actually on the modern farm, but counting all the people now employed in the food system who manufacture the tractors and fertilizer, process the food, etc., the total percentage engaged in the food system is about the same as it was in 1930–40.[11]

Fossil fuel consumption by our inanimate energy slaves in the global food system has grown to such an extent that it poses a threat to the very system it was designed to support. This threat is not, as some people suppose, because large quantities of energy are used to produce the food we eat, but rather, it is caused by the type of energy we are using, the effects of using only this type of energy (the fossil fuels) as our energy base, and abandoning many of the regenerative agricultural practices of our forebears. The amount of energy from the Sun which is consumed, not only in photosynthesis

---

During growing season about two billion kilocalories in the form of sunlight reach a one-acre cornfield; about 1.26% (26 million kilocalories) is converted into the corn plant and about .4%—8 million kilocalories—ends up as corn grain.

(which is vast), but in the evaporation, desalination, and purification of water from the oceans and elsewhere, lifting this water vapor to great heights, and then transporting it sometimes thousands of miles to then rain down upon crops, represents vast quantities of energy that are not recorded in our myopic economic accounting ledgers; and all this work performed by solar energy is only a fraction of that

performed for us by gravity. Almost nothing supplied by nature is on our accounting books, and, if it is, it is not in terms of what it cost nature to produce but as a "free" gift. We have known for quite some time that nothing is free, yet our accounting ledgers have their figurative heads in the ground.

The dangers posed by a heavy or sole reliance on fossil fuels are numerous:

1. The first is a result of the fact that our fossil fuels are finite. You can not base a regenerative or sustainable system on non-regenerative, finite resources. As long as our food production is based on fossil fuels it will not be sustainable; it will be used today with little thought for the future.

It takes as much energy to build a six passenger car as to grow an acre of cauliflower for a year.[12]

---

2. The second danger of a specialized and depleting energy source is that the supply is subject to the vagaries of international and national economic and political discord, upset, or imbalance. Increasing oil and gas prices are a case in point as are the threats of embargo. Farming uses more petroleum than any other single industry.[12] Ninety percent of all nitrogen fertilizer comes from the fossil fuel-subsidized manufacture of ammonia. Sixty percent of the cost of ammonia production is the cost of natural gas. As gas prices go up, fertilizer prices skyrocket. Prices in 1976 were four times what they were in 1973. Without a subsequent price increase in farm output the farmer is faced with the serious problem of his products costing him more to produce than he gets for them.

3. A third danger resulting from our intense use of fossil fuels is that it encourages agricultural practices that increase short-term productivity but also increase long term damage—such as the practice of monoculture or cropping (the planting of vast areas of land with only one crop). The danger inherent in monocropping is that large tracts of land devoted to single crops become open to attack from insects, fungus, rodents, and weeds that would not ordinarily be a problem with polyculture or multiple crops on a single piece of land. Nature loves, or fosters, diversity; the more diverse or complex a biological system is, the more stable it is. Monocropping eliminates diversity for the sake of increasing short-term production. The work performed by the diversity or complexity of the ecosystem is performed by the fossil fuel subsidy to the modern food

system. Instead of having many different plants growing on a given piece of land, some serving as food or havens for insects, others as shelter for insect predators, and still others as fertilizer for other plants, we now have a system where all the diversity of the "other plants" are in the form of fossil fuel based pesticides and fertilizers. There are alternatives to monocropping that may not be as profitable in the short-run but which are more productive in terms of long range stability. Crop rotation (growing different crops in regular succession on a given field or farm) and intercropping (planting two or more different crops in the same field to the mutual benefit of both and to the soil) are two such alternatives. For example, the International Rice Research Institute has found that the intercropping used by small farmers in Java is 30–60% more productive than monocultures, and that

a rice/corn combination is 80% more productive than separate plantings of each crop. This increased productivity can be explained in part by the higher total light interception of the two plants together and the resultant enhanced ability to surpress shade intolerant weeds.[5]

4. Other dangers result from the overuse of pesticides and fertilizers. Runoff, stream, pond, and lake eutrofication or contamination and loss of soil humus are some of the problems associated with synthetic pesticide and fertilizer over use. Details of these problems are included in the following sections on food production techniques.

5. Besides these uses of fossil fuel in the production of food, there are still others in the processing, distribution, and preparation of food. Gas fueled dryers for grains, petroleum or coal derived plastic packaging, the gasoline powered trip to the local supermarket, and the three hour oven roast all utilize their share of our limited fossil fuel supplies.

The above dangers or disadvantages of a fossil fuel subsidized food system are paramount, but there are advantages to using these sources as well. Among the advantages are:

1. Fossil fuels are, or were, widespread and readily available.
2. Fossil fuels are easily stored, handled, and transported.
3. The stored energy of fossil fuels is relatively easy to harness and release.
4. Fossil fuels were very inexpensive.
5. Fossil fuels were easily amendable to a wide variety of uses as a raw material for fertilizer

production as well as for pesticide production.

The extensive use of machinery can cause many problems, some related to the above energy use problems, and others intrinsic to the machinery.

Human Directed Energy Use in Typical North American Farming System[13]

Machinery
It takes about 24 kwh (20,680 kcal) to produce each kilogram of machinery, and the average North American farm has 20 tons of equipment; this amounts to 479 x 10³ kwh (412 x 10⁶ kcal) per farm.

Fuel
It takes about 7–8 gallons of fuel to produce and harvest each acre; there are about 52.3 kwh (45,000 kcal) per gallon of fuel.

Fertilizer To produce & process (exclusive of transportation to farm)	Application rates per acre (corn)
1 kilogram N requires 21.5 kwh (8400 kcal)	45 kg
1 kilogram P requires 3.9 kwh (1520 kcal)	23 kg
1 kilogram K requires 2.7 kwh (1050 kcal)	27 kg

Seed
Planting requires .33 bushels (26,000 kernels or 39.5 kwh (34,000 kcal) per acre.

Drying
It takes 14 gallons of propane to dry one acre of corn. There are 32.2 kwh (27,720 kcal) per gallon.

Labor
4 hours per acre

Yield
90 bushels of corn per acre and 1800 kcal per pound food energy value
50 bushels of wheat per acre and 1600 kcal per pound food energy value

1. The increase in size and weight of farm machines has resulted in increased problems of soil compaction.
2. The extensive use of the mouldboard plow can create an impervious layer of soil below the plowed depth.
3. Extensive tilling can result in soil degradation in the form of soil erosion.
4. Yields are lowered when wide spacing of crop rows are required to accommodate tractors.

Machinery advantages include:

1. The use of machines decreases the amount of coerced human labor.
2. Machines can work harder, longer, cheaper, and in more hazardous conditions than human labor.
3. Machines can do more with less resources than their human or animal counterparts.
4. Machines, and their capabilities, are mass-producible.
5. Machines can be improved as know-how increases.

There are many things that can and need to be done to cut down on fossil energy consumption in the global food system:

1. Alternative, non-depleting fuels such as hydrogen, methane, and alcohol can be utilized wherever gasoline, oil, or natural gas are currently being consumed, both as fuel for operating machinery and producing heat, and as a raw material for fertilizer production.
2. Energy conservation measures could reduce the amount of energy needed by the food system: from farm machinery that is kept in adjustment to more efficient tractors that get more miles per gallon (substitute diesel engines for gasoline engines), to combining farming operations (like harrowing, planting, and fertilizing in the same operation), to less energy intensive (high energy using) ways of processing food, to energy conserving practices in the distribution of food, such as moving food stuffs by train rather than truck as trains are significantly more efficient than trucks (700 BTU/ton mile vs. 3000), or the design of mass transit vehicles with provisions for passengers with packages.
3. Energy intensive materials for packaging could be replaced with less energy intensive materials—from paper used instead of aluminum foil to returnable bottles used instead of disposable bottles.
4. Energy intensive practices such as advertising, long distance shipping of non-essential food items, and the insistence on "perfect" or non-blemished vegetables and fruit could be drastically reduced.
5. Less energy intensive pest control methods such as polycropping and crop rotation, mechanical cultivation, and biological control of pests, as well as less energy intensive (and soil destroying) fertilizer, such as animal wastes, compost, green manure crops (like nitrogen fixing clover and alfalfa), sewage sludge, and crop rotation systems, could greatly reduce energy consumption in the gobal food system. So-called organic farms use one-third the energy of their non-organic counterparts.[14]
6. Locally more self-sufficient patterns of food production, in the form of backyard, rooftop, or neighborhood gardens and local truck farms around cities could cut energy costs of food production, processing, and transport.
7. Livestock feedlots could be integrated with feed producing areas to recycle waste and lessen transportation.
8. Livestock grazing could be substituted for feed; a 500 million BTU savings could result from the conversion of 20% of present feed grain and hay acreage to pastures for direct grazing by livestock. The savings would accrue because pastures require little fuel for field operations, and none for harvesting or distributing grain to stock.
9. New food sources could be developed that are less fossil energy dependent—for example, new crops that require less fertilizer or pesticide, mature faster, have a reduced moisture content, or better water efficiency than present varieties.
10. Unnecessary tillage could be reduced: 2.1 billion gallons of gasoline and diesel fuels are used each year for tillage in the United States. Extensive use of no-tillage farming could save as much as 100 trillion BTUs per year.
11. Where appropriate, and for a limited time, labor inputs could be increased or maintained instead of substituting machinery. For example, one application of herbicide to corn requires about 18,000 kcal/acre if applied by tractor, 300 if by hand.[5]
12. New machinery should be developed that is suitable for polyculture, for instance, machinery that can harvest intercropped fields and small scale tractors suitable for the small farms in developing countries.
13. Alterations in diet could perhaps reduce fossil energy consumption more than any other single item. U.S. meat consumption

averaged 250 pounds per person in 1974; this was roughly six times the amount recommended by the U.N. Food and Agricultural Organization. Fat consumption is over three times the recommended amount. Reducing these items to one half or one quarter of their present levels would result in no nutritional loss (and in the eyes of some, from a health standpoint, a nutritional gain), while also enabling the U.S. to double its grains and oil crop exports. Looking at the U.S. diet/energy interface more closely discloses that meat over-consumption is just one example of the more pervasive phenomenon of the overweight person and the energy costs to society incurred by that person.[15] It has recently been calculated that the amount of energy required to supply the extra food calories to maintain the excess body fat of all the overweight people in just the U.S. is about 47 billion kwh (about 1.3 billion gallons of gasoline).[15] About 900,000 average[16] U.S. autos could be fueled each year, or the annual residential electrical demands of Boston, Chicago, San Francisco, and Washington, D.C., or the entire energy demands of twenty million Indian people, could be supplied with the savings that would result from the reduction of the present overweight population of the U.S. to optimum body weight.

14. A global energy use division in the World Clearinghouse for Food Information (see Making the World Work: Strategies for a Regenerative Food System) could be established to collect, correlate, and disseminate appropriate energy information about the food system.

15. Every food product could list the energy tied up in that product.

16. Wind, bioconversion, and solar energy systems could be phased in to meet farm power needs.

17. Controlled agriculture in conjunction with carbon dioxide-producing power plants could increase yield.

18. Sustained production of fuel wood, particularly in rural village woodlots, along roadsides, etc., could be expanded.

History

8000–6000 B.C.	Bone and flint sickle invented for harvesting wild grains
8000–4000 B.C.	Use of animal power for plowing soil
6000–3000 B.C.	Invention of the primitive wood plow
3000 B.C.	Egypt: Primitive wood and stone implements of cultivation—hoes, sickles, plows
1000 B.C.	Western Europe: Bronze used for implements of cultivation
400 B.C.	Chinese use cast iron plow
900 A.D.	Europe: New harnesses developed allowing horses to pull plows—increased speed compared to oxen use
1066 A.D.	Europe: Cumbersome and crude wooden plows; only slight improvements made until 18th Century
1105 A.D.	Windmill
1300 A.D.	Europe: Wheelplough commonly in use
1500	Mechanized farming drill
1602	Europe: T. Cavalini, first wheeled seed drill for planting
1701	England: Jethro Tull seed drill
1780	Mass production of cast iron farm implements
1784	Drill plow
1786	England: A. Meikle, horse-propelled threshing machine invented
1794	U.S.A.: Whitney cotton gin
1797	U.S.A.: Neubold cast iron plow
1800	England: Salmon, hay feeder
1823	Europe: First plows of steel appear
1825	Germany: Hohenheim seed drill invented
1826	England: P. Bell, first successful design of reaper for cereal and grain harvesting
1831	U.S.A.: McCormick's reaper
1831	U.S.A.: Manning, mowing machine
1836	U.S.A.: Moore's combine harvester-thresher
1840	U.S.A.: Deere, steel plow
1840	England, U.S.A.: Portable steam engine applied to threshing machine and barn machinery
1840's	U.S.A.: Cravath's disc plow
1850's	Rail transport of beef
1850	Europe: Beginning of practical application of steam power to cultivation operations
1851	Combined threshing and stacking by steam power
1861	Meat freezers
1868	Europe: First steam-powered plowing
1870	U.S.A.: Improved combine using steam engine
1873	Meat slicer, pressure cooker
1875	Railroad refrigeration
1878	U.S.A.: McCormick Co., self-bind reaping machine first marketed—automatically tied sheaves with string

1880	Cream separator
1885	U.S.A.: Henry Ford, first steam-engine tractor used for haulage-plowing
1896	Electric stove
1901	U.S.A.: Internal combustion tractor
1902	Ivel tractor
1908	Caterpillar tractor
1911	Quick freezing
1905–19	Australia: Milking machine
1929	U.S.A.: Rust, mechanical cotton-picker
1936	U.S.A.: Completely automatic combine
1940's	U.S.A.: Inertia-type tree shakers for harvesting prunes and walnuts
1943	U.S.A.: Sugar beet harvester
1950	U.S.A., Europe: Automated field pick-up balers
1951	U.S.A.: Asparagus harvester
1960's	U.S.A.: Tomato harvester
1963	U.S.A.: Electronic color sorting
1964	U.S.A.: Lettuce harvester
1965	U.S.A.: Non-destructive measurements of the interior quality of fruit
1968	U.S.A.: Grape harvester
1968	U.S.A.: Cling peach harvester
1950's on	Dishwasher, toaster, mixer, blender, juicer, electric can opener, frostless refrigerator-freezer, self-cleaning oven, trash masher, etc.

Agribusiness

Food is big business; in fact, food is the largest business—over $531 billion in assets, $120 billion in annual sales and 18 million employed—in North America, where the world's largest businesses are located.[1] This is quite understandable, even though none of the large corporations most people are familiar with—Exxon, General Motors, A.T.&T., Ford, I.B.M., etc.—deal directly in food. There are many huge trans-national food corporations—Beatrice Foods, Unilever, General Foods, General Mills, Del Monte, Ralston Purina, Nestle's, Tenneco, Campbell's, H.J. Heinz, and Pillsbury, to name a few—that do deal directly with food.

"Agribusiness" is big business in the food industry. It is the industrialization and specialization of agriculture. Agribusiness is an interlocked web of businesses that buy and sell food, seeds, land, processing, packaging, and all the accoutrements of a global food system. It consists of essentially three components: an input industry that produces and sells seed, machines, fertilizer, and such; the farm that produces and sells the crops; and the food processing and distribution industry that buys and distributes the farm products.[2] Agribusiness, and "business" in general, is not found as we know it in centrally planned economies such as China. There, many of the functions of "business" are handled by the state.

The expansion of agribusiness (and all other modern industry) to its present proportions was furthered by those inventions and practices that enabled it to standardize, specialize, mass produce its products, and expand its markets. Mechanization as well as chemicals played a

Agricultural exports are the U.S.'s largest export—around $20 billion per year.[1] Food processing alone is a $62 billion industry in the United States.

big part in this. Besides fertilizers and pesticides that enabled the farmer to better standardize and regulate his output, chemical additives in the food processing industry made it possible to stabilize color and "freshness" for the extended storage and transport necessitated by wide regional, national, and international distribution. In the past, food markets had been localized due to food spoilage limits and the lack of a speedy and relatively inexpensive transport medium as that furnished today by rail and truck.

The large food corporation is not just a producer of food, or a processor, or a distributor, but all of these and more. A large agribusiness could produce and sell seeds; grow food; supply feed; process, package, distribute the food; and then sell it in its own chain of grocery stores or prepare it in its own restaurant chain. Almost every product in the modern supermarket—as well as the market itself—is a product of big business.

So far, big business has been most successful in processing and distributing food, not in growing it. Economies of scale are achieved in farming by buying supplies in large quantities at discount prices, keeping hired workers busy, and fully utilizing expensive mechanical equipment. When a farm gets too large, unforeseen things begin to go wrong—related to the uncertainties of weather, soil, seeds, and yields—that have in places driven conglomerate giants such as Gates Rubber Co.,

Great Western Ranches, Inc., Tenneco, and S.S. Pierce either out of the farming end of the business or into bankruptcy. Even though a larger farm can produce more food per unit of capital and labor input, the most efficient production unit in farming has been repeatedly shown to be quite small: for field crops such as corn, alfalfa, and barley, it is about 640 acres; for cling peaches it is about 90–110 acres.[3]

The concentration of farmland into larger and larger holdings and fewer and fewer hands—with the consequent increase of overhead, debt, and dependence on machines—is a matter of complex significance, and its agricultural significance cannot be disentangled from its cultural significance.

It *forces* a profound revolution in the farmer's mind: once his investment in land and machines is large enough, he must forsake the values of husbandry and assume those of finance and technology. Thenceforth his thinking is not determined by agricultural responsibility, but by financial accountability and the capacities of his machines. Where his money comes from becomes less important to him than where it is going. He is caught up in the drift of energy and interest away from the land. Production begins to override maintenance. The economy of money has infiltrated and subverted the economies of nature, energy, and the human spirit. The man himself has become a consumptive machine.[5]

The *functions* being performed by agribusiness are essential to the global food system, but some of the companions of those functions have severe disadvantages. Among these are:

1. Agribusiness encourages larger and larger farms, and they:
   a) are less efficient in terms of output per acre than small farms;
   b) are more costly to society; that is, the big farm employs fewer people, causing rural unemployment and migration to urban centers; in U.S. nearly 2000 farms and 300 rural businesses go out of business each week;[2]
   c) have a history of exploiting hired labor; clerks in air-conditioned Safeway markets earn up to $5.00/hour in parts of California, providing them with a greater return than the farmer receives for his labor and three times the earnings of the farm worker;
   d) attempt to maximize short term profits, often resulting in abusive practices such as soil and underground water depletion. The soil is "mined" of its nutrients rather than enriched.

2. By being so big, agribusinesses have a disproportionate influence in economic and political spheres. Four corporations account for more than 90% of cereal sales in the U.S. With such economic concentration the danger exists, as some charge, of overcharging the consumer.[2] With large resources at their disposal agribusiness can "maintain dozens of lobbyists in Washington and fly witnesses in and out of the capital during Congressional hearings" while "the organizations representing the small farmers, sharecroppers, small businesses, farm workers, the poor minorities, consumers and environmentalists cannot make such effort."[2] For example, through such efforts, the U.S. taxpayer has been forced to subsidize the American tobacco industry to the tune of $50 million each year.[4] Another problem of agribusiness is that because of their need to maximize profits, food industries spend more on advertising and less on research than any other industry in the U.S.

What Needs to be Done

1. Establish a Global Agribusiness Research Institute to research and develop solutions to agribusiness problems and to collect, correlate, and disseminate information dealing with agribusiness.
2. Have full disclosure of profits of multinational food corporations.
3. Allow tax credits for developing inexpensive and nutritious foods for children.
4. Allow tax credits for developing inexpensive and nutritious foods for food-short countries.
5. Allow tax credit for working with the Global Food Service (see Making the World Work: Strategies for a Regenerative Food system).
6. Allow tax credit for "adopting" developing country (that indicates receptivity to such a strategy) and participate/help in that area's food development.
7. Establish international regulations to regulate multinational food corporations.
8. Tax each multinational food company 1% of its gross profits to help fund the Global Food Service.

Irrigation/Drainage

Water is crucial to crops. Plant life evolved in an aqueous medium, adapting primarily to maintain that watery environment within leaves even though the plant is bathed in dry air. Most crops grow best and their yields are maximal only when they receive enough water throughout the life of the crop. Irrigated cropland constitutes about 15% of the total cultivated land on a global basis, but produces up to 30% of humanity's food.[1] Yield is about 50% higher with irrigation growing traditional varieties of crops, and even higher growing high-yield varieties.[2]

Irrigation and drainage are processes which attempt to maintain soil moisture within the range required for this optimal plant growth. In parts of the world, the moisture available in the soil from rain or from underground water is not enough for the requirements of plant life, either all the time or for part of the crop season. Irrigation is the supplying of this type of land with water from human-made streams or channels for growing crops or trees. In other areas, where ample rain falls annually but only in half the year, irrigation makes possible double or even triple cropping.

In contradistinction, there are parts of the world where the soil is either saturated with water or has more moisture than is healthy for plant life. Drainage refers to the removal of excess moisture from this type of soil.

Traditional irrigation usually delivers more water to the soil than crops use or is evaporated by the Sun; irrigation needs to be complementarily coupled with drainage so that the excess water is removed, or a bog will result.

There have been many types of irrigation used by humanity throughout history; each method reflects the unique water resources of the particular locality, e.g., rivers, lakes, springs, glaciers, and ground water. Some of these methods involved percolation wells, artesian wells, tub wells, springs, storage tanks, reservoirs, and pumping or lifting water from rivers and lakes.[5] Irrigation was first developed in level areas near streams that could be easily flooded; it was then expanded by levelling more fields and through the use of dams and canals. Water was distributed by open ditches, closed conduits, or even carried by hand.[6]

This type of surface irrigation depends on the flow of water over the soil surface to distribute water, requires a minimum depth of water to achieve coverage, and is usually synonymous with intensive human labor. Today, there are also other irrigation systems in use. Usually referred to as high frequency irrigation, these systems include set or travelling sprinklers, drip or trickle irrigation, and small basin irrigation. One type of sprinkler system—center pivot "irrigation machines"—has been called the "most significant mechanical innovation in agriculture since the replacement of draft animals by the tractor."[7] In these systems, water is pumped into the sprinkler pipe from a source at the center of the field and then it is carried around the central pivot by supporting towers. This system is the predominant method of automatically irrigating field crops available

today. Using such a system to apply relatively light irrigation frequently allows land that was previously limited in productivity because of limited water holding capabilities to become an intensively cropped land.[7] High frequency irrigation also saves about 50% of the water that would be used in surface irrigation, reduces or eliminates the need for drainage, reduces the energy required for land preparation, and increases yields over conventional irrigation by an average of 15%.[6] Such an irrigation system also allows for the administration of exact amounts of fertilizer at the right times by injecting these nutrients into the water supply. This saves both fertilizer and fertilizer run-off damage. As good as the center pivot sprinkler system may be, drip irrigation systems are even better from the point of view of water and energy use. A drip irrigation system only delivers water near the plant, and hence can supply plants with precise amounts of water, saving loss through evaporation, runoff, percolation, and blow-off which can result from sprinklers.[8]

The use of irrigation in the arid regions of the Earth could be a major new source of food (see map). In the Ganges Basin of India and Bangladesh, for instance, an integrated monsoon-control/crop-land irrigation plan could

World Irrigated Land 1976

Source:
1977 FAO Production Yearbook,
Vol. 31 (United Nations, 1978)

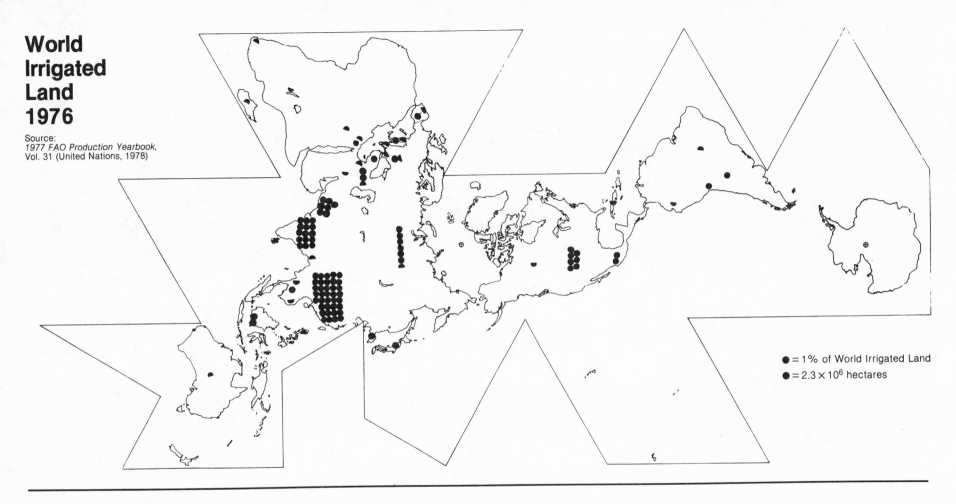

● = 1% of World Irrigated Land

● = 2.3 × 10⁶ hectares

result in an increased production of over 150 million metric tons of grain—enough to feed over 600 million people.[9] In many parts of Asia, intensively developing irrigation would be much easier and more economical than developing new land. Where there is a water supply that can be channelled into an arid or desert region with a warm, steady climate, the results have usually been good. There is no shortage of

About 15% of the world's farmland is irrigated with a little more than 1000 cubic kilometers of water—about 4% of the world's total river flow.[6]

water (see Chart 1). Clean, fresh water in the right place at the right time is another thing, but economical large-scale desalting of sea water

could change that. Presently, there are more than 244 million gallons per day of water produced in over 700 water desalting projects in the world (see Charts 1 & 2).[11] There are 50,000 miles of coastal deserts in the world (see map). With solar-powered water pumps and desalination plants, these lands could be irrigated and made productive. Another possible way for this to be accomplished would be to

Irrigated Land: Locations

Source:
Oxford Economic Atlas, 1972

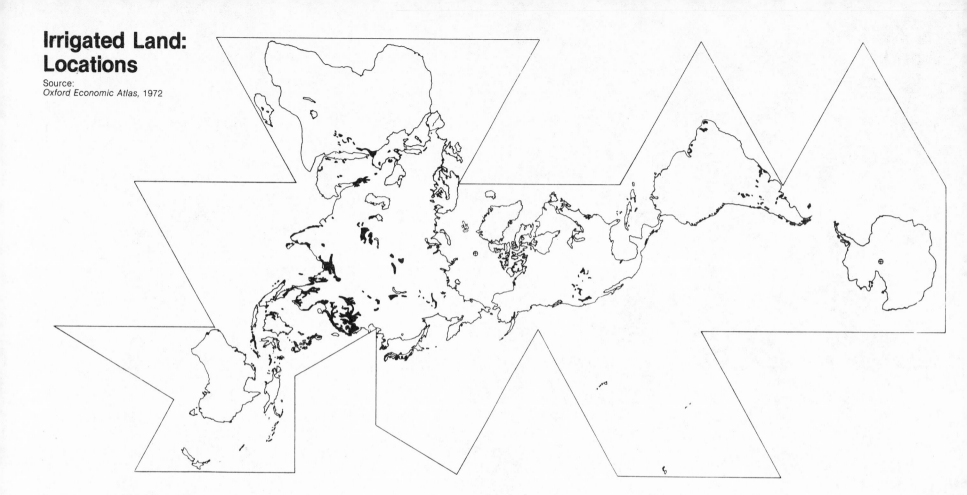

Total Irrigated Land in World 1974:	226.7
Africa:	7.7
North and Central America:	22
South America.	6.6
Asia:	161
Europe:	12.6
Oceania:	1.6
USSR:	14.5

All units in million hectares

Chart 1. The Hydrosphere.[10]

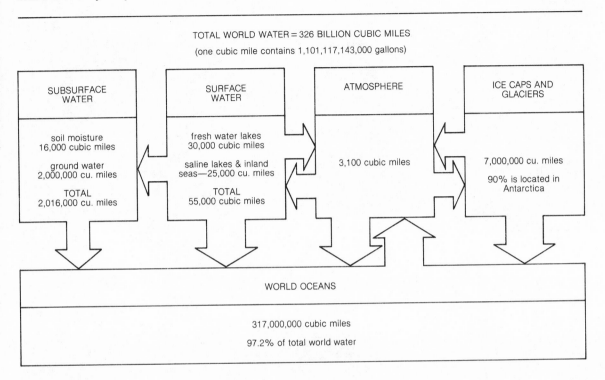

TOTAL WORLD WATER = 326 BILLION CUBIC MILES

(one cubic mile contains 1,101,117,143,000 gallons)

SUBSURFACE WATER	SURFACE WATER	ATMOSPHERE	ICE CAPS AND GLACIERS
soil moisture 16,000 cubic miles	fresh water lakes 30,000 cubic miles	3,100 cubic miles	7,000,000 cu. miles
ground water 2,000,000 cu. miles	saline lakes & inland seas—25,000 cu. miles		90% is located in Antarctica
TOTAL 2,016,000 cu. miles	TOTAL 55,000 cubic miles		

WORLD OCEANS

317,000,000 cubic miles

97.2% of total world water

70% of the Earth's surface is covered with water;

only 1% is fresh and 99% of this fresh water is underground.

Chart 2[11] Desalting Plants by Size

Size (thousands gpd)	No. Plants	Plant Capacity (mgd)
25–99	359	18.4
100–499	263	50.7
500–999	32	21.6
1000–4999	51	108.7
5000 and greater	7	45.2
Total	712	244.6

Chart 3[11] Desalting Plants by Geographic Location

Area	No. of Plants	Plant Capacity (mgd)
United States	301	43.1
United States territories	14	10.3
North America except USA and its territories	12	8.5
Caribbean	31	24.1
South America	23	4.1
England and Ireland	63	15.9
Europe (continental)	97	31.7
Union of Soviet Socialist Republics (USSR)	9	12.6
Middle East	78	69.1
Africa	50	19.7
Asia	27	4.2
Australia	7	1.3
Totals	712	244.6

further develop new salt tolerant crops that can be irrigated with sea water.[12]

Of the Earth's total land area (excluding Antarctica), about 10% is under cultivation. Forty percent of the land is in an arid climate where additional irrigation may favor the doubling of the agricultural produce; 15% is in a zone of semi-arid climate where irrigation may provide a threefold increase in agricultural produce due both to the extension of the cultivated areas and to the increase in crop yields; and another 5% of the cultivated area is in the arid desert zone where farming is impossible without irrigation.[13]

Warm waste water from industrial processes or electric power generating plants can also be used for increasing agricultural productivity. For example, by stimulating root growth through underground irrigation during cold weather, crop output has been shown to significantly increase.[14]

Much can be done to improve the efficiency of water usage by crops. At present, only about 30–40% of the water used in irrigation throughout the world is utilized by crops. This percentage can be doubled, as it has been in Israel, where water utilization from irrigation exceeds 80%.

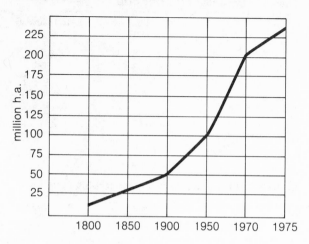

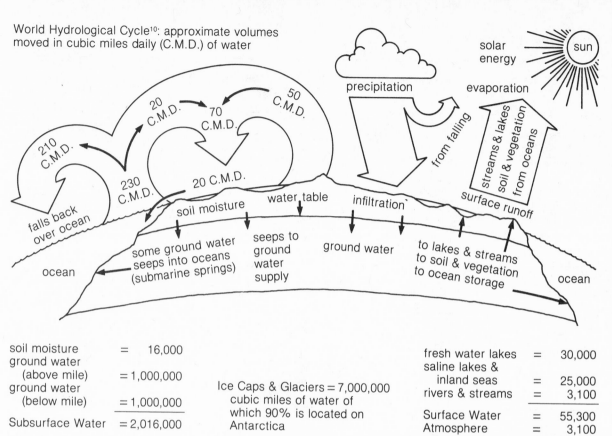

World Hydrological Cycle[10]: approximate volumes moved in cubic miles daily (C.M.D.) of water

soil moisture	= 16,000
ground water (above mile)	= 1,000,000
ground water (below mile)	= 1,000,000
Subsurface Water	= 2,016,000

Ice Caps & Glaciers = 7,000,000 cubic miles of water of which 90% is located on Antarctica

fresh water lakes	= 30,000
saline lakes & inland seas	= 25,000
rivers & streams	= 3,100
Surface Water	= 55,300
Atmosphere	= 3,100

Total World Water Supply = 326,071,300 cubic miles

One cubic mile of water contains 1,101,117,143,000 gallons

World Oceans = 317,000,000 cubic miles of water; 97.2% of Total World Water

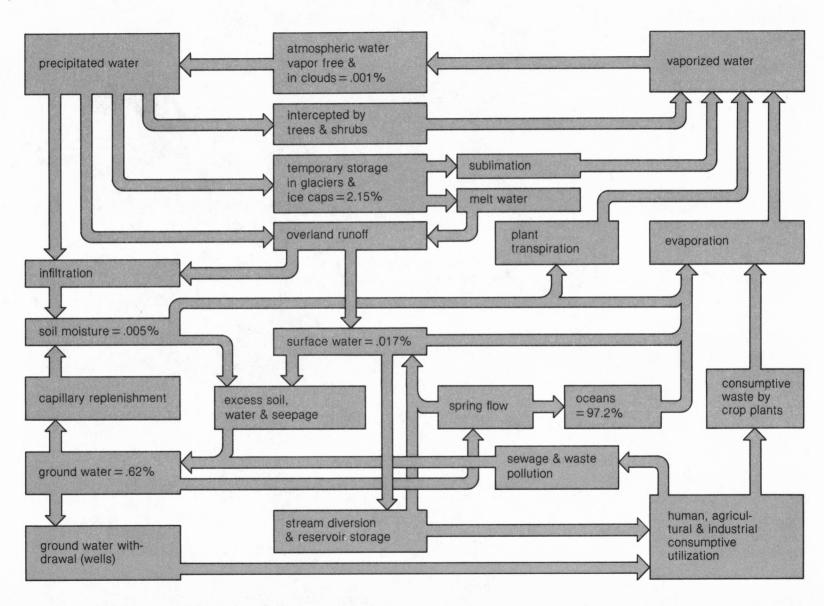

World Hydrologic Cycle

Note: numbers shown refer to percentages of total world water.

precipitated water

atmospheric water vapor free & in clouds = .001%

vaporized water

intercepted by trees & shrubs

temporary storage in glaciers & ice caps = 2.15%

sublimation

melt water

overland runoff

plant transpiration

evaporation

infiltration

soil moisture = .005%

surface water = .017%

capillary replenishment

excess soil, water & seepage

spring flow

oceans = 97.2%

consumptive waste by crop plants

ground water = .62%

sewage & waste pollution

ground water withdrawal (wells)

stream diversion & reservoir storage

human, agricultural & industrial consumptive utilization

Normal Mean Annual Precipitation

Source:
Time, April 4, 1977

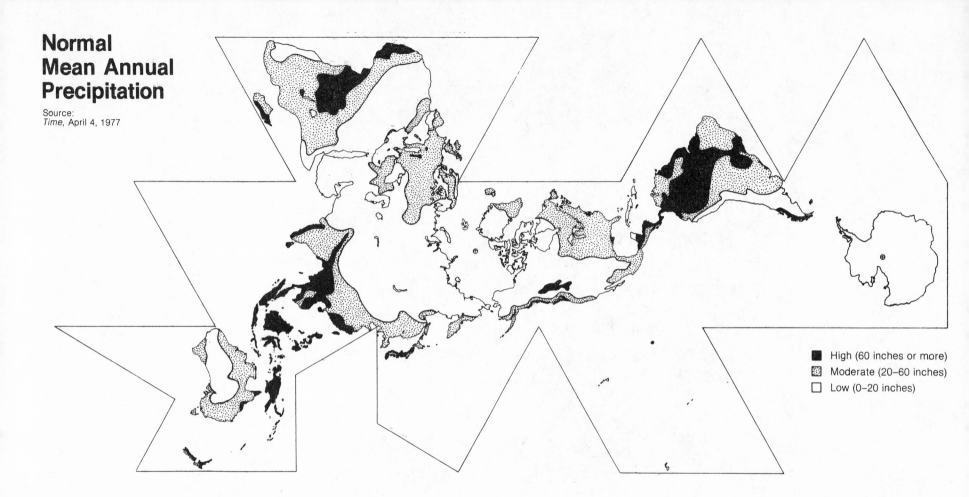

■ High (60 inches or more)
▨ Moderate (20–60 inches)
☐ Low (0–20 inches)

Drought
1976–77

Source:
"Droughts This Year"
Time, April 4, 1977

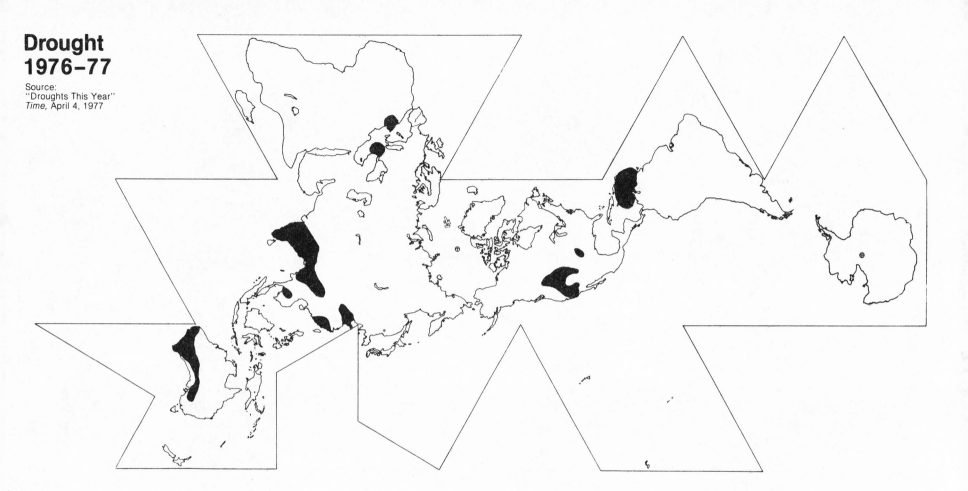

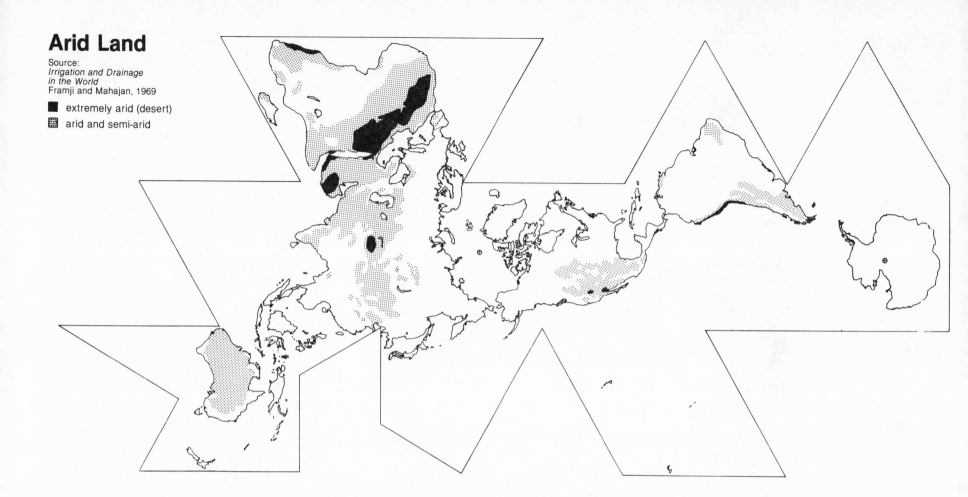

Arid Land

Source:
*Irrigation and Drainage
in the World*
Framji and Mahajan, 1969

■ extremely arid (desert)

▦ arid and semi-arid

Risk of Desertification

Source:
Ceres 5, March–April 1977

- ■ very high
- ▨ high to moderate
- ▦ desert

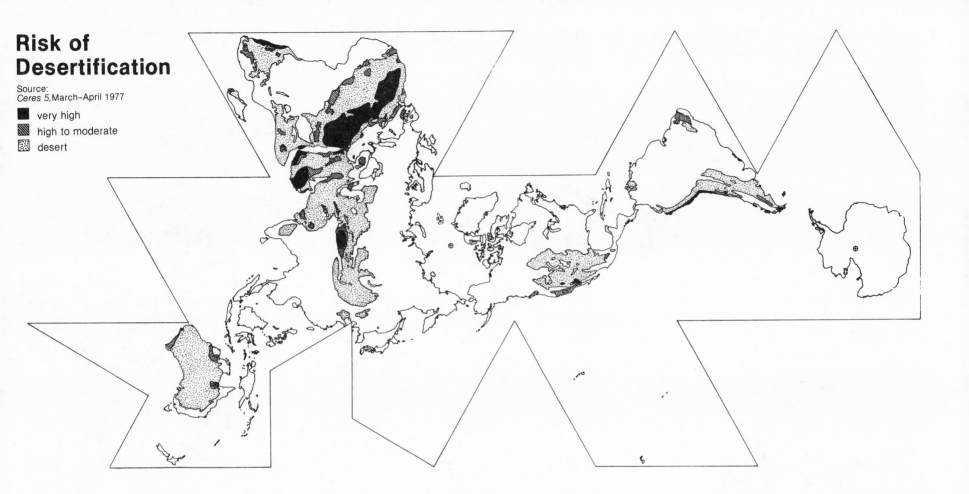

Coastal Deserts Which Could Be Irrigated with Desalinated Water from the Sea

Source:
Feeding the World of the Future
Hellman, 1972

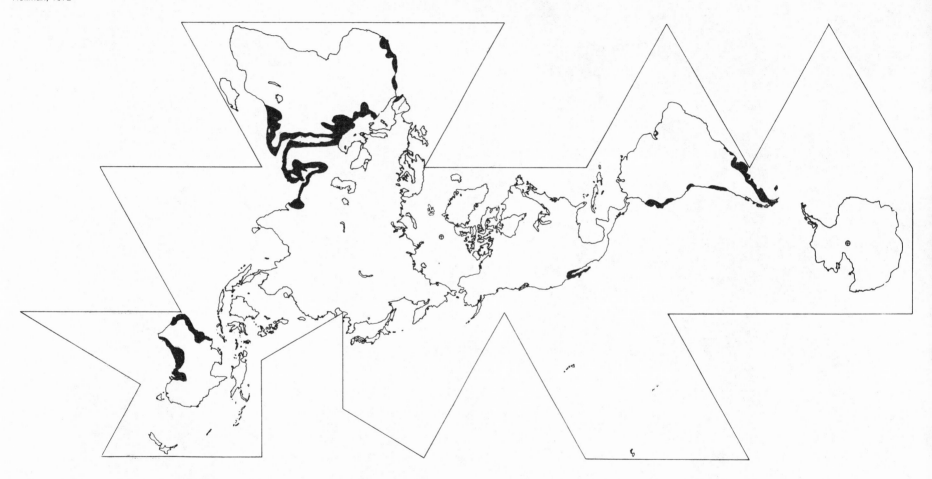

110

Two Types of Water Flows.[15]

A comparison of our present self-defeating linear system and a cyclical system of water use and pollution control

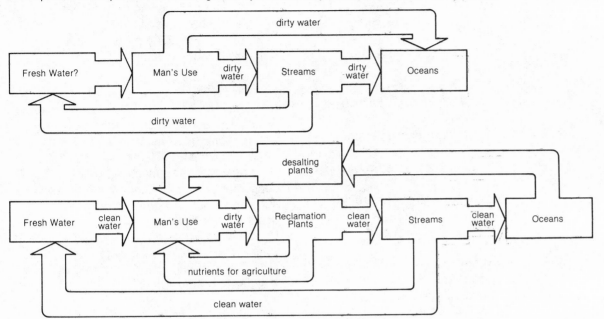

History

6000–3000 B.C.	Waterwheel for irrigation
3600 B.C.	Mesopotamia: Ditches and canals used for water transport and primitive irrigation
3300 B.C.	Egypt: Basin irrigation introduced on the Nile
3000 B.C.	Egypt: World's oldest dam (more than 100 meters long, 12 meters high) built to store water for drinking and irrigation
2300 B.C.	Great irrigation canals constructed in Babylon
2084 B.C.	Egypt: First diversion channel was constructed for the purpose of irrigating fields not on the Nile River
1500 B.C.	Middle East: Phoenicians construct numerous canals for irrigation purposes, soon practiced in North Africa as well
500 B.C.	India, Ganges Valley: Tanks and canals constructed for irrigation
300 B.C.	India: Water storage techniques allowed irrigation systems which supported two crops per season
250–200 B.C.	China: Li Ping and son Chen Tufu invent an elaborate system of canals, barriers, and ditches erected to utilize the waters of the Mino-Ho for irrigation
225 B.C.	China: Multipurpose scheme for flood control and irrigation on Minkiang River
212 B.C.	Greece: Archimedes invents the screw concept as a device for lifting water

200–1000 A.D.	Peru: Intensive agriculture based on elaborate irrigation systems and use of fertilizers
762 A.D.	Iraq: Founding of the city of Baghdad based on the restoration of ancient irrigation works
1325 A.D.	Mexico: City of Tenochtillan founded with a system of canals used for drainage and water storage or irrigation (peaked 1436–64)
1600	Spanish irrigate gardens surrounding their missions in Western United States
1810	South India: Large irrigation projects constructed
1825	North India: Yamuna canals for irrigation
1826	Egypt: Deep irrigation canals built
1840's	England: Reade invents pressed tubular drain pipes for irrigation
1847	Utah, U.S.A.: Brigham Young irrigates Great Salt Lake Valley—beginning of irrigation in the U.S. by Anglo-Saxons on community scale under conditions of modern practice
1850	India: Upper Bari Doab irrigation canals
1854	India: Ganges irrigation canal
1860's	Germany: Clay pipes laid about 8 meters below surface of soil in effort to combine irrigation and drainage as water table rose and fell during year
1873	India: Sirhind irrigation canals
1885	Moncrief, Egypt: Barrages and irrigation canals constructed across the Rosetta and Damietta
	distributaries of the Nile Delta
1901	U.S.A.: Opening of the Imperial Valley waterworks—irrigation from the Colorado River into California
1902	U.S.A.: Federal Reclamation Act first successful attempt of the government to make unused fertile lands available for colonization through economic use of irrigation on a national level
1911	Arizona, U.S.A.: Roosevelt dam completed—first large dam completed for storage of irrigation water
1930's	Australia: Peach orchards irrigated with galvanized pipes with holes cut in them; primitive form of drip irrigation
1940's	Development of siphon tubes for low-pressure drip irrigation
1952	U.S.A.: Zybach invents "walking sprinkler" for large scale sprinkler irrigation
1960's	Colorado, U.S.A.: Fully automated sprinkler systems with buried water supply lines and programmed, electrically operated valves
1960's	U.S.A.: First drip irrigation systems introduced
1977	U.S.A.: Solar-powered irrigation system for 100 acres begins operation near Willard, New Mexico

Advantages:

1. Irrigation results in more land capable of being cultivated more often, thus producing more food and increasing employment and farm income.

2. Irrigation is often coupled with flood control projects such as dams. These have the added benefit of reducing losses due to flooding ($32.8 million in 1971 in U.S.) and producing power (50.1 billion kwh in U.S., 1.2 trillion kwh world-wide).[16]

Disadvantages:

1. Irrigation can increase the salt content of soil with a consequent reduction in crop yields. As a general rule, the more arid the area, the more intense is the salinity problem.[5]
2. Water used for irrigation takes away from the supply that could be used for other purposes such as industry, recreation, sanitation, and domestic needs.
3. In areas where the primary or sole source of irrigation water is ground water, and where recharge is small, water tables are dropping steadily and face exhaustion.

Advantages of center-pivot and drip irrigation systems:

1. Automatic operation
2. Control of application rate and frequency
3. Accommodation to rolling terrain
4. Control over precise application of fertilizers and herbicides; use of less fertilizer and herbicides
5. Accommodation to coarse or sandy soils
6. 50–80% water savings
7. Reduction or elimination of need for drainage
8. Reduced energy needs for land preparation
9. Increased yields by an average of 15–50%
10. More uniform growth of crops
11. Cost is approximately the same as cost of

leveling, developing, and maintaining land for surface irrigation

Disadvantages of center-pivot and drip irrigation systems:

1. Irrigation pumps use a lot of energy—43% of the energy devoted to agriculture in Nebraska goes to pumping water for irrigation (drip irrigation, because of its lower water pressure needs, would require less energy for pumping)
2. Same as other types of irrigation

What Needs to be Done

1. Establish a Global Water Agency for irrigation research and development, to collect, correlate, and disseminate irrigation-related information, and to function as a water use/irrigation training center.
2. Inventory and map all lands that could be irrigated and all water sources.
3. Establish a global irrigation organization within a Global Water Agency to monitor and regulate irrigation, water table levels, soil salt content, etc.
4. Develop appropriate low-cost energy-efficient pumps for use in irrigation systems, e.g., wind, tidal, or solar-powered pumps.
5. Develop appropriate low-cost energy-efficient water distribution systems to reduce water loss through run-off and evaporation.
6. Develop appropriate low-cost solar-powered water desalination units.
7. Develop salt-tolerant crops.
8. Develop irrigation systems capable of using sewer effluent, warm power plant water, industrial effluent, and home effluent.
9. Wean the global irrigation systems from fossil fuels; inventory all areas where depletable resources are being used, and develop non-depletable energy source alternatives.
10. Develop new means of catching and holding rain water.
11. Develop and globally disseminate educational materials on water—supply, use, etc.
12. Develop monsoon control and irrigation in Ganges Basin.
13. Overhaul existing irrigation facilities that are operating at 50% or less efficiency; improve water availability and storage, and improve distribution methods.
14. Research methods of forecasting water requirements of given crops, and methods of forecasting water requirements for whole regions.

Fertilizers

A fertilizer is a substance added to soil or other culture medium to replace what is taken out by plant growth. Without the additions, the soil would soon be exhausted and crop output would drop drastically. The primary needs of the soil in modern agriculture are for nitrogen, phosphorus, and potassium. These elements are used in large quantities by plants and are the elements most likely to be lacking in the soil. Secondary needs in some cases are for calcium and sulfur, with manganese, iron, copper, magnesium, zinc, boron, and molybdenum also utilized by plants in trace amounts.[1] Without fertilizer, the world agricultural system would not be able to produce enough food to feed the people now alive. It has been estimated that fertilizer, through the increased yields it makes possible, is now responsible for feeding one billion people. With more fertilizer, especially in the developing countries that are plagued by chronic food shortage, the world agricultural system could easily produce enough food to vanquish hunger. If cereal crops grown around the world all produced the same yields as those grown in the highest yielding developed countries, the world cereal crop would be more than double (3286×10^6 mt vs. 1359×10^6 mt, or 859 kg per person vs. 340 kg per person).[2] It has been estimated that fertilizer can increase agricultural output by 50% in many developing countries.[3]

In 1974, there was a drastic shortage of fertilizers in the world. Driven by strong demand and limited production capacity, prices soared (see Chart 1). World trade prices for some fertilizers, such as urea, increased 700–800%

in the space of four or five years.[4] Hardest hit by these huge price increases were the developing countries who needed the fertilizer to alleviate or eliminate their food shortages, who could increase their crop yields the most from any increase in fertilizer use, and who could least afford any increase in price (see Chart 2). Grain production in these regions was reduced by an estimated 12 million metric tons due to this fertilizer shortage.[6] Fortunately, these shortages disappeared in 1975 and prices fell substantially, due primarily to weak demand (Charts 1 and 2).

The raw materials used to manufacture fertilizer by the fertilizer industry can be found in natural deposits, salvaged from sewage and industrial wastes, or manufactured synthetically. The primary nutrients (nitrogen, phosphorus, potassium) are obtained from various sources and the methods used to obtain them are unique to each. The raw materials are processed into acceptable fertilizer by chemical and mechanical means.

About 100 million metric tons of fertilizer was consumed in the world in 1976–77 (see Chart 3). Four-fifths of this was used by the developed countries (Chart 4). Because of the "law of diminishing returns" according to which improved crop yields resulting from fertilizer application reaches a plateau no matter how much more fertilizer is added to the soil, crop yields in the developing countries which use little or no fertilizer could greatly increase if their fertilizer use were to increase (see Charts 4, 5, and 6). Doubling fertilizer use in the United States would not greatly increase crop yields, but doubling fertilizer use in Bangladesh or other fertilizer-poor countries would almost double their outputs. (Rice yields in Bangladesh

are only 53% as great as the world average, 24% of those in America, and only 15% as good as can be obtained on experimental farms in Bangladesh. If Bangladesh were to raise its rice yields to the world average, its per capita production would be higher than Japan's at the beginning of the 1960's.[7]) It would take approximately 24 million metric tons more of fertilizer than is currently being used in a developed country to produce an increase in grain yields of 100 million metric tons. This same 100 million metric tons could be produced with only a 10 million metric ton increase in fertilizer use in the developing countries.[8] A positive development in the world fertilizer situation can be seen to be coming about through the fact that the developing countries are steadily increasing their share of world fertilizer consumption and production while the developed countries' share is dropping. The three largest fertilizer importers—China, Brazil, and India—should approach or achieve self-sufficiency in nitrogen and phosphates between 1976 and 1980–81 based on present commitments.[4] Several other developing countries will become significant exporters.

Nitrogen, as an essential element for life, is, along with water, the most frequently

encountered limiting factor in crop production. This is because most plants do not have the ability to use the nitrogen that is in the air, but instead require a form which is generally referred to as "fixed" nitrogen. The two major sources of nitrogen for food synthesis are biological nitrogen fixation and industrial chemical fixation (see Chart 5). About 175 million tons of nitrogen (about $35 billion worth) are extracted from the air each year by nitrogen-fixing bacteria and are converted into readily useable ammonia. In addition, about 10 million tons of useable nitrogen are annually washed into the Earth's soils in rainfall. These useable nitrogen compounds are made by lightning and ultraviolet light from atmospheric nitrogen. By comparison, the world agricultural system applies about 40 million tons of nitrogen in the form of inorganic chemical fertilizers, and fossil fuel combustion produces another 20 million tons.

The most common form of nitrogen used today is in the form of ammonia (NH_3). Nitrogen and hydrogen are plentiful; the atmosphere contains 75.5% nitrogen and the hydrosphere contains 62% hydrogen. With these ubiquitous sources, it seems strange to talk of nitrogen fertilizer shortages. One of the main reasons for shortages is that the source for the vast amounts of hydrogen used in the manufacture of ammonia is methane, derived from natural gas, oil, naphtha, or coal, and these items are in short supply (see Charts 9 and 10). There is also additional energy expenditure needed to maintain the temperature and pressure necessary for fertilizer synthesis, to transport the products to their destination, and to apply the fertilizer to the soil. Because these fossil fuels are finite in supply and are being depleted

Fertilizer Consumption

Source:
1975 FAO Fertilizer Yearbook,
Vol. 29 (United Nations, 1976)

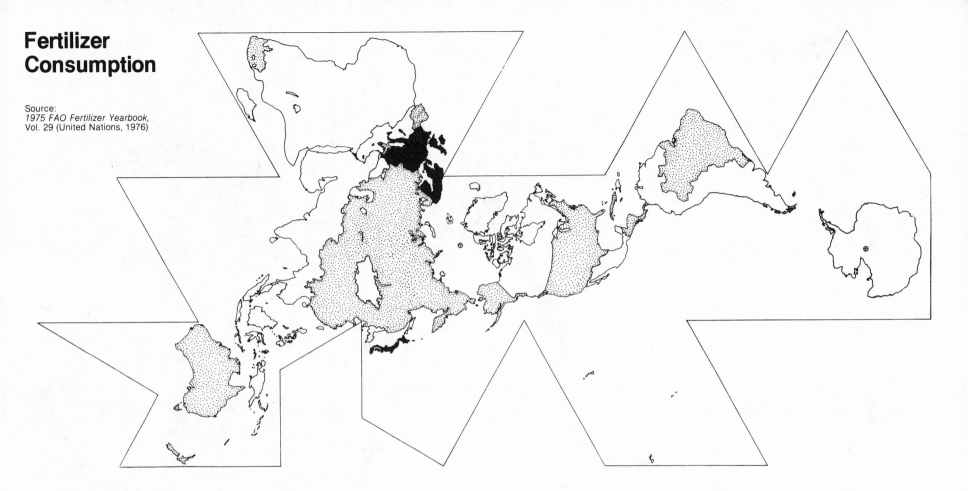

 ■ 150 kilograms per hectare and above

▨ 35–149 kilograms per hectare

□ 34 kilograms per hectare and below

Fertilizer Consumption

	1961–65	1974
N	14.9	38.8
P	12.7	22.7
K	10	19.9

All units in million metric tons

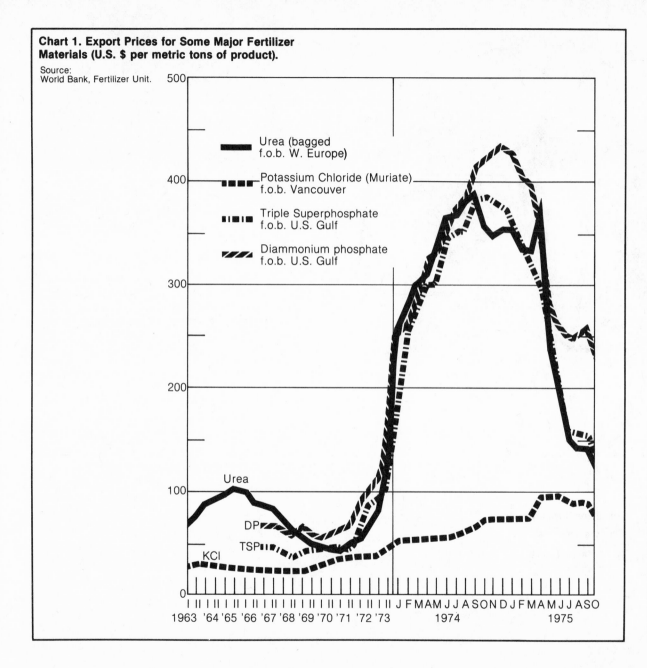

Chart 1. Export Prices for Some Major Fertilizer Materials (U.S. $ per metric tons of product).

Source:
World Bank, Fertilizer Unit.

Urea (bagged f.o.b. W. Europe)

Potassium Chloride (Muriate) f.o.b. Vancouver

Triple Superphosphate f.o.b. U.S. Gulf

Diammonium phosphate f.o.b. U.S. Gulf

Urea

DP

TSP

KCl

1963 '64 '65 '66 '67 '68 '69 '70 '71 '72 '73   J F M A M J J A S O N D J F M A M J J A S O
                                                        1974   1975

Chart 2. The Cost of Scarcity. Import of manufactured fertilizers by developing countries.

	1971	1972	1973	1974
NITROGEN				
million U.S. $	311	341	462	900
million tons	2.3	2.5	2.6	2.0
PHOSPHATE				
million U.S. $	126	183	275	380
million tons	1.0	1.2	1.4	1.1
POTASH				
million U.S. $	96	101	138	170
million tons	1.3	1.5	1.8	1.8

1450

875

625

533

TOTAL
million U.S. $

million tons

4.6   5.2   5.8   4.9

1971   1972   1973   1974

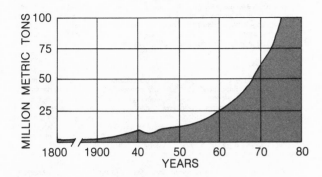

Chart 4. Fertilizer Consumption per Acre of Arable Land, Fifteen Most Populous Countries, 1972.

Country	Pounds/Acre
West Germany	363
Japan	347
United Kingdom	239
France	231
Italy	104
United States	72
U.S.S.R.	40
China	35
Brazil	32
Mexico	26
India	14
Pakistan	12
Indonesia	11
Bangladesh	7
Nigeria	1

Source: FAO, *Annual Fertilizer Review, 1972.*

Chart 5. Crop Yields with Fertilizer.

Country	Crop	Dosage kg./hectare (N-P-K)	Per Cent Increase in Crop Yield	Value/ Cost Ratio[a]
Turkey	Wheat	40—60—0	73%	2.5
	Corn	40—40—40	85	2.8
Morocco	Wheat	30—60—40	75	3.0
	Barley	30—60—40	91	2.5
	Beans	20—60—40	78	2.3
Lebanon	Wheat	20—25—7.5	101	7.0
Nigeria	Rice	22.4—22.4—0	30	4.0
Senegal	Rice	45—0—0	73	3.3
Ghana	Corn	44.8—0—0	120	3.3
	Rice	22.4—22.4—0	52	3.3
Ecuador	Corn	0—45—45	94	6.3
	Beans	0—45—0	93	2.2
Honduras	Corn	45—45—45	120	4.8
Costa Rica	Rice	45—45—45	80	4.5
	Corn	45—45—45	70	4.0
El Salvador	Beans	45—0—0	50	4.0

[a] Value of additional crop obtained/cost of fertilizer

Source: Review of Trial and Demonstration Results, 1961/62, FFHC Fertilizer Program, FAO, United Nations, January 1964

Chart 6. Corn-Yield Gains from Successive Fertilizer Applications.

Nitrogen Applied	Average Gain in Corn Yield per Pound of Nitrogen Applied
First 40 pounds	27 pounds
Second 40 pounds	14 pounds
Third 40 pounds	9 pounds
Fourth 40 pounds	4 pounds
Fifth 40 pounds	1 pound

Source: U.S. Department of Agriculture. Data from Iowa, 1964.

quickly, the fertilizer industry will have to obtain hydrogen from other, more direct methods such as the electrolysis of water into hydrogen and oxygen (as is currently done in Egypt[11] and in India at the Bhakra hydroelectric plant on the Sutlej River[12]), or photolysis, algae photosynthesis, or thermochemical cracking.[13]

In addition to these synthetic ways of obtaining nitrogen, there are natural sources such as organic fertilizers derived from plant and animal sources. Increasing the supply of biologically fixed nitrogen could be accomplished without the excessive energy expenditures needed by industrial nitrogen fixation. The biological fixation process is indirectly dependent on solar energy that is stored by plants, not upon fossil fuels. Also, biological nitrogen fixation takes place in the fields, forests, and oceans where the nitrogen is utilized. Large amounts of energy are not needed to transport the nitrogen, fossil fuels are not used in production, and capital investment required for chemical factories is not necessary.[11] The most prevalent method currently used for this type of fertilizer application is crop rotation. Before the advent of the synthetic nitrogen fertilizers, waste materials such as dried blood, oilseed meals, fish products, and slaughterhouse tankage were the main sources of nitrogen fertilizers.

Synthetic nitrogen fertilizer did not forge ahead of the organic fertilizers until the 1920's. In 1900, over 90% of the nitrogen in commercial mixed fertilizers was derived from organic sources.[1] Small quantities of nitrogen were derived as a by-product form coke oven gas in the form of ammonia. Production and utilization of this chemical was the crude beginning of today's synthetic fertilizer industry.

The Nitrogen Biogeochemical Cycle

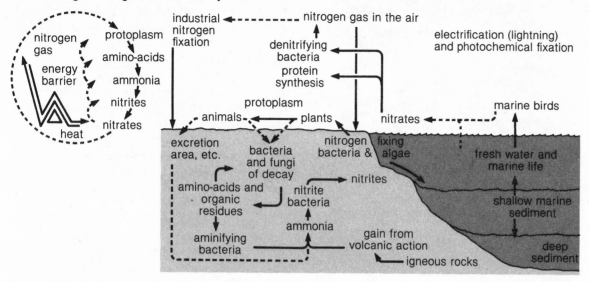

The Nitrogen Biogeochemical Cycle diagram: nitrogen gas, protoplasm, amino-acids, ammonia, nitrites, nitrates, energy barrier, heat. industrial nitrogen fixation, nitrogen gas in the air, denitrifying bacteria, protein synthesis, electrification (lightning) and photochemical fixation, protoplasm, animals, plants, nitrates, marine birds, excretion area, etc., bacteria and fungi of decay, nitrogen fixing bacteria & algae, fresh water and marine life, amino-acids and organic residues, nitrite bacteria, nitrites, aminifying bacteria, ammonia, gain from volcanic action, igneous rocks, shallow marine sediment, deep sediment.

The Phosphorus Biogeochemical Cycle

Phosphorus makes up about 0.1% of the earth's crust.

ocean water contains $6 \times 10^5\%$ phosphorus

The Phosphorus Biogeochemical Cycle diagram: agricultural fertilizers, protoplasm synthesis, animals, plants, excretion, soil, phosphating bacteria, fossil bone deposits, metamorphic rocks, igneous rocks, weathering and erosion, leaching, phosphate rock, exposed through geologic activity, guano deposits, streams, dissolved phosphates, marine birds, sedimentary rocks, fresh water and marine life, shallow marine sediment, deep sediment.

"The self-regulating, feedback mechanisms, shown in a very simplified way by the arrows, make the nitrogen cycle a relatively perfect one, when large areas or the biosphere as a whole is considered. Thus, increased movement of materials along one path is quickly compensated for by adjustments along other paths. Some nitrogen from heavily populated regions of land, fresh water, and shallow seas is lost to the deep ocean sediments and thus gets out of circulation, at least for a while.... This loss is compensated for by nitrogen entering the air from volcanic gases...."

"A portion of the earth's phosphorus is continually passing out of the mineral reserve into living substance, and similarly, phosphorus is continually passing out of living matter to re-enter the mineral reserve. This movement of the element has been pictured as taking place within two cycles, a land cycle and a marine cycle, or one general cycle with its complicated circulations of the element since the two cycles are definitely interrelated. Actually, the losses of the one cycle become the gains of the other. The cycle of matter is not completely reversible, that is to say, all matter is not restored completely to its original state, but it has a large measure of forward movement which permits a redistribution of chemical elements and states of matter.

"The cyclic phenomena of the life processes and the transport of phosphatic material by streams to the ocean waters give a broad picture of how biologically available phosphorus has been distributed over the face of the earth. The phosphorus content of sea water has been derived chiefly from soil erosion and the processes which dissolve fish bones, shells, and the vast amount of debris from dead tissues."

Chart 7. Typical Fertilizer Response Curve (Corn Yield in Iowa, 1964).

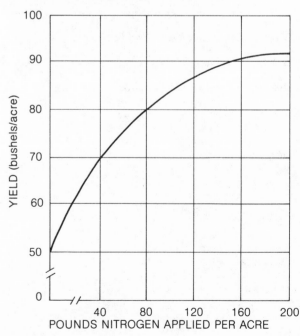

Graph: YIELD (bushels/acre) on vertical axis from 0 to 100; POUNDS NITROGEN APPLIED PER ACRE on horizontal axis from 40 to 200.

Source: U.S. Department of Agriculture

Sources:

(1) *Minerals in Industry*, W. R. Jones, (New York: Penguin Books), 1963.

(2) *Phosphate in Agriculture*, Vincent Sanchelli, (New York: Reinhold Publications Cor.), 1965.

(3) *Fundamentals of Ecology*, E. P. Odum, (New York: Holt, Reinhart, Winston, Inc.), 1959.

Over 90% of the nitrogen in commercial mixed fertilizers today comes from this source.

The oldest and principal source of phosphate is phosphate rock which is processed into phosphorus. Other sources are basic slag, bones, and guano. Phosphate rock after being dried and finely ground can be applied directly to the soil, but most is converted to more suitable forms by treating it with various kinds of acids. The product is then utilized in the production of mixed fertilizers.[1] Phosphate reserves which are, in current accounting standards, "economically" accessible (at 1974 prices) stand at over 16 billion metric tons,[14] an 800-year supply at 1971 use rates. Because of the finite supply of phosphate in concentrated sources (similar to fossil fuels), methods for recovering and recycling it need to be more thoroughly developed. So far, only tertiary sewage treatment recovers phosphate directly from our technological system.

Potassium is found in potassium chloride (a highly soluble salt), potassium-bearing silicates, and in marine and land plants. Potash originally referred to potassium carbonate recovered from wood ashes but today it has a more general meaning, referring to any material containing the element potassium. There is at least a twenty-three-hundred-year supply of potash based on present use rates.[14]

Other alternatives to the synthetic fertilizers currently in use include sewer sludge from cities, industrial waste, and the leguminous plants such as ground nuts, cowpeas, mung beans, alfalfa, and other grasses. A pharmaceutical factory in Connecticut is currently using its 1000 tons per week output of waste to fertilize soil used for growing corn

The average yearly manure production of one cow is 10 tons.[16] There are over 1.2 billion cows in the world. The average yearly production of cow manure is over 12 billion tons.[16]

silage and flowers.[15] Sewage treatment plants could be looked upon as fertilizer factories. There are approximately 1.6 million tons of sewage sludge produced each year in the United States alone. Milwaukee, Wisconsin, produces 75,000 tons each year of "Milorganite," which is a granular activated sewer sludge. This profitable product is used extensively on golf courses, lawns, parks, gardens, and orchards. The one million residents of Milwaukee are thus "producing" 2.5% of all the fertilizer now used on lawns and golf courses.[17] If all the human wastes from everyone on Earth were similarly treated, about 417 million tons of fertilizer could be produced annually,[18] four times the amount used by the whole world! The equivalent amount of fertilizers added to U.S. corn (50 kg nitrogen, 14 kg phosphorus, 27 kg potassium per acre per year) in the form of chemical fertilizer is available from the manure produced during one year by either one dairy cow, two young beef cattle, nine hogs, or eighty-four chickens.[12] Over 34 billion metric tons of manure were produced in 1975 by the world's cattle, horses, mules, buffalo, pigs, sheep, goats, chickens, ducks, and turkeys. Green manures—the young green plants that are plowed back into the soil—have numerous advantages. They add organic matter and nitrogen to the soil, they conserve water-soluble elements needed for plant growth, and they concentrate plant nutrients as well as improve the sub-soil through the decay of their

deep, penetrating root structures, and protect the soil surface, especially in winter and on slopes.[19] The natural fertilizers available in the world's developing countries during 1970–71 not only contained 7–8 times the nutritive elements of all the synthetic fertilizers used by these countries during the same year but their value, based on 1970's prices, exceeded $16 billion.[20] The great advantages of these types of fertilizer are the low amounts of energy which are needed for their production. The biological growth of the legumes, for instance, utilizes neither natural gas nor petroleum as its major source of energy, but is primarily dependent upon the sunlight captured through photosynthesis. About 68 kg of nitrogen per acre can be added to the soil by planting clover in the fall and plowing it under one year later; this results in an energy saving of 1.5 million kcal per acre. The substitution of cow manure for chemical fertilizer could save 1.1 million kcal per acre per year.[21] One other alternative to chemical fertilizer is the addition of nitrogen fixing bacteria to crops that do not normally have this ability—such as corn or wheat. Recent work in Brazil and Wisconsin has shown that it is possible to do just this, but further work

Alternatives to Chemical Fertilizers:
—*Legumes—green manure*
—*Animal wastes*
—*Sewer sludge*
—*Industrial waste*
—*Nitrogen fixation*
—*Inter-cropping and Companion planting*
—*Compost*
—*Seaweed*
—*Grass*
—*Silt*

Chart 8. Nitrogen Fixing on Earth.[9]

Nitrogen Fixing Process	10^6 tons	Dollar Value in Billions
Nitrogen Fixing Bacteria in Nature	175	35
Lightning & Ultra-Violet Light	10	2
Combustion	20	4
Inorganic chemical Fertilizers	40	8

Chart 9. Feedstocks used in world ammonia production, 1971.

	Natural gas	Naphtha	Fuel oil	Refinery oil	Coal	Electrolysis and other[a]
Ammonia, million tons	26.4	8.7	2.0	2.0	4.0	0.9
Percent of total	60%	20%	4.5%	4.5%	9%	2%

[a] Includes coke oven gas and byproduct hydrogen.

Source: R. P. Cook, "Fertilizer Production in the World from 1971 to 1980" UNIDO/ITD, October 3, 1973, p. 5.

World potash resources (million tons of K_2)[14]

Region	Known reserves	% of total	Other resources[a]	Total resources[b]
Canada	4,300	43	62,600	67,100
East Germany	2,400	25	2,400	4,900
West Germany	1,600	15	1,600	3,300
U.S.S.R.	700	7	900	1,600
Israel & Jordan	200	2	900	1,100
U.S.	200	2	200	400
Other	200	2	400	600
World	10,000	—	69,100	79,000

Source: Richard Reidinger, *World Fertilizer Review and Prospects to 1980/81.*

[a] Recoverable at higher prices or with improved technology.

[b] World potash production capacity was estimated at 29.8 million tons (K_2O basis) in 1975/76.

Chart 10. Percentage of production of primary synthetic ammonia obtained from various sources, 1971.

Country	Coal	Petroleum products	Gas	Electrolysis
Austria	35%	35%	30%	—
Spain	22	77	—	1
Finland	—	100	—	—
France	12	47	40	1
Norway[1]	8	65	—	27
Netherlands	—	—	100	—
Portugal	—	99	—	1
Sweden	—	80	—	20
United States	1	5	92	2
Canada	—	—	100	—
Japan	—	88	11	1

[1] 1969–70 and 1970–71 fertilizer years.

Note: The United Kingdom, not shown in the above table, now obtains 90 percent of its nitrogenous fertilizer from natural gas.

Source: OECD, the *Chemistry Industry 1971/72,* Table 24, except Canada which is from the 1970/71 issue.

World phosphate rock resources (million tons)[14]

Region	Known reserves[a]	% of total	Other resources[b]	Total resources	% of total
U.S.	2,300	14	4,100	6,400	8
U.S.S.R.	700	4	2,900	3,600	5
Africa	11,600	72	49,000	60,600	80
Morocco	9,100[c]	57	45,400	54,400	71
Spanish Sahara	1,500[d]	9	1,800	3,400	4
Tunisia	500	3	1,400	1,800	2
Other	600	4	400	1,000	1
Asia	300	2	1,800	2,100	3
Australia	900	6	1,800	2,700	4
Other	200	1	500	700	1
World	16,100	—	60,000	76,100	—

Source: Richard Reidinger, *World Fertilizer Review and Prospects to 1980/81.*

[a] Estimated recoverable reserves at 1974 price levels.

[b] Includes reserves recoverable at higher prices, with improved technology, etc.

[c] Reserves may be as high as 36,000 million tons.

[d] Reserves may be as high as 9,000 million tons.

is needed to make this technique widely available.[22]

China's agricultural policy seems aimed at preventing waste in any form; she probably has the world's most efficient system for utilizing human and animal wastes and crop residues. An estimated two-thirds of all crop nutriments in China are obtained from organic sources. About 1.7 billion tons, or 13 tons per hectare of cropped land, is produced each year from these sources.[23] Even though each county in China has had its own small to medium size fertilizer production plant operating since 1970 (with a total output of about 4 million tons[23]), pig, sheep, and human waste is in widespread use as fertilizer. Pigs are valued almost as much for their manure (they currently produce one-third of China's total organic fertilizer[23]) as they are for meat.[22,23] In Peking, night soil (human waste) is collected from underground storage by trucks with pumps, horse-drawn carts with tanks on the back, and even three-wheel bicycle carts with large drums, and then brought to rural communes where the sewage is mixed with straw and animal manure in compost pits for about two weeks, until the heat from the composting waste has killed all the bacteria and the compost is ready to be applied to the soil. Other sources of fertilizer in China include green manure, duckweed, river silt, grass, and even, in at least two reported instances, papermill and fertilizer plant waste water which is used for simultaneous irrigation and fertilization.[22] In the counties of Hangchow, Chiahsing, Ningpt, and Shaohsing, nearly all water surfaces, except for a central clearway for boat traffic, are covered with green water plants raised for use as fertilizer. Another rich source of nitrogen is a floating fern which can

yield up to 160 tons of green matter per hectare over its 100-day growing period.[23]

This waste-prevention ethic (as well as the pragmatic policy of generating employment for surplus rural workers) has gone so far as to engender the building of many small chemical plants in rural areas to use the former waste materials such as corn cobs, chaff, sugarcane residue, and cottonseed hulls to produce such things as alcohol, acetic acid, acetone, glucose, and antibiotics.[22]

History

8000–4000 B.C.	Rotation of crops is employed
B.C.	Wood ashes, manures, guano, fish, chalk, marl, and bones used as soil additives to increase crop yields
200 B.C.–100 A.D.	Romans recommend crop rotation, lime for acid soils, and manure and legumes
1600's	Germany: Glauber discovers large crop response to saltpeter
1600's	Europe: Seaweeds burned as source of ash for fertilizer use
1600's	Von Liebig discovers importance of nitrogen, phosphorus, and potassium for plant growth
1665	First use of chemical fertilizers
1750	Edinburgh, Scotland: Farm fertilized with sewage sludge
1800's	England: Bone dust fertilizer
1823	England: Faraday discovers that ammonia gas could be changed to a liquid by applying pressure
1840's	England: Guano and nitrate fertilizers; super-phosphate manufacture—the modern fertilizer industry is born
1849	U.S.A.: Mixed chemical fertilizers commercially on the market
1870	France: Phosphates mined in the Somme and Ardennes for use as fertilizer
1886	Hellriegel and Wilfarth determine that certain microorganisms in combination with leguminous plants fix nitrogen from the air
1915	Germany: Haber-Bosch process for obtaining atmospheric nitrogen commercially
1920	Germany: Sewage sludge pumped to farms using pumps powered by methane produced by the anaerobic digestion of the sewage
1960's	Israel: Fruit and vegetable production on the Negev Desert fertilized with sewage sludge
1978	Florida, U.S.: Major new phosphate rock mine opens
1978	Soviet Union: Discovery of potentially major phosphate rock deposits along new railroad route in Siberia
1979	Mexico and Soviet Union use their abundant natural gas supplies to produce ammonia; Mexico, until now a net importer of ammonia begins exporting about 600,000 mt/yr. Soviet Union begins exporting even larger quantities—700,000 mt in 1978, as much as 3 million tons by 1980. Phosphates & potash also in large supply
1978	Israel announces plans to build new 600,000 ton/yr. potash facility on the Dead Sea
1981	Brazil: one million ton/yr. potash facility begins operation

Advantages:

1. Fertilizer use increases crop yields.
2. Chemical fertilizers are highly concentrated (up to 200 times more than organic fertilizers), and therefore are more efficiently applied. Plant nutriment content of fertilizers is twice as high as in the early 1930's. This results in savings since transportation and handling account for 30–40% of the final costs of fertilizers.

Disadvantages:

1. Chemical fertilizer production (current methods) uses a lot of fossil fuel energy. U.S. production alone used an estimated 500×10^{12} B.T.U. in 1972–73.
2. Fertilizer run-off causes eutrophication of water bodies. On the average, crops utilize only about 50% of the nitrogen fertilizer that is applied.
3. Fertilizer use speeds up decomposition of soil organic matter (humus) unless corrective measures are taken. Loss of humus increases soil erosion and nutriment leaching.
4. Phosphate is often strip mined, thereby scarring the terrain.
5. Nitrogen fertilizer, through the process of denitrification which reduces nitrogen to gases, may be a threat to the ozone layer of the Earth. A recent study has shown that the main gas released in this process, nitrous oxide, behaves similarly to the ozone-threatening spray-can aerosols, and that a 15% destruction of the ozone layer would result if the current exponential growth of fertilizer use continued for a century or more.
6. Chemical fertilizer plants are capital intensive; a typical Haber-Bosch 1000 tons/day nitrogen production plant costs about $100 million.
7. Heavy fertilizer use may produce crops which are more susceptible to insect attack because they increase production of aromatic compounds that attract pests and also produce more succulent growth due to increased water retention capabilities.

What Needs to be Done

1. Establish a Global Fertilizer Agency for fertilizer research and development and as an information clearinghouse to collect, correlate, and disseminate fertilizer-related information.
2. Develop inexpensive ways of obtaining hydrogen for fertilizer use from nondepletable sources.
3. Develop more concentrated organic fertilizers.
4. Inventory all aspects of the fertilizer system that use depletable resources, e.g., potassium and fossil fuels, and develop nondepletable substitutes.
5. Develop plants that have self-fertilizing ability, such as nitrogen fixation in maize.
6. Develop plants that need less fertilizer.
7. Develop and refine all alternatives to chemical fertilizers.
8. Levy a tax on fuel consumption as raw material for fertilizer production; make hydrogen competitive with fossil fuels.
9. Phase out use of fertilizer on lawns, golf courses, etc.
10. Develop new fertilizer and fertilizer systems based on sewer sludge and industrial waste. Build "sewer sludge into fertilizer" plants in all urban areas.
11. Phase in use of alternatives to chemical fertilizers, e.g., crop rotation, green and animal manures, companion planting.
12. Build local fertilizer production plants in developing countries to increase their supply.
13. Supply fertilizer to poor farmers in developing countries at reduced rates or as payment for work performed during the off-season.
14. Encourage widespread development of home and community compost piles.
15. Develop and disseminate educational materials on fertilizer.
16. Begin extensive research into the ozone-depletion-by-fertilizer-denitrification theory; slow-release fertilizer; catalysts that work at lower temperatures and pressures for producing chemical nitrogen fertilizer; optimal plant-microorganism combinations; increase transfer of photosynthetic energy from plant to nitrogen-fixing organism; and improving efficiency of fertilizer uptake by plants (temperate zone crops utilize 50% or less of applied nitrogen; tropic zone plants utilize less than 35%).
17. Build fertilizer manufacturing plants in oil producing countries where natural gas is being burned as waste (flared). In 1972, more than 62% of all gas produced by OPEC—over 130 billion cubic meters—was flared. This was enough gas to produce five times as much nitrogen fertilizer as the total projected consumption for developing countries in 1980–81, and about as much as was used in the entire world in 1975.
18. Establish a "fertilizer pool" from which developing regions can draw.
19. Organize a technical assistance program to help impove fertilizer plant operations in developing regions by eliminating equipment failures, power shortages, obsolescence, and poor management.

Pesticides

Insecticides, herbicides, rodenticides, and fungicides all come under the general heading of pesticides, and are all chemicals that are added to crops or their environment to control the organisms which compete with humanity for the products of agriculture. These competing organisms include higher plants (weeds and poisonous plants), fungi, bacteria and viruses, birds, mammals, insects, mites and other arachnids, ticks, nematodes, and parasitic worms. All are lumped together as "pests."

Pesticides help control the environment of crops by eliminating or curtailing natural parasites. Ten to twenty percent of the total food crop planted each year in the developed world, and twenty to forty percent in the undeveloped world, is lost due to pests.[1,2] In the Sahel region of Africa where drought caused such widespread loss of agricultural productivity there is now a proliferation of rodents that are causing damage. Early reports say that in Senegal, 1.37 billion rats share the country with 4.31 million humans. Rats have reportedly been seen climbing stalks of corn to devour the ripening ears. Production in the rice fields in the Senegal River delta is said to be down 60%.[5] Modern agriculture seeks to reduce these losses, thereby increasing output, primarily through the addition of certain chemicals which seek to eliminate or control the pests or disease that is the cause of the loss. It has been estimated that the total world production of crops, livestock, and forests would be reduced by at least 25% without the aid of pesticides.[1] This success of chemical pesticides in contributing to the enormous increase in food

There are more than 160 bacteria, 250 viruses, and 8,000 fungi known to cause plant diseases; about 10,000 species of insects in the U.S. are destructive enough to be called enemies, and some 2,000 species of weeds cause economic losses.[1]

production over the last twenty-five years has encouraged farmers to increasingly practice monoculture. Before effective control of pests, mixed agriculture—or polyculture—was more practical as a precaution against pest losses and is still the prevailing practice in many parts of the world. Mixed agriculture allows a better balance of the insect population between beneficial and pest species. The more complex the eco-system, the more checks and balances there are to prevent any one organism from reaching unusually high numbers. If a single organism begins to increase in numbers, it is easier for its predators to "tune in" to it because it is easier for a predator to capture a numerous prey than a scarce one.[6] Once a chemical pesticide is used, the farmer is committed to using more and more as the natural enemies of the pests are killed off along with the pests for which the farmer was originally applying the pesticides.

There are four general types of pests:
1. Pests that complete their whole life-cycle within the agricultural eco-system, such as

"In 1967, the total world loss of stored cereals and rice for which rats are responsible is 33 million tons a year."[3]

"In one day a single swarm of locusts can eat enough food to feed 400,000 people for a year."[4]

soil organisms and weeds;
2. Pests which enter the system periodically from outside, such as cereal rusts, birds, rabbits, and locusts;
3. Pests that attack stored or transported products such as rats, mice, insects, and fungi;
4. Pests which cover large areas and prevent humans and their animals from entering or remaining in areas of otherwise useful country, for example, the tsetse fly, which has already effectively expelled agriculture from one million square miles of tropical Africa.

There are basically six pest management systems or methods:
1. Preventive methods, which include the production of weed- and disease-free seeds, cleaning of pest-infested seeds, inspecting nurseries, and using quarantines and regulations to prevent pests from entering regions where they do not already exist;
2. Genetic methods, which refers to the development of disease-resistant plants through breeding programs;
3. Chemical control methods, which include all chemical pesticides;
4. Cultural and physical methods, which include site selection, previous cropping history, seed purity, amount and kind of fertilizer, time of planting, degree of cultivation, irrigation, method and time of harvest, storage and distribution, as well as heat treatment of seeds, pest-resistant packaging, and low oxygen grain storage;
5. Biological control methods, which include the use of parasites, predators, pathogens, insect attractants, and the release of large

quantities of sexually sterile insects;
6. Integrated control systems, which include the co-ordinated use of all or some of the above to control pests.

Chemical pesticides are the most widely used of all pest control methods. In the United States, close to 1.4 billion pounds (631,000 mt) of synthetic pesticides were used in 1976;[8] this was enough to treat 52% of all cropland in the U.S. Some crops have an even greater pesticide use percentage. Corn, for instance, is about 90% and soybean acreage is 80% pesticide treated in the United States.[9] In China, chemical pesticides are also used, but not as intensely as in the United States. Other control methods used in China include rapid turnover of crops, especially vegetables, seed treatment, crop rotation, removal and destruction of diseased plants, and restrictions on the movement of infected seed.[10]

Chemical pesticides are non-specific poisons; that is, they do not just kill the particular insect, rodent, or weed that they are originally applied for, but will kill any weed or animal that ingests the poison, including the beneficial predators and parasites. As such, they pose a danger to human health. DDT and other pesticides have been found in measureable quantities in 73% of all dairy products, 77% of all meat, fish, and poultry samples, and the fatty tissue of almost all persons sampled.[9] Another serious problem with pesticides is the length of time that they

---

Soil is a living organism; treating the soil through pesticides often reduces the number and variety of soil microorganisms, which then results in the reduction of the quality of humus and humus-making capabilities.

---

remain in the soil (see Chart 1). For these reasons, a number of chemicals have been banned by various environmental protection agencies around the world. China has restricted both DDT and organic mercury compounds used for seed treatment.[11] DDT, Aldrin, Dieldrin, heptachlor, and chlordane are among the pesticides banned in the United States. The pesticides have been banned because of their link with cancer and widespread environmental dangers. However, these represent only a small fraction of the new chemical products available. There are about 32,000 products with over 1,000 active ingredients that are registered and sold in the United States. Since 1973, there has even been an insect virus used as a pesticide.

Because of the dangers associated with widespread pesticide use, new methods (or a re-examination of old methods) for controlling pests are being developed. One old method is the control of weeds through crop rotation or cultivation. Weeds can be effectively controlled through mechanical cultivation, herbicides, or a combination of the two. On an energy use basis, mechanical cultivation uses less energy than herbicides. Rotating crops not only helps reduce weed problems, but enriches the soil as well. Another method is the use of "natural" pesticides (in distinction to synthetic chemicals) such as diatomaceous earth, garlic sprays, cayenne pepper, etc.

A new method is the breeding of plants that are resistant to plant diseases and and insects. This has limits, as breeding new plants is slow, there is no resistance to weeds, birds, and mammals, and genetic diversity is decreased during the process of selecting desirable germ plasm. Biological control of pests is usually most effective in stable or predictable eco-

systems. Instead of attempting to eliminate the pest—a nearly impossible task when you consider the fact that, despite enormous efforts, no insect has been deliberately eradicated from the Earth by humanity—what is needed is to encourage the natural enemies of pests—their predators, parasites, and diseases.[12] Instead of elimination, what is needed is temporary suppression.[13]

As pointed out above, several methods of biological control are in use and being tested. One method is the use of a pest's natural enemy to control it, such as the use of praying mantises to control small insects, or lady bugs to control aphids. Flower crops, repellent crops, trap crops, hedgerows, and shelter belts are other viable present-day alternatives that utilize the natural diversity of an eco-system to achieve pest control.

Chart 1. Persistence of Insecticides in Soils

Insecticide	Years since treatment	Percent remaining
Aldrin	14	40
Chlordane	14	40
Endrin	14	41
Heptachlor	14	16
Dilan	14	23
Isodrin	14	15
Benzene hexachloride	14	10
Toxaphene	14	45
Dieldrin	15	31
DDT	17	39

Source: Nash and Woolson, *Science*, vol. 157, pp. 924–927.

As the following chart shows, biological pest control is not science fiction, but an established, effective procedure.

Pest	Crop Attacked	Type of Natural Enemy	Degree of Control
Alfalfa weevil	Alfalfa in California	Parasite (*Bathyplectes*)	S
Alfalfa weevil	Alfalfa in Mid-Atlantic States	Parasites	C
Avocado mealybug	Guava, avocado, fig, mulberry in Hawaii	Parasite (*Pseudaphytis*)	S
Black scale	Citrus in California	Parasite (*Metaphycus*)	S
Brown-tail moth	Deciduous forest and shade trees in Northeastern United States	Parasites	C
California red scale	Citrus in California	Parasites (*Aphytis spp.*)	S
Cereal leaf beetle	Grain in Michigan	Parasites	S
Chinese grasshopper	Sugarcane in Hawaii	Parasite (*Scelio*)	S
Citrophilus mealybug	Citrus in California	Parasites (*Coccophagus*)	C
Clover leaf weevil	Eastern United States	Parasites	C
Coconut scale	Coconut and other palms in Hawaii	Predator (*Telsimia*)	S
Comstock mealybug	Apple in Eastern United States	Parasites (*Allotropa*)	C
Cottony cushion scale	Citrus in California	Predator (*Vedalia beetle*)	C
European larch sawfly	Northeastern United States	Parasites	S
European pine sawfly	Eastern United States	Parasites	C
European pineshoot moth	Northeastern United States	Parasites	S
European spruce sawfly	Northern United States	Parasites	S
European wheat stem sawfly	Eastern United States	Parasites	C
Florida red scale	Citrus in Florida	*Aphytis holoxanthus* from Israel	S
Greenhouse whitefly	Vegetables and ornamentals in New York	Parasite (*Encarsia*) from Israel	S
Japanese beetle	Turf in Eastern United States	Disease & parasites	S
Larch casebearer	Northeastern United States	Parasites (*Tiphia*)	S
Linden aphid	Linden trees in California	Parasites (*Trioxys*)	S
New Guinea sugarcane weevil	Sugarcane in Hawaii	Parasite (*Ceromasia*)	S
Nigra scale	Ornamentals in California	Parasite (*Metaphycus*)	S
Olive scale	Olive, deciduous fruit trees, ornamentals in California	Parasite (*Aphytis*)	S
Oriental beetle	Sugarcane in Hawaii	Parasites (*Campsomeris*)	S
Oriental moth	Shade trees in Massachusetts	Parasite (*Chaetexorista*)	S
Pea aphid	Alfalfa in North America	Parasite (*Aphidius*)	S
Pink sugarcane mealybug	Sugarcane in Hawaii	Parasite (*Anagyria*)	S
Purple scale	Citrus in Texas and Florida	Parasite (*Aphytis*)	C
Rhodes grass scale	Grass in Florida	Parasite	C
Rhodes grass scale	Grass in Texas	Parasite	S
Satin moth	New England, Pacific Northwest	Parasite (*Apanteles*)	S
Spotted alfalfa aphid	Alfalfa in Southwestern United States	Parasites & resistant varieties	S
Sugarcane aphid	Sugarcane in Hawaii	Parasite, various predators	S
Sugarcane leafhopper	Sugarcane in Hawaii	Predator (*Cyrtorhinus*)	C
Taro leafhopper	Taro in Hawaii	Predator (*Cyrtorhinus*)	S
Torpedo bug plant hopper	Coffee, mango, citrus, etc., in Hawaii	Parasite (*Aphanomerus*)	S
Walnut aphid	English walnut in California	Parasites (*Trioxys*)	C
Western grape leaf skeletonizer	Grapevine in United States	Parasites (*Apanteles*)	S
White peach scale	Mulberry, papaya, etc., in Puerto Rico	Predator (*Chilocorus*)	S
Yellow scale	Citrus in California	Parasite (*Comperiella*)	S
WEED			
Alligator weed	Southeastern United States	*Agasicles* beetles	S
Klamath weed	Pacific states	*Chrysolina* beetles	C
Lantata rangeweed	Hawaii	Several moths and beetles	S
Prickly pear	Santa Cruz Island, California	Cochineal scale and coreid bugs	S
Puncturevine	California and Hawaii	*Microlarinus* beetles	S
Tansy ragwort	Pacific states	Cinnabar moth	P-C

Sources: From Debach, *Biological Control of Insect Pests and Weeds*; and the Council on Environmental Quality, *Integrated Pest Management* (Washington, D.C., 1972).

Note: S = Substantial Control, C = Complete Control, P = Partial Control.

125

History

100 B.C.	China: Natural pyrethrin powders (pesticide derived from vegetation) used
1800's	Smoke of pitch, sulfur, or tobacco lime used as pesticide on board ships at sea against lice, fleas, and other parasites
Early 1800's	First highly effective fungicide accidently discovered
1868	U.S.A.: Copper acetoarsenate used against potato beetle and major apple insects in Illinois
1886	California, U.S.A.: Use of hydrocyanic acid to control insects on citrus trees
1878	France: Paris Green first used as a pesticide on grape vines
1888	California, U.S.A.: First major success in biological control of pests in orange orchards
1892	Lead arsenate first used, proves effective as a poison against many chewing insects
1896–1908	Metal salts and mineral acids used to control broadleaf weeds in cereal production
1920–45	U.S.A.: Calcium arsenate chief insecticide used on cotton
1933	Sodium dinitrocreosylate used as herbicide for cereal, flax and pea production
1939	Switzerland: Müller develops DDT as pesticide
1944	U.S.A.: Discovery of dichlorophenoxyacetic acid (2,4-D) as growth regulator herbicide
1947	U.S.A.: Rust disease resistant wheat introduced
1948	Discovery of Wayfarin, an anti-coagulant used to reduce rat population
1962	Rachel Carson's *Silent Spring* published, leads to banning of DDT
1962	Africa: Desert locust plague
1970's	DDT banned in many developed regions
1978	Kenya/Tanzania: 22,000 tons of natural pyrethrins produced for world pesticide market
1979	U.S.A.: Herbicides 2, 4, 5-T and silvex banned because they are linked to miscarriages
1979	Red Sea area of Africa: Desert locust plague

Advantages:

1. Pesticides curtail crop loss and thereby increase crop output.
2. Pesticides reduce the labor needed to control pests.

Disadvantages:

1. Most chemical pesticides kill indiscriminately; both pest and helpful insects are eliminated, thereby upsetting the natural eco-system balances. Soil micro-organisms are reduced in number and variety.
2. Many chemical pesticides pose a threat to human health in that they have been linked to cancer and they do not degrade, but are transmitted along the food chain.
3. Chemical pesticides are expensive in terms of energy and materials needed to make them. U.S. pesticide manufacture used 10 trillion BTUs in 1971.[11]
4. Chemical pesticides are dangerous to the farm worker who has to apply the pesticide.
5. Long-term use of pesticides can lead to pesticide resistance. About two-hundred insect species have developed resistance to insecticides.[2] Cotton production in parts of

Mexico has been halted because the major pest has developed a resistance to all available insecticides.[1] Pesticide use can even increase the number of pests by freeing innocuous pests from their natural controls.

6. Some chemical insecticides reduce plant growth and yield.
7. Some chemical herbicides increase plant susceptibility to insect and disease pests.
8. Biological pest control can take weeks, rather than minutes to control any given pest.
9. Biological pest control often can not deal with very large infestations of pests.

What Needs to be Done

1. Establish a Global Pest Control Information Clearinghouse to monitor and forecast pest problems, set up quarantine programs on a world basis, and to collect, correlate, and disseminate pest control-related information.
2. Develop more effective biological pest control methods.
3. Develop polyculture agricultural techniques that are pest-resistant.
4. Develop food storage and transport systems that are pest-proof.
5. Develop more specific chemical pesticides; effective, biodegradable pesticides.
6. Develop tropical pest controls, especially for the tsetse fly.
7. Establish local research stations around the globe to research and design locally appropriate pest controls.
8. Tax chemical pesticide consumption; use the funds to support research into biological control of pests.
9. Phase out fossil fuel consumption in pesticide production.
10. Phase in use of crop rotation and cultivation for weed control.
11. Establish an emergency global pest relief agency to deal with serious outbreaks of pests, and to monitor, via remote sensing, migratory pests.
12. Establish regional reserve stocks of pesticides, application equipment, spare parts, etc. for emergency use.
13. Establish regional and local intensive training centers for teaching the safe and efficient use of plant protection methods.
14. Investigate aboriginal subsistence farming pest control methods for their possible modern day use.
15. Develop pest-resistant crops.
16. Develop insect mass culture and release methods for pest control.
17. Develop methods for avoiding pest resistance to chemical pesticides.
18. Develop controlled-release pesticides.

"Countries will expend large sums on tanks and planes to defend their territorial sovereignty but nothing on soil conservation. As a result, the country's topsoil is washed away, ending up in the floodplains of another country downstream. The barren wasteland mocks the very concept of sovereignty itself."[5]

Land Use/Soil

There are 13.39 billion hectares of land in the world.[1] Of this, 1.5 billion (11%) is arable land or in permanent crops, 3 billion (22%) is permanent pasture, 4 billion (29%) is forest and woodland, and 4.78 billion (35.6%) contains everything else, i.e., deserts, cities, towns, roads, etc. These figures are not static. In the last 20 years, 135 million hectares—an area over nine times the size of all Bangladesh—has been added to the world's arable and permanently cropped land.[3] Seventy percent of this growth took place in developing regions while Western Europe had a net loss of arable land in excess of 5%. More than three-fourths of all the world's food comes either directly or indirectly from the soil. The proper care of this priceless resource is one of humanity's prime responsibilities on board Spaceship Earth.

The U.S. has lost at least a third of the topsoil on its croplands in the last two-hundred years; nearly 96 million hectares have been ruined or impoverished for soil cultivation by soil erosion; more than one million hectares of arable cropland are lost to highways, urbanization, and other uses each year.[4] (See map.) Since 1945, the loss has been about 18.2 million hectares—

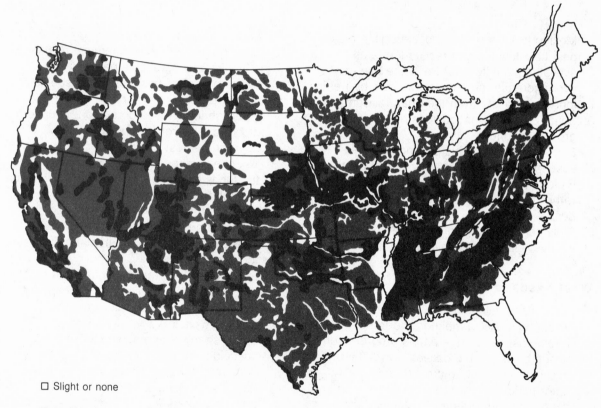

☐ Slight or none

■ Moderate

■ Severe
More than 75 percent of topsoil lost, may have numerous or deep gullies. Includes severe geological erosion in parts of low rainfall areas.

"Below that thin layer comprising the delicate organism known as the soil is a planet as lifeless as the moon."[2]

an area about the size of Nebraska. So far thirteen million hectares of the U.S. is covered with highways and roads, and sixteen million has been converted to urban use.[4] West Germany is estimated to be losing 1% of its agricultural land every four years.[6] Soil erosion loss in developing areas of the world is estimated to be even worse than in the U.S. Deserts are expanding in Africa, Asia, and South America (see map). In the past fifty years, 250,000 square miles (65 milion hectares) of arable land has been lost to the expanding southern edge of the Sahara Desert, with large losses also occurring in India, Argentina, and Chile.[7] This onslaught is caused by erosion that has been caused by over-cultivation, over-grazing, and the use of wood for fuel that in turn has been caused by the increase in population. This chain of events could continue but the point is that, whatever the cause, the deserts are growing, and that the approximately 630 million people who live off the arid and semi-arid lands immediately adjacent to these deserts are also endangered. More than 75 million people live on lands that have been rendered near useless by erosion, dune formation, changes in vegetation, and salt encrustation.[6] Over one billion tons of topsoil from the highlands of Ethiopia, nearly one half billion tons from fertile lands in Columbia, and an as yet unknown large quantity of soil in the monsoon areas of the world are lost to severe erosion each year. An estimated 6–12 million hectares of cropland are being lost annually, more, in effect, than are being added through increased cultivation, irrigation, etc.[3]

Land vs. Soil

Cities often grow in the exact spot where prime farmland occurs. Urban expansion is conservatively estimated to require 25 million additional hectares of cropland in the next twenty years.[6] In addition to expanding cities, other demands are being placed upon agricultural lands by our energy and transportation systems. Stripmines, oil refineries, hydroelectric dams and reservoirs, highways, gas stations and parking lots all need land. Given these competing demands, and given that the marketplace and other mechanisms of allocating resources do not seem able to deal adequately with the actual long term value of cropland, there needs to be *global* land-use regulations that will protect the world's prime farmlands and delicate ecosystems from destruction.

Because land is soil and soil is part of an ecological system, the use of land needs to be approached ecologically not economically. Often land use is mistakenly equated with space use. Land is more than just "space"; it is part of a complex web of interrelationships. Our awareness of our use of land should be expanded to include meteorology; seismology; bedrock and superficial geology; ground and surface water hydrology; physiography; limnology; agronomy; soil, plant, and animal

---

Soil is alive; one gram of fertile soil may contain tens of thousands of protozoan and algae cells, a million fungal cells, and more than 10 million bacteria.[8]

"We abuse land because we regard it as a commodity belonging to us. When we see land as a community to which we belong we may begin to use it with love and respect."[10]

ecology; and, where appropriate, oceanography and marine biology.[9] Nature and her needs should dictate where we do what and how, not how much money we will make how soon.

Because soil is being "used up" at alarming rates—the average annual loss of topsoil from agricultural land is estimated at 4.8 tons per hectare and the annual formation of soil under normal agricultural conditions is 0.6 tons per hectare[4]—soil conservation, rebuilding, and enriching practices need to be globally implemented. Besides the loss of soil and productive arable land, soil loss has detrimental effects on rivers, lakes, and reservoirs in the form of sediments that can silt up these bodies of water. Each year the U.S. spends about $300 million dredging up about 344 million cubic meters of sediment from its rivers, harbors, and reservoirs.[4] Eroded soils result in lower yields because of low nitrogen content, poor soil structure, low organic matter, and reduced availability of moisture. Soil productivity can be improved as well as destroyed. Examples of the former include the original croplands of Western Europe and Japan that were vastly inferior to what they are today.[11]

Soil conserving and enriching methods include contour plowing and planting, terracing, crop rotation, applying livestock and green manure, minimizing or eliminating tillage, planting cover crops during the 8–9 months when a crop is normally not on the field, intercropping or companion planting, mulching,

129

World Arable Land 1976

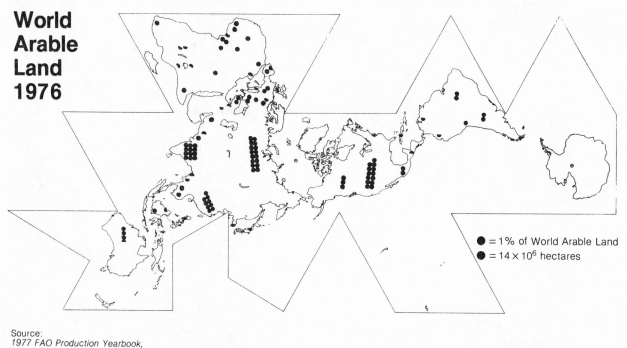

● = 1% of World Arable Land
● = 14 × 10⁶ hectares

Source:
1977 FAO Production Yearbook,
Vol. 31 (United Nations, 1978)

letting the land lie fallow every other year, and any combination of the above. To insure that future generations have soil to grow their food, all these practices need to be implemented as soon as possible and as extensively as possible. Most of these regenerative soil management techniques have the added benefit of reducing the fertilizer, pesticide, and energy needs of agriculture as well as maintaining or even increasing crop yields.

Many of the marginal and desert lands of the world could be reclaimed through a variety of techniques. One method is to stop and even reverse the onslaught of a desert by planting a "green wall" of trees. The trees would stop sandstorms and cool the upward atmosphere to seven times their own height, thereby increasing surface humidity enough to make the land productive again. In one such green wall experiment in Morocco, wheat and barley were grown in the shelter provided by twelve foot tall, four-year-old trees planted in the desert.[12] Using this method, the desert can be stopped from growing and then shrunk by planting inward. Even the Sahara desert could be planted almost all the way across. There is enough water beneath the surface and in the form of rain to keep an established tree alive.[12] In China, more than 870 miles of desert-containing green belts have been planted in the Gobi Desert. Reclaimed areas are presently being used as vineyards in Turfan country and as grasslands for livestock pasture in Inner Mongolia.[13]

Another method of stopping erosion in marginal lands is the use of shrubs. Many shrubs have the ability—similar to legumes—to fix their own nitrogen. They are thus able to grow in very marginal lands where most everything else would find it impossible. These

Cultivated Cropland

Source:
National Geographic, July 1975

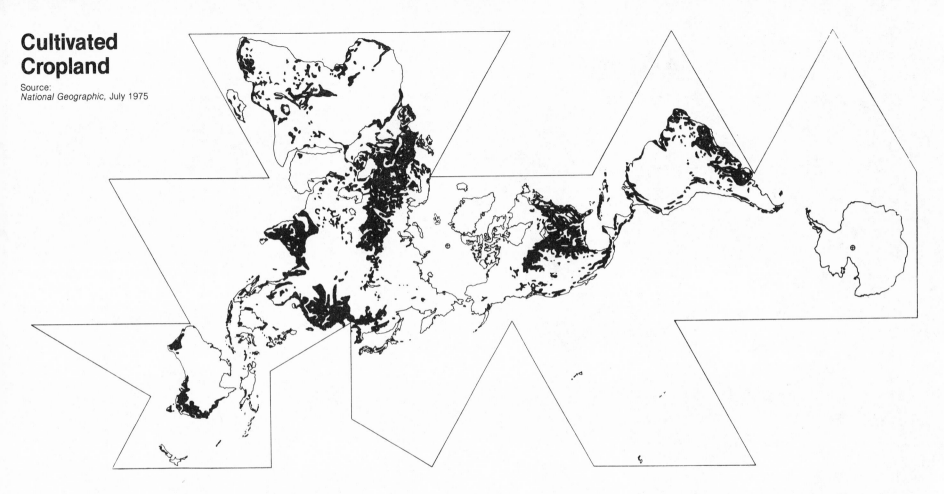

	Africa	North America	Central America	South America	Asia	Europe	USSR	Oceania
Arable and Permanent Cropland	209	272	481	104	476	142	232	47
Permanent Pasture Land	800	347	538	442	549	88	373	470
Forest and Woodland	640	714	604	924	596	153	920	186

All units in million hectares

Only about one fifth of the world's soils have actually been surveyed.[16]

1976

Total Arable and Permanent Crop Land in World:	1488
Total Permanent Pasture Land in World:	3058
Total Forest and Woodland in World:	4145

All units in million hectares

Potentially Arable

(25% or more potentially arable,
does not include cultivated cropland)
Source: *National Geographic,*
July 1975

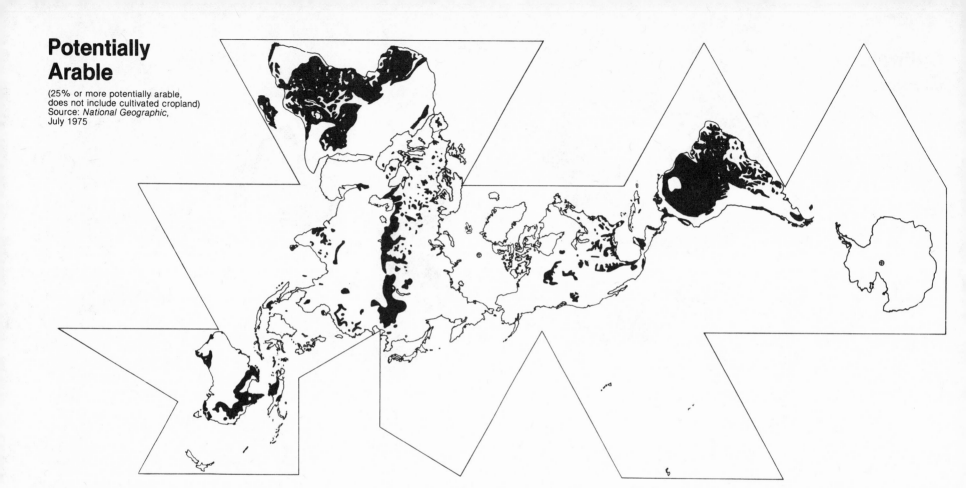

Forests

Source:
Goode's World Atlas, 1975

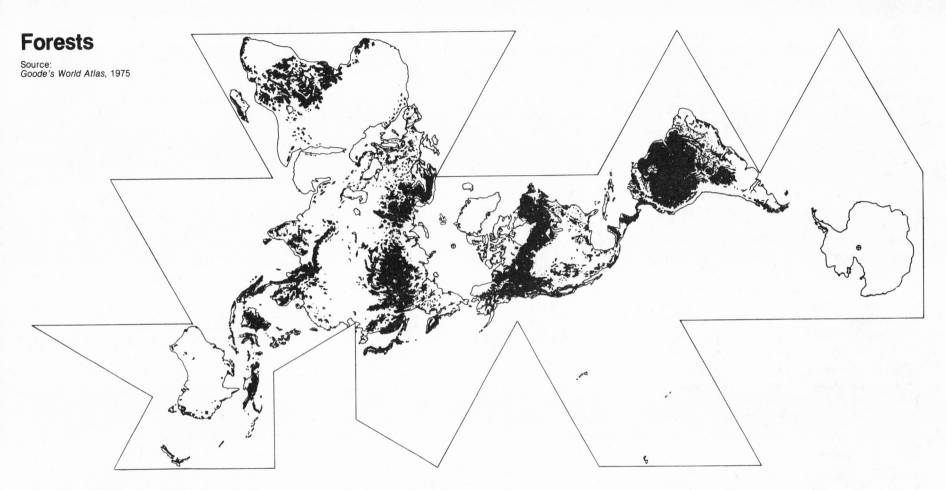

Lands having vegetation dominated by trees cover approximately 30% of the world's land area today; of this amount, 77% is in public ownership. The main types of forest are: tropical rainforests characterized by hardwoods, luxuriant undergrowth, and poor soil; mid-latitute hardwood (deciduous) forests quickly being depleted by exploitation and urbanization; arid Mediterranean or scrub forests with small trees and grassy areas; and coniferous (soft-wood) boreal forests of the northern latitudes with long, cold winters and sparse population. The ecosystem of the forests operates as an influence on the climate and water regime, providing shelter for wildlife, and potential utilization and/or exploitation for recreation, hunting and fishing, and the lumber industry.

shrubs could not only stop water and soil erosion, but aid in flood control, help rebuild the soil, and serve as a source of firewood. The areas of the world most in need of soil conservation, lumber, and firewood are those with a plentiful supply of manpower. Planting shrubs and/or trees could provide constructive employment for hundreds of thousands of people.

According to one estimate, the world has enough soil resources that are well or moderately well watered to more than double the present area of cultivation.[14] As the following chart and preceding maps indicate, there are large tracts of potentially productive cropland in many parts of the world, but especially in Africa and South America. (Africa alone has five times the area now farmed by the United States.[15]) The world's largest block of potentially arable soils are the vast tropical jungles and savannas that also abound in sunlight and offer a year-round growing season.[14] Because ". . . soils in the tropics are similar or equivalent to soils in temperate regions," they can, where appropriately farmed,

Cultivatable Land[14]

	Land now cultivated*	Land potentially cultivatable*	Difference
Africa	125	732	607
South America	77	647	570
North & Central America	289	556	267
Asia	476	560	84
U.S.S.R.	232	341	109
Europe	143	163	20

* In 10^6 hectares

"make a major and sustained contribution toward world food production. . . ."[16] Tropical deserts and semi-arid areas with fertile soils whose only need is for irrigation systems to bring in water exist. One of the major reasons that these lands are not now cultivated is that the necessary infrastructure needed for their development is missing. It would take enormous amounts of energy to prepare these new lands for cultivation. Most of the readily accessible prime farm land in the world is already in use.

One other aspect of land use is ownership. In many parts of the developing world—South and Central America, India, Africa—most of the land is owned by relatively few people. In some places, less than 10% of the people own more than 90% of the land. This arrangement is detrimental to those who are landless because they suffer the most when times are hard, and it is harmful to everyone because it effectively stops progress. One proposed solution to this inequality is land redistribution. In this scheme, large land holdings would be broken up by the government, either by direct seizure (as when China expropriated virtually all landlords' and rich peasants' lands in 1949–52) or through the purchase of the lands from the large land holder, and then redistributed to the landless farmer. "Land for the person who works it" is a rallying cry heard throughout the world. To achieve this, many other reforms are needed to help insure that small-scale farming is more economically viable. These reforms would include eliminating federal tax laws that encourage large or corporate farming, a minimum wage for farm workers that is equal to that of other workers, low interest farm loans, new small scale farming implements, and funds

When large corporations receive public assistance in the form of subsidies, "make-work" orders, or research expenditures, it is viewed as an investment; when the small farmers receive assistance, it is viewed as welfare.[17]

which are made available for extension programs for the small farmer and co-ops.[18]

What Needs to be Done

1. Establish World Land/Soil Institute to research and solve land use, soil abuse problems around the planet. Within the framework of a World Land/Soil Institute: a) establish a Global Soil Conservation Agency to monitor world cropland—soil lost due to erosion, land taken out of production, etc.—and to mount defensive and offensive campaigns to preserve, maintain, and reclaim the world's soil, marginal lands, and deserts; b) establish a Global Land Acquisition Agency that would assist in cooperative land reform around the world by securing land for landless or tenant peasants; c) map the geology, hydrology, soil, etc. conditions of the world for ecological land use planning and formulate global land use guidelines and regulations; d) develop more effective soil conservation techniques, especially for cultivated marginal lands; and e) transfer available erosion control technologies to soil-erosion regions.
2. Develop the arable lands of the Southern Sudan, and the Amazon and Mekong basins.
3. Adapt soil management practices to subsistence cultivation in developing regions.
4. Develop appropriate technology for crop production on problem soils.

Organic Agriculture

Organic agriculture, or what is called "biological agriculture" in Europe, refers to the growing of crops and animals without the assistance of synthetic chemical fertilizers or pesticides through the use of animal manure or green manure and the biological control of pests. Such agriculture uses about one-third less energy than conventional modern farms.[1] Besides using less energy, organic agriculture advocates claim that food grown without poisonous pesticides is much healthier than the crops grown with pesticides.

The orientation of organic agriculture is towards growing crops with Nature, not against her. Instead of trying to overpower Nature with massive inputs of energy intensive fertilizers and pesticides, organic agriculture uses the products and services provided by Nature and tries to channel or arrange these components in preferred ways.

In organic agriculture the soil comes first; building soil fertility is looked upon as a means of solving or reducing the severity of almost all farming problems. Pesticides, fertilizers, and mono-cropping are avoided. Because of its adversary position relative to conventional agriculture, organic agriculture and its oftentimes sensational claims have not been taken seriously by many conventional agriculturists, but recent studies showing the commercial competitiveness of organic agriculture may change this. One type of organic agriculture—called the "biodynamic French intensive method"—has recently shown that in relatively small lots, yields about four times those of conventional methods are produced. This system uses intensive plantings of symbiotic "companion" plants in well dug and raised soil beds that are heavily composted with locally available organic matter.

Advantages:

1. Organic agriculture requires much less energy.
2. Operating costs for organic agriculture are lower, primarily because farmers have no chemical fertilizer bills to pay.
3. Organic agriculture's use of manures instead of chemical fertilizers increases soil humus content, water retention of the soil, etc. (see "Fertilizer Disadvantages").
4. Organic agriculture's use of natural pest control methods does not destroy the soil bacteria, etc. (see "Pesticides Disadvantages").
5. Organic agriculture limits the vulnerability of the farmer to further energy price increases.
6. Organic agriculture, because of lower operating costs, is less vulnerable to crop price declines.
7. Organic agriculture has a low start-up cost: it does not require complicated and expensive machinery or fertilizers.
8. Certain types of organic agriculture (commonly referred to as "biodynamic French intensive") use one half to one sixteenth the water of conventional agriculture.

Disadvantages:

1. Organic agriculture may be more labor-intensive than conventional modern agriculture.
2. Organic agriculture may not be as productive per acre as conventional modern agriculture.

4

Animal Husbandry

Animal husbandry refers to the breeding, growing, and care of animals for human consumption. The most important species used by humanity in the United States are dairy and beef cattle, swine, sheep, and poultry; goats, horses, and species of pets, fur animals, wild game, and fish have somewhat minor roles. From a world viewpoint, many other species are important, including the elephant, camel, llama, donkey, water buffalo, reindeer, and caribou. Most domestic animals have been developed in the northern hemisphere where the bulk of the land is found in a temperate climate. Hence, most of our domestic animals are best adapted to temperate climates and are not able to withstand extreme temperatures.[1] There are approximately 860 million tons of livestock on Earth; this is 4.5 times the weight of all humans on Earth (187 million tons). These livestock eat about the equivalent amount of food that 14.5 billion people do. The world production of meat in 1977 was in excess of 126 million metric tons (277 billion pounds).[2] This was more than 86 grams per person per day for everyone on Earth. (The U.S. produced more than one-fourth of the total world red meat.) One-tenth of the

World Meat Production 1977

● = 1% of World Meat Production

126×10^6 metric tons

Source:
1977 FAO Production Yearbook,
Vol. 31 (United Nations, 1978)

---

world's calorie intake and one-third of its protein comes from animal products.

Animals such as cattle and sheep are often raised on ranges, with supplemental food provided during drought and winter. After 18–24 months on the range eating the natural forage, cattle are shipped to feed lots where they are fattened. They spend about 150 days in these lots and do little more than eat grain which is suitable for human consumption and gain weight. They are fed stimulants to make their production of meat more efficient, but this has the disadvantage of possibly being carcinogenic. Other methods are currently being developed and used on a limited scale to overcome this difficulty, such as feed additives and a plastic vaginal insert which through some as yet unknown mechanism stimulates weight gain. If the efficiency of feed conversion to meat could be improved 10%—as these additives do— more than 4 million metric tons of grain could be released to feed people who cannot afford to purchase beef.[6] As can be seen from Charts 1 and 2, some animals are more efficient than others in turning feed into meat. Eating eggs and milk, the products of poultry and cattle, is much more efficient than eating the animal

itself. As Chart 2 points out, 95% of the food fed to livestock ends up as either manure or as respiration loss. Livestock are better producers of fertilizer than they are of food.

"The present practice of feeding grain to animals developed because feed grains such as corn and soybean were in abundant supply and were thus an economical source of energy and protein. If grain feeding to ruminants were to be eliminated, the beef, dairy, and other ruminant industries could adjust to rations with higher levels of forages and to feed sources not consumed by humans such as food industry by-products and crop waste."[4]

Milk and milk products are of high nutritional quality. Dairy products, besides being rich in

137

Illustration 1[3]

	Giraffe	Elephant	Hippopotamus	Antelope
Environment	open forest	open forest, rain forest, marshes	all rivers and lakes	open forest, savanna
Feeding habits	browses treetops, high shrubbery	browses, breaks down forest	eats water plants	browses and grazes
Adaptability to Harvesting	good	excellent	excellent	excellent
Equivalent to	40 sheep	80 sheep	60 sheep	3–12 sheep

There are large areas of the African continent which appear to be basically unsuited to intensive farming and from which substantial crops of wild animals could be harvested for meat. This would dramatically enlarge Africa's ability to add to the world's food supply. Among these animals are the giraffe, elephant, hippopotamus, and more than twenty varieties of antelope. The environment inhabited by these animals, their feeding habits, adaptability to harvesting and food-equivalent when compared with sheep are shown diagrammatically in the above chart. All these animals are capable of living in territory unsuitable for conventional animal husbandry and eating fodder which is unsuitable either as human food or as feed for other animals.[4] For example, the large horned African antelope, the oryx, is well adapted to marginal living conditions. It needs only a third to a quarter of the water cattle need to survive, converts food to weight twice as efficiently, and is immune to many diseases that attack cattle. Production of these animals could be greatly increased by the development of watering places, improved ranges, disease-control centers, and meat packing facilities.

China raises large numbers of animals, largely sheep and goats, on land that is unsuitable for intensive agriculture. They exist on waste materials such as vegetable refuse, ground and fermented rice hulls, corn husks, soybean vines, water hyacinths, etc.[7]

The edible portion of animals:
  63% for hogs
  59% for beef cattle
  48% for sheep
An additional 15% consists of useful products such as hides, tallow, glue, and bloodmeal. The remainder, about 25%, of the total is left as waste.[5]

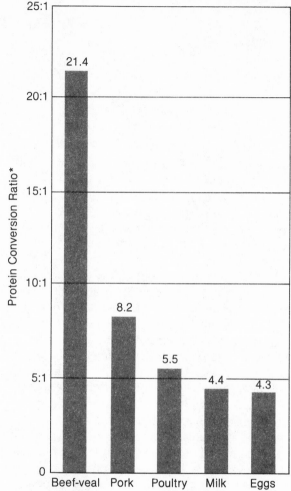

Chart 1. Livestock Protein Conversion Efficiency.

Protein Conversion Ratio*

- Beef-veal: 21.4
- Pork: 8.2
- Poultry: 5.5
- Milk: 4.4
- Eggs: 4.3

Poultry and pigs possess important advantages over cattle: they convert grain and other food concentrates into meat much more efficiently; they lend themselves far more easily to production by small-scale farmers; and they can make an important addition to their incomes and a valuable improvement to their families' diet.

*No. of lbs. protein fed livestock to produce 1 lb. protein for human consumption.

Extensive Grazing or Stock Raising

Predominant Economy
Source:
Oxford Economic Atlas, 1972

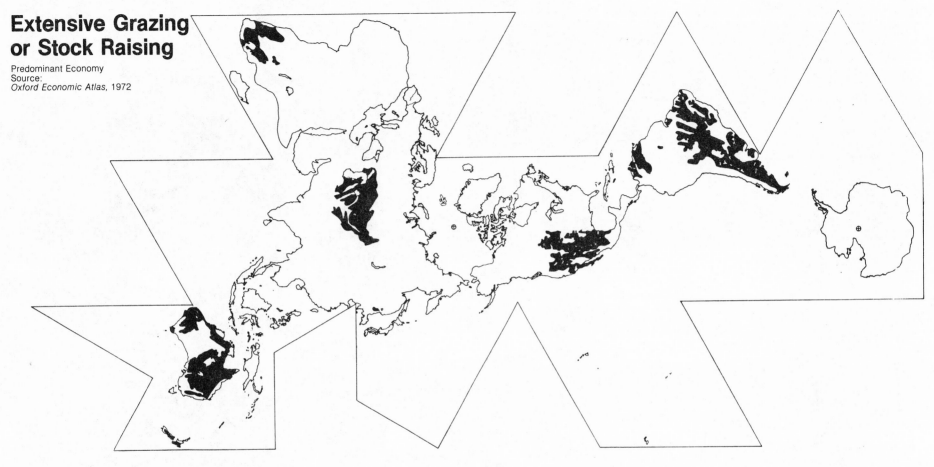

Animals in World—1977

Horses:	61.5
Mules:	11.7
Asses:	41.9
Cattle:	1212.8
Buffaloes:	130.8
Camels:	13.8
Pigs:	666.3
Sheep:	1027.9
Goats:	401.3
Chickens:	6335.1
Ducks:	155.2
Turkeys:	89.8
TOTAL:	10148.1

All units in million head

139

Cattle

One dot represents 100,000 head
Source:
Oxford Economic Atlas, 1972

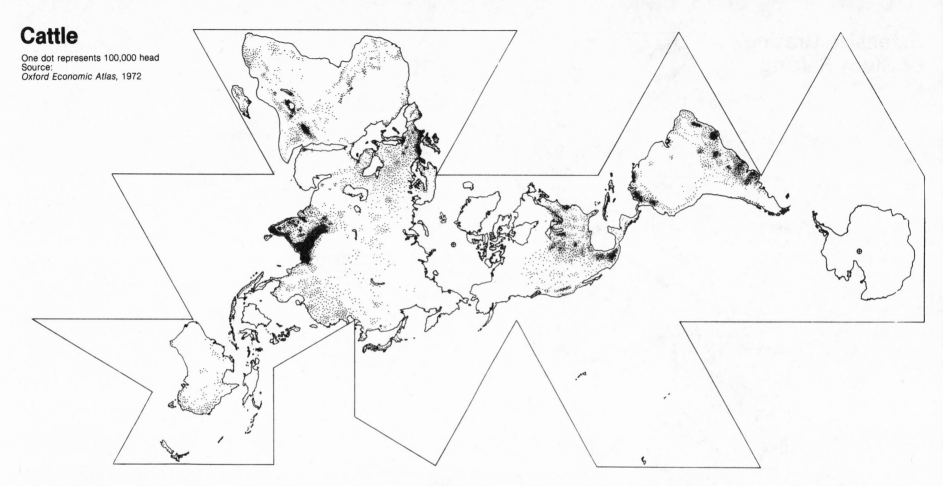

Beef (and veal from cattle 6 months or younger) accounts for about 53% of the world's red meat consumption, and is much valued for its high protein content, essential amino acids, B vitamins and minerals. One of the earliest of animals to be domesticated (6500–5000 B.C.), cattle are thought to be descended from the Aurochs, a large European ox, and a smaller Asian variety. They were brought to the New World by Columbus on his second voyage. Breeding for improvement of beef and dairy qualities began in Roman times but wasn't done scientifically until the 1800's in England, where the principal beef breeds today, Angus and Hereford, had their origins. Cattle are ruminants and are usually fed a combination of green forage on the range and yellow grain in the feedlot, often supplemented with vitamins and minerals.

Cattle research: International Center for Tropical Agriculture, Palmira, Colombia, and International Livestock Center for Africa (ILCA), Addis Ababa, Ethiopia

Cattle—1977

World:	1212
Africa:	162
North and Central America:	186
South America:	220
Asia:	358
Europe:	134
Oceania:	42
USSR:	110

All units in million head

Dairy Farming

Predominant Economy
Source:
Oxford Economic Atlas, 1972

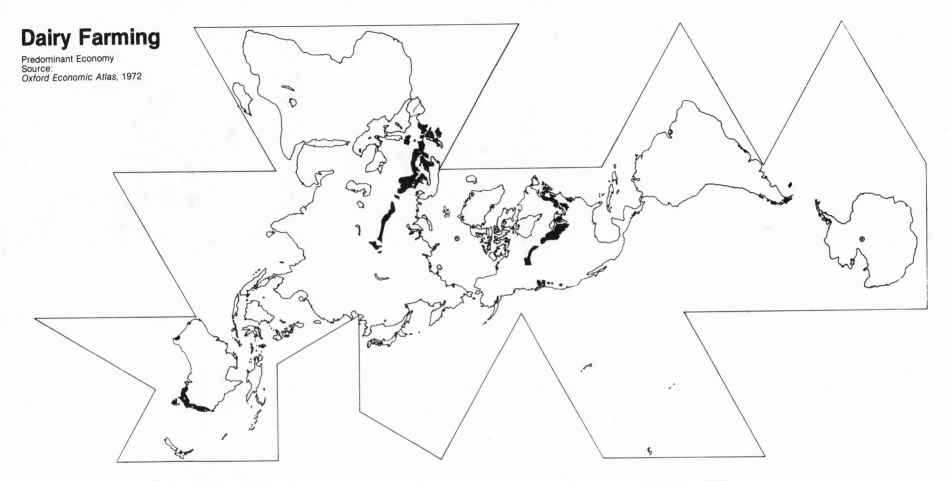

Ninety per cent of the world's milk comes from cows, the remainder from other ruminants: goats, buffaloes, sheep, reindeer and yaks. Cows may have been domesticated as early as 9000 B.C. in Libya. According to written records, dairying was already highly developed by 6000 B.C. in Old Mesopotamia. Although Columbus brought cows to the New World in 1495, it wasn't until 1850 that dairying became an industry, developing very quickly with the first cheese factory in Oneida, N.Y. (1851), Gail Borden's invention of the condensed milk process (1856), the first butter factory in New York (1856), the first creamery in Iowa (1871), the invention of the separator by Gustav DeLaval (1878), refrigeration (1880), the pasteurizing machine (1895), and the first compulsory pasteurization law in Chicago (1908). Today, one fifth of U.S. agricultural income derives from dairying, with one third of production output butter, one third milk and the rest of the output production of cheese, powdered milk, etc. Principal dairy breeds include Ayrshire, Brown Swiss, Guernsey, Holstein-Friesian, and Jersey, which produce 10–20 lb. of milk each day (on a diet of 2 lb. of hay or 6 lb. of silage per 100 lb. of body weight).

Cow Milk—1977

World:	409
Africa:	9.4
North and Central America:	72
South America:	24
Asia:	28
Europe:	168
Oceania:	12.5
USSR:	94

All units in million metric tons

141

Pigs

One dot represents 100,000 head
Source:
Oxford Economic Atlas, 1972

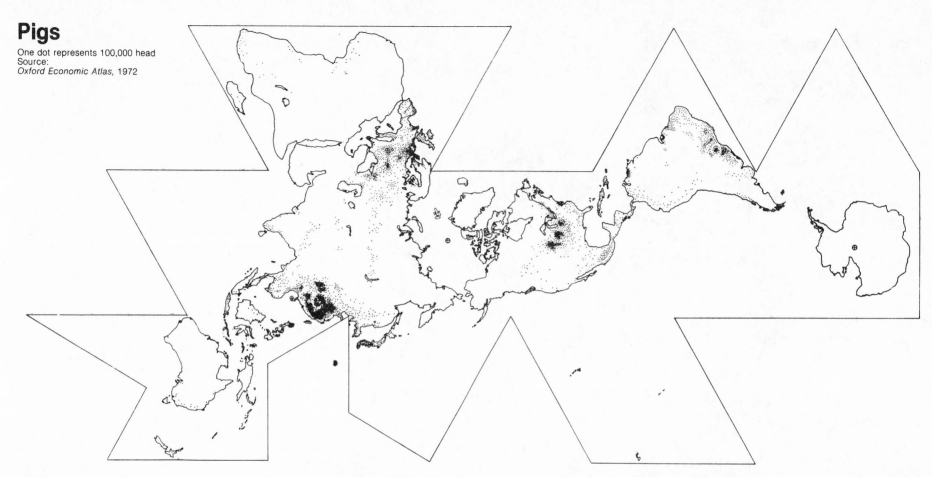

Pigs were first domesticated in Europe and India in the Neolithic period. It is believed the modern pig is descended from the wild boar which was domesticated in Northern Europe in 1500 B.C. and a smaller Asiatic boar domesticated in China in 3000 B.C. The most important products from swine producton are meat and lard (about 15% of the total calories consumed as food in the U.S.), hides, bristles (for brushes), and some pharmaceutical products. Swine, as nonruminants, use large quantities of concentrated feed in the U.S. (about 30% of the corn produced is for hogfeed) and, although pigs will eat almost anything, they are generally located close to sources of high-energy feedstuffs. In China, pigs are fed waste products and their manure is prized for fertilizer use. Over one third of China's organic fertilizer is supplied by pig wastes.

Pig research: International Center for Tropical Agriculture, Palmira, Colombia, and ILCA

Pigs—1977

World:	666.3
Africa:	8.5
North and Central America:	80.6
South America:	53.3
Asia:	296
Europe:	160
Oceania:	4.3
USSR:	63

All units in million head

Sheep

One dot represents 100,000 head
Source:
Oxford Economic Atlas, 1972

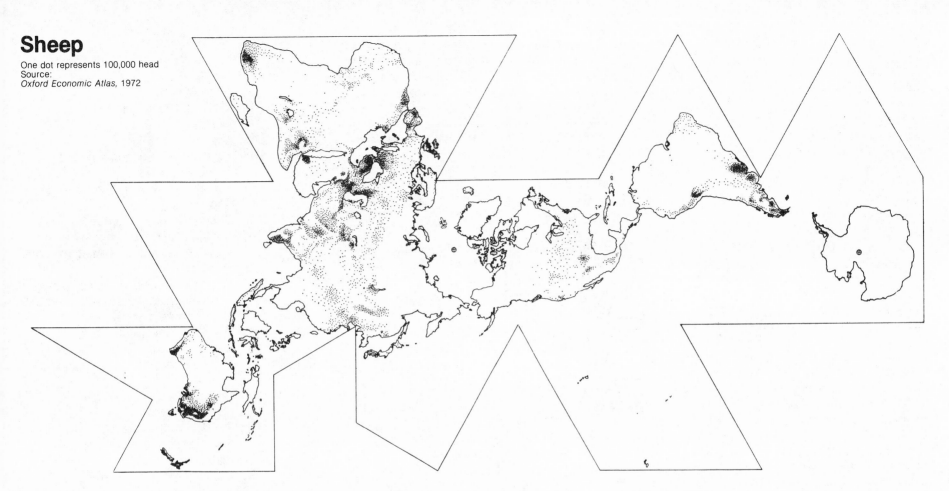

Among the first animals to be domesticated (11,000 B.C. in Southwest Asia), sheep were much prized for their meat and became part of the religious and domestic life of the people. The first known use of their fleeces for wool was about 4000 B.C. The modern domesticated sheep varieties were developed from wild sheep of Sardinia, Corsica, and the Urals of Asia. They are bred for their wool, meat (lamb, mutton from older sheep), oil (lanolin), skins, and milk (which is used to make cheese in the Near East and parts of Europe). Forage, which consists mostly of leguminous plants, makes up 95% of sheep diets.

Sheep research: International Center for Agricultural Research in Dry Areas, Lebanon, and ILCA

Sheep—1977

World:	1027.9
Africa:	160.5
North and Central America:	22
South America:	103
Asia:	282
Europe:	126
Oceania:	194
USSR:	140

All units in million head

Chart 2[5]. Materials Balance for Livestock in U.S.

(Dry weight x 10[6] tons)

Inputs of feed and forage	515.0
Output:	
Milk	9.6
Eggs	1.0
Meat and poultry (edible)[a]	6.6
Hides, lard, and other animal products	2.8
Wool, hair, and fur	0.4
Animal feed (recycled)	1.0
Bone meal and slaughterhouse waste	2.1
Manure and respiration losses (approximate)	490.0

Source: Estimates derived from U.S. Department of Agriculture statistics.

[a] "Edible portions" include some bone, skin, and fat which is later discarded in home preparation and appears as garbage.

protein and energy, supply key nutrients that are important for health. Over 400 million metric tons of cow milk were produced in the world in 1977. The retail cost of dairy protein is relatively low: 20 grams of dairy protein costs 23 cents (U.S. retail price 1975). This is about half the cost of the same amount of protein in sirloin beef steak and about twice the price for protein in dry beans.[4] Dairy proteins can improve the protein quality of diets based on vegetable proteins and starchy staples; as such they are very significant for bridging the nutritional "protein-gap" which divides the developing from the developed world. Secondary dairy products such as casein, cassinates co-precipitated with milk proteins, whey, modified whey proteins, and proteins from fermented whey contain highly nutritious proteins. Dairy processors alone produce an estimated 4.5 million metric

tons of whey; the total waste whey (including that from soybean processing) from the United States food processing industry alone amounts to 11×10^6 mt, the amount of protein produced from two million steers (113,000 mt).[9]

Whey is 94% water, 5% lactose (sugars), and 1% high grade protein.

History

Before 13,000 B.C.	Domestication of the dog
9750 B.C.	Thailand: Stockbreeding
8920 B.C.	Iraq and Romania: Sheep domestication
7000 B.C.	Jericho: Goats and sheep
7000 B.C.	Iraq and Romania: Pig domestication
6000–3000 B.C.	Domestication of oxen
6100–5800 B.C.	Turkey: Cow domestication
4000 B.C.	Domestication of the horse
3000 B.C.	Asia: Domestication of the goose
2000 B.C.	India: Jungle fowl (ancestor of modern hen) domesticated
1000 B.C.	China: Domestication of the duck
1000 B.C.	Mediterranean: Domestication of the rabbit
1000 B.C.	Domestication of the camel
1000 A.D.	Massachusetts area, North America: First cattle to reach Western Hemisphere brought by Norsemen who landed by sea
1493	Western Hemisphere: Columbus' second voyage brought hogs and other animals from Canary Islands to Haiti
1530's	Argentina: European pioneers bring cattle to the Western Hemisphere
1539	U.S.A.: DeSoto introduces hogs to North America
1540	U.S.A.: Coronado introduced to Western U.S. 500 cows and 5,000 sheep from Mexico
1569	Argentina: Horses introduced by Europeans
1611	Jamestown, U.S.A.: First sizeable importation of cattle
1633	Sheep to North America
1725–1795	England: Bakewell endeavors to improve cattle by breeding to yield more meat
1750	Britain: Selective animal breeding
1780	U.S.A.: Long-horn cattle imported from Europe by boat
1797	Australia: Sheep introduced
1850	Western U.S.A.: Cattle drives
1865	U.S.A.: Cattle trails established to railheads
1860's	France: Pasteur develops pasteurization
1871	U.S.A.: Commercial stockyards built for cattle, hogs, sheep, horses, and mules
1873	U.S.A.: American Poultry Association founded
1874	Barbed wire
1880	Cream Separator
1890	U.S.A.: Milk first pasteurized commercially
1895	Denmark: Milk control societies started
1905	Michigan, U.S.A.: First U.S. cow testing organized to control milk industry

Chart 3[3]. Composition of various meats (per 100 g of edible material).

	Water	Kilo calories	Protein	Fat	Carbo-hydrate	Calcium	Phos-phorus	Iron	Vitamin A	Thiamine	Ribo-flavin	Niacin	Ascorbic acid
	%		g	g	g	mg	mg	mg	iu	mg	mg	mg	mg
Bacon	19.3	665	8.4	69.3	1.0	13	108	1.2	0	0.36	0.11	1.8	0
Beef carcass	60.3	263	18.5	20.4	0	11	171	2.8	40	0.08	0.16	4.4	0
rib	51.7	352	16.2	31.4	0	9	148	2.4	60	0.07	0.14	3.9	0
steak	49.1	380	15.5	34.8	0	9	142	2.3	70	0.07	0.14	3.7	0
Brains beef, pig or sheep	78.9	125	10.4	8.6	0.8	10	312	2.4	0	0.23	0.26	4.4	18
Chicken light meat	73.7	117	23.4	1.9	0	11	218	1.1	60	0.05	0.09	10.7	0
dark meat	73.7	130	20.6	4.7	0	13	188	1.5	150	0.08	0.20	5.2	0
Duck domestic	54.3	326	16.0	28.6	0	10	176	1.6	0	0.08	0.19	6.7	0
wild	61.1	233	21.1	15.8	0								
Goose domestic	51.1	354	16.4	31.5	0	10	176	1.6	0	0.08	0.19	6.7	0
Heart beef	77.5	108	17.1	3.6	0.7	5	195	4.0	20	0.53	0.88	7.5	2
lamb	71.6	162	16.8	9.6	1.0	14	231		100	0.21	1.03	6.4	trace
pig	77.4	113	16.8	4.4	0.4	3	131	3.3	30	0.43	1.24	6.6	3
Kidney beef	75.9	130	15.4	6.7	0.9	11	219	7.4	690	0.36	2.55	6.4	15
lamb	77.7	105	16.8	3.3	0.9	13	218	7.6	690	0.51	2.42	7.4	15
pig	77.8	106	16.3	3.6	1.1	11	218	6.7	130	0.58	1.73	9.8	12
Lamb leg	60.8	262	16.9	21.0	0	10	152	1.3	0	0.15	0.21	4.9	0
loin	52.0	351	14.7	32.0	0	9	127	1.0	0	0.13	0.18	4.3	0
shoulder	55.9	318	14.7	28.3	0	9	127	1.0	0	0.13	0.18	4.3	0
Liver beef	69.7	140	19.9	3.8	5.3	8	352	6.5	43,900	0.25	3.26	13.6	31
lamb	70.8	136	21.0	3.9	2.9	10	349	10.9	50,500	0.40	3.28	16.9	33
pig	71.6	131	20.6	3.7	2.6	10	356	19.2	10,900	0.30	3.03	16.4	23
Pork carcass	33.4	553	9.1	57.1	0	5	88	1.4	0	0.44	0.10	2.4	0
loin	57.2	298	17.1	24.9	0	10	193	2.6	0	0.83	0.20	4.4	0
Rabbit domestic	70.0	162	21.0	8.0	0	20	352	1.3	0	0.08	0.06	12.8	0
wild	73.0	135	21.0	5.0	0								
Reindeer side	63.3	217	20.5	14.4	0								
forequarter	67.4	178	21.8	9.4	0								
hindquarter	59.6	256	19.4	19.2	0								
Sweetbreads (thymus) beef	67.8	207	14.6	16.0	0								
lamb	79.5	94	14.1	3.8	0								
Tongue beef	68.0	207	16.4	15.0	0.4	8	182	2.1	0	0.12	0.29	5.0	0
lamb	69.5	199	13.9	15.3	0.5								
pig	66.1	215	16.8	15.6	0.5	29	186	1.4	0	0.07	0.29	3.5	0
Tripe beef	79.1	100	19.1	2.0	0	127	86	1.6	0		0.15	1.6	0
Veal loin	69.0	181	19.2	11.0	0	11	195	2.9	0	0.14	0.26	6.4	0
Venison	74.0	126	21.0	4.0	0	10	249		0	0.23	0.48	6.3	0
Whale	70.9	156	20.6	7.5	0	12	144		1,860	0.09	0.08		6

1905	Milking machine
1919	U.S.A.: Mass production of poultry made possible by development of mammoth incubators and effective means of controlling disease
1930– 1970	U.S.A.: Average annual milk production of U.S. dairy cow increases from 4,508 pounds to 9,388 pounds
1949	Australia: First large-scale transport of beef by airplane
1960	Artificial insemination; growth hormones
1960's	U.S.A.: Beefalo—combination of the buffalo and cow—developed
1970	U.S.A.: 110 million cattle on farms compared to 60 million in 1925

"Blood contains approximately 17% protein and the total recovery of this material as food could result in the production of over 180,000 mt of protein in the U.S. alone."[4]

Advantages:

1. Many animals are able to eat foods which humans cannot, and then convert this food into useable food for humanity. They convert low quality, non-concentrated protein into high quality concentrated protein.
2. Many animals can be raised where no other food source or production technique will work, e.g., cattle, sheep, and goats can forage on steep slopes or on soil too rocky to farm.
3. Animals can furnish more than just food, e.g., hides, skins, and pelts for clothing; tallow, lard, manure, etc.

Disadvantages:

1. Animals often compete for food with humans; sometimes on a local level but mostly on an inter-regional basis, i.e., animals of a developed region vs. humans in a developing region.
2. Intensive and concentrated meat and egg production and processing industries (feedlots, slaughterhouses, etc.) cause environmental problems in the form of accumulated organic wastes, suspended and dissolved solids and grease in wash water effluents, air pollution from smoke, odors and dust, and problems in the disposal of solid waste.

What Needs to be Done

1. Set up a Global Animal Husbandry Research Institute to research and develop animal production systems to solve animal related problems and to collect, correlate, and disseminate accurate animal husbandry information.
2. Develop non-grain animal feeds, e.g., insects, algae, manure, and farm wastes.
3. Develop new breeds of animals suitable for grazing the marginal rangelands of the world and in the Southern Hemisphere.
4. Improve animal reproduction and growth efficiency.
5. Develop new dairy products.
6. Perfect automated rapid cheese production and ripening process.
7. Develop new milk processing and preservation methods that would increase milk's useful storage life, reduce bulk, and make a significant protein resource suitable for worldwide shipment.
8. Develop whey products as protein supplements for world market.
9. Sponsor research into stopping the loss of 36,000 mt of cattle lives.
10. Develop increased utilization of slaughterhouse by-products.
11. Tax grain consumption by animals; use funds in developing alternative animal feeds.
12. Integrate feedlots with feed producing areas.
13. Eradicate or control the tsetse fly-borne diseases of tropical Africa; this could result in this area supporting about 120 million head of cattle—or about 1.5 million tons of meat per year, and reducing the serious health risk to 35 million people who reside in this area.
14. Modernize existing slaughterhouses and milk plants, and build new ones.
15. Develop cooperative refrigeration storage facilities for meat.
16. Train farmers, veterinarians, slaughterhouse staff, hygiene inspectors, etc. in modern methods of livestock management.
17. Establish development goals for livestock for each country/region; targets also should be specific in form of milk yield per cow, meat output per head of cattle, eggs per hen, etc.

5

Fishing

Commercial fishing is the catching of fish from the ocean, lakes, and rivers in large quantities for human and animal consumption. About 70 million metric tons of fish are caught each year (Chart 1 & 2). Much of this is caught by the 20–30 million people in the world who are engaged in or dependent on small-scale fisheries.[1] This comes to 17.5 kg (38.5 pounds) per year per person on Earth (48 grams per person per day)—more than world beef production. Over 90% of this is finfish, the remainder being whales, crustaceans, mollusks, and other vertebrates. Two-thirds of this is used directly for human consumption while the other third is indirectly consumed in the form of fish meal that is fed to poultry and hogs in developed countries.[2]

Modern commercial fishing consists almost exclusively of three types: trawling, purse seining, and gill netting.[3] Trawling catches more fish in less time than either of the other methods. A trawl is a conical net that captures fish as it is dragged across the sea bottom or, with recent developments, through medium depth waters. Purse seining is used to catch fish swimming on the surface by surrounding

147

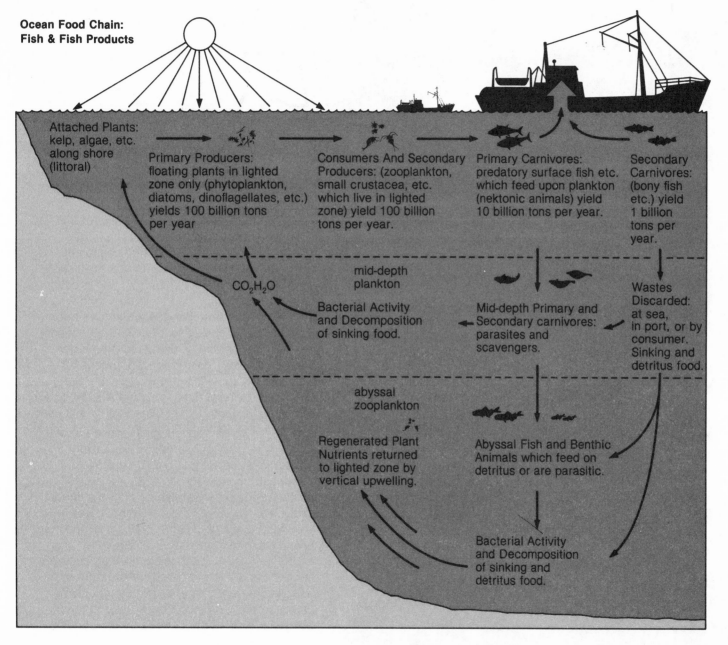

Ocean Food Chain: Fish & Fish Products

Attached Plants: kelp, algae, etc. along shore (littoral)

Primary Producers: floating plants in lighted zone only (phytoplankton, diatoms, dinoflagellates, etc.) yields 100 billion tons per year

Consumers And Secondary Producers: (zooplankton, small crustacea, etc. which live in lighted zone) yield 100 billion tons per year.

Primary Carnivores: predatory surface fish etc. which feed upon plankton (nektonic animals) yield 10 billion tons per year.

Secondary Carnivores: (bony fish etc.) yield 1 billion tons per year.

mid-depth plankton

CO_2H_2O

Bacterial Activity and Decomposition of sinking food.

Mid-depth Primary and Secondary carnivores: parasites and scavengers.

Wastes Discarded: at sea, in port, or by consumer. Sinking and detritus food.

abyssal zooplankton

Regenerated Plant Nutrients returned to lighted zone by vertical upwelling.

Abyssal Fish and Benthic Animals which feed on detritus or are parasitic.

Bacterial Activity and Decomposition of sinking and detritus food.

73.5 million tons (World Catch) of Live Weight Marine Products in 1976

Discarded at sea, in port or by consumer	5–50%
meal, oil, etc.	31%
Edible Weight consumed	68.5%
fresh	26.5%
frozen	18%
canned	13%
cured	11%

Commercial Catch, Ten Leading Fishing Nations,

	Thousand Metric Tons Live Weight
Japan	10,620
U.S.S.R.	10,134
China	6,880
Peru	4,343
Norway	3,435
United States	3,003
Korea Rep.	2,406
India	2,400
Denmark	1,911
Thailand	1,640
World Total	73,500

Source: FAO, *Yearbook of Fishery Statistics, 1976 Vol. 42.*

Chart 2. World Fish Catch, 1940–73.

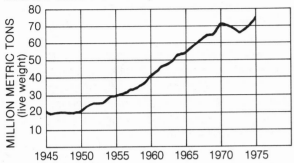

Chart 4. Peruvian Anchovy Catch, 1960–76

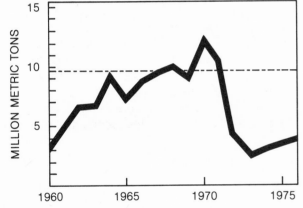

Major Fisheries

Source:
Goode's World Atlas, 1975

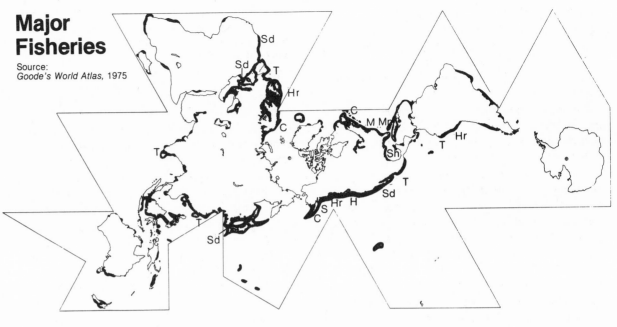

C—Cod
H—Halibut
Hr—Herring
M—Mackerel
Mn—Menhaden

S—Salmon
Sd—Sardine
Sh—Shrimp
T—Tuna

them with netting whose ends are drawn together to trap the fish in a purse-like web. Gill netting is the least efficient method and catches fish by entangling them in a slack upright netting as the fish attempt to swim through the water.

Successful commercial fishing depends not only on the size of the fish stocks but also on their concentrations and on locating them.

The fish populations which are taken from the ocean and fresh water fisheries replenish themselves from year-to-year unless the fish stock is over harvested. If more fish are taken than are gained through the natural reproduction of the fish crop, then the total fish population decreases. If the harvest continues to increase, sooner or later a point is reached where the amount of fish available for harvesting plummets, as in the case of the anchovies off Peru and the sardines off the coast of California (see Chart 4). "Sustained yield" is the balanced state when the fish stock stays at the same level because only a certain amount of the fish are taken. The rest are left to replenish the crop. It has been estimated that the largest sustainable world catch is between 100 and 200 million metric tons,[5] almost two to three times the present world catch. This does not mean, though, that the present fish stocks currently harvested in great quantities could be much further exploited but rather that new varieties could be fished. The overfished stocks include tunas, herring, haddock, cod, perch, and whale in the north Atlantic, and anchovy in the southeastern Pacific. Despite new fish resources that have been opened up in the Indian and eastern Pacific Oceans and additional stocks that have been discovered in

---

The progress made in fishing methods since 1930 alone has been greater than that made in the previous 3,000 years.

---

fishing areas with a long history of intensive fishing, as in the North Sea, within ten years very few substantial stocks that are of current commercial interest and accessible to knowable fishing methods will remain under-exploited. For the world fish harvest to double in size, fish that are presently thought to be commercially undesirable (such as squid in the U.S.) and the direct use of the smaller organisms that constitute the diet of the fish now caught need to be utilized. Methods now known for improving fish stock concentration also need to be more fully developed and used. By harvesting smaller organisms the theoretical limit for a potential yearly harvest from the sea is closer to 150 *billion* metric tons as opposed to 100–200 million metric tons.[5] Most smaller organisms from the sea and the fish not considered edible or desirable by humans are made into fish meal that is then fed to livestock. Fish meal has a protein content of 60–75%. Since 1948, fish meal use has climbed about ninefold, from 571,000 metric tons to 4.8 million in 1968. Less than 10% of the world fish catch was transformed into fish meal prior to World War II; by 1967, this figure rose to 33%.

Another way of utilizing these same organisms and fish in a way that makes them available for human consumption is in the form of a tasteless and odorless fish protein concentrate (FPC). This whitish fish flour is high in protein (80%) and minerals, can be shipped and stored easily, can be added to a variety of

foods as a protein supplement, but requires a large energy subsidy to produce—more than twice the energy of production of grass-fed beef or eggs.

The largest source of animal protein in the world is krill, a small shrimplike crustacean that is found in abundant supply off the coasts of Antarctica. Krill is the sole diet of the large toothless whales, whose population has in recent years been almost decimated, (reduced by 90%) causing a corresponding increase in the numbers of its prey. Russian scientists, who are actively developing this food source and have been marketing it since 1970, estimate the Antarctic krill stock to be from 800 million to 5 billion tons. Catches of up to 30 tons per hour have been reported by a number of Japanese, Russian, German and Polish fishing fleets.[6] An annual catch of 70 million tons of krill could provide 20 grams of animal protein per person daily for one billion people. Catches to date are around 20,000 tons per year.[6] The Japanese are testing krill in frozen fish cakes, dumplings, soups, pet foods, and protein concentrates.

History

B.C.	Fishing exists as a form of primitive hunting; methods include hand and thrown spear fishing, beach nets, fishing from canoes and outriggers, and fishing with bait at the end of a line
1300 A.D.	Marco Polo observes the making of fish flour and the drying of fish in China
1850	Trawlers introduced
1880	Commercial canning of fish is begun
1900	Purse seining introduced
1900's on	Steam propulsion in fishing vessels; power equipment for handling fishing gear
1924	U.S.A.: Patented method of preserving fish products
1945	Sonar used for fish location
1946 on	Long-range navigation with radio, man-made fibers used for nets, use of airplanes to locate fish, pumps to unload fish
1955	Reduction of fish to oil and meal gains importance
1970	Krill marketed by Russians

Advantages:

1. The ocean covers three-quarters of the Earth, harboring large sources of protein for human consumption.
2. Fish protein is readily assimilated by human beings.
3. Fish are a regenerative food resource if properly exploited.

Disadvantages:

1. Over fishing seriously damages the ecology of the oceans.
2. Distant fishing requires a large energy subsidy.

What Needs to be Done

1. Establish a global organization to monitor and regulate ocean fish stocks and their exploitation.
2. Set up Global Fish Research Institute to research and solve fish related problems and to collect, correlate, and disseminate accurate fish and fishing related information to fishermen, fish processors, and consumers.
3. Sponsor research into alternative species for commercial food sources.
4. Monitor and protect all the endangered mammals and fish of the seas. Attempt to communicate with those species with larger brains than humankind (whales, dolphins).
5. Inventory all places where depletable resources are being used in the global fishing industries and develop non-depletable alternatives.
6. Design and produce locally appropriate small scale fishing vessels for use in coastal waters in developing regions.
7. Develop ways of making the fish stocks that currently have little or no commercial appeal accessible to the palates and pocketbooks of the world.
8. Develop low-cost ways of making fish protein concentrate that is appropriate to low protein areas of the world.
9. Develop ways of fertilizing and then harvesting the vast stretches of biological desert in the ocean.
10. Eliminate waste by using the "trash fish" normally thrown back into the sea. For example, shrimp fishermen in the Gulf of Mexico discard 5–10 pounds of trash fish for every pound of shrimp marketed. It has been estimated that 10 million tons are thus wasted in the world.
11. Fresh water fishing in Africa (currently 1.4×10^6 mt/year) should be further studied: fish populations, abundance, distribution, and maximum sustainable yields should be deduced and the appropriate methods for harvesting and distribution should be developed.
12. Build fish preservation and storage facilities to prevent spoilage in developing countries where losses are highest.
13. Develop inexpensive and effective means of wrapping fish, or other means of repelling beetles and microorganisms during storage.

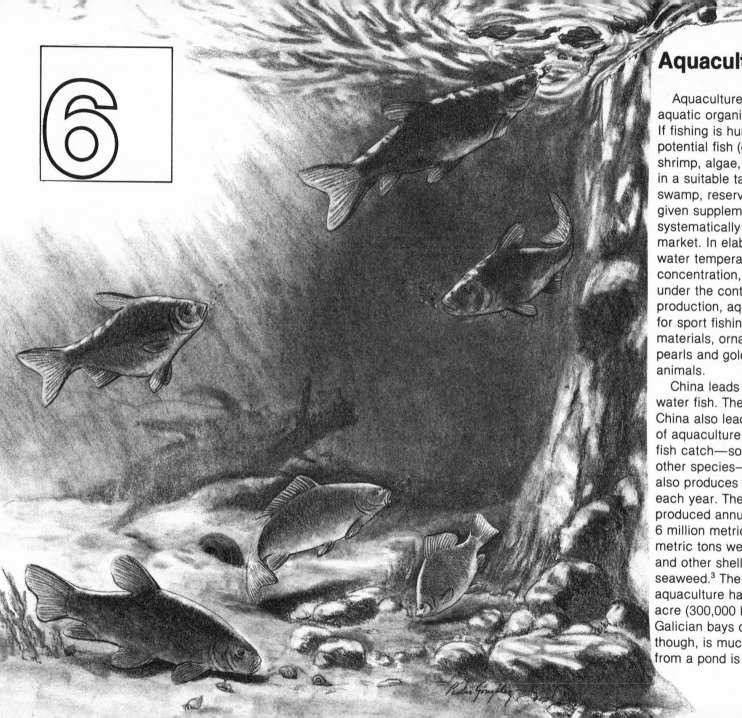

6

Aquaculture

Aquaculture is the husbandry or cultivation of aquatic organisms under controlled conditions. If fishing is hunting, aquaculture is farming. A potential fish (or oyster, prawn, frog, turtle, eel, shrimp, algae, seaweed, etc.) crop is enclosed in a suitable tank, pond, lagoon, mangrove swamp, reservoir, small lake, or estuary and given supplemental feed. The crop is then systematically harvested when large enough for market. In elaborate aquaculture enterprises the water temperature, light, nutriments, oxygen concentration, pests, and disease all come under the control of the farmer. Besides food production, aquaculture is used to supply game for sport fishing, fertilizer, industrial raw materials, ornamental fish and plants, as well as pearls and goldfish reared for laboratory animals.

China leads the world in the catch of fresh water fish. The primary reason for this is that China also leads the world in the development of aquaculture (Table 1). About 40% of China's fish catch—some 2.2 million tons of carp and other species—come from aquaculture.[1] China also produces 100,000 metric tons of seaweed each year. The total world tonnage of fish produced annually through aquaculture is about 6 million metric tons.[2] Of this, about 4 million metric tons were fish, one million were oysters and other shellfish, and 300,000 tons were seaweed.[3] The highest yield yet attained through aquaculture has been about 336,000 pounds per acre (300,000 kg/ha) of mussels, raised in the Galician bays of Spain (Table 2).[4] Average yield, though, is much lower. In China, average yield from a pond is about 3,000–5,000 kg/ha per year. One advantage aquatic animals have over their terrestial relatives is that their body density is nearly the same as that of the water they inhabit, so they are spared the energy consuming task of supporting their own weight and can thus devote more food energy to growth than land animals. Also, fish are cold blooded animals and thus do not use energy in keeping themselves warm. Carp, for instance, accumulate flesh per unit of assimilated food one-and-one-half times as rapidly as swine or chickens and twice as rapidly as cattle or sheep.[4]

The Chinese were also the first to develop polyculture—the growing together of different species or age groups. This technique recognizes that a body of water is a three dimensional growing space and that different types of fish inhabit different strata of water. It also takes advantage of the fact that a fertile body of water produces a variety of food organisms and that for an efficient utilization of these organisms it is necessary to have a variety of species to feed on them. To stock only one species is to waste both space and food (Illustration 1). Polyculture has been developed to the point where the waste products of one species furnish the food for the organisms that another fish species consumes. An example of this in Chinese polyculture is that the grass carp feces act as a source of fertilizer for plankton which nourish the silver and big head carp in the same pond.[7] The ecology of polyculture can extend beyond the body of water that is the growing medium to include the surrounding countryside in an aquaculture-agriculture symbiosis.

Illustration 1. Habitat and feeding niches of the principal species in classical Chinese carp culture.

(1) Grass carp (*Ctenopharyngodon idellus*) feeding on vegetable tops. (2) Big head (*Aristichtys nobilis*) feeding on zooplankton in midwater. (3) Silver carp (*Hypophthalmichtys molitrix*) feeding on phytoplankton in midwater. (4) Mud carp (*Cirrhinus molitorella*) feeding on benthic animals and detritus, including grass carp feces. (5) Common carp (*Cyprinus carpio*) feeding on benthic animals and detritus, including grass carp feces. (6) Black carp (*Mylopharyngodon piceus*) feeding on mollusks.[4]

The tiny shrimplike Daphnia can produce nine tons per acre in 34 days—ten times the production rate of soybeans at one-tenth the cost per unit of protein—from sewage-nourished algae cultures.[5]

Acres of Catfish Ponds in U.S.

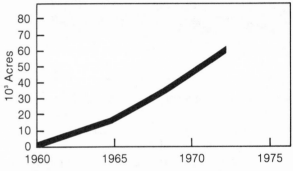

Yields from Catfish Ponds.

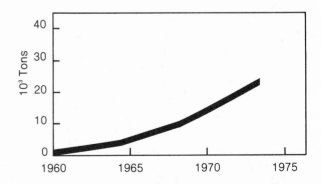

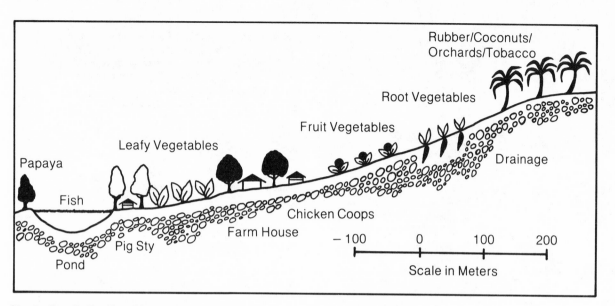

Illustration 2. Profile of integrated aquaculture system used in Singapore.[7]

Labels on illustration: Rubber/Coconuts/Orchards/Tobacco; Root Vegetables; Fruit Vegetables; Leafy Vegetables; Papaya; Fish; Drainage; Chicken Coops; Farm House; Pig Sty; Pond; Scale in Meters (−100, 0, 100, 200)

As the diagram illustrates, excess fertilizer, compost, and solid minerals from all the land crops as well as chicken, human, and pig waste eventually flow downhill to the fishpond. Manure from the pig sty is periodically washed into the pond which in turn becomes a dilute solution of fertilizer that is then applied to the land crops. The sludge at the pond bottom is dug out periodically and incorporated into vegetable gardens. In some locations in China and Thailand pigs or ducks are kept in cages overhanging the pond; even human waste has been utilized by having latrines built over fish ponds.[7] Illustrations 3 and 4 diagram another aquaculture set-up, this one in the U.S. near Woods Hole, Massachusetts, developed by the New Alchemy Institute.

Seaweeds, that is, large marine algae, can be valuable aquaculture crops. They are used as food, particularly condiments, animal feed, fertilizer, food additives, and in numerous medicinal and industrial processes. Over one hundred species of seaweed are utilized by the Chinese, Japanese, and Hawaiians.[8] Even the U.S. uses about 500 tons of seaweed products annually in everything from microbiology, bakery goods, and laxatives, to desserts and beverages. In Japan about 70,000 growers produce over 120,000 metric tons annually of just one type of seaweed: "nori." Total tonnage of all types of seaweeds approaches 400,000 metric tons. Nori is 30–50% protein, which makes it superior to rice and soy and comparable to beef, if eaten alone, which it never is.[4] The amount of useable protein is increased by the eating of rice and soy and nori in various combinations (Tables 4 & 5). Seaweeds are used as fodder for pigs, sheep,

cattle, and poultry. About 50,000 tons per year of seaweed meal are produced in Canada, the U.S., France, Great Britain, Ireland, Norway, and South Africa.[4] Seaweed also has the potential to be developed for grains, alcohol, and chemicals. China has the potential to greatly expand her seaweed production. There is an estimated 123,500 acres (50,000 ha) of coastal waters suitable for culture of which only about 12,350 acres (5,000 ha) are being utilized.

Another polyculture technique that should be mentioned is the growing of fish, shrimp, and crayfish in rice fields in Japan, Southeast Asia, and the southern United States. This form of aquaculture/agriculture has unfortunately become less prevalent with the spread of insecticide in rice farming.

The yield from *existing* aquaculture installations could be increased tenfold to over 40 million tons per year in the next three decades[4] but there is also room for vast expansion of aquaculture into *new* areas. The greatest potential and need for aquacultural development is in the developing countries. There are huge regions of presently unutilized brackish swamps in the tropics and elsewhere (14–17 million acres [6–7 million hectares] in southeast Asia alone) that could be utilized for aquaculture. There are one billion acres of undeveloped coastal wet lands in the world. If 10% were developed, they could yield about 100 million metric tons annually using simple techniques.[10] It has been estimated that by using advanced techniques this figure could be increased as much as tenfold to one *billion* metric tons. It would only take about 12 million hectares (45,000 sq. miles) of high yielding aquaculture to meet the world's present (4 billion + people) protein needs.[11]

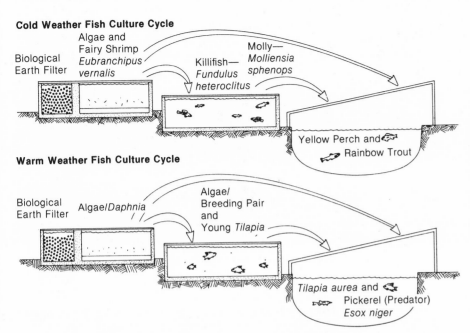

Cold Weather Fish Culture Cycle

Biological Earth Filter → Algae and Fairy Shrimp *Eubranchipus vernalis* → Killifish—*Fundulus heteroclitus* → Molly—*Molliensia sphenops* → Yellow Perch and Rainbow Trout

Warm Weather Fish Culture Cycle

Biological Earth Filter → Algae/*Daphnia* → Algae/Breeding Pair and Young *Tilapia* → *Tilapia aurea* and Pickerel (Predator) *Esox niger*

Illustration 3.[8] Biological relationships in the backyard fish farm.

Illustration 4.[9] New Alchemy's backyard fish farm, with solar heater, reflectors, and night covers for cool-season culture.

N.A.I.'s 5,000 Gallon Fish Rearing Complex Adapted to Northern Climates.

Table 1. Estimated Production of Fin Fish in Aquaculture.[6]

Country	Area (hectares)	Production (metric tons)
1. China (Mainland)	700,000	2,240,000
2. India	607,915	480,000
3. U.S.S.R.	—	190,000
4. Indonesia	266,300	141,075
5. Philippines	164,414	94,573
6. Thailand	—	87,764
7. Japan	508	85,000
8. Taiwan	39,234	56,185
9. U.S.A.	28,300	40,200
10. Pakistan and Bangladesh	30,780	37,540
11. Malaysia	90,473	25,648
12. Hungary	22,000	19,697
13. Italy	—	18,000
14. South Vietnam	2,500	16,500
15. Yugoslavia	9,747	15,840
16. Ceylon	10,000	15,000
17. Rumania	6,400	12,000
18. Denmark	—	11,000
19. Poland	62,791	10,909
20. Czechoslovakia	42,798	10,641
21. Israel	4,904	10,220
22. Brazil	—	9,967
23. Mexico	12,650	9,026
24. Khmer	—	5,000
25. Germany, East	—	3,669
26. Germany, Federal Republic	11,824	2,627
27. Burma	2,920	1,494
28. Zaire	4,058	1,406
29. Bolivia	25,502	1,400
30. Austria	3,000	780
31. Hongkong	629	690
32. Zambia	—	689
33. Uganda	410	670
34. Madagascar	1,280	615
35. Norway	—	600
36. Singapore	890	554
37. Nigeria	—	127
38. Kenya	610	122
39. Spain	—	50
40. South Korea	76	40
41. Ghana	204	30
42. Puerto Rico	135	25
Total	2,153,252	3,657,373

Table 2. Production of Shrimps and Prawns in Aquaculture.[6]

Country	Area (ha)	Production (tons)
1. India	4,000	3,800
2. Indonesia	—	3,328
3. Philippines	—	2,500
4. Thailand	—	2,500
5. Japan	—	1,800
6. Malaysia	870	250
7. Singapore	—	120
Total		14,298

All estimates are not for the same year. In all cases the most recent figures available have been used. The tables were compiled by FAO.

Table 3. Production of Mollusks in Aquaculture.[6]

Country	Production (tons)
A. OYSTERS	
1. United States	350,500
2. Japan	194,600
3. Korea	45,700
4. Mexico	43,500
5. France	34,200
6. Taiwan	12,700
7. New Zealand	10,700
8. Australia	9,800
9. Canada	4,100
10. Portugal	2,900
11. Spain	1,800
Total	710,500
B. MUSSELS	
1. Spain	109,700
2. France	39,800
3. Korea	16,800
4. Italy	13,700
Total	180,000
C. CLAMS	
1. Malaysia	28,600
2. Korea	16,800
3. Japan	10,800
4. Taiwan	60
Total	56,260
D. MISCELLANEOUS	
Korea	19,700
Total for Mollusks	966,400

Table 5.[4] Nutrient Composition of Nori, a Food Prepared from the Red Alga *Porphyra* in Japan (Contents per 100 g of Algal Sheets).

Water	Protein	Fat	Carbohydrate	Ash
11.4 g	35.6 g	0.7 g	44.3g	8.0g

Provitamin A	Vitamin B₁	Vitamin B₂	Niacin	Vitamin C
44,500 IU	0.25 mg	1.24 mg	10.0 mg	20.0 mg

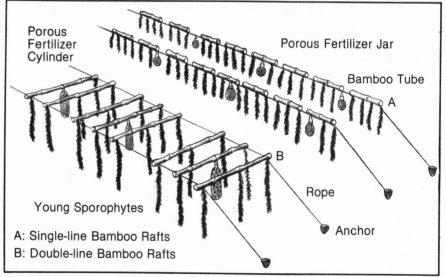

Bamboo tube rafts used for kelp culture in China. (After Cheng, 1969).[4]

Table 4.[4] Selected Examples of Aquacultural Yields by Ascending Intensity of Culture Methods.

Culture Method	Species	Yield[kg/(ha)(year)] or Economic Gain
Transplantation	Plaice (Denmark, 1919–1957)	Cost: benefit of transplantation, and other social benefits
	Pacific salmon (U.S.)	Cost: benefit, based on return of hatchery fish in commercial catch
Release of reared young into natural environment	Pacific salmon (Japan)	Cost: benefit on above basis
	Shrimp, abalone, puffer fish (Japan)	Not assessed; reputed to increase income of fishermen
	Brown trout (Denmark, 1961–1963)	Maximum net profit/100 planted fish: 163%
Retention in enclosures of young or juveniles from wild populations, no fertilization, no feeding	Mullet	150–300
	Eel, miscellaneous fish (Italy)	
Stocking and rearing in fertilized enclosures, no feeding	Shrimp (Singapore)	1,250
	Milkfish (Taiwan)	1,000
	Carp and related spp. (Israel, S.E. Asia)	125–700
	Tilapia (Africa)	400–1,200
	Carp (Java, sewage streams) (¼–½ of water area used)	62,500–125,000
Stocking and rearing with fertilization and feeding	Channel catfish (U.S.)	3,000
	Carp, mullet (Israel)	2,100
	Tilapia (Cambodia)	8,000–12,000
	Carp and related spp. (in polyculture) (China, Hong Kong, Malaysia)	3,000–5,000
Intensive cultivation in running water; feeding	Clarias (Thailand)	97,000
	Rainbow trout (U.S.)	2,000,000 [170 kg/(liter)(sec)]
	Carp (Japan)	1,000,000–4,000,000 [about 100 kg/(liter)(sec)]
Intensive cultivation of sessile organisms, mollusks, and algae	Shrimp (Japan)	6,000
	Oysters (Japan, Inland Sea)[a]	20,000
	Oysters (U.S.)	5,000 (best yields)
	Mussels (Spain)[a]	300,000
	Porphyra (Japan)[a]	7,500
	Undaria (Japan)[a]	47,500

[a] Raft-culture calculations based on an area 25% covered by rafts.

Table 6. Some of the Common Commercial Preparations of Seaweeds Used by the Japanese are Listed Below.

Porphyra tenera	Nori gohen	Seasoned and eaten with rice
Dried Porphyra tenera	Hoshi Nori	The famous Japanese Sushi is prepared by rolling cooked rice with algal sheet
Powdered dried Porphyra tenera	Mominori	Eaten with rice
Porphyra tenera mixed with salt, spices, etc.	Chazuke Nori	Eaten with cold rice
Nostoc sp. (common in Kyushu island—fresh water form)	Chusenji Nori	Eaten with rice
Dried Kelp	Doshi kombu	Boiled in water to prepare Japanese soup
Dried Kelp	Oboro kombu	Used in soup for breakfast
Undaria pinnatifida	Wakame	Eaten as it is or with vinegar
Dried Kelp	Su kombu	Eaten as it is
Dried Kelp	Oyatsu kombu	Eaten as it is
Dried Kelp	Tororo kombu	Used in soup or eaten with vinegar
Dried Kelp	Koshi kombu	Eaten as it is
Porphyra tenera	Nori matsuba	Sandwich of squid and Porphyra
Giant Kelp	Kobu matsuba	Sandwich of squid and kelp
Giant Kelp	Kombu tsukudani	Seasoned in Japanese sauce, sugar, etc. Eaten with rice.

Tidal Sites

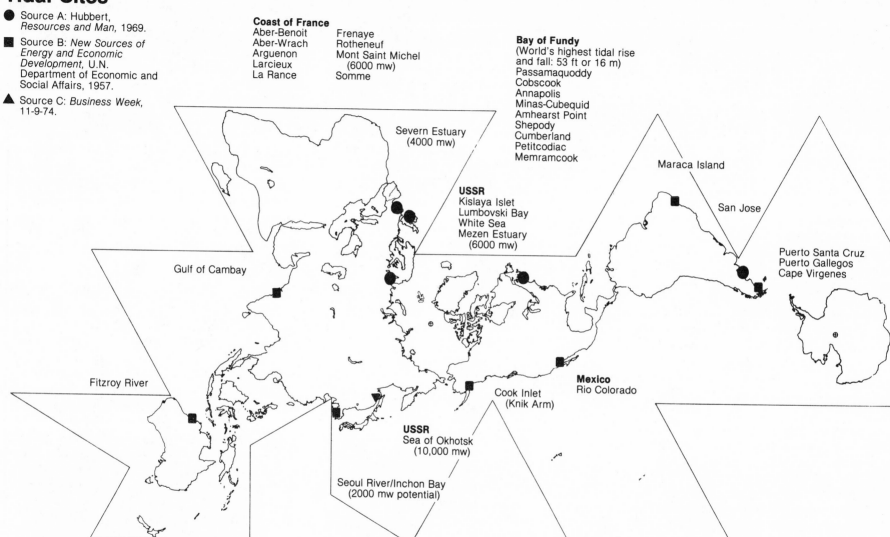

● Source A: Hubbert, *Resources and Man,* 1969.

■ Source B: *New Sources of Energy and Economic Development,* U.N. Department of Economic and Social Affairs, 1957.

▲ Source C: *Business Week,* 11-9-74.

Coast of France
Aber-Benoit
Aber-Wrach
Arguenon
Larcieux
La Rance

Frenaye
Rotheneuf
Mont Saint Michel
(6000 mw)
Somme

Bay of Fundy
(World's highest tidal rise and fall: 53 ft or 16 m)
Passamaquoddy
Cobscook
Annapolis
Minas-Cubequid
Amhearst Point
Shepody
Cumberland
Petitcodiac
Memramcook

Severn Estuary
(4000 mw)

Maraca Island

San Jose

USSR
Kislaya Islet
Lumbovski Bay
White Sea
Mezen Estuary
(6000 mw)

Puerto Santa Cruz
Puerto Gallegos
Cape Virgenes

Gulf of Cambay

Fitzroy River

Cook Inlet
(Knik Arm)

Mexico
Rio Colorado

USSR
Sea of Okhotsk
(10,000 mw)

Seoul River/Inchon Bay
(2000 mw potential)

The open sea, 90% of the ocean and almost three-fourths of the Earth's surface, is essentially a biological desert. Nearly all of the productivity of the oceans comes from three types of regions—upwelling regions where nutrient-rich deep water fertilizes the surface waters (these total no more than one-tenth of one percent of the ocean surface—an area about the size of California—and produce 50% of the ocean's total catch), coastal waters, and a few offshore regions of relatively high fertility.[12]

Irrigation projects have frequently demonstrated that the addition of water makes the desert bloom. Adding nutrients to the ocean has much the same effect, but without the limits that are imposed by scarce fresh water supplies on land irrigation. This is because the deep ocean holds a vast supply of nutrients that are constantly being renewed.[13] Because natural upwelling increases the productivity of the open ocean almost 50,000 times, there are a number of serious plans for stimulating upwelling artificially to increase the productivity of surface waters. In one such plan, nutrient-rich deep ocean water is pumped to the surface and dumped into adjacent shallow coral atolls where the nutrients are kept from sinking back down and which serve as natural pens for fish and other aquatic organisms. It has even been suggested that whales be raised in such a manner.

Producing power and food could be combined in the one hundred odd *large* tidal basins of the world (see map) where tidal power plants could be constructed by placing a causeway or dam across the mouth of the basin. The dam would house turbines that would generate power with the incoming and outgoing tides as well as

Occurrence of Kelp in Quantities Sufficient for Harvesting

Source:
Science, Vol. 182

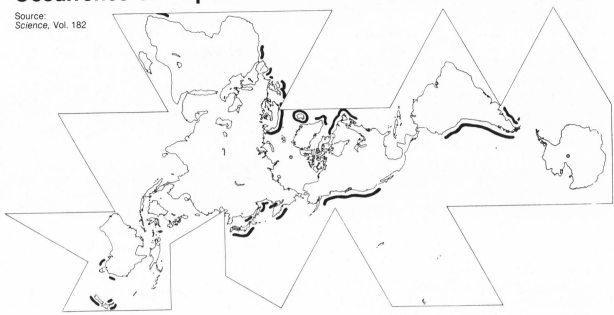

enclose the fish, seaweed, shrimp, etc. culture. There are also proposals and designs for coupling wave harnessing power plants with food production.[14]

In other plans the production of food and energy would be developed by cultivating areas of unutilized open ocean for seaweed or harvesting the already existing quantities of kelp (see map). The oceans possess five to ten times more "potentially arable" area than the land. Some of the 80–100 million square miles of arable surface water would be cultivated with rapidly growing and easily harvested types of seaweeds on lines attached to floating supporting structures. The water surrounding the crop would be fertilized by pumping up the

cool nutrient-rich deep waters. Crops would be harvested periodically and converted into foods, fodder, fertilizers, methane, alcohol, and industrial materials at processing plants. An initial prototype of seven acres has already been built; the next stage is to develop a 1,000 acre facility and the third would be a full-scale farm of about 100,000 acres.[15]

The cold deep ocean water could be coupled with the condensor cooling systems of power plants, refrigeration units, or for the production of power through temperature differentials.[13,16] Also possible are the use of sewage effluent from urban areas in combined aquaculture/waste processing plants as well as small-scale basement fish ponds for supplying the protein

2. Breed and hybridize disease and pollution resistant and faster growing aquatic organisms.
3. Further develop large scale aquaculture/sewage treatment units that produce high quality protein from local sewage.
4. Develop small scale—backyard and basement—aquaculture production units (some that process household waste).
5. Establish regional aquaculture research stations and locally appropriate production facilities and techniques, for South America, Africa, Asia, Europe, North America, etc. Research into:
    a) milkfish and yellowtail spawning
    b) an aquaculture fish for South America
    c) inventory and trials with previously uncultured species
    d) genetic improvements.
6. Establish instruction facilities at appropriate locations for local farmers, teachers, and officials, especially for the proliferation of advanced and efficient management of present practices.
7. Establish special credit and tax arrangements to encourage aquaculture development.
8. Develop aquaculture infra-structure and service industry, e.g., specialized engineering, tools, feeds, processing, disease control, etc.
9. Make global inventory of prime areas for aquaculture with special emphasis on developing regions.
10. Develop high protein fish foods from insect and other "non-human" foods.
11. Develop milkfish ponds in tropical mangrove swamp regions.

12. Develop and spread Chinese and Japanese aquaculture techniques where applicable world wide.
13. Develop the seaweed culture potential off Australia, South America, and the West Coast of North America.
14. Develop efficient, inexpensive hatcheries for developing regions.
15. Develop efficient production and processing techniques for algae for animal and human food.
16. Improve aquaculture technology, intensify culture, introduce new species to culture, increase the total area devoted to culture.
17. Develop easier and more efficient ways of cutting and collecting seaweeds.
18. Design and develop new aquaculture ponds with feeding and harvesting methods "built in."
19. Increase yield of existing aquaculture installations.
20. Develop coastal wetlands and brackish swamps for aquaculture.
21. Develop ocean fertilization/aquaculture in shallow coral atolls and other appropriate locations.
22. Develop seaweed cultivation in areas of the open ocean.
23. Develop, if appropriate, major salmon fishery in South Pacific.

Controlled Environments/ Greenhouses

A greenhouse is a glass or other transparent material structure in which the cultivation and protection of plants takes place. A greenhouse is a means of controlling the environment of plants with much more thoroughness than that possible with traditional or modern agriculture methods. Modern agriculture seeks to control the environment of plants through such mechanical means as plowing, weeding, and irrigation, and chemical means such as the addition of fertilizers, pesticides, and fungicides to crops and their immediate surroundings. Greenhouses are closed environments where insects and other plant attackers or inhibitors are excluded and warmth, sunlight, moisture, and sometimes carbon dioxide are enhanced thus allowing for optimum plant growth. A greenhouse allows sunlight into its enclosure and keeps the long-wave radiation (heat) within, thus keeping the structure and plants warmer throughout the year. The growing season is lengthened and more food can be produced in more areas. Because greenhouses can be located anywhere, city or country, large amounts of present costs that arise from

needs of the single family. In Equatorial Africa, where there are over 50,000 aquaculture ponds, it has been shown that a one acre pond will produce a metric ton of fish a year with a daily feeding of sixty pounds of Manioc leaves or eleven pounds of peanut pressings (what is left of the nuts after the oil is extracted).[17] As in China, this contributes an essential addition to the diet at little additional cost other than the labor of the farmer and his family.

Another plan for increasing the productivity of the ocean is to establish a major salmon fishery in the southern Pacific. The warm equatorial seas prevent the northern hemisphere salmon from migrating to the equally hospitable southern hemisphere. There are ideal salmon breeding conditions as well as feeding grounds off the coast of South America. The plan calls for the ferrying of northern salmon in special hatchery ships across the equator and then the establishment of the new salmon in Chile.

History

2500 B.C.	Egyptian culture of the tilapia fish
2000 B.C.	Aquaculture practiced in Asia
500 B.C.	Chinese breed carp in ponds
100 B.C.	Rome and Gaul: Artificial culture of oysters
618–904 A.D.	Chinese institute polyculture (the stocking of more than one species in a single pond) thereby greatly increasing fish culture
1227	Europe: Carp production begins in Austria
1600	Japan: Culture of seaweed in Tokyo Bay
1600	Europe: Production of soda and potash from the ash (called "kelp") of burned brown seaweeds
1800's	Europe: Brown trout raised in fish farms for restocking purposes
1920's	U.S.A.: Development of first shell-fish hatcheries
1930's	Chinese spawn carp by artificial insemination
1934	Brazil: Development of "hypophysation" of fish, that is, a technique that permits the controlled breeding of fish
1934	Japan: First spawning and hatching of shrimp eggs
1947	Africa: Belgians start fish culture in Belgian Congo
1960's	Japan: Large commercial fish farms use heated waste water from adjacent electric power plants
1960's	Arkansas, U.S.A.: First catfish farming
1961	China: Mass production of artificially produced carp fry

Advantages:

1. Aquaculture has very high productivity in many situations. A body of water is a three dimensional growing space.
2. Aquatic crops are primarily protein crops; as such, they are better converters of primary food than ruminants (beef), fowl, or pigs.[1]
3. Aquaculture can cut protein distribution costs by being able to produce moderate volumes of meat in a wide variety of places.
4. Many aquaculture products—fish, shrimp, etc.—have a wide cultural acceptance as a food source.

Disadvantages:

1. Possible pollution: water, as the universal solvent, is easier to pollute than soil; physical and chemical contamination of bodies of water have detrimental or lethal effects on aquatic organisms or their consumers and are much more difficult to prevent or control than is the case for expanses of land. Also, aquaculture organisms tend to concentrate pollutants. Pollution is often heaviest in some of the places where ocean-based aquaculture would thrive best.
2. Aquaculture is limited to regions with enough water in the desired form (temperature, salinity, etc.) for a specific crop.
3. Costs for large scale industrial production of aquaculture tend to make the product available only as high price luxury food; pumps, tanks, feed, and labor costs are high.
4. Fish disease is difficult to control because of the water medium and crowded conditions.
5. The waste products from ten pounds of trout is almost equal to one human; a million pound culture facility produces the same kinds and quantities of waste as a city of about 100,000 people. Properly utilized, this is a valuable resource; improperly dealt with it is a liability.
6. Fresh fish spoil quickly without refrigeration and/or processing.

What Needs to be Done

1. Set up a Global Aquaculture Research Institute to research and develop aquaculture systems and to collect, correlate, and disseminate accurate aquaculture related information.

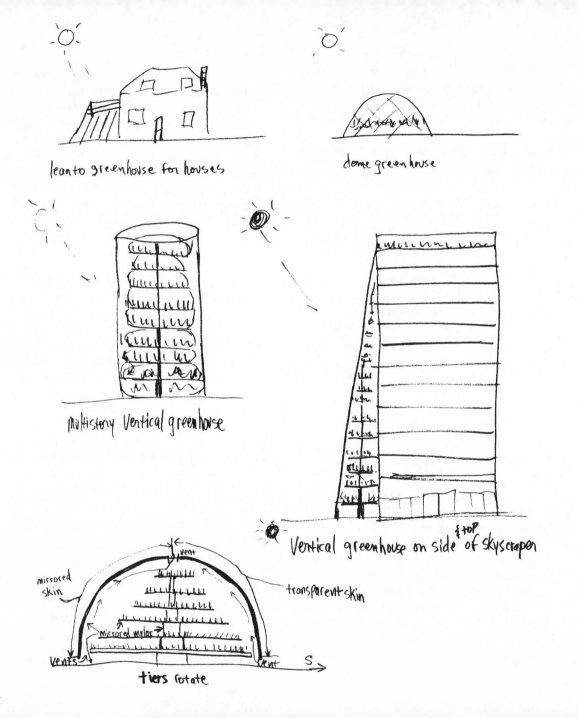

leanto greenhouse for houses

dome greenhouse

multistory vertical greenhouse

Vertical greenhouse on side of skyscraper & top

mirrored skin

transparent skin

vent

mirrored mylar

vents

vent

S

tiers rotate

transportation, harvesting, preservation, packaging, and storing can be eliminated. Greenhouse "food factories" could be constructed in close vicinity to or in cities because of their low ground area requirements, structural adaptability, and environmentally clean operations. They could be coupled with other industrial, commercial, or residential processes to utilize waste heat from power plants or fertilizer from sewage treatment plants.[1] Geothermal power is currently in use to heat greenhouses in Japan, Iceland, New Zealand, and the U.S.S.R.

There are a number of greenhouse designs. The conventional design is the horizontal or "on the ground" type; there are, though, designs for vertical (or tower) greenhouses (see illustrations). A vertical greenhouse will enjoy some advantage of increased available solar radiation during periods of very low sun angle. It has been shown that for sun altitude angles below 17°40' (areas of higher latitudes) the vertical greenhouse receives more solar radiation per wall surface area than the horizontal greenhouse.[2] From preliminary evaluations, vertical greenhouses do not appear to be suitable for low latitude arid areas where large land areas are available and sun altitude angles are generally high.[3] There are 20,000 miles (2.6 million sq. miles) of desert coasts in the world (see map, Irrigation Section).[4] Putting up greenhouses on only 1 percent of this land and irrigating with water from solar powered desalinization plants could potentially produce enough vegetables to feed the entire world. In air-inflated, controlled environment greenhouses it is possible to grow 200,000 pounds per acre of most vegetables. Cucumber yields of 900,000 lbs./acre have been obtained.[5] Many of the world's most hungry areas are in regions which are or are near coastal deserts.

History

1st Century	Rome: Tiberius Caesar (Nero) raised cucumbers year-round in special house glazed with mica
1599	Holland: Botanical greenhouse in Leyden for cultivating tropical plants for medicinal value
1619	Heidelberg, Germany: First greenhouse on record producing year-round crop
1717	Europe: First all glass greenhouse
1736	U.S.A.: First greenhouse in America, built by Andrew Fanevil
1885	U.S.A.: First large-scale production of greenhouses in U.S.
1975	Prince Edward Island, Canada: The New Alchemists develop self-contained fish farm greenhouse utilizing natural food chains and renewable energy sources

Advantages:

1. The growing season is lengthened thereby increasing crop yields.
2. Crops grow faster under the optimal conditions furnished by greenhouses.
3. Pesticides and herbicides are often not necessary.
4. Greenhouse installation is free of region's soil and weather conditions.

Disadvantages:

1. The greenhouse structure is expensive to build and operate.
2. Climate control in the greenhouse can be an expensive energy cost.
3. Because there are usually no insects, pollination must be done mechanically by hand.

What Needs to be Done

1. Set up a Global Controlled Environment Research Institute to research and develop controlled environment systems and collect, correlate, and disseminate greenhouse related information.
2. Develop low cost greenhouses for developing countries.
3. Develop low cost, mass produced, light weight greenhouses for urban roof-top food production.
4. Provide tax credits for gardening materials.
5. Develop automated vertical greenhouses.
6. Develop automated cultivating, harvesting, etc. controls for greenhouses.
7. Design and build housing, apartment buildings, and condominiums with integrated solar heated greenhouses.
8. Develop urban food factories in combination with sewage treatment and aquaculture production units.
9. Develop greenhouses in combination with power plant waste heat and CO_2 utilization.
10. Develop large greenhouses for coastal desert utilization with solar powered irrigation.
11. Develop and mass produce small scale greenhouses for houses, apartments, offices, etc.

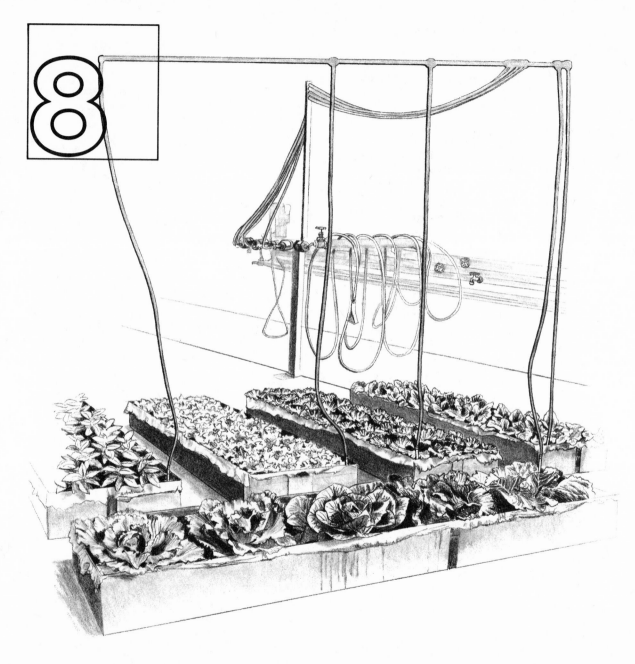

Hydroponics

Hydroponics is the cultivation of plants without soil. With conventional agriculture, plants obtain their nutrients from the soil; in hydroponics, the plants obtain nourishment from a nutrient-rich water solution. Plants are grown supported in a matrix of peat or some other similar material on a wire screen with their roots immersed in a solution containing the necessary nutriments for growth. In another method, plants are rooted in a medium of sand or gravel contained in a shallow tank through which the nutritive solution is pumped. Hydroponics is a closed irrigation system that often gives higher yields because nutrients are abundantly and continuously available for uninterrupted growth. The chemical elements that are necessary for plant development (in currently detectable amounts) are carbon, oxygen, hydrogen, nitrogen, phosphorus, sulfur, potassium, magnesium, calcium, iron, manganese, boron, copper, zinc, and molybdenum. The first three are obtained by the plant from the air or water absorbed from the soil. The others are all absorbed in the form of mineral salts from the soil or, in the case of hydroponics, in the nutritive solution.

Hydroponics can be used with or without greenhouses but almost all projects have utilized the environment-controlling advantages of enclosed farming (see Greenhouses). Large quantities of quality fruit and vegetables can be grown in relatively small confines because with enclosed farming, production is dependent on environmental control and not on the site's variable weather patterns. Hydroponic farms could be established on residential rooftops, highrise buildings, in and on top of supermarkets as well as basements, back yards, and in conventional greenhouses.[1] Any plant that can be grown in soil can be grown hydroponically, but high initial capital investment costs have limited the widespread use of hydroponics for most crops. Hydroponics is ideally suited for areas with poor soil and scarce water, such as the desert. Hydroponic food production in desert areas is currently operating in Abu Dhabi, along the Arabian Gulf. This facility has its own desalinization and power plant and produces vegetables for the sheikdom as well as for export. Barley grass grown to a height of six inches and used as a food supplement for cattle, horses, and poultry with yields per acre of 30,000 tons per year[2] as well as a wide variety of vegetables used for commercial consumption—such as tomatoes, green beans, cucumbers, eggplants, peppers, radishes, onions, lettuce, turnips, mustard greens, chard, celery, spinach, asparagus, beets, Brussels sprouts, carrots, cauliflower, muskmelons, peas, potatoes, squash, corn, and turnips as well as seedlings, saplings, herbs, medicinal plants, flowers, and fruits have been successfully produced hydroponically.

Commercial hydroponic food production has begun with emphasis on cucumbers and tomatoes. One commercial hydroponic grower supplied over four million pounds of tomatoes in 1973. One commercial unit 26 × 128 feet can yield as much tomato poundage in a year as four to eight acres of land because it operates all year round.[6] Production is independent of site and season and continuous plant production is possible with an "assembly line" method where cyclic, continuously moving conveyor belts transport plants into separate culture rooms,

Gross Yields per Acre per Year.[3, 4, 5]

Crop	Conventional Agriculture	Hydroponics
Soya	600 lb.	1,550 lb.
Snap Beans	10,000 lb.	42,000 lb.
Wheat	600 lb.	4,100 lb.
Rice	1,000 lb	5,000 lb.
Lettuce	16,000–19,500 lb.	50,000 lb.
Potatoes	16,000 lb.	140,000 lb.
Tomatoes	15,000 lb.	342,000 lb.
Oats	7,000 lb.	30,000 lb.
Cucumbers	7,000 lb.	565,000 lb.
Peas	2,000 lb.	18,000 lb.

Comparative Yield for a Single Crop Grown in Sadiyat Greenhouses vs. Field Grown.

Type of vegetable	Yields (tons/ha/crop)		
	Sadiyat greenhouse	Good yield field grown U.S.[Z]	Al Ain government farm[Y]
Cabbage	70	27	49–70
Cucumber	229	27	20
Eggplant	240	19	30–49
Lettuce	56	24	20–30
Okra	52	11	30
Tomato	159	67	15–26
Turnip	157	22	15–20

[Y]Yields supplied by Mr. Omar Baki of the Al Ain Department of Agriculture, Abu Dhabi.
[Z]From: J. E. Knott, (3).

each with specific environmental conditions. Extrapolating from a NASA guideline that 30% of a person's food needs could be produced from 42 square feet of hydroponics (or 100% from 153 square feet including 10% excess for support machinery) the Earth could provide for

its present population with 5.66 million hectares (or less than .4% of its presently used arable land). If 10% of a city's surface was used for hydroponic culture, it would provide support for 18,200 people per square mile of city area. The population densities of some city areas (Chicago—15,000; Indianapolis—11,000; New York—26,000) suggest that many cities could be much more self-sufficient in food production than most people realize.

Hydroponic food production is currently being used on nuclear submarines with artificial lights because it sharply cuts requirements for storage space and oxygen. Other places where hydroponics is used are in remote strategic areas such as the desert, arctic, or on offshore drilling rigs. Standard Oil operates one of the largest hydroponic installations in the world on the island of Aruba. Even the U.S. Army has a hydroponics branch that grew eight million pounds of fresh produce in 1952.[7]

History

1500's	Mexico: floating gardens of Xochimileho
1699	England: Woodward grows spearmint in several kinds of water
1800	France: J. Bousingault grows plants in sand, quartz, and charcoal by adding nutritious solutions of mineral salts
1840	Leibig publishes findings on fact that plants are made of chemical elements derived from air, water, and soil
1865	U.S.A.: Sach and Knop develop soil-less cultivation

1921	U.S.A.: Pember and Adams find that carnations grow in sand in which nitrogen, potasium, and phosphorus have been added
1929	U.S.A.: Gerich grows hydroponic tomato vines up to twenty five feet high—word "hydroponic" is coined
1936	Eaton develops automatic system of sand culture with nutrients supplied under pressure from perforated pipes laid on beds of sand in watertight containers
1940's	Wake Island and Ascension Island: Pan-American Airlines and U.S. Army/Navy set up and successfully operate large scale hydroponic installation for feeding U.S. troops
1940's	Florida, U.S.A.: Large scale commercial operations
1946– 1957	Bengal, India: Development of the Bengal system of hydroponics— outstanding results produced over 400% yield of soil culture
1950's	Development of commercial operations throughout world (South Africa, Israel, England, France, Sweden, U.S., Holland, Germany, Rhodesia, Japan, Spain, Puerto Rico, Norway, Italy, British Guiana, Netherlands, Antilles, Aruba)
1972	Hydroculture Inc. markets four million pounds of hydroponic tomatoes (.17% of total tomato consumption in U.S.)

Advantages:

1. Hydroponics gives higher yields per acre than conventional agriculture (500 people can be fed from one acre vs. 1 person per acre conventional farming). The growing season is extended or is continuous.
2. Hydroponics has a high water conserving efficiency; there is no water run-off; water requirements are $\frac{1}{8}$ to $\frac{1}{30}$ those of surface irrigation.
3. There is no fertilizer run-off or leaching out into surrounding streams, ponds, lakes, and rivers resulting in nitrate and phosphate pollution.
4. Hydroponics farming can take place most anywhere, not just in places where the soil is good as in agriculture. Hydroponics farming can also be easily automated and multi-storied.
5. There is no need for insecticides, weeding, or heavy labor. Pest control is minimized by growing plants in an inert substance that is hostile to insects.
6. Hydroponics furnishes fresh produce year round.
7. Transportation and storage losses and costs could be reduced if food were grown near to where it was to be consumed.

Disadvantages:

1. Hydroponics is energy and materials intensive; that is, it uses more energy and material than conventional agriculture.
2. Hydroponics is monetarily expensive.
3. Skilled technical expertise is necessary to make hydroponics successful.

What Needs to be Done

1. Set up a Global Hydroponics Research Institute to research and develop hydroponic systems and to collect, correlate, and disseminate hydroponics related information.
2. Develop and mass produce wide-scale hydroponics for home, office, etc.
3. Develop roof-top hydroponics units for grocery stores, highrise buildings, etc.
4. Develop educational materials for hydroponics utilization.

Insects

Insects are humanity's greatest competitors for food. There are more insects than any other form of animal life: 80% of all animal species are insects. There is an incredible variety in the size, shape, and color of insects—from small beetles able to crawl through the eye of a needle, to the tropical "walking sticks" over a foot long. Only a few insects are injurious either directly (physically) or indirectly (economically) to humanity. In North America there are about 600 harmful species which result in an annual 10-20% loss of all crops and livestock.[1] Modern agriculture seeks to control injurious insects mainly through dangerous insecticides which disrupt the ecological balance of other forms of life (see Pesticide section). Given present economic accounting perspectives, chemicals are the "cheapest" method of insect control but they are also the least specific in that they do not just kill harmful insects but all insects as well as other life.

Insects have been used productively by humanity since antiquity. Silk from the silkworm, honey and wax from the bee, and the bodies of insects have been used for pigments, fish bait,

". . . the locusts went up over all the land of Egypt . . . so that the land was darkened; and they did eat every herb of the land, and all the fruit of the trees, and there remained not any green thing in the trees, or in the herbs of the field, through all the land of Egypt."
—*Exodus, 10:14–15*

Locusts are 46.2% protein.

bird food, and even food in the diets of some people. Insects can be used as fertilizer, animal feed, pet food, or human food. Several insects were considered delicacies in classical times in Europe, and a number are still eaten with pleasure in China, Africa, and Australia today.[2] The major way in which insects contribute to humanity is by pollinating our crops. At least fifty agricultural crops depend on insects for pollination, or yield much more abundant crops when insects are present.[3] They also destroy weeds and other injurious insects, improve the physical condition of the soil, and some are important in scientific endeavors. Humanity is, in fact, dependent upon insects for its survival. Aside from the use of termites in Australia, Africa, and America, caterpillars in Africa, silkworms in China and Japan, and locusts in Africa and America, various types of lice, grubs, moths, water beetles, grasshoppers, dragon flies, bees, and ants have been used or consumed ubiquitously throughout history and to the present. Insects for human consumption can even be purchased in the marketplace in some areas of the world. They are raised commercially for this purpose.[3] Many crops are increased through the eating of the insects which prey on the crops. For example, in Thailand, peasants eat the beetles and caterpillars which damage coconut and sugar palms and coffee plants. In this way not only is crop productivity increased but the peasants have an increased supply of protein from the insects. One hundred thirteen thousand to 340,000 metric tons of animal protein in the form of honey bees are destroyed each fall by apiarists in the colder regions of the United States and Canada. In the spring, new bee colonies are purchased from the south. This is done because if the bees were allowed to survive they would consume most or all of the honey they produced.[4] Also, more than seventy pounds of high protein pollen can be harvested from a single beehive each year. With over 50 million beehives in the world, 1.6 million metric tons of pollen can be harvested annually. Termites could be used to recycle the wood and paper wastes that are today burned or buried. Working under controlled conditions the termites could dispose of this waste while simultaneously producing high quality proteins, lipids, vitamins, and minerals. The housefly (63% protein) could be used in advanced waste treatment processes that could produce food as a by-product.[3] Another system for sewage waste disposal is lagoon disposal. This method is advantageous for small and larger towns where standard systems have become overloaded. Properly engineered lagoon systems will convert 100% of the waste materials into plants and animals. The harvest from such a lagoon has twice the protein content of the animal feed, alfalfa meal.[3]

Given humanity's long standing appreciation and utilization of insect food (i.e., honey), and the avowed taste of fried insects (recalling shrimp), our aversion to eating insects is less than logical. There is no technological, ecological, or health reason why certain types of insects could not be raised on a mass production scale in closed, automated,

---

"The flavor of sauteed silkworms makes you think of cashew nuts."

—Joseph Alsop

"insectary" production facilities. To date, the only large insect colonies that have been raised have been for use in entomological research laboratories, and for biological control of crop pests. At the U.S.D.A. screwworm laboratory in Texas, approximately 190 million flies (13.6 tons) are produced each week. This is about 8.6 tons of protein per week.[4] About one hundred of these production facilities would supply everyone in the U.S. with over 60 grams of protein per day. One hundred grams (3.5 ounces) of fried termites contain 561 calories, placing them among the richest of foods, superior to other animal foods and approaching the value of ground nuts (peanuts).

Insects as Food[5]

Food stuff	Moisture	Fat	Protein	Ash	Calories/ 100 gm
Fried Termites	13%	36.2%	45.6%	5%	561
Meat	75.2	6.6	16.9	1.3	127
Dried Salt Fish	32.4	3.1	43.7	20.8	203
Smoked Caterpillars	15.7	13.7	38	40	268
Silkworm Pupae	60.7	14.2	23.1	—	207
Fresh Locust	10.5	9.6	46.2	—	—
Dried Locust	—	20	75	—	—
House Fly	3.9	15.5	63.1	5.3	225
Dry Night Crawler	—	—	72	—	—

Advantages:

1. Insects are plentiful, hardy, and grow and breed quickly; large yields in short time spans with minimum upkeep are possible. One female aphid could produce in one season 1,560 sextillion offspring, the weight of which would be more than the entire human population of the Earth.[3]

2. High nutritive content; certain insects are high in protein and calories which makes them ideal as a human food supplement or as a directly consumed food item by animals such as pets or livestock, thereby freeing vast quantities of grains fed to animals which could be fed to humans.
3. Many areas of the world that are protein deficient are in the tropics, where insect fauna is very rich.
4. Numerous insects are cleaner than many of the animals that are regularly consumed by humans.

Disadvantages:

1. There are some cultural biases towards the direct consumption of insects by humans.
2. The economic feasibility of insect mass production has not yet been demonstrated.

What Needs to be Done

1. Set up a Global Insect Research Institute to research and develop insect food/feed systems and to collect, correlate, and disseminate insect related information.
2. Develop large and small scale automated insect production facilities for animal feed.
3. Research which insect species are ideally suited to mass production.
4. Develop processing facilities for the 100–225 tons of bees disposed of each year in North America.
5. Develop termite and other insect production systems that feed off sewage.
6. Develop and disseminate educational materials about insects and their utilization.

Table 1. The Insect Orders.[4]

	Order Name	Common Name	No. World Species	No. Species North America
APTERYGOTA Primitive, Wingless	Thysanura	Silverfish	350	20
	Diplura	Japygids	400	30
	Protura	Proturans	100	30
	Collembola	Springtails	2,000	325
PTERYGOTA Winged and Secondarily Wingless — **EXOPTERYGOTA** Simple Metamorphosis	Orthoptera	Grasshoppers	22,000	1,100
	Dermaptera	Earwigs	1,100	20
	Embioptera	Webspinners	150	10
	Plecoptera	Stoneflies	1,500	350
	Ephemeroptera	Mayflies	1,500	550
	Odonata	Dragonflies	5,000	425
	Isoptera	Termites	1,700	45
	Psocoptera	Booklice	1,100	150
	Zoraptera	Zorapterans	19	2
	Mallophaga	Bird Lice	2,600	320
	Anoplura	Sucking Lice	250	65
	Thysanoptera	Thrips	3,000	625
	Hemiptera	Bugs, Aphids	55,000	8,750
ENDOPTERYGOTA Complete Metamorphosis	Neuroptera	Lacewings	4,700	350
	Mecoptera	Scorpionflies	350	70
	Trichoptera	Caddisflies	4,500	950
	Lepidoptera	Butterflies	200,000	10,500
	Diptera	Flies	85,000	16,700
	Siphonaptera	Fleas	1,100	250
	Hymenoptera	Bees, Ants, Wasps	105,000	14,600
	Coleoptera	Beetles	277,000	27,000
	Strepsiptera	Strepsipterans	300	100

Source: Adapted from D. J. Borror and D. W. DeLong, *An Introduction to the Study of Insects* (Holt, Rinehart and Winston, 1971).

Leaf Protein

Leaf protein refers to protein that has been extracted from fresh green leaves. In one method developed in England, the leaves are passed through a pulper, the juice drained, and then heated to 70–80° C. causing the leaf protein to coagulate which is then separated in a filter press. What remains is a dark green cheese-like protein which can be used directly as a food, stored in a refrigerator, or dried and ground into a powder. It will then keep indefinitely if put in airtight containers to protect it from oxygen. Another method involves harvesting a crop such as alfalfa and putting the crop into a machine that separates a juice from the fiber. This juice is then spray-dried to form a green powder containing 35% protein.[1]

About 80% of a leaf is water and up to 25% of the dry matter consists of protein. In addition, leaf protein is a rich source of both vitamins and minerals, and the by-product of the extraction is a protein rich (16%) fibrous residue that is a viable cattle fodder. Current leaf protein extraction facilities obtain a yield of 30 kg (66 lb.) of protein per ton of foliage. These facilities can process three tons of leaves each hour. With crops grown for the purpose of protein extraction (see chart for comparative yields per acre) yields can be as high as 1400 lb./acre (1,590 kg/ha) in temperate climates or 1.2 tons/acre (3,060 kg/ha) in the tropics.[3] In addition to land crops there are many water plants which can be used. There are an estimated 21 million

Green leaves are the largest producers of protein in the world.

> *There was twice the protein in the alfalfa used as hay in the U.S. in 1974 as was produced in the 12.5 million metric tons of soybean meal used domestically that year.[2]*

tons of leaf waste in the U.S. alone in the form of carrot and beet tops, bean plants, and potato vines.[4] From this, 620,000 metric tons of protein could be extracted using the above technique (8.5 grams per day per person in the U.S.). There are currently pilot leaf protein plants in the U.S., France, Hungary, and England. Research for a low cost on-the-farm type leaf protein recovery system is underway.

Typical Protein Yields under Good Management

	Yield per Acre, dry wt	Protein
Alfalfa	4.0 tons	1500 lbs
Grass	1.2 tons	600
Soybeans	20 bu	450
Peanuts	1300 lbs	350
Maize	55 bu	280
Wheat	35 bu	220
Hogs (maize and alfalfa meal)	800 lbs	160
Milk (grass, silage, alfalfa)	3000 lbs	120
Beef (grass, maize)	300 lbs	50

History:

1773 France: what we now call protein first extracted from leaves by chemist Rouelle

1941 England: first large scale extraction of protein from leaves

1968 England: commercial-scale leaf protein extraction plant built and operated

1975 India: first large scale comparative feeding trial of leaf protein

Advantages:

1. Leaf protein is biologically very efficient; the green leaf is the most efficient biological system for synthesizing protein. A field of green grass during its period of most rapid growth in warm and wet weather synthesizes protein faster than any other system in Nature.
2. Leaf protein as a protein supplement is very inexpensive; in India it costs $1/5$ as much as soybeans, $1/17$ as much as milk or meat.[1]
3. Leaf protein will make available to humanity vast new stores of protein in the form of 300,000 green plants that have heretofore never been treated as edible.
4. Leaf protein, because green plants grow everywhere, is ideally suited for allowing every locality to be self-sufficient in protein. Undernourished communities in remote tropical areas, which constitute some of the world's most malnourished spots, could extract from their own environment the protein they now go without.
5. Machinery for protein extraction from leaves is currently available.

Disadvantages:

1. Straight leaf protein is not palatable or acceptable as food to most people.
2. Exact cost of leaf protein production for use as a human food is unknown, as no one has produced it on a continuous basis.

What Needs to be Done

1. Set up a Global Leaf Protein Research Institute to research and develop leaf protein food systems and to collect, correlate, and disseminate leaf protein related information.
2. Develop, test, and mass produce large and small scale leaf protein production facilities.
3. Develop and disseminate educational materials about leaf protein use, production, etc.
4. Develop ways of processing leaf protein to increase its availability and acceptability.

Non-Photosynthetic Single Cell Protein

Non-photosynthetic single cell protein refers to the numerous varieties of one-celled organisms such as fungi, yeast, and bacteria which are currently being grown or which can be grown from petroleum and its byproducts, cellulose (such as waste paper, wood pulp, sawdust, and hay), waste manufacturing plant residues such as the sulphite liquors discharged by paper mills, urine, alcohol, or any starches, and which are used as a source of high quality protein for human or animal consumption. The raw material chosen for single cell protein (SCP) production depends largely on local availability. There is no single raw material or organism that will provide the ultimate SCP process.

Over 1.3 billion gallons of oil bilge are dumped into the world's oceans each year by oil tankers as they flush their holds.[5] Certain yeast and bacteria strains can convert this waste petroleum into high quality protein. It has also been estimated that nearly 20 × 10⁶ tons of protein could be produced from the paraffins found in the present annual world production of crude petroleum.[7, 8]

A 1,000-pound steer produces 1 pound of protein in 24 hours. 1,000 pounds of soybeans produce 92 pounds of protein in 24 hours. 1,000 pounds of single-cell organisms produce 1,000 pounds of protein in 24 hours.

Single cell proteins have been in the human diet since antiquity. Any fermented food will contain significant quantities of cellular organism. Yogurt, cheese, and bread yeast are primary examples. Charles Darwin even reported that the staple food of the natives of Tierra del Fuego was a green fungus which grew abundantly in that environment.[1] Yeast has a protein content of 50% as well as being rich in vitamins and enzymes. From the waste liquor from each ton of beech pulp produced, 200–240 pounds of yeast can be grown.[2] There exist a number of large SCP plants in operation for animal feed production. In Sweden, a large factory that produces powdered mashed potatoes and french fries has had its starchy waste water processed into edible protein through the symbiotic activity of two yeasts.[3] In Russia, a wood pulp fed yeast industry produces an estimated 900,000 metric tons per year. A "yeast factory" with ten large sized fermenting tanks could furnish ten tons of yeast per day on a continuous basis. It would be necessary to kill 80 pigs a day or 30,000 a year to provide the same amount of protein.[4] In another design, all the world's protein could be continuously provided by a SCP plant occupying an area equivalent to about fifteen square kilometers (six sq. miles) of the Earth's surface.[5,6]

Bacteria, cultivated in urine, was pursued as a food source for astronauts. Large cultures of the bacteria Hydrogenomanas entropha

Average Composition of Single-cell Proteins

	Bacteria %	Yeast %	Mold mycelium %	Lean beef %
Water	75	75	80	67
Protein	14	12	8	19
Fat	3	3	2	13
Ash and cellulose	8	10	10	1
Protein in 1 lb. of dry matter				
In ounces	9	7.5	6.5	9.5

Time for One Doubling in Mass

Bacteria	½–1 hour
Yeast	1–2 hours
Single cell algae	12 hours
Grass and some plants	1–2 weeks
Chickens	2–4 weeks
Cattle	1–2 months
People (babies)	3–6 months

(consisting of 70% protein) would take the urea, the result of human protein metabolism, and convert it back into protein.

History

1864	France: Pasteur discovers bacteria
1916	World War I, Germany planned large scale production of yeast from molasses, but molasses supply failed and the newly-built yeast plants were shut down
1930	League of Nations proposes yeast as a means of feeding the malnourished

1940's	Germans use tortula yeast as food supplement
1967	France: Single cell protein pilot production plant capable of producing 225 tons of single cell protein/year from petroleum waste
1967	U.S.S.R.: 10,000 tons of single cell protein produced from petroleum for use as cattle feed
1978	Singapore: Single cell protein produced from pig wastes

Advantages:

1. Single cell protein is a vast untapped source of protein.
2. Single cell protein is a highly efficient source of protein, e.g., it is very low on the food chain. Yeast and fungi are superior to animals in protein production. Yeasts can do in a few hours and in a more concentrated way what it takes plants and animals an entire growing season to accomplish.
3. Single cell protein can be produced from wastes.
4. Single cell protein can be produced quickly.
5. Single cell protein is not dependent on the weather; yields can be had year-round.
6. There is no need for pesticides or other chemical toxins.
7. Single cell protein production process is not limited to surface land; tanks are used.
8. Single cell protein production makes few demands on skilled labor.
9. There are few waste disposal problems because nearly everything is used.

Disadvantages:

1. Single cell protein grown on waste petroleum and its by-products have been limited by problems of carcinogenic contamination in many of the more economically desirable processes.
2. The protein nutritional quality of SCP is below that of animal proteins, with particular deficiencies in the sulfur amino acids.
3. There might be a problem of human intolerance to high concentrations of SCP which do not exist in animals. Yeast contains high concentrations of RNA that presents a digestability problem to some people.
4. Economically, SCP processes are limited by the high cost of cell harvesting.

Photosynthetic Single Cell Protein (Algae)

"Photosynthetic single cell protein (algae) is comprised of the cells of microscopic plants which grow in suspension in shallow, illuminated ponds. The algae feeds on carbonates, nitrates, and phosphates dissolved in water. Depending on the type of algae, the cells can be separated from the growth medium by screening, filtration, or coagulation either by flotation, sedimentation, or centrifugation. Separated algae form a dark green slurry or paste containing 5–15% solids which may be consumed directly by animals, used for fertilizer, or preserved by freezing or dehydration. When a 10–15% solids paste is heat dried on a smooth, non-adhering surface, fragile green flakes are obtained; when sun dried, coarse chips are produced. Either flakes or chips can be ground to a very fine green flour. Finely ground dry algae can be stored indefinitely at a moisture content below 7%. Depending on the type of algae, the latitude, and the temperature, potential yields of crude protein of 10–20 metric tons dry weight per hectare per year may be expected. This is 10 to 20 times those attainable with soybeans."[1]

Plankton, which often covers hundreds of square miles of ocean area is about 25–30% high quality protein dry weight.[2] According to one estimate, a one-acre algae tank could produce enough protein, vitamins, and minerals to take care of 300–400 people.[3] Based on the lower figure, it would take 5.38×10^6 hectares to provide these needs for all of humanity— about 2.6% of the arable land in the U.S., or about .35% of the world's arable land.

Another use of algae is as feed for livestock. Less than 5.5 million hectares of algae culture could supply 100% of the feed and forage requirements of the 1974 U.S. livestock.[4] There are a number of techniques currently in use that utilize algae in small scale man-made ecosystems for waste recycling and food production. In these multi-stage systems, algae feed on sewage that is pumped into their tanks. The algae is then siphoned off into another tank that contains trays housing oysters. The oysters feed on the algae and their waste products are consumed at the bottom of the oyster tank by worms that are eventually sold for bait. The algae-cleaned water is purified once again by passing over beds of filtering seaweed before it is released. The seaweed can also be sold and used for a variety of purposes. Another technique has the sewage fed algae used as cattle feed and the resulting purified water used for irrigation.

Protein Percentage of Algae

Algae	% Protein
Spirulina	68
Chlorella	40–60
Scendesmus	40–60
Conyaulax Polydedra (Red Tide)	25–30

Protein Production Per Acre Per Year in Kilograms

Chlorella	6363
Peanuts	191
Beans	168
Peas	160
Wheat	122
Rye	118
Oats	105
Milk	41
Meat	25

History

Prehistoric to Present	Some communities in Chad consume algae by harvesting and then forming into pancakes to dry in the Sun
1500's	Mexico: Aztecs consumed algae that grew in lakes
1870's	Jules Verne suggests using algae for human food
1961	Mitsuda, Japan: Chlorella (algae) is sold to Japan as an additive to yogurt, ice-cream, and related products
1966	Czechoslovakia: Lab set up to produce algae as a supplemental supply for animal feedstuff
1972	Mexico: One-ton-per-day plant to produce algae for human food opened
1978	Singapore: Algae ponds for pig and poultry feed

Advantages:

1. Algae is a vast untapped source of protein. Spirulina, a type of blue-green algae that grows in ponds, contains between 60–68% protein, six times as much as wheat and three times as much as beef.
2. Algae is a highly efficient source of protein; it is very low on the food chain.
3. Algae can be produced quickly.
4. Algae can be grown year-round.
5. There is no need for pesticides or other chemical toxins.

Disadvantages:

1. Like most vegetable proteins, green algae is deficient in certain amino acids (cystein and methiomine).
2. Harvesting and processing of algae is expensive.
3. Because algae is so efficient in converting air, water, and sunlight into organic compounds it is also very efficient in concentrating pollutants.
4. Algae has poor keeping qualities, even after processing.

What Needs to be Done

1. Set up a Global Single-Cell Protein Research Institute to research and develop Single-Cell Protein systems and to collect, correlate, and disseminate Single-Cell Protein related information.

2. Develop, test, and mass produce large and small scale SCP production facilities.
3. Develop new processing techniques for algae; to produce spun algal protein, etc.
4. Develop algae preservation techniques of solar dehydration, canning, freeze-drying, etc.
5. Develop new methods of increasing productivity.
6. Prototype SCP production systems that process mill and other industrial, commercial, and residential waste.

Sprouting

Sprouting refers to the process of eating seeds a few days after they have sprouted a shoot. This is in contradistinction to eating the seed just as it is before it sprouts (such as sunflower or pumpkin seeds) or long after it sprouts—when it has fully grown and one eats the fruit of that seed (tomatoes, fruits, etc.). Seeds are highly concentrated sources of food; within each seed are packaged all the nutrients which the emerging embryo seed needs to begin growing. It is the best food value that a plant has to offer. Proportionally, protein is higher in the seed than in any other part or stage of growth of the plant, and vitamins, minerals, oils, and carbohydrates are also in plentiful supply. Virtually any type of seed can be sprouted; each has its own unique flavor and texture. Sprouting is done by washing seeds in water, then soaking them overnight and keeping them moist for a few days until the sprout portion is long enough to suit the individual's taste.

History:

Chinese and Japanese have used sprouts for thousands of years.

Advantages:

1. Seeds store well; whole seeds do not have to be frozen or preserved to prevent spoilage.
2. Seeds are relatively inexpensive; each serving costs less than a penny.
3. Seeds are highly concentrated; a cupboard is large enough to store all the seeds a family would need for months. Eight pounds of sprouts result from every pound of seeds.
4. Seeds and sprouts are highly nutritious.
5. Sprouting uses very little energy; there is no need to plow, cultivate, harvest, heat or process, grind into a flour, nor cook. Only moisture is needed.
6. Seeds, when they sprout, increase in nutritional value. Vitamins greatly increase when the sprout begins to grow.
7. Sprouting transforms seeds previously used mainly as cattle feed into high-quality food for people.
8. Sprouting is mainly suited for local, decentralized production but can be produced in large quantities on a farm as well.

Disadvantages:

1. Sprouts are not palatable to many people.

What Needs to be Done

1. Set up a Global Sprout Research Institute to research and develop sprout systems and to collect, correlate, and disseminate sprouting related information.
2. Develop, test, and mass produce large and small scale foolproof sprouting production kits and facilities.
3. Develop and disseminate educational materials about sprouts and their use, production, etc.

Synthetic Nutriments

Synthetic nutriments refer to food products that are manufactured in factories rather than grown "on the farm." These nutriments have been primarily used as food additives, not as a replacement for conventional foods. Synthetic fats, carbohydrates, proteins, alcohol, vitamins, and flavorings have all been developed and used, and in the case of the last two items, are in actual widespread use.

Germany developed and widely used a synthetic fat for human consumption during both World Wars. Several manufacturing processes were developed for synthesizing fatty acids from carbon dioxide derived from petroleum. The least expensive process produced a product for about 20¢ per kg. Today, even complex proteins can be produced. The only "synthetic" protein that has found its way into the human diet to date has been the meat substitutes currently in wide use in institutional food services and also available in North American grocery stores. These products use mostly soybeans as their basic raw material. The beans are dehulled, pressed, and turned into flakes, then their oil is removed and they are ground into a flour that is more than 50% protein. Further processing

results in a powder that is 90% protein which is then mixed with an alkaline liquid, fed under high pressure into a "spinning" machine, and spun into threads of protein. These threads are then stretched, bound, flavored, colored, cut, cooked, and shaped into the final product.[1] Even with this tremendous amount of processing, these meat substitutes are less expensive than their four-legged feed-lot analogues.

There are also processes for manufacturing proteins from "scratch," that is, without starting with soybeans but with more basic compounds. These proteins are manufactured either through a step by step procedure, as in the case of the amino acids lysine, melonine, and tryptophan, or through a silica or spark gap technique. The former is a molecule building technique where the chemist starts with a basic compound and builds upon it. The second technique is one where gases are passed over hot silica, or run through a spark gap, to produce a number of simpler amino acids simultaneously. These techniques essentially duplicate, or try to duplicate, the vast amount of work done for humanity by the soybean/sun/soil/etc. combination and hence require a lot of energy.

The protein value of foods—most dramatically the cereals—can be improved through the addition of synthetic amino acids. These amino acids can be produced by chemical synthesis or by fermentation. The amount of utilizable protein in wheat increases 66% with the increase of the amino acid lysine; cornmeal increases 70% with the addition of lysine and tryptophan; and rice increases 78% with lysine and threonine.

There are a number of relatively simple chemical reactions that yield useable sugars or starches as their products. Synthetic sugars

may be produced from formaldehyde from a gas works or petrochemical plant which has been treated with an alkaline or heated. These processes can produce glucose, fructose, galactose, ribose, and a number of other sugars. Starch has been synthesized in the laboratory through the use of non-organic starting material and organically produced enzymes.

Synthetic vitamins were the first synthetic food components to be successfully marketed. There are now at least ten vitamins that are produced by chemical synthesis—Vitamins A, C, E, K, thiamine, riboflavin, niacin, pyridoxine, flocin, choline, and pantothenate.

History

1914	Germany uses synthetic fat
1932	Haworth synthesizes Vitamin C
1935	Kuhn and Karrer synthesize Vitamin B_2
1936	Williams synthesizes Vitamin B_1
1939	Kuhn, et al. synthesize Vitamin B_6
1940	Folkers synthesizes pantothenic acid
1940's	Germany uses synthetic fat
1947	Isler synthesizes Vitamin A
1949	Boyer introduces first vegetable-protein fiber
1950	Miller produces first amino acids by electrical discharge through gas of methane, hydrogen, water vapor, and ammonia[2]

Advantages:

1. Protein supply could be expanded.
2. Synthetic proteins (textured vegetable protein) are free of cholesterol and low in saturated fats.
3. Synthetic proteins are less expensive than real meat. Institutional administrators find that they can save as much as 50% in costs by using meat substitutes that are half as expensive and contain more protein per pound than real meat.[3]

Disadvantages:

1. Synthetic manufacture of nutriments from scratch is very expensive.
2. Yields from scratch are not very high.
3. Taste and texture are not yet perfectly compatible with human consumption.
4. Totally synthetic nutriments are a long-range undertaking; there are no currently operating chemical synthesis plants.

What Needs to be Done

1. Set up a Global Synthetic Nutriments Research Institute to research and develop synthetic nutriment systems and to collect, correlate, and disseminate synthetic nutriments related information.
2. Develop, test, and mass produce large and small scale synthetic nutriments production facilities.

Decentralized Food Production/Home Gardens and Urban Self-Sufficiency

Decentralized food production refers to the growing of food by individuals, families, or communities—primarily for their own use—in backyard home-gardens in the suburbs and rural areas as well as in urban areas on vacant lots and roofs. In a recent Gallup survey, it was found that more than half—nearly 36 million—of American households in 1976 had their own backyard gardens. Another 30 million Americans revealed that they would garden if they had a place to do it. Ten percent of the gardens were community gardens—that is, they were on public land or property not owned by the gardener. Pennsylvania alone had over 300,000 gardens on public land. The home garden is gaining in popularity because many people are seeing it as a viable way to save money and eat good food. With about $10 worth of seeds, a home gardener can produce about $250 worth of vegetables. If all the gardens in the United States produced that much, it would amount to $9 billion worth of food. Given an average production of 100 pounds of food, U.S. home

gardens produced 1.6 million metric tons of food in 1976. Assuming a similar or smaller proportion of people in the world had home gardens, the world production would be close to 30 million metric tons. A relatively small home garden—10 feet by 16 feet—has the potential of supplying an individual with a year's supply of vegetables and soft fruits by using the previously described "biodynamic French intensive method." Using this production technique on a world-wide basis would nearly quadruple home garden production. Food production in the urban environment holds great promise for increasing the availability of nutritious foodstuffs in the inner city and amongst the urban poor. It may even be possible for many cities and/or neighborhoods to be self-sufficient in many foods. Just the Bronx in New York City has over 200 hectares of empty, devastated land that could be reclaimed for urban agriculture.[1] China currently produces a lot of her vegetables in urban or near-urban environments. Most consumers in Chinese cities are supplied fresh fruits and vegetables that come from nearby areas.[2] China has urban gardens in parks, roadway medians, backyards, and behind factories. There are garden plots next to apartment complexes and even division and regional army units grow some of their own food.

Besides vacant lots, backyards, and abandoned or rundown parts of cities (such as parts of the Bronx) that could be used to grow food crops, there is the additional possibility of cultivating rooftops. There are hundreds of hectares of unused flat rooftops in most urban environments that could add to the amount of space available for cultivation. Rooftop gardening can be done in containers, cold frames, in greenhouses, or hydroponically. Major problems concern the lack of easy access to many rooftops and the increased snow loads that would accrue to a building through drifting if the rooftop was only partially covered with a structure such as a greenhouse. Covering the entire roof would avoid this problem.

Advantages:

1. Home gardens produce food at lower cost.
2. The nutritional quality of fresh food is higher than most store-bought food.
3. Home gardens can provide the city dweller with a link to nature.
4. Home gardening is a constructive recreational activity for the individual or the whole family.
5. Home gardens provide a valuable use for organic household wastes.
6. Home food production reduces the need for fuel for processing, packaging, retailing, and transporting farm-grown commodities.
7. Home gardens require less pesticides.
8. Home gardens cut down on food waste in that people who would not buy a blemished tomato will eat one out of their own garden.

Disadvantages:

1. Home gardening is time-consuming.
2. Home gardens use space that could possibly be used for other purposes.

What Needs to be Done

1. Establish local Information clearinghouses for locally appropriate home gardening techniques, seeds, etc., and interlink them with regional and global information networks for home gardens.
2. Make available facilities to local communities for processing—canning, freezing, etc—as well as marketing local gardening produce.
3. Offer courses in gardening, food self-sufficiency, food preservation, etc. in school systems—grade schools, high schools, colleges, and adult education courses.
4. Unilaterally declare vacant lots community garden property.
5. Research at local colleges which home garden plants grow best, when to plant, harvest, etc. in their unique locale.
6. Make land available by commerce and industry for its employees for vegetable gardens.
7. Set aside land for gardens at apartment complexes, subdivisions, and urban redevelopment projects.
8. Develop and test lightweight rooftop gardens.
9. Develop and test efficient ways of year-round storing of the home gardens' summer produce.
10. Establish a Decentralized Food Production Research Institute to research and develop small scale food systems. (Research needs to be devoted to the home garden by the agriculture research community—instead of just researching large-scale farming for agribusiness.)
11. Develop window and balcony gardens for urban dwellers.

New Foods

As pointed out in Section One, most of the world's population lives on only a few staple crops. Also, 90% of the world's animal protein comes from six species: cattle, sheep, goats, chickens, hogs, and fish. Relying on a small number of food sources is dangerous because "monocultures are extremely vulnerable to catastrophic failure brought about by disease or variations in climate."[1] As pointed out in the Animal Husbandry and Fish sections, there are many other types of animals and fish than those currently being exploited that could be. There are also many other crops than those mentioned above—new foods—that could be developed, especially in and for the poorer tropics that could provide food, forage, raw materials, and protection from over-reliance on too few crops.

Channel millet, a cereal plant from the Australian desert, can grow with just one watering and could be grown in other tropical deserts; quinua, a grain rich in protein, was the staple of the Incas before the Spanish conquest;

"The greatest service that can be rendered any country is to add a useful plant to its culture."

—Thomas Jefferson

another plant rich in protein is the "soybean of the tropics," the winged bean. This incredible nitrogen-fixing plant is 34–39% protein and 17–20% polyunsaturated fat. The entire plant can be used as livestock feed.[2] The Amaranthus, a South American plant, is rich in protein (especially the essential amino acid lysine). Amaranthus can be milled and the grain used for pancakes, gruel, or a drink and its high protein leaves can be eaten as a kind of spinach.[3]

The babassu palm, which grows wild over millions of hectares in the Amazon basin, yields kernels that taste, smell, and look like coconut meat, but contain more oil. After the oil has been extracted, the remains can be fed to animals while the hard shells can be used for fuel.[3]

The tarwi, from the Andes region of South America, is richer in protein than the soybean and groundnut; is easy to plant; is frost, drought, and pest tolerant; and can be cultivated in a wide range of soils.[2]

The marama bean, from semi-desert regions of Southern Africa, is also the nutritional rival of the soybean and groundnut.[2]

The opuntia cactus—commonly called the prickly pear—can produce over 4 tons of nutritious fruit per hectare when cultivated. This can be accomplished on soils unfit for conventional farming.[4]

Forage crops include the leguminous tree tamarugo that grows in the northern Chilean desert, and salt-brush; both plants can tolerate high salinity. Two crops can even be grown in salt water—the grain zostera marina and the silt grass Paspalum vaginatum. Recent work on barley has also developed strains that can be irrigated with sea water.

"The 1970 oilseed production contained on the order of 55 million tons of protein—enough to meet, several times over, the total protein requirements of the world."[3]

There are also fruits, fiber, oil, wax, and rubber plants that could be developed and utilized. For example, the jojoba plant, capable of thriving in desert-like conditions, produces an odorless liquid wax that is almost identical chemically to the oil of the near extinct sperm whale. Several hundred hectares of jojoba plants are currently under cultivation in the U.S. Southwest. Another desert plant—the guayule bush which is nearly one-fourth rubber and can be harvested mechanically—holds promise of relieving natural rubber shortages.[5] One successful *newly* developed plant is triticale, a synthetic species that was derived from the cross of wheat and rye. Other possibilities include crosses of wheat and barley and barley and rye.

Besides these relatively new plants—either "brand new" in the case of triticale or new in the sense of recently discovered and re-evaluated—that could be more widely cultivated, there are new uses for some of the plants that are currently in widespread use. One recent development has enabled the cotton seed to become a source of low-cost protein for human consumption. The new process removes a substance in the cottonseed which heretofore made it indigestable for one-stomach animals. The resulting cottonseed flour is 60–70% protein, bland in taste, can be added to everything from hamburger, bakery products, and soft drinks and costs about 20¢ a pound to produce.[6]

Another similar development is the harvesting of mature okra seeds instead of the immature pods. Okra is traditionally eaten like string beans—as immature green pods—but if the okra pod is allowed to mature its seeds grow to about soybean size and can then be dried, pressed for oil, or ground into flour that is 20% high quality protein. Okra protein contains the valuable amino acid lysine that corn and wheat are deficient in so when okra flour is mixed with either of these, the resulting protein is much more nutritious. Okra, native to West Africa where it is known as gumbo, grows on marginal land and in low rainfall regions where other high protein crops do not fare as well. Grown in many parts of Africa, India, Malaysia, the Philippines, Central America, and the Middle East, okra yields about the same per hectare as do soybeans, requires less fertilizer, and bears fruit continuously as long as there is no killing frost.

Another high protein food product that could be produced (or more widely produced) from an already existing crop that is in widespread cultivation is tofu—a cheese-like food made from soybeans. Tofu is already in widespread use in the East: there are as many or more tofu shops per person in Japan and China as there are bakeries in the U.S.[7] Tofu is often used in the East as meat, eggs, and dairy products are used in the West. There are a variety of tofu preparations, each sharing an uncommonly high complete protein content (from 8 to 53% protein by weight), a high degree of digestability, low calorie and cholesterol count, high amount of minerals and vitamins, easy use, and relatively low expense.[7]

Other "new foods" or improved foods could be developed from old plants through genetic engineering; that is, by manipulating the plant stock on the genetic level rather than on the plant level as plant breeding and hybridization do. Genetic engineering is becoming more of a possibility with each advancement in biology. The possibilities are enormous. For instance, by increasing the protein content of corn by 1%, we would reduce the need for two million tons of soybean meal in the United States for animal feed.[8] The near total re-design of food crops might be undertaken. One such re-design envisions "an ideal new crop species [that] would produce the edible portion of the plant with a photosynthetic efficiency two or three times higher than that of any existing food grain; it would fix its own nitrogen, preferably in the leaves rather than in the roots; protein in the edible portion would have the balance of amino acids needed by human beings, and the plant would be water saving . . . look and taste like a present-day cereal and be capable of being made into bread or pasta or chapati."[9]

Advantages:

1. The more crops humanity gets its food from, the safer we will be from a catastrophic failure of any one crop due to climate change or plant disease.
2. New plants (referring to new, non-traditional plants) are often heartier than hybrids.
3. New plants could be more ideally suited to certain developing areas than imported crops from the developed world.

Disadvantages:

1. People are unfamiliar with growing, processing, and eating new foods.
2. The new taste of new foods could be deterrant to their widespread adoption.

What Needs to be Done

1. Establishment of a Global New Foods Research Institute to research and develop new food systems and to collect and disseminate new foods related information.
2. Undertake a comprehensive inventory of plants suitable for cultivation as food, forage, or raw material crops.
3. Set up pilot programs around the world for growing, processing, and utilizing new foods.
4. Establish educational programs describing the techniques for utilizing new foods.
5. Develop and build okra seed processing plants.
6. Grow channel millet and other new crops wherever appropriate in the world.
7. Genetically improve cereals, potatoes, legumes, cassava, sweet potato, fruits, and vegetables so that these crops are more nutritious.

Alternative Animal Feed

Freeing grains from animal consumption so that they are available for human consumption is an important strategy for feeding the people of the world. Animals can eat many things people cannot. A comprehensive and humane utilization of foodstuffs would preclude feeding human food to animals when humans are hungry. The following are alternative food sources for animals.

1. Animal Feed from Animal Waste

Cattle waste has a high protein content in the form of undigested plant protein, protein from the body of the animal discarded in the metabolic process, and single cell protein from micro-organisms involved in the digestion process. There is a recent development whereby this protein is preserved and recycled as cattle feed. In this process animal wastes are gathered before they begin decomposition, processed through a biochemical system similar to a sugar refinery operation that extracts and improves nutrient materials and then treats these materials with chemicals and pasteurization to make them into sanitary feed for animals. There is about 600 million tons of cattle manure produced each year in feedlots in the U.S. alone; the protein from this equals the protein contained in the total U.S. yearly soybean crop.[1] Because the U.S. grows 75% of the world's soybeans and then proceeds to feed them to livestock while many humans in developing countries cannot afford to purchase them, this savings of protein is of no little significance. There is presently one full scale plant operating in Colorado that processes

Protein Content of Some Animal Wastes[2]

Dried poultry manure	10.6 to 12.9%
Dried poultry house litter	12.9 to 21.9%
Cattle	12.0 to 23.2%
Sheep	12.4 to 18.3%
Pigs	8.2 to 12.6%

about 200,000 pounds of raw manure per day from over 10,000 head of cattle. The only residues are clean water vapor and ash; everything else is used either as silage, feed supplement, or fertilizer. Other advantages include odor, dust, and water discharge elimination or reduction, cost reduction for feed ($70/ton for 30% protein content vs. $206/ton for 44% protein soybean meal) and increased sanitary conditions for the livestock in that their pens are continuously cleaned. Disadvantages include high capital cost ($550,000 for 10,000 cattle) and energy intensiveness. Recycled animal waste is currently used in the United States, Canada, and the United Kingdom.

2. Stakes into Steaks

A high pressure, high temperature hydrolysis process changes poplar wood, which is high in cellulose, into a form of feed that is easily digested by calves. This has the potential of turning the wood lot into cattle feed and releasing the human-digestible grains that cattle currently consume for human consumption.

3. Non-Protein Nitrogen

Ruminants have bacteria in their digestive systems that can synthesize protein from nitrogen. Currently, more than 1.5 million tons of urea—a commercial nitrogen fertilizer made from ammonia and carbon dioxide—are fed to animals as a protein substitute. Urea ranks second in the world, behind soybeans, as a source of nitrogen for feedstocks. Because humans do not have the ability to synthesize protein from nitrogen, feeding nitrogen directly to ruminant animals and the humanly-edible grain or soybeans to people would lead to more food for people.

4. Sludge

There are about five trillion tons of wet sewage sludge generated in the U.S. each year. Sludge is rich in carbohydrates and protein as well as the more undesired viruses, bacteria and parasites. By drying and irradiating sewage sludge, these microorganisms are killed and the sludge can be used as a feed supplement. Cattle are currently being fed irradiated dried sludge mixed with grain sorghum, urea, and small amounts of molasses and cottonseed meal to improve taste. Dried irradiated sludge is about half as expensive to produce as regular cattle feed supplement.[3]

5. Leucaena

The leucaena is a tropical legume that has the incredible potential for furnishing livestock forage, firewood, and fertilizer as well as improving the soil. Often regarded as a weed, the crop is highly palatable, digestible, and nutritious for cattle, water buffalo, and goats; is hardy, resistant to drought, grows rapidly, adapts easily to steep hillsides and marginal soils, provides excellent wood for use as firewood, charcoal, pulp, paper, and construction materials, fixes nitrogen, provides exceptionally high quality green manure with its foliage, and provides young pods and seeds which are even consumed by humans in Central America and Indonesia.[4] Leucaena is an excellent plant for reforestation efforts, erosion control and energy plantations.

6. Cement Dust

Cement dust, which is high in minerals, particularly calcium, is a by-product of the manufacture of portland cement. Some 33,000 tons are produced each year. Recent tests in the U.S. indicate a 30% increase in the rate of gain of weight in cattle fed cement dust as a feed supplement.[5]

7. Other Alternative Animal Feeds

Insects, single cell proteins, new food sources, and leaf protein, covered earlier in this section, are also suitable for animal feed.

Exotic Food Sources

There are many other food sources or production techniques. Some are on the drawing boards, some are actually in use, all will strike at least someone as pie-in-the-sky and all deserve more serious attention, research, and development. For lack of a better catch-all these sources and production techniques are called exotic. This term was chosen over the "unconventional" because most of the previously mentioned sources/production techniques in this section are unconventional. The following are even more unconventional than the unconventional, hence "exotic."

1. Chicken Feathers

The National Swedish Environment Protection Board is subsidizing the construction of a plant to process chicken feathers and eventually hoofs, bristles, and other hard-to-dispose-of animal waste from slaughterhouses and tanneries into protein. This first plant will produce 3,000 tons of protein from 8,000 tons of feathers.[1]

2. Space Farm

So-called because it was developed by NASA to feed astronauts in deep-space, the "space farm" is a machine that rotates plants—turns them upside down—so that gravity is partially nullified. A lot of a plant's energy is devoted to overcoming gravity; by lessening gravity the plant can now grow more quickly. The space farm rotates plants that are growing from a central cylinder so that they are facing downwards, towards the pull of gravity, half the time, and the rest of the time they are either on their way to this position, returning from it, or in the normal upright position. Water and nutrients flow from the central cylinder that the plants are attached to. The advantageous claims for this system include: plants grow 25% faster and produce four times the yield of a flat growing bed, photosynthesis and respiration are accelerated, the rotating plants absorb five times as much light, and space is conserved because of the concentration. NASA's growing machine was three feet on an edge and could continuously provide a three man crew with all their fresh vegetable requirements, 10% of their total calorie requirements, and all of their water soluble vitamins. Disadvantages include the fact that the cylinder uses electricity to rotate, a number of vegetables are not suited for rotation, and a special treated soil that will not fall out as the cylinder is rotated is needed.[2]

3. Snails

The Nigerian Institute for Oil Palm Research is developing small-scale snail farm prototypes for small rubber, cocoa, or palm tree farmers. With the proper balance of males and females it should be possible to produce 150 pounds of meat (or about $115 of cash income) yearly from snail farming in shaded enclosures under the canopy of mature palm trees.

4. Outer Space Agriculture

Because of the twenty-four-hour-per-day sunshine factor plus the possibility of concentrating carbon dioxide and water vapor, one study has estimated that "vegetables, cereals, poultry, ham, and dairy products for a North American population of 10,000 could be grown on a total area of about 450,000 square meters (111 acres) on an orbiting space colony."[3] Growing food in this way, it would be possible to produce all the food for 4 billion people on less than 18 million hectares (about 1.2% of Earth's arable land). The most obvious disadvantage of such an undertaking is the enormous transportation cost from the orbiting farm to the Earth and the fabrication of the space station.

5. Heating the Soil

Coupling power production with agriculture could increase agricultural productivity and reduce thermal pollution. Heating the soil with power plant waste water or geothermal power in pipes under the soil has been found to dramatically increase crop productivity. Corn silage growth increased 45%, tomatoes 50%, and soybeans 66% in one study. Besides utilizing waste heat, crop productivity could be increased still further by using the CO_2 discharge from coal, oil, or gas fired power plants to increase the concentration of this growth-encouraging ingredient.

6. Altering Taste

Food shortages often refer to shortages of food people like to eat, not actual shortage in humanly nutritious foodstuffs. People run out of food they like or are willing to eat long before all the food in a given environment is totally gone. World food supply could possibly be increased through the increased understanding of the mechanisms and psychology of taste. Taste may affect the efficiency of the individual's food utilization by triggering the release of digestive reactors and thereby preparing the digestive system for the food it is about to receive. By altering our or our animals' taste receptors we could possibly increase world food and feed availability by making large quantities of food materials available that are currently not utilized because of their taste.[4]

All the Food Needed
to Feed the World
(4 Billion People)
Could Be Produced From:

☐ 1,507 million hectares, using the same production techniques that are currently in use throughout the world (this is the amount of land now in use).

☐ About 1,200–1,300 million hectares (10–20% less than present) with the same production techniques currently in use by eliminating 70–90% of post-harvest loss.

☐ About 740 million hectares by feeding all the world's cereal crops to people instead of animals and distributing these cereals efficiently (49% of present land).

☐ About 650 million hectares using Chinese production techniques (43% of present land).

☐ About 170 million hectares using North American production techniques and a vegetarian diet (11% of present land).

☐ The southern half of Sudan, if it were drained, the proper infrastructure developed, and the nomadic cattle raisers of the region changed to sedentary farmers (or farmers brought in from other regions).[2]

☐ About 60 million hectares of greenhouses using North American production techniques with three crops per year (3.9% of present land).

☐ About 50–100 million hectares using the "bio-dynamic intensive" method of food production (3.3–6% of present land).

☐ About 6 million hectares using hydroponics (.4% of present land).

☐ About 5.4 million hectares growing algae (.35% of present land).

All the Protein Needed
to Feed the World
Could Be Produced From:

☐ 3,044 million hectares using the same production techniques and pasture lands of the world as are now being used.

☐ The world's annual fisheries catch (approximately 70 million mt) if fed to humans and distributed with little loss (each person would get 48 g per day).

☐ 12 million hectares of high yielding aquaculture.

☐ 5.5 million hectares growing algae.

☐ About 30 *thousand* hectares using leaf protein extraction techniques.

☐ 1,300 hectares using single cell protein (yeast) production techniques.[5]

☐ 8,300 factories of the same design/size as the La Choy Food Products factory that produces its bean sprouts.

☐ Single cell protein made from one-seventh of the world's oil production waste products.[5]

185

References

Food Production Techniques

1. Lappe, F. M., Collins, J., "More Food Means More Hunger," *Development Forum,* UN Centre for Economic and Social Information, Geneva, Switzerland, Vol. IV, No. 8, Nov. 1976.

Aboriginal Agriculture

1. Dasmann, R. V., *Environmental Conservation,* John Wiley & Sons, 1976, excerpted in *CoEvolution Quarterly,* Fall, 1976.

2. Wortman, S., Cummings, R. W., *To Feed This World: The Challenge and the Strategy,* Johns Hopkins University Press, 1978.

3. Stewart, G. F., Amerine, M. A., *Food Science and Technology,* Academic Press, 1973, pp. 2–3.

Modern Agriculture

1. Dasmann, R. F., *Environmental Conservation,* John Wiley & Sons, 1976, excerpted in *CoEvolution Quarterly,* Fall, 1976.

Energy and Mechanization

1. Shenkin, P., Friend, G., "Food Report," World Man/World Environment Workshop, Dept. of Design, Southern Illinois Univ., Carbondale, IL, 1972.

2. Wittwer, S. H., "Food, Fiber and Energy," *Congressional Record,* 5-14-75, S7987.

3. Nelson, L. B., "Manufactured Physical and Biological Inputs," *The World Food Problem,* Vol. III, Ch. 4, pp. 95–217.

4. Geno, L. M., "Energy, Agriculture, and the Environment," Policy Branch, Policy Planning and Evaluation Directorate, Planning and Finance, Environment, Ottawa, Canada, Aug. 1975.

5. Pimentel, D., et al., "Food Production and the Energy Crisis," *Science,* Vol. 182, 11-2-73, pp. 443–49.

6. Commercial energy either involves a technology of energy conversion or enters commercial channels. Noncommercial energy is consumed directly, without technological conversion and without being formally marketed.

7. Abercrombie, K., "Which Energy Crisis," *Ceres,* FAO Review of Agriculture and Development, FAO, Rome, Italy, Sept.–Oct., 1978, pp. 13–18.

8. Fuller, R. B., "How to Maintain Man as a Success in the Universe," *Utopia or Oblivion,* Bantam Books, 1969, p. 214.

9. Butcher, W., et al., "Alternative Agricultural Strategies—Energy Aspects of World Food Problems," Report to the Institute of Ecology Founders' Conference, Morgantown, WV, 4-16-75.

10. *Food Update,* GAO, Community & Economic Development Division, May 1977, Vol. 2, Issue 2, Washington, D.C.

11. Perelman, M., "Efficiency in Agriculture: The Economics of Energy," *Radical Agriculture,* Ed. Merrill, R., Harper & Row, 1976, p. 65, Table 1, and p. 66.

12. Heichel, G. H., "Agricultural Production and Energy Resources," *American Scientist,* Vol. 64, Jan.–Feb. 1976, pp. 64–72.

13. Stevenson, K. R., Stoskopf, N. C., "Energy Efficiency in Crop Production," Proceedings of the Ontario Institute of Agrologists, 15th Annual Conference, Guelph, Ontario, Canada, 4-22-74.

14. Lockerety, W., et al., "A Comparison of the Production, Economic Returns, and Energy Intensiveness of Corn Belt Farms that Do and Do Not Use Inorganic Fertilizers and Pesticides," Center for the Biology of Natural Systems, Washington Univ., St. Louis, MO, 7-20-75.

15. Hannon, B. M., Lohman, T. G., "The Energy Cost of Overweight in the U.S.," *American Journal of Public Health,* Sept. 1978, Vol. 68, No. 8, pp. 767–77.

16. Assumed average: 14 miles per gallon; 12,000 miles per year; 125,000 BTU per gallon.

Agribusiness

1. Press, F., "Science and Technology: The Road Ahead," *Science,* Vol. 200, 5-19-78, p. 739.

2. Sinha, R., "Agribusiness: A Nuisance in Every Respect?" *Mazingira:* The World Forum for Environment and Development, No. 3/4, 1977.

3. Madden, J. P., "Economics of Size in Farming," Agricultural Report No. 107, (A 93.28.107), United States Dept. of Agriculture.

4. Eckholm, E. "The Unnatural History of Tobacco," World Watch Institute, 1977.

5. Berry, W., *The Unsettling of America: Culture & Agriculture,* 1977.

Irrigation

1. Wittwer, S. H., "Food Production: Technology and the Resource Base," *Science,* Vol. 188, 5-9-75.

2. Gavan, J. D., Dixon, J. A., "India: A Perspective on the Food Situation," *Science,* Vol. 188, 5-9-75.

3. Geno, L. M., "Energy, Agriculture, and the Environment," Policy Branch, Policy Planning and Evaluation Directorate, Planning and Finance, Environment, Ottawa, Canada, Aug. 1975, p. 6.

4. Pimentel, D., et al., "Land Degradation: Effects on Food and Energy Resources," *Science,* Vol. 194, 10-8-76, pp. 149–55.

5. Irrigation, Drainage, and Salinity, An Internation Source Book, FAO/UNESCO, 1970.

6. Rawlins, S. L., Raats, P. A. C., "Prospects for High Frequency Irrigation," *Science,* Vol. 188, 5-9-75, pp. 604–10.

7. Splinter, W. E., "Center Pivot Irrigation," *Scientific American,* 6-19-76, pp. 90–99.

8. Shoji, K., "Drip Irrigation," *Scientific American,* 11-77, pp. 62–68.

9. Revell, R., Lahshminarayana, V., "The Ganges Water Machine," *Science,* Vol. 188, 5-9-75, pp. 611–16.

10. McHale, J., *World Facts and Trends,* Braziller Pub., 1972.

11. H. W. Gehm, J. I. Bregman, *Handbook of Water Resources and Pollution Control,* Van Nostrand-Reinhold Co., 1976, p. 647.

12. Morenarco, S., "Growing Plants with Seawater," *Science News,* Vol. 105, 6-22-74, p. 406.

13. Revelle, R., "The Resources Available to Agriculture," *Scientific American,* Oct. 1976, p. 174.

14. "Warm Water for Agriculture," *Science News,* Dec. 1974.

15. Miller, G. T., *Living in the Environment,* Wadsworth Pub., 1975.

16. Gabel, M., *Energy, Earth, and Everyone,* Straight Arrow Books, 1975, p. 109.

Fertilizers

1. "Fertilizer Industry Chemicals," *Chemical Week,* July 1971, p. 2.

2. Gordon, L., Pryor, C. A., Letters, "Food, Energy and Population," *Science,* Vol. 193, 10-17-76, pp. 1070–73.

3. *Fertilizer Manual,* UN., United Nations Industrial Development Organization, New York, 1967, No. 67, II B, p. 1.

4. Redinger, R., "World Fertilizer Review and Prospects to 1980–81," Economic Research Service, U.S. Dept. of Agriculture, *Foreign Agricultural Economic Report,* No. 115, Feb. 1976.

5. Berg, A. D., "The New Foods," published in "National Nutrition Policy: Selected Papers on Technical Agricultural Advances and Production," June 1974, U.S. Government Printing Office.

6. UN, *Assessment of the World Food Situation, Present and Future,* World Food Conference, Rome, UN, 1974.

7. Eberstandt, N., "Myths of the Food Crisis," *The New York Review of Books,* 2-19-76, p. 35.

8. Brown, L., *By Bread Alone,* Praeger Publishers, 1974.

9. Table adapted from: Hardy, R., Havelka, U., "Nitrogen Fixation Research: A Key to World Foods," *Science,* Vol. 188, 5-9-75, pp. 633–43.

10. McHale, J., *The Ecological Context,* World Resources Inventory, Human Trends and Needs, W.R.I., 3500 Market Street, Phila. PA 19104.

11. Evans, H. J., ed., "Enhancing Biological Nitrogen Fixation," Div. of Biological & Medical Sciences of the National Science Foundation, Washington, D.C. 20550, June 1975.

12. "Nitrogen Fixation in Maize," *Science,* Vol. 189, 9-1-75, p. 368.

13. Gabel, M., *Energy, Earth, and Everyone,* Straight Arrow Books, 1975, p. 95.

14. Wortman, S., Cummings, R. W., *To Feed This World: The Challenge and the Strategy,* Johns Hopkins Univ. Press, 1978, p. 71.

15. "Former Waste Product Grows Plants," *The New Haven Register,* 4-6-75, Connecticut Agricultural Experiment Station, New Haven, CT.

16. Heichel, G. H., "Agricultural Production and Energy Resources," *American Scientist,* Vol. 64, Jan.–Feb. 1976, pp. 64–72.

17. Goldstein, J., "The Wastes to Fertilizer Connection," *Environment Action Bulletin,* 10-5-74, Rodale Press, Inc., Emmaus, PA.

18. Milwaukee has a population of 717,372, and it produces 75,000 tons; a population of 4×10^9 would produce 416,666,250 tons (75,000 tons

$= 10.4\%$ of 720,000; 10.4% of $4 \times 10^9 = 416 \times 10^6$).

19. Stout, P., "Power: The Key to Food Sufficiency in India?," *Bulletin of the Atomic Scientists,* Nov. 1968, pp. 26–28.

20. "Organic Fertilizer to Alleviate Shortages," *Ceres,* FAO Review of Agriculture and Development, FAO, Rome, Italy, Mar.–Apr. 1975, p. 7.

21. Pimentel, D., et al., "Food Production and the Energy Crisis," *Science,* Vol. 182, 11-2-73, pp. 443–49.

22. Sprague, G. F., "Agriculture in China," *Science,* Vol. 188, 5-9-75, p. 549.

23. "Waste Recycling Has Become a National Industry," *Ceres,* FAO Review of Agriculture and Development, FAO, Rome, Italy, Sept.–Oct. 1978, pp. 5–7.

Pesticides

1. Bunting, A. H., "Pests, Population and Poverty in the Developing World," *Journal of the Royal Society of Arts,* 3-19-72, pp. 227–39.

2. Waterhouse, D. F., Wilson, F., "Biological Control of Pests and Weeds," *Science Journal,* Dec. 1968, pp. 31–37; Ennis, W. B., et al., "Crop Protection to Increase Food Supplies," *Science,* Vol. 188, 5-9-75, p. 593.

3. World Health Organization, Report in *Development Forum,* May 1976, p. 8, Center for Economic and Social Information, UNICEF.

4. Haskell, P. T., "The Hungry Locust," *Science Journal,* Jan. 1970, p. 61.

5. Giban, J., "Sahel—Drought and Now Rats," *Development Forum,* May 1976, Center for Economic and Social Information, UNICEF.

6. Geno, L. M., "Energy, Agriculture, and the Environment," Policy Branch, Policy Planning and Evaluation Directorate, Planning and Finance, Environment, Ottawa, Canada, Aug. 1975, p. 6.

7. *Food Update,* GAO, Community & Economic Development Division, June 1977, Washington D.C.

8. *FAO 1977 Production Yearbook,* Vol. 31, FAO/UN, Rome, Italy, 1978.

9. Cook, L., "U.S. Farmers Using More Pesticides than Ever Before," USDA, government spokesman, in the *Vancouver Sun,* Associated Press, 8-13-75.

10. Sprague, G. F., "Agriculture in China," *Science,* Vol. 188, 5-9-75, p. 553.

11. Merrill, R., "Towards a Self-Sustaining Agriculture," *Radical Agriculture,* Harper & Row, 1976.

12. Wade, N., "Insect Viruses: A New Class of Pesticides," *Science* Vol. 181, 9-7-73, p. 925.

13. Olkowski, H., Olkowski, W., "Insect Population Management in Agro-Ecosystems," *Radical Agriculture,* ed. Merrill, R., Harper & Row, 1976.

Land Use/Soil

1. *FAO 1977 Production Yearbook,* Vol. 31, FAO/UN, Rome, Italy, 1978.

2. Jacks, G. V., Whyte, R. O., *Vanishing Lands: A World Survey of Soil Erosion,* Doubleday, Doran, NY, 1939, quoted in Brink, R. A., et al., "Soil Deterioration and the Growing World Demand for Food," *Science,* Vol. 197, p. 625.

3. "How Much Good Land is Left?" *Ceres,* FAO Review of Agriculture and Development,

FAO, Rome, Italy, Sept.–Oct., 1978, pp. 13–18.

4. Pimentel, D., et al., "Land Degradation: Effects on Food and Energy Resources," *Science,* Vol. 194, 10-8-76, pp. 149–55.

5. Brown, L., "Redefining National Security," *Development Forum,* Nov.–Dec. 1977, Center for Economic and Social Information, UNICEF.

6. Brown, L., "Vanishing Croplands," *Agenda,* AID, Dec. 1978, Vol. I, No. 11, pp. 5–12.

7. Hill, G., "United Nations Study Says Spreading Deserts are Caused by Man's Misuse of the Land," *New York Times,* 2-25-76, p. 17.

8. Revelle, R., "The Resources Available for Agriculture," *Scientific American,* Sept. 1975, p. 170.

9. McHarg, I., "Towards a Comprehensive Plan for Environmental Quality," 12-16-73, Wallace, McHarg, Roberts & Todd, Architects, 1737 Chestnut St., Phil. PA 19103.

10. Aldo Leopold, quoted in *Ecoscience,* Ehrlich, Ehrlich & Holdren, W. H. Freeman, 1977.

11. Wittwer, S. H., "Food Production: Technology and the Resource Base," *Science,* Vol. 188, 5-9-75, p. 582.

12. "Counterattack on Deserts," *Manas,* Vol. 28, No. 47, 11-19-75, Manas Publishing Co., Los Angeles, CA.

13. "Chinese Report Success in Effort to Turn Deserts into Vineyards," *New York Times,* 8-31-77.

14. Kellogg, C. E., Orvedal, A. C., et al., "World Potentials for Arable Soils," 1969.

15. Canby, T. Y., Raymer, S., "Will There Be Enough?" *National Geographic Magazine,* July 1975.

16. Sanchez, P. A., Buol, S. W., "Soils of the Tropics and the World Food Crisis," *Science,* Vol. 188, 5-9-75, pp. 598–603.

17. Hightower, J., "Hard Tomatoes, Hard Times: The Failure of the Land Grant College Complex," *Radical Technology,* ed. Merril, R., Harper & Row, 1976.

18. Barnes, P., "Land Reform in America," *Radical Technology,* pp. 26–38.

Animal Husbandry

1. Park, et al., *Agriculture: Food and Man,* Brigham Young Univ. Press, Provo, UT, 1975, p. 60.

2. *FAO 1977 Production Yearbook,* Vol. 31, UN, Rome, Italy, 1978.

3. Pyke, *Man and Food,* McGraw-Hill, New York, 1970.

4. *Protein Resources and Technology: States and Research Needs,* Dept. of Nutrition & Food Science, MIT, Cambridge, MA, RANNNSF grant AEN 75-13072, Dec. 1975, p. 58

5. Kneese, A. V., et al., *Economics and the Environment—A Materials Balance Approach,* Resources for the Future, Washington, D.C., 1973.

6. Maugh, III, T. H., "The Fatted Calf: More Weight Gain with Less Feed," *Science,* 2-7-76, p. 454.

7. Sprague, G. F., "Agriculture in China," *Science,* Vol. 188, 5-9-75, p. 555.

8. Wittwer, S. H., "Food Production: Technology and the Resource Base," *Science,* Vol. 188, 5-9-75.

9. Boyce, R., "Food Processors in Race," Copley News Service, 2-10-74, (report on Ohio State University/NSF Whey Processing Development Project).

Fishing

1. Roedel, P. M., "Fishing for the Future," *Agenda,* AID, Dec. 1978, Vol. I, No. 11.

2. Brown, L., *By Bread Alone,* Praeger Publishers, New York, 1974.

3. *Yearbook of Fishing Statistics,* FAO/UN, Vol. 36, 1973.

4. McHale, J., *The Ecological Context,* World Resources Inventory, Human Trends and Needs, Vol. 6, W.R.I., 3500 Market Street, Philadelphia, PA 19104.

5. Holt, S. J., "Food Resources of the Ocean," *Scientific American,* Sept. 1969, Vol. 221, No. 3.

6. "Caution Signal on Krill," *Ceres,* FAO Review of Agriculture and Development, FAO, Rome, Italy, Mar.–Apr. 1978, pp. 5–6.

Aquaculture

1. Brown, L., *By Bread Alone,* Praeger Publishers, New York, 1974.

2. "World Development of Aquaculture," *Ceres,* FAO Review of Agriculture and Development, FAO, Rome Italy, May–June 1977, p. 5.

3. Sullivan, W., "Aquaculture Scrutinized for Protein-Poor Lands," *New York Times,* quoting FAO of United Nations, 10-9-73.

4. Bardach, J., Ryther, J., McLarney, W., "General Principles and Economics," in *Aquaculture—The Farming and Husbandry of Fresh Water and Marine Organisms,* John Wiley & Sons, 1972, pp. 1–27.

5. "Food Production in the Nation's Coastal Zone," working paper, Institute of Ecology, Coastal Zone Commission Report, Chairman, John Clarke, 4-15-75.

6. Pillay, T. V. R., "The Role of Aquaculture in Fishery Development and Management," FAO/UN, 1973.

7. "Chinese Carp Culture," FAO/UN, pp. 75–119.

8. Druehl, L. D., "Past, Present and Future of the Seaweed Industry," *Underwater Journal,* Oct. 1972, pp. 182–191.

9. Todd, J., "A Modest Proposal: Science for the People," in *Radical Agriculture,* ed. Merrill, R., Harper & Row, 1976, pp. 259–83.

10. Ryther, J. H., "Mariculture: How Much Protein and for Whom?," *Oceanus,* Winter 1975, Vol. 18, No. 2.

11. Based on yields given in No. 9 and 40g/day protein needs.

12. Ryther, J. H., "Photosynthesis and Fish Production in the Sea," *Science,* Vol. 166, 10-3-69, pp. 72–76.

13. Pinchot, G. B., "Marine Farming," *Scientific American,* Dec. 1970, pp. 15–21.

14. Bott, A. N. W., "Power Plus Proteins from the Sea," *The Royal Society of Arts Journal,* London, England, July 1975, pp. 486–503.

15. Wilcox, H. A., "The Ocean Food and Energy Farm Project," paper presented at the International Conference on Maine Technology Assessment in Monte Carlo, Morocco, 10-26-75, published in supplement to Calypso Log, Vol. 3, No. 2, Cousteau Society.

16. Gabel, M., "Temperature Differentials," *Energy, Earth, and Everyone,* Straight Arrow Books, 1975.

17. "Fecundity of Fish Aids Congo's Diet," *New York Times,* 3-2-59, p. 18.

Greenhouses

1. Ruthner, O., "Habitat: Feeding Human Settlements," *International Development,* May, 1976, pp. 47–52.

2. Hodges, C. N., "Ruthner Tower Greenhouse Discussions," *U.N. Development Programme,* New York, May 15, 1968.

3. Hodges, C. N., "Calculation of Period of Solar Advantage of Ruthner Tower Type Greenhouse," prepared for Bureau of Operations and Programming, *U.N. Development Programme,* May 2, 1968.

4. Peveril, M., "Geography of Coastal Deserts," *UNESCO Arid Zone Research 28;* UNESCO, Paris, 1966, p. 140.

5. Hodges, C. N., and Hodge, C. O., "An Integrated System for Providing Power, Water and Food for Desert Coasts," *Horticultural Science,* Vol. 6 (1) Feb. 1971, pp. 30–33.

Hydroponics

1. Ruthner, O., "Habitat: Feeding Human Settlements," *International Development,* May 1976, pp. 47–52.

2. Hodges, C. N., and Hodge, C. O., "An Integrated System for Providing Power, Water, and Food for Desert Coasts," *Horticultural Science,* Vol. 6 (1) Feb. 1971, pp. 30–33.

3. Bentley, M., *Commercial Hydroponics: Facts and Figures,* Benton Books, 1959.

4. Annual Report 1971–72, Environmental Research Laboratory, Univ. of Tucson, Tucson, AZ 85706.

5. Hodges, C. N., Kassander, A. R., "Extending Use of Available Supply—A Systems Approach to Power, Water and Food Production," in Post and Seale, *Water Production—*

Using Nuclear Energy. Univ of Arizona Press, 1966.

6. *Wall Street Journal,* 6-29-73, p. 1.

7. Fox, S., "Hydroponics," S. Fox, Station A, Albuquerque, NM.

Insects

1. Park, et al., *Agriculture: Food and Man,* Brigham Young Univ. Press, Provo, UT, 1975.

2. Bodenheimer, F. S., *Insects as Human Food,* The Hague, 1951.

3. Taylor, R. L., *Butterflies in My Stomach: Insects as Human Nutrition,* Woodbridge Press, 1975.

4. Olkowsky, H. W., "Insect Population Management in Agro-Ecosystems," in *Radical Agriculture,* ed. Merrill, R., Harper & Row, 1976.

5. Mattson, H. W., "Food for the World," *International Science and Technology,* Dec. 1975, p. 31.

Leaf Protein

1. *League for International Food Education Newsletter,* 155 16th Street, N.W., Washington, D.C. 20036, Mar. 1975, p. 2.

2. Scrimshaw, N. S., Wang, D., "Protein Resources and Technology: Status and Research Needs," Dept. of Nutrition and Food Science, MIT, Cambridge, MA, RANNNSF grant AEN 75–13072, Dec. 1975, p. 58.

3. "Leaf Protein Extraction Plant Demonstrated," *The Engineer,* 7-26-68, p. 133.

4. "Good Juice," Science and the Citizen, *Scientific American,* Apr. 1975.

Non-Photosynthetic Single Cell Protein

1. Tannahill, R., "Food in History," Stein & Day, New York, 1973.

2. Schmidt, E., "Food and Feed Yeast in Germany," *Unsylva,* Volume III, No. 11, December, 1953.

3. "Yeasts Turn Factory Waste to Food," *New Scientist,* June 15, 1972, p. 625.

4. Borgstrom, G., "The Human Biosphere and Its Biological and Chemical Limitations," *Global Impacts of Applied Microbiology,* John Wiley & Sons, 1964, p. 156.

5. Scrimshaw, N. S., Wang, D., "Protein Resources and Technology: Status and Research Needs," Dept. of Nutrition and Food Science, MIT, Cambridge, MA, RANNNSF grant AEN 75–13072, Dec. 1975, p. 58.

6. Green, H., "Feed the People," *New York Times,* June 16, 1975, p. 27.

7. Wolff, A., "The Supa Oil Diet," *World* Magazine, 1973, p. 4.

8. Cousteau, J., "What Song the Sirens Sing," *Saturday Review,* 2/19/77, pp. 48–50.

Photosynthetic Single Cell Protein

1. Scrimshaw, N. S., Wang, D., "Protein Resources and Technology: Status and Research Needs," Dept. of Nutrition and Food Science, MIT, Cambridge, MA, RANNNSF grant AEN 75–13072, Dec. 1975, pp. 58.

2. Patton, S., et al., "Food Value of Red Tide," *Science,* Vol. 158, 11/10/67, pp. 789–90.

3. Lawlor, R., "Algae Research in Auroville," *Alternative Sources of Energy,* pp. 2–9.

4. Based on Greeley, R. S., "Land and Fresh Water Farming, Capturing the Sun Through Bioconversion," Conference Proceedings March 10–12, 1976, p. 197.

5. *Unconventional Foodstuffs for Human Consumption,* OECD, Paris, 1975.

Synthetic Nutriments

1. Hellman, H., "The Story Behind Those Meatless 'Meats'," *Popular Science,* Oct. 1972, pp. 78–80.

2. Miller, S. L., *Science,* Vol. 117, 1953, p. 528.

3. Mayer, J., "Textured Vegetable Proteins: Actually Nothing New," *Washington Post,* 9-10-72.

Decentralized Food Production/Home Gardens and Urban Self-Sufficiency

1. Sterne, M., "South Bronx Project Hopes to 'Green' 500 Acres," *New York Times,* 5-6-78.

2. Richmond, F., "Food in China," *Food Monitor,* July–Aug. 1978, pp. 16–17.

3. Alward, S., Alward, R., Rybczynski, W., *Rooftop Wastelands,* Minimum Cost Housing Group, School of Architecture, McGill Univ., Montreal, Quebec, Canada.

New Foods

1. Hopson, J. H., "Praise for Pummelo, High Score for Soursop," *Science News,* 4-10-76, p. 237.

2. Vietmeyer, N. D., "The Plight of the Humble Crops," *Ceres,* FAO Review of Agriculture and Development, FAO, Rome, Italy, Mar.–Apr. 1978, pp. 23–27.

3. "The Forgotten Amaranth," *Ceres,* FAO Review of Agriculture and Development, FAO, Rome, Italy, Sept.–Oct. 1977.

4. "The Fruit of the Prickly Pear, A Troublesome Cactus, Is Hailed as Food Source," *New York Times,* 9-6-77, p. 33.

5. Broad, W. J., "Boon or Boondoggle: Bygone Rubber Shrub Is Bouncing Back," *Science,* Oct. 1978, Vol. 202, p. 410.

6. Reed, R., "New Process Makes Cottonseed Oil a Source of Low Cost Protein for Humans," *New York Times,* 7-10-73.

7. Shurtleff, W.; Aoyogi, A., *The Book of Tofu,* Ballantine, New York, 1979.

8. Pimentel, D., et al., "Food Production and the Energy Crisis," *Science,* Vol. 182, 11-2-73, p. 447.

9. Worgen, J., "Possible Solutions to the World Food Problem," *Appropriate Technology,* Vol. II, No. 2, Aug. 1975.

Alternative Animal Feeds

1. *Farmers Weekly,* 2-8-74.

2. "Unconventional Foodstuffs for Human Consumption," OECD, 1975, Agricultural Products and Markets.

3. "Irradiated Sludge Showing Potential as Food for Cattle," Energy Insider, D.O.E., Oct. 1978, p. 5.

4. "The Rediscovery of a Wonderful World," *Ceres,* FAO Review of Agriculture and Development, FAO, Rome, Italy, Mar.–Apr. 1978, p. 5.

5. "Cattle Gain Weight Eating Feed Mixed with Cement Dust," *New York Times,* 12-16-77.

Exotic Food Sources

1. Quigg, P. W., "World Environment Newsletters: Global Report, Stockholm," *Saturday Review* 3-8-75, p. 56.

2. Gravi-Mechanics Co., Dept. MVH, 22 Arrow Lane, Hicksville, NY 11801.

3. "Space Colonies: Home, Home on Lagrange," *Science News,* 10-6-74, p. 149.

4. "To Understand Taste Is to Have More Food," *Technology Review,* Feb. 1979, pp. 82–83.

All the World's Food

1. Revelle, R., "The Resources Available for Agriculture," *Scientific American,* Sept. 1976, p. 174.

2. Hopper, W. D., "The Development of Agriculture in Developing Countries," *Scientific American,* Sept. 1976, p. 201.

3. Based on Lawlor, R., "Algae Research in Auroville," *Alternative Sources of Energy Journal,* pp. 2–9.

FOOD DISTRIBUTION

Processing, Storage, Packaging, Preparation and Delivery

Food Processing

The natural state or tendency of fresh food is to decay and spoil. To overcome or retard this eventuality, food is processed in such a way that the agents of spoilage—microorganisms, enzymes, oxygen, insects, rodents, spillage, excessive heat, cold, humidity, or fumes—are removed. As pointed out in the Overview section of this document, food is processed so that its nutritional content or complexity is maintained. In some instances, food is processed for aesthetic reasons. From an economic perspective, food is also processed to transform surpluses of perishables that would otherwise go to waste into storable products, e.g., tomatoes into tomato paste, oranges into frozen juice; and to provide additional employment both in the processing plants and in servicing those plants. In addition, processing increases the range of products the consumer has to choose from and which the farmer can produce.[1] This is necessary if food is to be stored or transported long distances. Food is stored so that a continuous supply can be assured. Stored food serves as a reservoir to the fluctuations of production, both seasonal and longer term. The larger the amount of stored food, the longer the time period can be that a given area can survive without new food inputs. The more extensively developed a region's transportation and storage facilities, the easier it is for a food-short area to obtain food from a food rich area. A rural population can subsist on the food it produces locally, but an urban population depends on the surrounding countryside for its food supply. The larger the urban population and the further distance it is from the sources of food, the greater will be the need for modern food protection techniques.[1]

In the developing regions of the world most farmers produce food primarily to meet their own immediate requirements. In developed regions, farmers tend to specialize in crops that will provide the greatest amount of financial return. Crops are grown for cash, not subsistence. When crops are consumed locally by the people who grow them, processing is minimal; highly perishable foods tend to be consumed seasonally and locally; animals are moved long distances on foot and slaughtered under primitive conditions; meat is commonly consumed within twenty-four hours of slaughter because of lack of refrigeration facilities.[1] Processed foods are a luxury in developing rural regions and a necessity in developed and urban regions. Processed food is often priced beyond the purchasing capacity of most people in a developing region.

The reason why foods are processed is to protect them from loss. Micro-organisms consume an estimated 1% of the world's grain harvest;[2] insects take another estimated 3–50%, depending on local conditions;[1] rodents take an estimated 5–60% in tropical areas—world around, it is estimated that 3.82×10^6 tons are lost to rodents each year[3]; mycotoxins, harvesting before maturity, mechanical damage—bruises in harvesting, storage, etc.—and primitive processing techniques also result in nutritional loss. Surveys in India show minimum storage losses from all causes to be 10% for cereals and oil seeds, 30% for pulses, and 12% for rice;[4, 5] one survey showed that

were it not for rodents, pests, and poor storage, India would be a food surplus country;[6] in Africa, it is estimated that one-third of all harvested cereals are lost to pests;[7] in Tanzania, an estimated 88,000 tons of corn—enough to feed one million people for a year—is lost annually to insect damage;[6] in Brazil, 15–20% of stored grains are lost;[8] 50% of the harvested fruits and vegetables are lost to spoilage in developing countries as well as 15–20% of the meat, poultry, fish, and dairy products.[9] In developed regions food losses are kept down through the protection of food through processing and effective storage. But, unfortunately, losses that have been reduced to insects and other pests have seemingly been more than made up in losses due to waste: about 20% of all food produced in the U.S.—some 137 million tons—is lost or wasted annually.[10] "66 million acres of land, 9 million tons of fertilizer, and the equivalent of 461 million barrels of oil were used to produce food that was ultimately lost, either at some stage of the food system or by the consumer."[10] It has been estimated that the combined loss of U.S.-produced grains, meat, vegetables, sugar, fruits, nuts, and oilseeds in 1974 could have fed about 49 million people.[10]

The process of protecting foods and eliminating waste can thus be seen to be very important. If only half of the estimated *cereal* crop loss were prevented there would be almost a pound per day of extra grain for one *billion* people.

The way foods are preserved is through the development of a physical-chemical environment wherein spoilage organisms cannot grow or where the foods are sterilized and then sealed in containers so they cannot become recontaminated.[1] Because the preservation of food can change the taste, color, texture, or composition of the original product, a lot of further processing is devoted to restoring these qualities artificially. In the Western world, food processing has often been carried to such an extreme that some people claim that the modern food processor has lost sight of the basic purpose behind food processing—preserving nutritional content. Nutritional content is often processed out of foods, sacrificed for greater shelf life, appearance, palatableness, or convenience in preparation. In some circles processed food has almost become synonymous with non-nutritive or even dangerous food. Problems with over-processed "junk" foods—eatables that are predominantly sugar or fat—are compounded by the large amount of resources devoted to advertising them as well as some of the targets of this advertising. Four billion dollars are spent annually on food advertising in just the U.S.[11] More than 70% of the ads on weekend morning television—watched overwhelmingly by young children—are action-packed advertisements for junk foods—usually in the form of candy, sugar-coated cereals, and chewing gum.[12] Results of this pervasive and effective "educational" campaign are reflected in the somewhat frightening statistics that in the U.S. during the years 1959–70, milk consumption dropped 20% while that of soft drinks went up 79%; fruits, vegetables, and potatoes declined by more than

50% while unenriched commercial bakery products went up 67%, potato chips 85%, ice cream 29%, and artificially-flavored fruit-punch 750%.[13] And to top it off (or rather to recover), Americans spend over $460 million on over-the-counter stomach preparations.[14]

Besides basic protection, food processing can flavor, color, concentrate, improve texture and consistency, add nutritional substances, and change the form of the raw food stock. Chart 1 lists the many food processing techniques in use and the functions they perform; Chart 2 lists some of the operations involved in the food processing.

There are more than 3,000 intentional additives used by the food processing industry to aid and abet the operations listed in these charts. There are also many unintentional additives, e.g., insecticides and other environmental pollutants as well as manufacturing plant impurities such as rodents

Processed and Fresh Fruit and Vegetable Consumption in the United States[15]

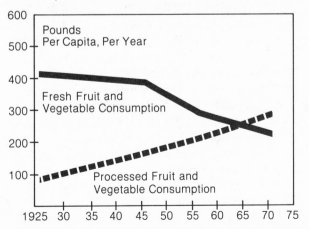

and insects that get into the raw food stock and are also processed. The functional use of food additives can be seen in Chart 3. From just a cursory glance at these charts, the magnitude and complexity of the modern food processing industry becomes apparent.

Part of food processing is packaging the food product to further protect it and to prevent spillage and waste in distribution outlets and homes. Packaging serves the purpose of:

1. furnishing mechanical strength for protecting foodstuffs from handling, impact, piercing, temperature, and humidity;
2. facilitating exact weighing and ready handling;
3. protecting against infestation, contamination, oxygen, odor uptake, and light;
4. facilitating flavor retention and stabilization of preservative influences; and
5. serving as a medium for education as to the product's use, preparation, and content.

Chart 5 lists the types of packaging materials most often used. As with food processing, a lot of food packaging has seemingly lost its functional basis and is now being subjected to attacks pointing out its wastefulness. The cost of a food container is sometimes more than the farmer receives for the food packaged in it. The packaging industry is exceeded only by the automobile and construction industries in its use of steel and aluminum resources; it uses 50% of the paper and paperboard produced in the United States; 20% of all plastic; 10% of all lumber; 96% of all non-flat glass; and 90% of all aluminum foil. This amounts to about 124 billion boxes, 29 billion new glass containers, 45 billion returnable bottles, 51.3 billion metal cases, and 42 billion grocery bags in the United States alone.[21]

One of the alternatives or improvements to conventional packaging that is used successfully in Europe is modular packaging. In conventional packaging there are a wide variety of container sizes. One survey of just the dry goods section of a food warehouse disclosed close to 2,600 different shipping containers out of 5,000 stocked items.[24] When shipped, these various-sized containers do not always fit together very well (see illustration). This results in wasted space, damage, and reduced productivity. Modular packaging solves these problems by having just a few basic container sizes all in geometric proportion to one another and related to one or more basic unit load sizes, such as a pallet.

Throughout the entire food system there are enormous opportunities for reducing wastes. The opportunities in the food processing and packaging industry are monumental, and more often than not, result in increased economies. By redesigning food processing techniques to be more resource efficient, more of the incoming raw food product emerges from the plant as finished products of high quality.[25]

Between 1963 and 1971, food consumption in the U.S. increased by 2.3% by weight on a per-capita basis; in the same period, the tonnage of food packaging increased by an estimated 33.3% per capita and the number of food packages increased by an estimated 38.8% per capita.
—U.S. Environmental Protection Agency

Chart 1

Food Processing Methods	Function
Drying	preservation, concentration
Aging	preservation, increase tenderness
Smoking	preservation, flavor
Salting	preservation, flavor enhancement
Curing	preservation, flavor, tenderness
Pickling	preservation, flavor enhancement
Fermenting	change characteristics of food
Cooling	preservation
Milling	change characteristics, texture
Canning	preservation
Freezing	preservation

Food Processing Methods	Function
Freeze drying	preservation, concentration
Baking	preservation, flavor
Frying	preservation, flavor
Heat sterilization (pasteurization)	preservation
Sugaring	flavor, color
Starching	preservation, improve texture and consistency
Radiation	preservation
Additives	all of the above, plus can add nutritive value

Chart 2. Unit Operations in Food Processing.

Mechanical Separation	Physical Chemical Separation	Mixing Operations	Disintegrating Operations	Forming Operations
centrifuging		agitation		casting
deaeration	distillation	beating	breaking	extruding
defeathering	evaporation	blending	chipping	flaking
dehairing	dehydration	dispersing	cutting	rolling
draining	crystallization	diffusing	crushing	molding
evacuating	freezing	emulsifying	grinding	sawing
filtering	leaching	homogenizing	milling	shaping
percolation	extraction	kneading	macerating	slicing
pitting	ion exchange	stirring	pulverizing	splitting
pressing	electrodialysis	whipping	shredding	
screening	membrane permeation	working	spraying	
sedimentation	reverse osmosis			
sifting				
skinning				
sorting				
trimming				
washing				

Chart 3.[18, 19]

Functional Use of Food Additives	Examples
acidifiers	citric acid
alkalies	calcium carbonate
anti-caking agents, drying agents	silicon dioxide
antimicrobial agents	benzoic acid
antioxidants	BHA
binders, fillers, plasticizers	polyethylene glycols
bleaching, oxidizing agents	hydrogen peroxide
bodying, bulking agents	glycerin
buffers, neutralizing agents	aluminum potassium sulfate
carriers, disintegrating agents	magnesium carbonate
dispersing agents	pvp
chewing gum base components	betadiene-styrene 75/25 rubber
clarifying agents	tannic acid
color fixatives	potassium nitrate
color retention agents	sodium nitrate
components in the manufacture of other food additives	stearic acid
defoaming agents	decanic acid
dough conditioners	potassium bromate
emulsifiers; foaming, whipping agents	acetylated monoglycerides
enzymes	papain
firming agents	calcium carbonate

Functional Use of Food Additives	Examples
flavor enhancers	monosodium 1-glutamate
flavoring adjuncts	formic acid
flavoring agents*	clove oil
humectants, moisture retaining agents	sorbitol
leavening agents	sodium bicarbonate
lubricants	mineral oil
maturing agents	calcium acolate
mold and rope inhibitors	propionic acid
non-nutritive sweeteners	saccharin
nutrients, dietary supplements**	ascorbic acid
preservatives	sodium benzoate
salt substitutes	1-glutamic acid
sequestrants	tartaric acid
solvents	acetone
stabilizers	mono- and diglycerides
surface-active agents	propylene glycol
surface finishing agents	petrobatum
texturizers	mannitol
thickeners	pectin
yeast foods	calcium oxide
stimulant	caffeine
decolorizing agent	activated carbon
miscellaneous	methyl formate

*There are over 225 separate chemicals used as flavoring agents.
**There are over 75 separate chemicals used as nutrients.

Chart 4. Raspberry Flavor Formulation

Ingredient	Parts
Ethyl methylphenylglycidate	400
Benzylidene isopropylidene acetone	100
Methoxyacetoxyacetophenone	60
Benzyl acetate	50
Phenethyl alcohol	50
Essence of Portugal	50
Isobutyl acetate	40
Vanillin	30
Methylionone	25
beta-Ionone	25
Coumarin substitute	10
Iris concrete essence	15
Ethyl acetate	10
Ethyl caproate	10
Isoamyl caproate	10
Hexanyl acetate	10
Hexenyl acetate	10
Methyl salicylate	10
Ethyl benzoate	10
Methyl butanol	10
Bornyl salicylate	10
Essence of clove	10
Essence of geranium	10
Hexyl alcohol	5
Hexenol	5
Anisaldehyde	5
Benzaldehyde	5
Acetylmethylcarbinol	3
Biacetyl	2

Chart 5. Types of Food Packages.

1. Metal Containers
   a. tin cans
   b. steel cans and barrels
   c. aluminum cans

2. Glass Containers

3. Paper Containers
   a. cardboard boxes, cartons
   b. bags

4. Flexible Containers
   a. tin foil
   b. polyester film
   c. wax paper and paper

5. Plastic Containers

6. Steel, Concrete, etc., i.e. stores, grain bins, etc.

Chart 6. Food Distribution Mediums, Industries, or Organizations.

Transport Medium	Predominant Foods Carried
ship, barge	grains, processed foods
train	vegetables, processed foods
truck	vegetables, processed foods
car, cart, wagon	food for home/market
pipeline	grain, catsup, etc.
conveyor belt	processed foods
airplane	highly perishable foods
animal	food or market, home, etc.
human	food for home, etc.

Food Service Industry Outlets	Predominant Foods Carried
warehouses	all food types
grocery store	all food types
supermarket	all food types
farmers market	all food types
roadside stand	all food types
restaurants	prepared foods
cafeteria	prepared foods
canteen/vending machines	prepared foods
vendor—e.g., milk truck, ice cream truck, etc.	specialties

Organizational Distribution Aids	Means of Food Procurement
food stamps	produce
"bread lines"	purchase
"care package"	trade
foreign aid	earn
price controls	gift
	steal

After food is processed and packaged, it is then distributed. Chart 6 lists the various ways and institutions through which food finds its often circuitous route to the home. As with processing and packaging, delivery has its inefficiencies and new alternatives. One such alternative is the giant airship. New advances in lightweight high-strength metal alloy geodesic air frames and multiple wall leak-proof plastic air bags have made the airship a viable and safe transport medium. The ancient (judged by contemporary possibilities) Graf Zeppelin could lift 75 tons of cargo and get to its destination at least as quickly as a ship of the sea. The advantages of the airship include its lift capability, energy efficiency (power is not needed to raise the cargo off the ground as this is accomplished by the lighter-than-air lifting medium of helium or hydrogen; in addition, there are even designs for solar-powered airships that would run off of photovoltaic cells), ability to dock or land without extensive airport facilities or even roads, and the synergetic bonus that as the ship rises into the air, the temperature decreases, thus refrigerating or even freezing the perishable foodstuffs on

---

Twice as much energy is consumed outside the farm in processing, packaging, transporting, distributing, refrigerating, and cooking food as farms consume in growing it.

758 trillion BTUs were used in the major food processing industries in the United States.

---

board. The airship has the capability of being both transport and storage medium simultaneously.

After each step of harvesting, processing, and delivery, food is most often stored. Food storage is essential to the survival of humanity on Earth because food production is not constant. The only place where storage is perhaps not needed is in the archetypal tropical paradise where the food is always being produced. By storing food, humans increase the amount of free time that they can reinvest in pursuits other than searching for food. The more food stored and preserved, the longer can a human go without having to spend his time in food gathering. The root cellar, grain bin, pantry shelf, and refrigerator all perform the similar function of

Allocation of U.S. Food Dollar Budget[22]

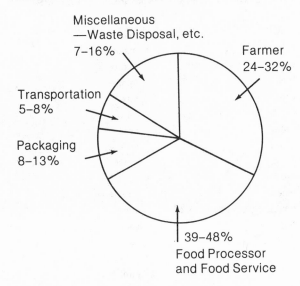

Miscellaneous
—Waste Disposal, etc.
7–16%

Transportation
5–8%

Packaging
8–13%

Farmer
24–32%

39–48%
Food Processor
and Food Service

Allocation of U.S. Food Energy Budget[23]

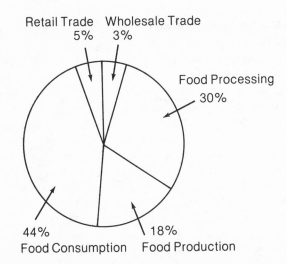

Retail Trade
5%

Wholesale Trade
3%

Food Processing
30%

44%
Food Consumption

18%
Food Production

storing surplus food for later consumption. In a sense, storage is just a slowdown in the rate of delivery.

The minimum amount of food that needs to be in storage is a function of nutritional needs per day times the maximum number of days that production can lag behind consumption. The maximum amount of food that is stored is usually a function of production capacities and the costs of storage. Conventional grain storage in developed areas costs about five cents per bushel per year for maintenance, operation, and fixed expenses.[1] This amounts to millions of dollars per year and is one of the reasons the U.S. disposed of its large grain reserves in the early 1970's. Another reason included the abhorrence of the then ruling administration for government involvement in business (or at least the businesses of their campaign contributors).

Under normal conditions, the longer food is stored, the more is lost, both in quantity and nutrition. The longer food is to be stored, the more processing it needs. An ideal storage system from this perspective would be one where food was in storage the least amount of time; from the perspective of maximum food supply stability, the ideal would be a huge storage—enough to sustain a region five or more years to guard against prolonged drought or other severe climatic fluctuations. A small storage is only desirable when production is predictable. In the situation the world is in presently—with widely varying climatic regions and predictions of impending climatic change—large storages are needed. The only alternative to large food storage is to industrialize food production—move it indoors into the factory (see Single Cell Protein and

Chart 7. Food Storages.

> Grain bin, silo
> Barn
> Shelf, pantry, cellar
> Root cellar
> Refrigerator, freezer

Hydroponics sections)—and thereby insure a steady supply.

Besides the conventional means or places of storing food listed in Chart 7, there are other alternatives.

Livestock could be viewed as a storage for grain. We dump grains into livestock and retrieve them, in altered form, when the animals are butchered. This is probably the most inefficient form of food storage known; for every ten pounds of grain "stored," we lose nine. Another storage for grains, and perhaps even meats, that is more efficient in terms of loss, is in the −40° to −50° F. deep freeze of the Antarctic continent. Parts of Antarctica could be a global "grain bin" where food could be preserved almost indefinitely, and possibly at lower cost than current storage costs. Because the low environmental temperature would freeze all the food for "free," and the size of the storage would be much, much larger than anything ever done before, and the length of storage could be much longer than conventional food storage, the per unit cost would be lower than conventional bulk food storage.

The major problem is how to get the large amounts of food to and from the Antarctic. One alternative to this difficulty is the previously mentioned airship. Such a venture could even possibly be synergetically connected with the production of energy in the Antarctic. The wind power potential of certain parts of the Antarctic is enormous. One proposal is to harness this potential with a virtual forest of wind turbines that generate electricity which would then turn water into hydrogen and oxygen through electrolysis. The hydrogen would then be transported to other regions of the planet where it would be used as a fuel, electricity source in a fuel cell, or as a raw material for nitrogen fertilizer production.[26] One way of transporting this hydrogen from Antarctica would be via the airships that come to Antarctica to drop off food for storage. On the return voyage, the ships could carry liquid hydrogen. As pointed out, the airship could conceivably function as a storage medium as well. Such "mobile warehouses" could be anchored like balloons in chronic food-short areas of the planet; they could float high above the land in the cold atmosphere and descend when and where needed to bolster diminishing food supplies.

Another exotic food storage technique, related to the airship warehouse, is the possibility of using one- to three-mile-diameter atmospheric floating geodesic spheres. The weight of the air in a sphere increases eight times every time the size of the sphere is doubled. At one-half mile in diameter, the weight of the air in the sphere outweighs the structure itself. Raising the temperature one degree above the outside air temperature raises the whole structure off the ground. The higher the sphere gets, the colder it gets. Preliminary calculations for a one-mile diameter structure indicate that at 30 km, it would not only stay aloft through the capture of solar energy, but produce at least 100 megawatts (at 10% conversion efficiency) of surplus net energy, and

be able to lift 10,000 tons.[27] For a two-mile diameter structure these figures would go up exponentially. Such a structure could be used for atmospheric study, astronomy, Earth resources study, communications relay, as well as food storage and energy production. It would essentially be a colossal sized, low-orbiting satellite that could even be tethered for wire transmission of power to Earth. Yet another variation of this outward food storage, the farthest out, in fact, is the actual storage (and production) of food in the vacuum of outer space. Even with the space shuttle, this would be outrageously expensive, but the possibility does exist.

Deep-sea storage could also be used for food storage. Here, the lowered temperature plus the ocean pressure retard food spoilage; yet another alternative is hypobaric, or low pressure, storage. In this technique, foods are kept in an insulated container and air pressure is lowered by a small vacuum pump. Units can be built ranging from the size of a home appliance to warehouse size.

In today's world, storage is the weakest link in the chain of distribution. Food is stored on the individual family level, community level, regional, and national level. Each level is a back-up for the ones before it. What is needed in the world now is a global storage network to back up the regional storages as well as new, more effective storage techniques on the family, community, and regional levels. A multiple year supply of food for the entire globe could be stored in the Antarctic and banish the specter of hunger from the Earth. This will be discussed in greater detail in the following section on Global Food Strategies.

After the harvesting, storage, processing,

Chart 8. Common Food Preparation Techniques.

age	leaven
bake	marinate
barbeque	mash
blend	microwave
boil	mince
broil	mix
braise	pare
bread	peel
brown	pressure cook
chop	roast
cream	season
dice	shell
double boil, parboil, poach	shred
fry	slice
freeze	steam
grind	stew
garnish	stuff
heat	tenderize
knead	wash or dry

Chart 9. Common Food Utensils.

knife
chopstick
fork
spoon
hands, fingers, palms
cups, bowls
glasses
bottles
plates
pot
leaf

packaging, and distribution of food comes the preparation and finally the eating. Food preparation is often the last stage of food processing—mixing, blending, seasoning, heating, etc. all add their unique qualities to the food product and are determined by local culture. Chart 8 lists some of the various food preparation techniques; Chart 9 lists food utensils found around the world that are used in consuming food.

One of the major problems in food preparation is the use of inefficient stoves that consume valuable wood. The use of fuel wood—branches, twigs, forest floor debris, etc.—for cooking amounts to about 1 kg per person per day in developing areas. This is about twice the amount in heat value used by the developed world for cooking.[28] The reason for this difference is the gross inefficiency of the open fire and stoves currently in use in developing areas. The widespread destruction of forests for firewood can cause serious environmental problems including soil erosion, water runoff, flooding, and, ultimately, desertification.[29] The burning of dung and crop residues also has its problems in the fact that the nutrients in these materials are lost to the soil if they are burned. The use of wood, dung, and crop residues needs to be drastically reduced and suitable alternatives substituted.

Last but not least, food waste, both what is eaten and eliminated as well as what is lost along the way, needs to be considered. With waste the loop is closed; we can put back into the food production system some of the resources it needs to produce food. As stated or implied throughout, there is much waste in the processing, delivery, and consumption end of the food system. It should be borne in mind,

though, that waste is only waste if it is not utilized; all waste is valuable resources in the wrong place. There are wastes in processing, packaging, storage, delivery, preparation, consumption, and elimination. How much food is thrown out each day in the restaurants, cafeterias, and homes of the world? Approximately 32 million tons of food are thrown out each year in the U.S.; 21 million tons from the household sector and the rest from hospitals, prisons, and other institutions.[10] How much valuable nitrogen is lost and how many gallons of clean water polluted each day when all the toilets of the world flush? Strategies for dealing with these problems follow in the Strategy section of this document.

Even though refrigeration and deep freezing are excellent means to preserve food quality, extend shelf life, and expand the distances that perishable foods can be transported, they are not in widespread use in the areas of the world that could benefit the most from them because the infrastructure that is needed to support such a technique—refrigerated warehouses in rural areas, refrigerated train and truck transport, as well as refrigerated storage and display facilities in urban areas—does not exist. Nor does the energy to power all those refrigeration units or the trained personnel to repair them, or the roadways, or the purchasing ability by the local populace exist. Before industrial food processing can commence there need to be reliable supplies of raw material, water, processing equipment, packaging materials, fuel, and waste disposal facilities, and storage for finished products as well as distribution networks and education for the consumer as to the uses of the new product. When we talk of developing food processing capabilities in

developing areas, past experience informs us that we are in fact speaking of total economic and social development; we're talking about the possible radical shift away from survival/subsistence agriculture and possibly toward cash-crop, specialized, or a new type of agriculture—abundance agriculture; away from the poor farmer and possibly toward the food manufacturer or well-off farmer; away from the cycle of local feasts and famine to regional interdependence and plenty; away from the coerced time spent in maintaining survival and toward the increased "reinvestable time" that can come with the successful production of more food than can be consumed locally. Past experience has also furnished us with numerous examples of how not to go about this inevitable evolutionary transition to the "better life," and the negative qualities of freeing people from their total dependence on the good earth and her fickle weather, but not furnishing them with any other connection to the well-springs of life.

The establishment of technologically self-reliant and energy self-sufficient local food conservation and processing industries in rural developing regions could be a great tool for development. Such industries could employ surplus rural workers and improve rural income, increase food supplies with little additional cost in natural resources, stimulate production, open new opportunities for investment, result in better quality food for consumers, and positively change trade balances.[30]

The most "economically" efficient way, according to traditional economic theory, of providing increased food processing and storage techniques for developing regions today—and thereby cutting down on food losses—is to shift to centralized large scale operations. As pointed out in the Long Ranger section of this document, what is economical in terms of dollars does not always make sense in terms of people's values and culture or resource use from a larger perspective. A more appropriate approach would be to simultaneously upgrade the subsistence farming system as well as prepare the infrastructure needed for larger scale food production. The use of decentralized processing and storage facilities instead of a sole concentration on the large processing plant would help the local farmer to increase his wealth and reinvestable time instead of sending him packing to the shanty towns of the city in search of a job. Food processing plants can be located in rural areas providing both jobs for surplus rural labor and a shorter distance for highly perishable food to travel. The farmer in India, Africa, and South America is mainly interested in preserving his food resources to last until the next harvest. Rodent, insect, and moisture proof storage bins could be developed and mass produced with surplus rural and urban labor. More efficient food distribution and preparation techniques can be implemented along with the overall development of human life-support services—health care, education, water supply, roadways, flood control, energy production, and shelter construction.

History

Before 15,000 B.C.	Roasting, pounding, drying
15,000 B.C.	Dried fish, boiling, smoking, steaming
9000 B.C.	Alcoholic fermentation, salting, baking, sieving, primitive pressing, seasoning
8000–6000 B.C.	Pottery making, bread making, and some meat preservation exists
5000 B.C.	Stomach of animals used as pouches to carry liquid—milk in contact with renin enzymes and bacteria forms first cheese
3500 B.C.	Filtration, lactic acid fermentation, more types of flavoring, flotation, leavened bread
3000 B.C.	Sailboats begin commerce and trade, distributing food, tools, and ideas
3000 B.C.	Fermentation of fruit wines increases their storage
600 B.C.	Greece and Rome: Corks with pitch and beeswax used to seal glass and earthenware jars
1600 A.D.	Europe: Cured cod commercially packed and shipped abroad
1679	England: Papain invents autoclave (early pressure cooker)
1735	Germany: First case of botulism identified, named from *botulus* meaning sausage indicating disease relationship to infected sausage
1780	England: Steam engine applied to flour milling
1785	U.S.A.: Evans develops conveying system; first continuous-flow flour mill
1795	France: Masson and Challet invent first vegetable dehydration room with stream of 40° C hot air flow over thin slices of vegetables
1809	France: Appert develops heat treatment and appertization (packaging in sealed container)
1810	England: Durand awarded first patents for glass and metal containers for food canning
1819	U.S.A.: Underwood and Kennett begin commercial canning operations
1830	England: Coffey and Coffey still (made volume production of spirits and wine possible)
1830	U.S.A.: Rellieux invents the triple-effect evaporation
1834	Beginning of food chemistry—idea of varied molecular structure for three essential components: carbohydrates, fats and proteins
1834	England: Perkins invents first vapor compression refrigeration system (similar to those used today)
1835	Switzerland: Sultzberger invents roller milling (flour)
1840	U.S.A.: Tin food containers in widespread commercial use
1842	England: Benjamin develops food freezing by immersion in ice and salt brine
1850	England: Perkin steam-heated oven
1850	Australia: World's first refrigerated warehouse (salt and brine)
1851	France: Chevalier and Appert develop autoclave for sterilization of food for canning—lessening

dangers from steam/pressure vessels

1855 England: Roller drying of milk

1856 U.S.A.: Borden Co. develops first condensed milk process

1857 U.S.A.: The use of ice made summer packing of perishables possible—facilitating the shipment of pork instead of live hogs

1858 U.S.A.: Mason awarded first patent for glass jar with screw top

1860 France: Carre invents absorption refrigeration system

1861 Australia: Mort and Nicolle establish first meat freezing factory

1865 U.S.A.: Fish being frozen for local use

1873 U.S.A.: Ick invents meat slicing machine

1873 Tellier, with ice-making industry, makes commercial refrigeration possible

1874 U.S.A.: Shriver designs retort

1875 Ginde introduces ammonia refrigeration system

1875 U.S.A.: Armour Meats builds first refrigerated (ice) rail car

1876 U.S.A.: Knott introduces freezing in hermetically-sealed containers

1876 South America to France: First successful transport of meat by sea (refrigeration)

1877 Sweden: Centrifuged cream separator invented by de Laval

1880 New Zealand: First meat freezing plant starts operations

1894 Rostosnik invents revolving slicer

1900 England: Jam boiling thermometer

1905 U.S.A.: First commercial cold pack process implemented (salt and ice)

1908 Australia: First international institute of refrigeration formed

1908 U.S.A.: Baker develops fruit freezing

1910 U.S.A.: Locker plants, where individual families can store frozen food supplies, are opened

1911 Denmark: Ottesin develops quick-freezing process

1925 U.S.A.: Birdseye first freezes fruit in hermetically-sealed cans

1929 U.S.A.: First "paper bottles" commercially used for frozen juices and vegetables

1930 U.S.A.: Vita-Fruit Products freezing 30,000 gallons of juice per day

1930 U.S.A.: First commercial shipment of frozen food by mail

1930 U.S.A.: Instant-seal vacuum-capping machine in use

1930's U.S.A.: Dry ice used in storage, transportation and the actual freezing process

1931 U.S.A.: Birdseye introduces multi-plate freezer

1932 U.S.A.: Hold introduces eutectic filled plate for transport of frozen foods by truck

1932 U.S.A.: Birdseye uses silica gel refrigerated cars to ship frozen meat across country

1934 U.S.A.: Finnegan develops cold blast freezing tunnel for frozen food

1938 U.S. Food, Drug and Cosmetic Act

1940 U.S.A.: Deep Freeze Corporation introduces first home freezer commercially available

1945 U.S.A.: Flosdorf invents freeze-drying

1950's England: Quick fish freezing

1953 U.S.A.: Staple machines used to close cartons of frozen food

1957 U.S.A.: First containerized cargo ships

1958 U.S.A.: Delaney Amendment to the 1938 Food, Drug and Cosmetic Act state that any chemical additive capable of causing cancer is specifically prohibited from food products

1960's U.S.A.: Freeze drying commercially begins

U.S.A.: The "Truth in Labeling" Act instituted; stipulates that all food packages bear uniform and accurate representation of weight, volume, or count of the package

1965 Adoption of standard-sized cargo containers for world-wide use aboard ships and trucks

1965 U.S.A.: Non-destructive measurements of the interior quality of fruit available

1970 First refrigerated containerized cargo ship transports perishable food

Advantages

1. Preserving food insures a steady supply.
2. Large scale food processing enables food by-products to be utilized; for example, individual animal slaughter for immediate sale of fresh meat often results in the loss of blood, bones, and other useful animal products that are recoverable for food or feed products in large slaughterhouses; also analogous losses occur when primitive equipment is used for milling grain, extracting raw sugar, or pressing oil from seeds. In some areas of India 1/3 of the rice is lost through antiquated rice mills.[31]

Disadvantages

1. The processing of foods is energy and capital intensive.
2. Food processing and distribution requires specialized know-how and experience, often lacking in developing regions.
3. Over-processing of food removes a lot of nutritional content.
4. Over-processing of food adds some ingredients that may not be totally safe for human systems.

What Needs to be Done

1. Establish a Global and Regional Food Processing and Storage Research Institute to research and develop solutions to food loss, processing, storage, distribution, preparation, and waste disposal problems.
2. Establish global food quality identification standards for production, processing, and purchasing of food.
3. Develop a global, satellite-assisted food production monitoring network.
4. Develop and mass-produce resource efficient large and small scale storages for grains.
5. Develop and mass-produce solar-powered small-scale grain drying processes.
6. Develop and mass-produce resource efficient community refrigeration units.
7. Develop and test procedures for long term storage of foods in the Antarctic and under sea.
8. Develop and test large airship transport and storage of food stuffs.
9. Develop technologically self-reliant and energy self-sufficient food processing industries in rural areas.
10. Develop new, low cost, and simple techniques for home and community food preservation.
11. Develop new low cost stoves that do not utilize valuable firewood.
12. Modernize the cereal milling industry in developing regions.
13. Reorganize urban food distribution; eliminate the middleman.
14. Develop educational programs to reduce household food waste.
15. Develop food packaging materials (possibly edible) from parts of the plant formerly discarded, and from plastics made from vegetable oils.
16. Develop and mass-produce locally, appropriate pedal-powered transport vehicles for transporting heavy loads.
17. Establish local organizations—Food Conservation Units—to train local specialists in assessing and preventing post-harvest losses.

References

Food Processing

1. "Marketing, Processing, and Distribution of Food," The World Food Problem, Vol. II, pp. 539–67.

2. International Symposium on Mycotoxins in Foodstuffs, M.I.T., 1964; Mycotoxins in Foodstuffs, proceedings, Cambridge, MA., M.I.T. Press, 1965, p. 291.

3. Ling, L., "Man Loses a Fifth of the Crops He Grows," Atlantic, special issue for FAO for Freedom from Hunger, 1961. Using Ling's figure of 3.55% loss (of 1961–62 production) on 1975 production, this figure was arrived at.

4. Rice in India: A Techno-Economic Review, Mysore, India, Central Food Technological Research Institute, 1965.

5. FAO of the UN, Regional Conference for Asia and the Far East.

6. Development Assistance Group, International Division, U.S. GAO, "Hungry Nations Need to Reduce Food Losses Caused by Storage, Spillage, and Spoilage," Food Update, GAO, Community & Economic Development Division, Oct. 1977, Washington, D.C., p. 7.

7. Hall, D. W., FAO Informal Working Bulletin No. 24, 1963. Jordan, R. C., U.N. Conference on the Application of Science and Technology for the Benefit of the Less Developed Area, Vol. V, Geneva, 1963.

8. Weitz-Hettelsater Engineers, Economic and Engineering Study—Marketing Facilities for Grain and Tuberous Crops (an economic survey for ETA), Weitz-Hettelsater, 1963, 2 vols.

9. Jordan, R. D., New Techniques for Temperature Control of Perishable Goods in Transport and Storage Applicable to the Less Developed Area. In U.N. Conference on the Application of Science and Technology for the Benefit of the Less Developed Area, U.S. papers, Washington, D.C., U.S. Government Printing Office, 1962, Vol. V, pp. 120–32.

10. Stemlieb, S., "Food Waste: An Opportunity to Improve Resource Use," Food Update, GAO, Community & Economic Development Division, Oct. 1977, Washington, D.C., pp. 5–6.

11. Robbins, W., "Nader Assails Spending for Food Ads," New York Times, 8-18-73.

12. Waters, H. F., "Television," Newsweek, 2-21-77, p. 69.

13. George, S., How the Other Half Dies—The Real Reasons for World Hunger, Penguin Books, 1976, in Ceres, FAO Review of Agriculture and Development, FAO, Rome, Italy, May–June 1978, p. 47.

14. Chemical Marketing Reporter, 7-18-77

15. "Trends in Fresh Fruit and Vegetable Consumption, Nutritional Qualities of Fresh Fruits and Vegetables," Futura Publishing Co., Mount Kisco, New York, 1974, in Dietary Goals for the U.S., Superintendant of Documents, U.S. Government Printing Office, Washington, D.C.

16. Neil and Joslyn, Fundamentals of Food Processing Operations.

17. Stewart, G. F., Amerine, M. A., Food Science and Technology, Westport, CT, N. Potter, Inc., 1973.

18. Food Chemical Codex, National Academy of Sciences, Washington, D.C., 2nd Edition, 1972.

19. Ibid.

20. Stewart, G. F., Amerine, M. A., Food Science and Technology, Westport, CT, N. Potter, Inc., 1973.

21. 1965 figures.

22. "Food in Space: Orbiting Black Markets," Technology Review, Feb. 1979, p. 85.

23. Kinne, I., McClure, T. A., "Energy in the Food System," Encyclopedia of Food, Agriculture, and Nutrition, McGraw-Hill, New York, 1978.

24. U.S. GAO, "Redesigning Shipping Containers to Reduce Food Costs," Report to the Congress of the U.S. by the Comptroller-General, CED-78-81, Apr. 1978.

25. Hoover, S. R., "Prevention of Food-Processing Wastes," Science, Vol. 183, 3-1-74, pp. 824–28.

26. Gabel, M., Energy, Earth, and Everyone, Straight Arrow Books, 1975.

27. Okress, E. C., "The Franklin Institute Has High Hopes for Its Big Balloon," IEEE Spectrum, Dec. 1978, pp. 41–46.

28. Kotz, N., "Agribusiness," Radical Agriculture, ed. Merrill, R.; Harper & Row, 1976, pp. 41–51.

29. Business Week, 3-8-76.

30. Parpia, H. A. B., "More than Food Should Be Saved," Ceres, FAO Review of Agriculture and Development, FAO, Rome, Italy, Nov.–Dec. 1977, pp. 19–24.

31. The World Food Conference: Selected Materials for the Use of the U.S. Congressional Delegation to the World Food Conference, Rome, Italy, 11-5-74; Compiled for the Sub-committee on Agriculture and Forestry, U.S. Senate, p. 164.

Strategies for a Regenerative Food System

There are a number of different responses or approaches to solving the world food problem. One of the traditional responses by political leaders and bureaucracies to all problems is to do nothing and hope the problem will either go away or solve itself. With the food problem this is not entirely irrational or counter-productive because food problems *are* in the habit of taking care of themselves—either the weather gets better and more food is produced and temporarily "solves" the problem, or ingenious and industrious farmers develop solutions to the problems they have access to and temporarily "solve" the problem, or the weather gets worse and famine then "solves" the problem. This "do nothing" approach to the food problem is often accompanied by fatalistic indictments of anything that has ever been either tried or proposed in the past and even more vehement denunciations of anything proposed in the present. Setting up an ad hoc committee to study the problem is usually the most daring action taken. Related to this approach but even more conservative or reactionary is the silent insistence (through ignorance or avoidance) that there really is no problem. Another classic response is to do more of whatever was being done in the past. When confronted by a seemingly insurmountable problem, double whatever it was that wasn't working before and your opposition is decreased fourfold. "If money won't solve it, more money will" is the rationale. Agricultural planning is often permeated by scarcity models—the "there isn't enough to go around" syndrome—and further constrained by a short-range focus that ignores large-scale and long range patterns. Both the faulty models and focus grew out of the milleniums-long preoccupation of agriculture with the short yearly cycles of coping with shortages.

The predominant way resources have been allocated in solving large-scale social development problems in the developed world is through a type of industrialization often referred to (scatologically?) as the "trickle down" approach. In this approach, emphasis is on centralized planning and control, the development of a "modern sector" of heavy industry and major capital intensive projects such as power plants, highways, etc., the rapid growth of gross national product, extensive development of private corporations and multinational enterprises, increased access to foreign capital to purchase equipment, artificially induced low prices for food and other agricultural goods, inflated prices for manufactured goods, and a "free" market economy. Those in possession of investment capital—the rich—are the ones who benefit first and the most from such an arrangement. Benefits to the rest of society—increased employment, health benefits, education, etc.—trickle down from the top to the bottom. This approach is coming under increasing fire by those who claim that the trickle dries up before it reaches the poor who need it the most and that a trickle, even if it is reaching some, is not nearly enough to bring about constructive change or to meet the startling shortfalls of 120–145 million metric tons of staple food crops projected for 1990 (over three times the shortfall that occurred in the good production year of 1975).[1] A Niagara waterfall or avalanche is more in line with what is needed to solve the problems of the hungry poor. We have to do more than just continue to eke by. To meet the basic human needs and expectations of all of humanity on Earth requires an approach to solving problems, to development, essentially different than traditional methods.

To design a system which will meet the specifications of the preferred state described in the first part of this book involves being both comprehensive and anticipatory, as well as taking an approach that is both global in its scope and local in its considerations. It needs to include three basic elements: 1) emergency measures to relieve the dangers of the immediate crisis; 2) conservation measures to reduce or stabilize demand on the food system, to reduce loss of limited resources, and to increase production; and 3) long-term measures to make sure the problem does not recur.

As with the world's energy problem, there is no one answer to the world's food needs. The exploitation of single-cell protein, increased fertilizer supplies, the Antarctic krill, better storage facilities, land reform, appropriate technology, family planning, violent revolution, or any other single item will not ensure all of humanity, both those alive today and our future generations, of a regenerative supply of food.

As pointed out earlier, the food problem is a complex web of interconnected parts and processes. The intimate links between food, energy, transportation, health care, population, education, and communication dictate that agricultural development, especially in rural developing areas where these links are more apparent and direct, be part of an overall program of general development. The purpose of development is to increase the life-support

". . . development is not so much economic growth as it is the cultivation of the capacity to respond to new challenges."[2]

capacities and individual freedoms of any particular locale, region, or even the planet as a whole. The purpose of agricultural development, then, is to increase the life-support capacity, the amount of forward-days, that an area is organized to provide for itself. The benefits of development should be shared as widely as possible not only for humanitarian or ethical reasons but also because a healthy and educated populace can not only help themselves to ever higher attainments that can then be globally shared, but they also create new markets for the world's manufacture and service industries. Additionally, the inter-dependence of population growth and economic affluence is widely documented.[3] As affluence goes up, birth rate goes down (see charts on page 000). Development is not a closed system nor a machine, it is a biological growth, an open system. Development is not a limited pie, with just so many pieces. An orchard—where proper cultivation brings in more and more fruit on a regenerative basis—is a better model for development than a pie. It is time to replace our images of scarcity with those of abundance. The fruits of development are *multiplied,* not divided, by being shared.

Currently, somewhere between a quarter and a half of the population of developing regions and up to one quarter of the planet's population is being bypassed by the forward march of development.[3] (See chart.) Primarily, two groups have been bypassed: those unemployed in towns and those in the countryside who don't have the capability to tap the fruits of the green revolution. To help remedy this situation, development priority or emphasis will be on increasing the income to the small farmer in the developing regions of the world. Here, development will have the largest effect on increasing the amount of available food. By focusing on the small farmer, by designing systems to meet the needs of the small farmer, all farmers will benefit (something that does not work in reverse). By increasing production and income for large numbers of small family-farmers, demand for goods and services increases, which generates economic activity and employment in rural trade centers as well as domestic markets for urban-based industries.[4] Increased small family-farm income will also empower the rural poor to provide themselves with the basic human needs for

Global Poverty: Unmet Basic Human Needs[5]

Undernourished (below suggested calorie/protein levels; inadequate diet to insure that each person is able to work mentally and physically in good health)	400–930 million
Inadequate Drinking Water	1200 million
No Access to Effective Health Care	800–1500 million
Inadequate Housing (lacking minimum socially acceptable dwellings)	800–1030 million
Illiterate Adults	800 million
Children Not Enrolled in School	250–300 million
Less than $90.00 Income Per Year	1300 million
Life Expectancy Below 60 Years	1700 million
Life Expectancy Below 50 Years	1260 million
Life Expectancy Below 40 Years	31 million
Unemployed Landless or Marginal Farmers	283 million

such things as clean water, clothing, shelter, sanitation facilities, etc. Because development is an ongoing process, this will foster a region's self-reliance instead of a central government dependence. In the context of overall development, increasing income is the quickest, most equitable, participatory, and flexible way of meeting human needs. Development does not mean total self-sufficiency or independence, but rather a self-reliant sufficiency with a synergetic interdependence with other locales and regions where each locality has more degrees of freedom after development than before.

Development planning and the concept of "progress" today is pervaded by an underlying image of what it is to be "developed"; "successful"; a "have" rather than a "have-not"; that is based on a Western urbanized model. "Developed" implies large cities with tall buildings, concrete superhighways with automobiles, and lots of "action"—the Tokyo, New York, Mexico City, Paris, Hong Kong image that comes through the movies (and television for those with access to it). This underlying image of success or full development is the "city of the future." The rural poor of the world need new images of their possible futures. There is no reason why the highest standard of living possible—measured by such things as access to desirable food, clothing, shelter, clean water, sanitation facilities, health care, education, transportation, communication, recreation, cultural facilities, and self-fulfilling employment—higher than *anyone* anywhere currently enjoys, couldn't exist in a rural setting. The vision of the present-day rural poor or the small farm family in developing regions of the world living at a higher standard of living— better educated, more leisure time, more access to cultural activities, etc.—than the urban North American or European is not incompatible with present-day technology, know-how, and resources. There is no reason the rich cultural heritage of over two billion rural people of the Earth needs to be disrupted or destroyed by development. There is no inherent reason for the rural poor to go to the city if development is carried out from the position of allowing the rural populations to develop themselves to standards of living that are equal to (but culturally distinct from) those of the city dweller. It is past time to end the world-wide second-class image of the farmer and make him or her a first-class hero.

To adequately deal with the world's food problems, we need to deal with all aspects of the global food system. This is not as impossible as it may first sound because we are already dealing with everything. What is necessary is to emphasize certain things, develop new structures to coordinate existing parts into synergetic wholes, and to coordinate the whole towards goals that are beneficial to 100% of humanity.

The overall guiding principles or values of development used here are to maximize diversity, flexibility, participation, and stability, that is, to furnish a regenerative structure for

human growth. The decision-making criteria listed in the first part of this book are the specific guidelines for development used in formulating the strategies in this document.

Given these general overall values and guidelines, the following section outlines a design science plan that attempts to deal holistically with the world's food problems. It is a synergetic synoptic, view of the variables that affect the world food system and is intended to give a feel for the whole strategy rather than the details of a few parts. Details follow in part four of this section—Critical Paths.

The Chinese/American Alternative

The two most visible (and successful) models that the world presently has for feeding itself could be summarized as the North American model and the Chinese model. The following chart compares these two systems.

American Agriculture
The North American model is probably better known to most people reading this book; it involves the intense use of energy, machinery, high-yield seeds, fertilizer, pesticides, processing, centralization; relies on a wide availability of a large consumer choice of products; and is very efficient in terms of output per man-hour. Relatively few people (3%) are engaged in agricultural production and agriculture itself has a low development priority relative to industry. The U.S. uses more than three and one-half times as much fertilizer, over four times as much energy, and has over twenty-three times the total number of farm machines as China.

Chinese Agriculture
The Chinese food system model differs from the North American model in its emphasis on

doing more with less and on measuring efficiency in terms of output per unit area rather than per man-hour invested; agriculture is labor intensive, cropping intensive—as many as twelve vegetable crops are grown in one year in some places[7]—and decentralized, with each separate locale being highly self-sufficient and self-reliant.[8] Most of China's population (63%) is engaged in agriculture, and agriculture has development priority over everything, including industry. The way to reach the goals of development—more food, shelter, transportation, communication, education, etc., in the Chinese model is through agricultural development.[8] In the North American model, raising the standard of living is achieved through emphasis on industrial development.

China has only two-thirds as much arable land as the U.S., but four times the total population to feed. It successfully accomplishes this task by having almost seventy times the agricultural population that the U.S. does. Each person in the U.S. has almost one hectare of arable land while the Chinese have less than one fifth of a hectare per person. Crops are grown much more intensely on Chinese land

Chart 1. China/USA Agricultural Portrait.[6]

	China	Percent of World	USA	Percent of World	World	Units
Total Population	866	21.1	216	5.3	4103	million
Agricultural Population	539	27.7	5.4	.3	1947	million
Percent of Total Population	62.2		2.5		47.5	per cent
Arable Land	129	9.2	187	13.4	1398	million hectares
Hectares/person	.15		.87		.34	
Irrigated Land	85.2	36.9	16.6	7.2	231	million hectares
Percent Irrigated	66		8.9			
Synthetic Fertilizer Consumption						
Nitrogen	3.82	9	8.28	21.3	38.8	million metric tons
Phosphate	1.39	5.7	7.6	19	24.1	million metric tons
Potash	.53	2.5	4.61	22.2	20.7	million metric tons
Work Animals	20.3	16.5	9.4	7.6	122.6	million head
Farm Machinery	20×10^4	1.1	44×10^5	24	183×10^5	tractors
Energy Consumption	590.1	7.1	2485.5	29.9	8318.4	mmt coal equivalent
Cereal Production	242	16.6	262	18	1459	million metric tons
Cereal Yield/HA	2061		3667			kilograms
Wheat Production	40	10.3	55	14.2	387	million metric tons
Rice Production	131	35.7	4.5	1.2	367	million metric tons
Cattle Production	2.1	4.4	12	25	48	million metric tons
Pig Production	10.4	23.6	6	13.6	44	million metric tons
Milk Production	3.8	.9	55.7	13.6	409	million metric tons
Egg Production	3.862	15.6	3.820	15.5	24.70	million metric tons
Aquaculture Production	2.39	60	.041	1.03	3.98	million metric tons

All figures 1976–77 from FAO *Production Yearbook*, Vol. 31, 1978.

than in the U.S.; irrigation is widespread—over five times the amount in the U.S.—with 66% of the arable land irrigated in China and only 9% in the U.S. Aquaculture is also widely developed in China: 60% of the world's aquaculture products are produced there, while the United States accounts for only 1% of production. By increasing the use of fertilizer and mechanization (currently China uses twice the number of work animals as the U.S.), as well as the continued use of intensive, coordinated, massive human labor projects, China hopes to greatly increase her total yields per hectare, which now average only 56% of those in the U.S. In the highly praised and emulated Tachai county in China, yields are already nearly twice the U.S. average yield per hectare (6820 kg. vs. 3440 kg./ha). This same mountainous county, in ten years and with 83 households and a population under 500, built 183 stone dams across seven gullies, 9.3 kilometers of earthen embankments on the eight ridges of their hillside, combined more than 4700 small farm plots into 1500 bigger plots, flattened 33 hills of varying size, filled in 15 small gullies, moved nearly 700,000 cubic meters of earth and stone, reshaped all sloping land into contour-terraced fields, dug a 7 kilometer mountain-skirting irrigation canal, built three large water storage ponds, broadened mountain trails and roads to make way for tractors, cooperated with professional research workers in designing and building farm machinery suitable for local use, forested nearly 27 hectares of formerly barren hillside, and now have over 40,000 fruit trees.[8] Such labor intensive projects, and the obvious planning that goes along with such undertakings, has enabled China to feed its people. Planning has an integral part in Chinese agriculture. All counties are required to map out over-all plans, in stages, for farm construction, improving soil, and water conservation.

The type of foods consumed by North Americans and Chinese are also indicative of the differences between the two systems. In China, each person is adequately fed on an estimated 204 kilograms (450 lbs.) of grain per year; of this, 160 kilograms (350 lbs.) are consumed directly as cereal or cereal products, and 45 kilograms (100 lbs.) are fed to animals. In the United States, each person consumed more than 900 kilograms (2000 lbs.) of grains per year; of this, 68 kilograms (150 lbs.) are eaten directly, and the rest, 840 kilograms (1850 lbs.), is fed to animals which are then eaten. The Chinese people eat 77% of their grains, while the U.S. feeds 90% to animals.

Conventional or North American agriculture and/or business tells us that, to solve the world's food problems, what is needed is to industrialize agriculture, to export western or advanced technology to developing regions: build four hundred new 1000 ton/day fertilizer manufacturing plants, quadruple the amount of irrigated land in the world, bring a third or more of the world's potentially arable land into cultivation, plant vast tracts of individual crops, use high yielding varieties of seeds and use machines and automation where possible for more efficient cultivation, harvesting, processing, etc., control pests with chemical pesticides and population growth with birth control programs, and take advantage of the increased economies of large scale centralized food production and processing. Estimates vary on how much could be produced with the wide scale application of these modern food production techniques, but one recent estimate says that about fifty billion people could be fed a nutritious, largely vegetarian diet if these techniques were used.[10]

Alternative Agriculture

New insights into our global food system—neither Chinese or American—tell us that heavy use of chemical fertilizers can burn out or deplete soils and cause serious pollution problems with run-off; that to bring new lands under the plow as well as build those fertilizer plants and farm machines would be enormously expensive in energy (one estimate finds that it would take a three-fold increase in the amount of energy used for agriculture to double the world's food production[11]); and that chemical pesticides are dangerous to human survival and are breeding insects that are immune to these poisons. Alternatives proposed by the later insights are "natural" fertilizers and pest control methods; soil conservation and reclamation; appropriate food technologies for each specific locality instead of one technology; diversification of crops, both in terms of genetic diversity in the same crop as well as in the actual planting, i.e. multi-cropping instead of monocropping; income energy sources instead of a heavy dependence upon the diminishing supply of fossil fuels; and a basic decentralization of the food system.

All three viewpoints—conventional North American agriculture, Chinese agriculture, and "alternative" agriculture—admittedly abstracted and maybe overcategorized, are nevertheless operative and, perhaps ironically, all are "right." We do need fertilizer plants, but we also need to build them as efficiently as possible, and also to preserve our soil for the future. Essentially, the various approaches can be seen as either short term tactics to solve a pressing problem or as long term solutions to our regenerative survival. The same dichotomy can be observed in the energy systems of the world. In the short term—next month, next year, the next few years—we have critical energy needs that must be met by our fossil fuels, but in the long run, the regenerative solutions—conservation, solar, wind, bioconversion, etc.—must be implemented if we are to have a continuing supply of energy. If the regenerative solutions to our problems can also take care of the immediately pressing critical and emergency needs, then so much the better.

The two different food systems of China and conventional North America can be viewed as two methods of developing a region's human life-support capacities. The differences are caused by geography, climate, relative sizes and demographic make-up of populations, and organizational structures. Because most of the developing world is closer to China's conditions—with large populations and relatively little good arable land (the U.S. is a relative "freak" of nature with her incredibly fertile, productive, and large amounts of arable land and small population)—the Chinese model of development through its basic and primary emphases on agricultural development and doing more with less would be the more logical place to start in developing food system plans for other regions. Building upon the good points in both systems, dropping the items that are not suitable for a given area, and incorporating both what a given locality has learned about producing food in its specific geography and climate and what the latest contemporary research has learned (that goes beyond either the Chinese or North American model) about nutrition, soil conservation, the dangers of pesticides, overuse of fertilizer, depletable energy sources, monocropping, overprocessing, storage, and generally doing more with less resources would be a firm basis for insuring a regenerative supply of food for the world. The following is a world food plan which, along with

some new perspectives, tactics, and the synergetic combination of some already known strategies, integrates these three approaches into one world food development strategy with critical short term needs and equally crucial long term mandates.

Dare to be Ethical: People First

As was seen in Section II, there are many sources of food that could be but are not utilized, and many that are utilized but could be much further developed. There are also many ways of increasing the efficiency of the food distribution system so that everyone has access to more foods as well as increasing the efficiency of food processing, storage, and preparation systems in use throughout the world.

The global food system development strategy calls for the simultaneous development of decentralized and centralized food production, storage, processing, and distribution facilities. The purpose of the large centralized units of the global food system is to synthesize, coordinate, and absorb the surplus of the decentralized units, and to take advantage of the increased efficiencies of some large scale processes. The purpose of the decentralized units is to make as many households, communities, and regions as self-sufficient in food and as much in control of their lives and life-support systems as possible.

As they are used here, the words "centralized" and "decentralized" are descriptive of *one* developmental process; two sides to the same coin. Neither is good or bad in itself, but both can be abused. Large scale centralized production, processing, and distribution units can be optimally functional only if they are locally appropriate, and can achieve long term viability only if they are in tune with the decentralized local environments that they coordinate, are dependent upon, and, in fact, in a very real sense, are composed of. Centralization needs to be looked upon as more than just "large." It also plays an integrative role. Centralization/integration has to be looked upon as a means of increasing the efficiency and self-sufficiency of the locality, not vice-versa. Centralization should foster decentralized, self-sufficient synergy. Decentralization needs centralized coordination and synthesis or it degenerates into chaos.

Centralization does not have to mean "big." Although it can be big, it starts off small. It is an integrative function. In terms of the time frame of development, centralization comes first and involves the pulling together of numerous diffuse factors—energy, materials, and process—and combining them into one functioning unit that is more efficient than even the sum of all its parts. For example, Thomas Edison pulled together many diverse elements to build the world's first electric utility in New York. At the time, Consolidated Edison was a revolutionary organization that brought light to the people of New York. As time goes on, a small centralizing/integrating process can become large, rigidified, or bureaucracized and be unresponsive to the needs of the people it is serving. When the know-how that enabled this centralization to coalesce becomes widely known, then the process of decentralization begins. New know-how, new needs, or different systems may re-engender the centralizing process. Because "everything is connected to everything else," one part of a technological, social, or economic system could be in the midst of a decentralizing process while another part could be becoming centralized, as for instance in food production—home gardens are a decentralizing process, but the seeds the home gardener uses (at present) come from increasingly centralizing seed manufacturers (e.g., Burpee Seeds). Centralization primarily involves energy and materials—because they can easily be collected in one place—and decentralization primarily involves information or know-how—educational processes. Viewed in this way, the centralization/decentralization phenomenon is a pulsating process that runs throughout the entire developmental process on all its levels. It makes no sense to advocate either half of this process by itself as an ideology or goal. Both processes can and have been abused; too much, or a misuse of, centralization can lead to oligarchy or monopoly; an abuse of decentralization can lead to deprivation of the benefits—such as polio vaccine, communication facilities, etc.—of the centralizing process. There are certain things that make sense—with present day needs, technology, resources, and know-how—to do on a large centralized/integrated scale; others make sense on a decentralized scale. Which is which is subject to steady transformation.

Feeding Humanity

The strategy is divided into two overall stages. The first has as its goal the elimination of famine, hunger, and the reaching of sound nutritional standards for everyone on Earth. The second stage is more long range and involves the reaching of a regenerative agricultural system; that is, one which is not based on depleting the stock of fossil fuel subsidies or other depletable resources or practices and that is efficient in all stages of food production and distribution. The time frame for the first stage is ten years; for the second, twenty-five years.

In ten years, there will be about five billion people on Earth.[12] To feed this many people will take about 5500×10^{12} calories and 73 million metric tons of protein each year (@ 3000 calories and 40 grams of protein per person per day[13]). As has been seen in previous sections, this is well within the productive and distributive capabilities of the world food system.

Between 1967 and 1972, North American wheat acreage was cut back from 193 to 166 million acres. More than 100 million tons of additional grain would have been available in 1972 if these 27 million acres had not been cut back. This grain would have been more than enough to ride out the crop failures of 1972 and 1974 without significant price increases.[14] In 1960–61, North American grain reserves amounted to about 120 million metric tons. By 1965, they were down to 90 million metric tons; 1974 saw the stocks dwindle to 43 million metric tons, and in 1975 they were down to a

Chart 2. Global Food Service.

MAJOR SUBDIVISIONS:	Emergency Relief Agency	Food Information and Management	Agricultural Resources Development Agency	Food Research Agency
PRIMARY FUNCTIONS RESPONSIBILITIES:	1. Famine and Food Relief	1. World Clearinghouse for Food Information 2. Global Food Monitoring/Famine Early Warning System 3. Global Food Education 4. Planning and Coordination of Global Food Service 10 and 25 Year Plans	1. Conventional Sources/Techniques 2. Unconventional Sources/Techniques 3. Fishing and Ocean Resources 4. Soil Conservation/Reclamation 5. Land Reform 6. Food Storage/Distribution/Preservation 7. Urban Food Production 8. Water Resources 9. Agriculture Training 10. Energy/Food Interface	1. New Sources of Food 2. Increased Efficiencies of Food System 3. Genetic Breeding of Plants/Animals; Genetic Resources Bank 4. Energy Systems

precarious 27 million tons, less than enough to feed humanity for one month. To adequately deal with and overcome problems such as these that arise naturally in the now global food system, an organization is needed that has as its special interest all of humanity, not the maximization of profit for a specific and minute subset of the overall global food system. Maximizing profit in the short term is a rational thing to do given the perspective of immediate corporate survival, but this is not always (and perhaps never) the case if the perspective is widened to include maximizing the survival of the species.

The *Global Food Service* is intended to be such an organization. It would be formed during the first five years of the global food system development strategy and would help coordinate all the various activities of the strategy. While in some ways similar to the Food and Agriculture Organization of the United Nations, the Service would be significantly different to warrant calling it something different here for the sake of distinguishing it.[15] Its clients would be 100% of humanity; its prime directive would be to service the food needs of its clients as efficiently in as short a time and with the least costs to the environment and consumer as possible. It would be non-political and non-profit. Every five years it should review its operations to see which operations could be better performed by existing or new services in the open market so as to progressively phase itself out of existence, if possible and desirable. It would (and could) dare to be ethical.

Given that there are currently over four billion people on Earth who need food each day and that 400 million of these people do not get enough food to be adequately nourished even though there is plenty of food produced for everyone's needs, a strong case can be made that there is an overwhelming mandate from the people of the world for an organization such as the Global Food Service.

Without an organization like the Global Food Service to look out for the needs of the entire global food system and its users, especially the most globally disenfranchised, the rural poor, there is the danger that agricultural "surpluses" in the developed areas of the world would result in another cycle of acreage restrictions (as is *again* happening in the U.S. in the late 1970's), grain stock reductions, price increases, etc. The Global Food Service will help insure that the "world food problem" is not looked upon as being just the problem of the poor, particularly those in the densely populated regions of South

Asia or the remote areas of South America and Africa. The Global Food Service will be partly composed of and help coordinate the activities of the already global food corporations and the regional and local food cooperatives, companies, farms, research and educational organizations, governments, and international agencies. It will assist in decentralizing, where necessary, large centralized bottlenecks of the food system, and coordinating the already local food production and processing units of the world into one synergetic whole. Each nation will be encouraged to formulate its own agricultural development goals for the short, medium, and long term for specific commodities important to each country and for each region within the country; these goals will include specific quantities for productivity increases, loss reductions, research priorities, numbers of farm families benefitted, and manpower requirements as well as goals to measure the success or failure of meeting the basic human needs of the respective populations. Such indicators as population growth rate, infant mortality rate, literacy, housing conditions, etc. will be monitored. Once goals are established for each region and the primary crops within those regions, specific strategies would be developed to meet the stated goals.

The Global Food Service will coordinate local, regional, and industrial planning into global food development plans, as well as coordinate the development of "out of the way" food resources such as ocean and desert farming, Antarctic storage of food, or new modes of bulk transport of food. It will blend all sources of food production, distribution techniques, etc. into one functional system. One of the basic tasks of the Global Food Service will be to help all the food producers of the world to utilize the large body of agricultural technology that has been developed from both the biological and physical sciences and is ready for immediate application. This transfer of appropriate technology will be aimed predominantly at the developing regions of the world.

The Global Food Service will be composed of the four functional areas shown in Chart 2.

The *Emergency Relief Agency* of the Global Food Service will be responsible for getting emergency food, shelter, and health care supplies to natural disaster and famine victims throughout the planet, but especially in the developing areas. This agency will coordinate the work of the existing emergency relief groups such as the International Red Cross, CARE, Project Hope, Catholic Relief Services, etc. into one functioning unit with a diversity of approaches. Taking its cue from the Famine Early Warning System of the Global Food Service, it will deal anticipatorily with potential and actual food shortages. The Agency would train people from every country, draft contingency plans that would list likely food and other requirements and sources of food, medicine, transportation, communication, and personnel, develop disaster and famine relief manuals, and stockpile essential supplies. The Emergency Relief Agency will have access to *all* the grain and other food reserves of the Food Service and be responsible for eliminating famine and starvation in the world. In a famine-

stricken area, the Emergency Relief Agency would immediately move to control prices so that the poor, those most in need, would not be discriminated against; public kitchens would be set up, and "famine hospitals" established in large numbers to vaccinate, delouse, disinfect, treat the starving sick, monitor the situation, and act as a check on panic. Law and order would be maintained to prevent looting and other abuses, and planning would begin at once for rehabilitation and development.

In order to ensure that food aid does not discourage a recipient area from necessary agricultural development, each area that receives emergency relief aid would have to "pay" for it through long-term commitments to agricultural development—over and above what they had already planned—that would be undertaken in each recipient region as soon as the emergency was over, or sooner if possible. The area would have to allocate funds for its food system's development so as to avoid future emergencies. Such projects as locally appropriate irrigation and flood control, fertilizer production facilities, rural roads, and storage facilities would be undertaken with the resources and unemployed of the food-short area. Food could be used as payment in such public works projects.

The *Food Information and Management* section will perform four distinct functions. The first will be as a clearinghouse for all the information that is relevant to the world's food problems. All relevant statistics from the various local, regional, national, and international organizations which document world food production, processing, and distribution (e.g., U.N. Food and Agriculture Organization, U.S. Department of Agriculture, etc.) will be collected, correlated, and made available to the public. A world inventory of all agricultural technology—including the technologies' function, performance, energy and material use, environmental constraints, scale, and cost—would be undertaken, updated, and made globally available. A global decentralized information network that would hook up every agricultural field worker, farmers' cooperative, agricultural college, and research institute via computer terminal and satellite telephone relay would be developed to facilitate the use and evolution of this and other data. Information on all food production, storage, and processing techniques, tactical alternatives, food resources and their locations, and researchers will be available to assist the decision-maker. In addition, decentralized educational projects for instructing (and learning from) rural farmers in new agricultural techniques will be carried out to insure that the increased benefits that come from new, advanced agricultural practices are maximized. Such things as crop variety, best planting rate, date, depth, fertilizer use, supplemental water use, pest and weed control, soil preparation, and such considerations as determining how the new crop fits into the rest of the farmer's cropping system, sequences of crop usage and how to determine maximum income wil be presented to the farmer in a wide variety of educational mediums, including the previously mentioned computer tie-in and,

where appropriate, agricultural field technicians to teach farmers in their own fields, radio, film, newspapers, pamphlets, posters, village meetings, field demonstrations by farmers at harvest, television from satellite broadcasts, agricultural education institutions such as agricultural colleges, rural secondary schools, extension and vocational schools, community centers, rural cooperatives, and traditional media such as village theater, traveling story-tellers, etc.[4]

The second area will monitor the global food situation through satellite and on-the-ground reconnaissance. A famine early warning system would have high priority; global weather reports and forecasts, crop forecasts, food reserves, retail prices, children's height-to-weight ratios, skin fold thicknesses, and height-to-arm circumference ratios would be monitored to warn in advance of impending famine.[16] This real time data will be used to avert famine or any food shortages that may arise due to local or regional crop failures. If a crop failure appears imminent or threatens, corrective measures can be taken to either save the crop, or, if that is impossible, to begin the shipment of food to the soon-to-be-needy area. In this way, the worst impacts of a food emergency or shortage can be averted or lessened. The monitoring section will also closely monitor the key indicators (see Section I) of the global food system to keep a constant check on the progress or lack of progress that the programs that the service has initiated are having. This feedback will guide future actions and programs. In this capacity, the food information clearinghouse will constantly monitor, display, and forecast local, regional, and world food needs and supplies. It will set up a

computerized "World Food Game"[17] that will model the world food situation and allow for the testing of new strategies for feeding the people of the world. This "World Food Game" would preferably be highly accessible and readily "played" on various levels by experts and grade-school children alike.

The third function of the Food Information and Management section of the Global Food Service will be in *global food and nutrition education.* Primarily local in focus, proper nutritional information as well as family planning and improved ways of producing, processing, and storing food will be disseminated via locally produced television, radio, films, posters, pamphlets, books, school curricula, lectures/demonstrations, etc.

The fourth function of the Food Information and Management section will be the development of plans and the *coordination/ management* of all the functional divisions of the Global Food Service. As pointed out before, the Global Food Service, because it is a meta-system to the nation-state and trans-national corporation, could do things that neither of these institutes seem capable of. It could be ethical. For example, given the power to regulate food imports and exports, it could tax—as long as there were groups of malnourished people in the world—the consumption of grains by livestock to such an extent that the poorest people in the world could compete with the richest people's animals. Besides the previously mentioned coordination of regional and country goals and plans, the Global Food Service, with the assistance of the various countries involved, will undertake the preparation of multi-country plans to take advantage of possible synergies between regions and countries brought about by common watersheds, shared coastline, similar climate, topography, etc.

Agricultural Resources Development will be the agency primarily responsible for coordinating the development of the world's food potentials so as to insure that 100% of humanity has all the food that it needs. It, in distinction to the Emergency Disaster Relief that will deal with food shortages, would be responsible for eliminating malnutrition in the world. It will view the planet as one entity with certain food requirements and certain methods and resources for meeting those needs. The Agricultural Resources Development Agency (ARDA) will be responsible for developing all the out-of-the-way food resources such as those of the ocean, desert, and Antarctic, as well as providing assistance and co-ordination in the planning and execution of local and regional agricultural development programs, and in the global processing and distribution of foods. It will also be responsible for amassing a global food storage.

The Emergency Relief Agency would deal primarily with food aid; Agricultural Resources Development would deal primarily with developing the means for producing and storing food locally through fertilizer production, high yield seeds, soil reclamation, storage building, education, and research. Food aid will continue to be necessary until each developing region has reached a point where its food needs can be met internally or through its own purchased imports. Food aid will assist the overall economic development of a region by eliminating undernourishment that, as evidence indicates, is a major factor in the low level of human productivity in many developing countries.[14]

Agricultural Resources Development Agency (ARDA) will deal with ten main areas: 1) Conventional Food Sources/Techniques, 2) Unconventional Food Sources/Techniques, 3) Ocean Resources and Fishing, 4) Soil Conservation/Reclamation, 5) Land Reform, 6) Food Storage/Processing/Distribution, 7) Urban Food Production, 8) Water Resources, 9) Agricultural Training, and 10) Energy/Food Interface.

The *Conventional Food Sources/Techniques* division of the Global Food Service will aid and abet the diffusion of current tried and proven agricultural techniques for increasing food production. Agriculture in developing regions is often divided into two sectors—a relatively small progressive modern sector that provides a major portion of the commercial agricultural products on a small percentage of the total land (in Mexico, 45% of the food is produced on 20% of the land), and a large, comparatively

Chart 3.[4] Average and Record Yields, 1975.

Food	Average Yield		
	Developing countries	U.S.	World record yield
Maize (kg/ha)	1,325	5,398	21,216
Wheat (kg/ha)	1,295	2,085	14,526
Soybeans (kg/ha)	1,544	1,883	7,398
Sorghum (kg/ha)	867	3,295	21,521
Oats (kg/ha)	1,199	1,722	10,617
Barley (kg/ha)	1,154	2,367	11,405
Potatoes (kg/ha)	9,129	26,632	94,153
Milk (kg/cow)	624	4,725	22,500
Eggs (per hen)	—	230	365
Cassava (kg/ha)	9,113	—	60,000
Rice (kg/ha/crop/112 days)	—	2,500	14,400
Sugarcane (kg/ha/year)	—	50,000	150,000
Sugarbeets (kg/ha/year)	—	50,000	120,000

"... most large-scale mechanized agriculture is less productive per unit area than small-scale farming can be."[2]

unproductive subsistence and semi-commercial farming sector that is primarily concerned with producing enough food to survive until the next harvest.[18] Because of this, the primary focus will be on raising the productivity of the poor subsistence farmers who are the majority of the world's farmers and whose increased productivity would have the largest effect on eliminating starvation and malnourishment.[18] Average yields of all major crops are well below the records in productivity (see Chart 3). In the tropics, it is reasonable to expect 100% gains in productivity. If the potential for multiple cropping in the tropics is tapped, world output of cereal crops could increase five or six times above its present level.[19] India has about the same area under cultivation as the United States, a comparable soil and water potential, but produces only about two-fifths as much food.[20] Instead of nearly six metric tons per cropped hectare, the average Indian or Pakistani farmer harvests only a little more than a ton of wheat or rice per hectare. Mexico could quadruple its production of corn with more complete utilization of available technology.[18] Indonesia could increase its rice production five-fold (to yields comparable to the average U.S. and Japanese yields) with more fertilizer.[10] Developing regions produce an average of 14 kg of beef and veal per head of cattle; developed regions produce 75 kg per head of cattle.[9]

The use of large tractors, spray planes, and other high technology and expensive facilities of the green revolution are not needed to dramatically raise crop yields. With nothing else but a few simple hand tools, good seed, a little pesticide, fertilizer, manure, land, and know-how, a poor but diligent farmer can produce higher yields per hectare than those now harvested in developed regions.[3]

This section of the Global Food Service will also help initiate, coordinate, and assist in whatever ways possible large-scale and long-range ecologically considerate development projects such as the draining of the southern Sudan; preparing the infrastructure needed for turning the grassy plains north and south of the Amazon basin into highly productive ranch lands; opening up the millions of hectares of semi-humid land south of the Sahara closed to human habitation by river blindness disease; controlling the diseases caused by the tsetse fly in Middle Africa; harnessing the glacial waters and rainfall of the Indus-Ganges-Brahmaputra plain of Pakistan, Bangladesh, and India; developing the Mekong Delta; or harnessing the rivers and ground waters of the semi-arid Sahelian zone of Africa.

The amount of fertilizers, irrigation, appropriate technologies, animal production systems, and new high-yield and pest-resistant seeds that are suited to each soil, climate, and consumer preference will be increased. Successful technologies in use elsewhere around the world will be studied and possibly modified to match the needs of a new region.

75% of the world's chemical fertilizers and 85% of the pesticides are used in developed countries on only 30% of the world's arable land.[9]

Fertilizer production plants will be constructed immediately, either near the supply of the needed raw materials—e.g., the flare gas around the Persian Gulf—or in the needy areas.

Specialized farms will be established to produce the seeds of high yielding crops. Dams, barrages, canals, water courses, wells, and levees will be built where appropriate to store, divert, and distribute river and ground waters for irrigation and protection against floods. Drainage channels or land grading will be done to see that farmlands are properly drained. Farm-to-market roads for bringing harvests to market and fertilizer and other supplies to the farm will be constructed or improved. Large numbers of pest and moisture proof and heat resistant food storages will be built. Food processing plants and energy-producing facilities (to process either farm waste or surplus that may arise in the future) will be built in rural areas. These plants will then contract with local farmers for their marketable surplus, thereby creating a market for the farmers' produce. Wherever possible the artifacts needed for this development—farm machinery, motors, pumps, pipes, casings for wells, storage facilities, etc.—will be constructed by small machine shops in rural towns, using steel and other materials produced in centralized mills.[21]

To facilitate all this, the Global Food Service, along with the specific countries affected and perhaps other international institutions such as the World Bank, will:

1. establish an international system of credit that favors the small farmer and small businessman, and that will, in effect, get those people out of the clutches of rural usury;

2. make crop insurance and low-interest loans available to the world's small rural farmers as well as provide a place where the farmers can invest their savings;

3. help form rural farm cooperatives for purchasing supplies and selling produce that will help solve the problem of the small farmer by making him a member of a larger, more viable unit, not as a hired worker, but as an active member with a stake in the success of the enterprise;

4. help establish food system field extension classes to speed and ease the adoption of new technologies or improve old ones;

5. help establish, perhaps in conjunction with rural health care facilities (see Population section), educational facilities that will teach farm children how to read, write, and do arithmetic;[21]

6. help diversify and expand the farming activities of the rural community to include forestry, fisheries, animal husbandry, energy production, industries based on serving agriculture, and essential social and welfare services;[9]

7. help foster the realization among rural people of the extent to which they can attain self-reliance.[9]

Unconventional Food Sources/Techniques will involve the developing of large- and small-scale prototypes and then full-scale automated mass-production facilities for the production and processing of leaf proteins, single-cell proteins, sprouts, seaweeds, insects, and synthetic nutriments. It will develop small- and large-scale greenhouse, hydroponic, and aquaculture techniques for use on both land and ocean in tropical, semi-tropical, and temperate climates.

Unconventional Food Sources/Techniques will also develop integrated systems like those in Illustrations 1, 2, and 3 for possible use throughout the world. Various versions of these integrated, whole, or ecologically closed systems approaches to agriculture are widely in use throughout China. Besides the systems described in the aquaculture section—where fish feed on excess fertilizer, compost, and animal manure and the water from the pond is in turn used as fertilizer for land crops—Chinese agriculture employs many others. For example, in silkworm production, mulberry leaves are picked and fed to silkworms whose waste products are then fed to fish who are periodically harvested. Silt from the fishpond bottom is used to fertilize the mulberry trees. Other crop waste is fed to pigs whose droppings in turn are used to cultivate mushrooms. This approach to agricultural production can be expanded to include all facets of the food system and industrial processes whose waste by-products would be suitable as inputs into the food system.

Ocean Resources and Fishing is the third area that ARDA will oversee. It will deal comprehensively with the ocean and its potential for producing food, including commercial fishing and ocean farming. All waters over twelve miles from any shore will be in the sole jurisdiction of the ARDA. All fishing and other exploitation of the ocean for food purposes beyond the twelve mile limit would only be possible through the ARDA. In this way, fish stocks will not be over-exploited, endangered species will be protected, separate countries will not be forced to compete for scarce resources, and a maximum sustainable yield can be harvested. The ocean and its food

Illustration 1. An idealized polyculture farm and research center.[22]

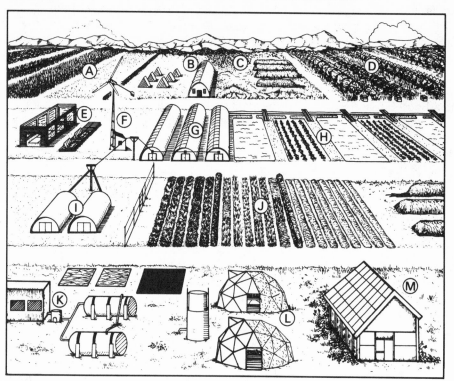

A = Grains, green manure, and forage crops.
B = Solar grain-drying structures.
C = Windrow compost piles on fallow section.
D = Diverse, multi-storied orchards with undergrowth of refuge plants and green manure crops.
E = Fish-food stocks; aquaculture insectary and worm cultures.
F = Wind generator.
G = Solar-heated quonsets for rearing warm-water fishes and crustaceans.
H = Outdoor fish ponds and row-crop fields.
I = Agriculture insectary for rearing beneficial insects.
J = Experimental vegetable/herb/flower/weed beds for investigating diverse cropping systems.
K = Poultry shelter with methane digesters, sludge ponds, and gas storage tanks.
L = Dome-greenhouses.
M = Solar-heated laboratory/homesite.

products will be viewed as belonging to the whole world; the most pressing human food needs will receive the highest priorities. For example, pet food for the developed regions will come after human food in the developing areas. Today's commercial fishers and fisheries will continue their present regenerative activities, but be licensed and coordinated by the ARDA.

Ocean farms for growing kelp and other sea plants as well as fish will be developed in appropriate localities. Other projects include the fertilization and cultivation of the ocean's

biological "deserts" and the building of floating food factories to cultivate and farm the more productive areas of the ocean. A floating food factory, especially in tropical waters, has the potential of producing large quantities of energy as well as food. One proposed scheme is shown in Illustration 4.

Soil Convervation and Reclamation will deal with all the areas of the planet that are suffering from or endangered by soil erosion or deserts. It will include the cessation, reversing, reclamation, and enrichment of damaged,

N.A.I.
SOLAR HEATED
GREENHOUSE-AQUACULTURE
COMPLEX

Illustration 2. The Ark: The New Alchemy Institute's solar-heated greenhouse-aquaculture complex.[23]

Illustration 3. Cutaway of the Ark showing the interior.[23]

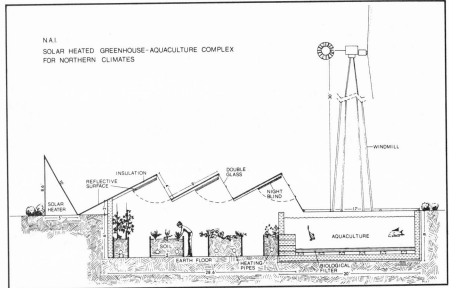

N.A.I.
SOLAR HEATED GREENHOUSE-AQUACULTURE COMPLEX
FOR NORTHERN CLIMATES

destroyed, or desert lands. Some of the 20,000 miles of coastal deserts will be reclaimed by irrigation with waters from solar-powered desalination plants or through the growing of salt-tolerant crops and irrigation with sea water. Large public works programs utilizing the labor of the seasonally and chronically unemployed will undertake reforestation of the vast areas of watershed vital for soil protection that have been cut for firewood in recent decades in developing regions.

The *Land Reform Agency* section will undertake to support every country and region in their efforts to institute effective reform of land ownership.

An important fact to realize is that land reforms, like population stabilization and other large scale social problems, are often solved not by direct frontal attack, i.e., birth control campaigns, sterilization, etc. in the case of population control, but indirectly through reduced infant mortality, increased social security, etc. One way around the generally debilitating situation brought about by very few people owning nearly all the land, or large numbers of landless laborers or tenant farmers, is to bring the "have-nots" into economic well-being through other methods than land redistribution. Land-owning is not the only way to attain higher standards of living or social position or power. The U.S. is a good example. There is no widespread clamor for land reform in the U.S. because land ownership is not the sole determinant of wealth. Increasing rural employment opportunities—such as food processing, fertilizer manufacturing, fuel

Illustration 4. Ocean-Based Solar/Wind/Algae/Fish/Power and Food Plant.

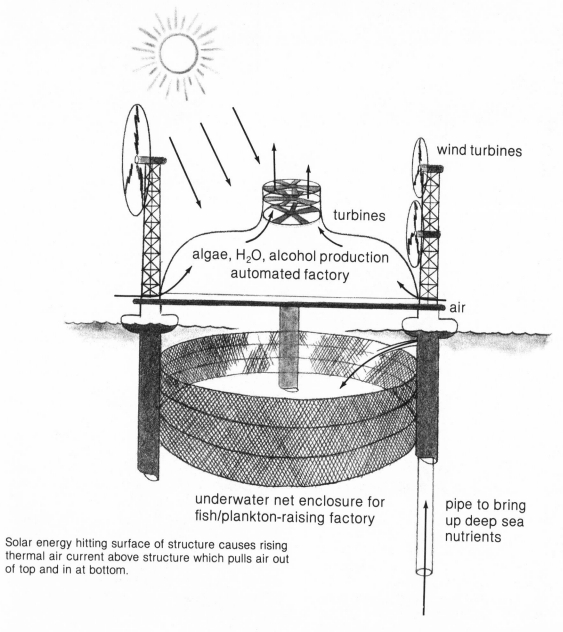

wind turbines

turbines

algae, H₂O, alcohol production automated factory

air

underwater net enclosure for fish/plankton-raising factory

pipe to bring up deep sea nutrients

Solar energy hitting surface of structure causes rising thermal air current above structure which pulls air out of top and in at bottom.

production, etc.—in developing countries where land reform is most needed could bypass the power base of the rural land baron. Making everyone "middle-class" (not in the Western sense of that word, but something more in tune with the realities of the specific developing region) would destroy the power of rural large landholders almost as much as land redistribution. The long term answer to almost all our specific basic human need problems is to raise the general level of well-being of the entire social structure to levels above those currently enjoyed by anyone. Nevertheless, because of long historical abuse and emergency situations, land redistribution is the only, or one of the only, tactics that will lead to rapid increases in food production. To help bring this about, the Land Reform Agency will actively facilitate, through voluntary sale, the conversion of public land holdings and unproductive landlord-dominated agriculture to high productivity, small, family-owned or co-op-owned farms. One non-violent-revolutionary path that land reform can take is for a government of a particular country to buy large landowners' land with cash and long term government bonds and then make this land available, at little or no cost, to the farmers who are working those lands. This tactic is often opposed by the landowner because he does not perceive the government as having the resources to pay the bonds off. The Land Reform Agency would guarantee these bonds, acting as a type of "Federal Deposit Insurance Corporation" thereby assuring the safety of the landlords' money and effectively eliminating his opposition to land reform.[24] The ex-large-landowner would be required to invest some of the compensation he received for his lands in rural agricultural support industry. Government bonds would be retired with the proceeds that come in from a small tax on the new small land-owning farmers. This tax would be substantially less than the previous rent payments. Another tactic that would be instituted in appropriate regions (where governments were not powerful enough or the large landowners were too powerful a political force) would be to progressively buy up the lands of the land-owners. This would be accomplished by using an initial grant from the Global Food Service (or other international agency) to purchase a tract of land whose farmers would then pay for (again at lower annual costs than they were paying in rent for land they didn't own or couldn't benefit from improving). The farmers' land payments would go into a revolving fund that would purchase more lands. Another possible source of funds for this would be a graduated tax on large land holdings—the larger the land, the larger the tax. Over a certain size, the tax would equal a certain size tract of land (at minimum, the amount needed for one family to farm), purchased at the going rate on that country's market. Such a land "breeder" program would continue until all large land holdings were owned by those who farmed them.

Food Storage/Distribution/Preserving will deal with the surpluses of the global food production system and the means of getting the foods that are needed to those areas in need. It will also develop and coordinate a global food reserve. In order to more fully explain the vital functions of this section of the Global Food Service a little background is needed.

For a system to survive, or to maximize its survival capability, it has to be able to deal with changes in its environment. Not all the changes are or will be small. One way to view the way

> *"Worldwide weather trends will have more to do with the supply of grain than all the governments' policies of the world laid end to end."*[26]

nature orchestrates events is in terms of relative magnitudes: small magnitudes occur very often, large events occur rarely.[25] In other words, mosquitoes occur more often than tornadoes; raindrops occur more often than severe drought. Big events are least frequent but have the highest stress when they do occur. If a system is not flexible enough to be able to adapt to the big changes that come along relatively infrequently, it becomes extinct. In this way, the ice age eliminated many previously viable organisms from Earth that could readily adapt to the small and frequent changes in their environments but did not have the general adaptability to get by the very large change that occurred once. All of this is just to say that humanity on Earth faces—as it always has—a relatively unknown future. According to the latest evidence pertaining to humanity's presence on Earth, we have already been through at least two ice ages. A big difference between then and now is that in prehistoric times there was always room to migrate to another, more hospitable location. A growing number of scientists have forecast or warned of an impending large magnitude change in our climate.[27] "Even the most conservative of climatologists can now see processes at work that may radically alter world climate."[28] Of more immediate threat than even large scale global climate change (but with essentially the same dire consequences) is the ever present danger of a staple food shortfall caused by local

or regional weather problems. These once minor, localized disturbances of the 1950's and before have increased to the larger regionalized shortfalls of the 1960's, and on to the world shortfalls of the 1970's. They are also more prevalent than most people realize. The probability of a major shortfall between now and 1985 is alarmingly high. "Three major shortfalls occurred during 1950–70, suggesting a probability of about 15% in any given year."[29] Considering the period 1960–78, we could expect 2–3 shortfalls per decade, or a probability of up to 33% in any given year.[29] Additionally, a period of greater variability in traditional weather patterns would lead to a decrease in the use of marginal lands and the less hardy high yield seeds, thereby possibly decreasing food production.[30] Because of this growing threat of climate change, the already mentioned possible shortfalls in world grain (and oil) supplies in the 1980's, and because our agricultural system is dependent upon approximately the current weather patterns to maintain itself (with any large scale change possibly being cataclysmic), we need to do some extra-ordinary planning and preparation for these very extraordinary contingencies.

For humanity to maximize its survival, for most or all people to survive in the best possible way, humanity has to be prepared for the rare, large magnitude change as well as the frequent, small magnitude changes. We should be prepared for the worst so that we can enjoy the best. Or, rather, we should be prepared for the worst of what our scientific experts have cautioned us is a definite possibility, even if it is not to our liking. We need to exhibit the same care and consciousness in our design, planning, and action on the societal, planetary scale as we do when putting a man on the Moon. Spaceship Earth needs the consciousness devoted to her problems that was needed to solve the problems of our human-made spaceships. (One of the hidden benefits of the erstwhile space program was the development of various methodologies for tackling large-scale problems.) In airplane and spacecraft design, "worst possible" cases are simulated and prepared for. Back-up systems are designed into critical systems. On the whole, more care, time, intelligence (measured by person-years of time), and forward-looking has gone into the building of our spaceships than into the solving of our food problems.

One "worst" possible scenario could be something like the following: a major and extended drought hits North America, China, and India decreasing grain harvest by one quarter the first year. North American and Chinese grain surplus is quickly exhausted; China and India begin rationing and famine is narrowly averted in China through a massive relief program, exhaustion of food reserves, and slaughter of large numbers of livestock. India and Bangladesh are not so lucky; famine strikes, social order breaks in some regions, and millions die. Drought continues for the next six years. During this time a world-wide influenza epidemic strikes; 500–1000 million people die world-wide from malnutrition and disease. Social order breaks down in many parts of the world; communications are cut off to many spots. Border skirmishes break out between roving armies. Violent revolutions are almost weekly occurrences in the harder-hit regions. War breaks out in scores of locations. Russia, China, Japan, and then the U.S. are drawn in. Someone somewhere, no one

remembers where, presses the button and over 3000 intercontinental ballistic missiles, with over 12,000 nuclear warheads, are launched, land, and devastate most of the world's northern hemisphere. At least two billion people die directly and indirectly in the chaos that follows. . . .

There are many, many other possible scenarios. Not all need to have as severe a starting point as a multiple-year drought to three major food producing areas to have the end result be either massive famine and/or world-wide thermonuclear war.

One way pointed out in the Food Storage section of "preparing for the worst" would be to store a multiple-year supply of food stocks. Such a stock could avert even the largest famine and its attendant social devastations, keeping the world social fabric relatively stable in the wake of such a large magnitude change as severe and extensive drought. A world food reserve has never before existed. Individual countries have maintained reserves but a truly world food reserve is as yet on the drawing boards. Because of ever increasing interdependence the planet now needs a world food reserve as much as the individual subsistence farm family needs its seasonal food storage to get it through to the next harvest. A large global food storage would greatly increase the adaptability and survivability of the species.

Developed countries, primarily the U.S. and Canada, have serious economic problems with their agricultural surplus. Developing countries have very serious problems with their agricultural shortages. Shortage is obviously more serious than surplus because it is a threat to survival. Choosing between the lesser of two "evils"—surplus over shortage—the U.S. and

Canada (and the rest of the world) should develop globally rational methods for dealing with this problem. The developed countries are in much better positions to deal with surplus than poorer developing countries are in for dealing with shortages. The planet should develop mechanisms for dealing with surplus rather than artificially creating scarcity. The agriculture of abundance needs to replace the economics of scarcity. In a world as small as planet Earth, there is no other way.

Food storage has to be globally based; it has to be for 100% of humanity, not, as some have proposed, for just those who are already well off. There might as well not be any storage if that were the case. Selective storage, or selective murder or triage or the "lifeboat ethic" as it is colloquially masked, is impossible in a world of intercontinental ballistic missiles and thermonuclear warheads. What is to stop a famine threatened country (or area—North Dakota would be the third largest nuclear power in the world if it seceded from the U.S.) from using its weapons to survive? When threatened with survival a system will do whatever it can do to prevent extinction. "Whatever it can do" definitely includes all military options. Triage— the selective feeding of some people rather than all people—is inherently suicidal in an interdependent closed system. It is no more possible in the world of today than it is possible for an individual to direct that its food should only nourish its arms and not its legs. The world is one system; for a part to try to dictate that another part is not to receive the resources it needs to survive—in other, more plain words, that it is to die—is schizophrenic and suicidal. The specious argument that triage is as sane a policy as is cutting off a gangrenous leg does not hold up because it 1) falsely equates the lives of human beings with a malignant growth, 2) falsely equates a country with a malignant growth, and assumes a country is as easy to dispose of as a dead leg, and 3) falsely assumes that conditions are as bad in the world as in a person's gangrenous leg. As has been pointed out repeatedly in this document, many options exist for the elimination of hunger on Earth. Triage is not only not necessary, it is irrelevant, and maybe, depending on your definition, insane.

One other related reason why a food storage program needs to be global in scope rather than local is that the whole purpose of food storage is violated if storage isn't for everyone. Food is stored for security; there is no security if there are food storages that one group of armed people attempt to keep another group of armed and hungry people from getting. And last, but not least,

the U.S. advocates of triage and the lifeboat ethic like to apply the concepts only to food, as though it could somehow be treated apart from all other resources. The notion that a country which is already importing 40% of its petroleum and which is projected by the end of the century to be primarily dependent upon imports for twelve of the thirteen principal minerals required by an industrial society, should somehow isolate itself either economically or politically, from the rest of the world makes no sense whatsoever.[31]

As just pointed out, simultaneous or successive crop failures in different parts of the world could possibly lead to famine unless there are adequate reserves of food in stock. Because

private food reserve holders can't be expected to bear the cost of storing these stocks ($1 billion was spent in the U.S. alone for grain storage in 1970[3]) the Global Food Service would purchase and store surplus grain stocks. These would be over and above the usual privately held carry-over stocks that currently act as a small buffer against food shortage. These foods would only be released for famine and disaster relief in developing regions and when world food prices become abnormally high.

Location of short-term food storage facilities would be primarily in the food-poor countries and as decentralized as possible, i.e., either farmer, co-op, or village-held storages. The reasons for this are twofold, one logistical, the other psychological. If food is stored near to where it most likely will be needed, then the time, energy, and organization required to get it when it actually is needed will be reduced. The second reason is that the comfort of knowing that your family is not going to go hungry or starve will have an unknown but powerful psychological effect on the entire world. The fear of hunger has haunted humanity since its beginning. This weight is today most pressing in the lands where, to many, hunger is an actual daily threat. The developed world does not need huge grain storages to bolster its confidence or quench its fears of hunger. The hungry developing areas do. One food storage tactic the Food Service could engage in would be to help local governments build grain storage facilities for the individual farmer or his community. Crops would be stored at minimal cost to the farmer (paid for in grain) and would be sold by the farmer when prices were what he wanted. As will be detailed later, if prices didn't rise, the farmer could then sell his crop to the Global Food Service at a price that would give him a fair return on his work.

Besides these storage facilities in the developing and developed regions, where up to a year's supply of food would be stored for emergency uses, the Food Storage/Distribution section of the Global Food Service would develop storage facilities for a multiple year supply of food for the entire planet in Antarctica. Here the food would be naturally frozen by the −30° to −50° Antarctic temperatures and preserved until such a time that a part of the planet needed a larger supply of food than was in the more readily accessible local or regional storages. The Antarctic storage would be a buffer against any lengthy drought such as the recent seven-year drought which hit the African Sahel region or other unknown catastrophes that could strike the world's food system and exhaust our present food surpluses.

A large food storage would give humanity the time it needs in a crisis to develop new sources of food, new locations for food production, and effective conservation measures to reduce food losses. As will be shown later, amassing a large food storage could also be instrumental in raising the standard of living in all the poverty-stricken areas of the planet.

The only way to amass a multiple-year storage of food for the entire planet in a limited amount of time is to produce a large surplus each year. One of the best ways of furnishing the incentive to produce a surplus is to guarantee a market for the producer/farmer. Establish a price before the crop is planted. Armed with the knowledge that a bumper harvest will not lower the prices that he will receive for his produce, the farmer can bring all his resources to bear on producing as much food as possible. The surplus would be purchased to stock food reserves in the developing countries around the planet and, when those are full, in Antarctica. The farmer would not be faced with drastic drops in prices for his product after he has successfully produced a lot of food. If the food producer knew that he could sell all of his product and would not drastically force down the market price by producing a lot of a certain crop, he would be willing and able to grow all the food that he could. The tragic vicious circle that has the farmer being punished every time he is successful will be broken. The Global Food Service would essentially buy up all the surplus storable food crops at an established fair price.

If a food producer could sell his crops at a higher price, then he could do that. The Global Food Service would be a "buyer of last resort." "A buffer stock would serve the interests of the farmers as well as the consumers in both exporting and importing countries. It would support farm incomes when prices are low while avoiding excessively high prices."[14] It would also stop wild speculation that drives up food prices in times of shortage. In this connection, the Global Food Service would be engaged in the distribution/shipment of grains and other basic foodstuffs around the planet. The Global Food Service would *not* concern itself with luxury items, gourmet foods, pet foods, etc., but rather the basic food needs of people.

Because of the serious threats to humanity

"The idea of a buffer stock of grain is as old as the story of Joseph in Egypt. There is no record that Pharoah inquired about storage costs. Costs are a minor consideration when the issue of holding or not holding reserves becomes a matter of survival."[14]

that exist without any or little food storage—the situation we find ourselves in currently—the first priorities will be to quickly amass a storage of about a six to twelve months' supply from all farmers using all types of food production techniques. Once this initial buffer stock is stored, and ready for use in combating local shortages around the world, the buying organization would put preferences or priorities on the crops it would purchase. Priorities for purchase could be set up so that the poorest farmers and the small farmers had the highest priorities. The Indian farmer—who makes the equivalent of $12 or less per month—would have all his surplus wheat purchased before the North American or rich Indian farmer's surplus wheat was bought. The price paid for the wheat would be geared to guarantee the poor a good return for their produce. As storages increased further, another priority would be established that would place the purchase priority on foods grown with production techniques judged to be regenerative—such as good soil and water management, biological pest control, non-depletable energy sources, etc. As time went on, only those foods grown with regenerative practices would be purchased. This would have the effect of stimulating the widespread adoption of these techniques and their resultant beneficial effects upon the environment and our future.

As just pointed out, a large food storage is needed for the world to insure against the indeterminacies of weather, climate, and possible famine. Also, the poor of the world need to have their needs for excellent shelter, clothing, health care, education, and social security met. In addition, the urban and rural unemployed of the world need constructive work. The strategy proposed here would synergetically combine all these elements into one development plan. The Global Food Service would buy all the surplus storable food stocks from all the farmers of the world, but with priority on the poor farmers' surplus crops. The money or credit received for the food stocks would allow the rural poor to purchase the needed shelter, clothing, health care, education, etc. to upgrade their condition (as well as those who are supplying those materials, products, and services to the poor). Urban and rural unemployed could be constructively employed in building local roads, houses, schools, health care facilities, decentralized energy harnessing artifacts, and storages for food.

Energy/Food Symbiosis

Obviously, buying all the surplus food stocks of the world could not go on forever, nor would it be desirable even if it were possible. If climatic and other conditions were right, a multiple year stock of food should be accumulatable within a 12–20 year period. If it happened more quickly, so much the better. Once the stock was gathered, the types of crops purchased would gradually switch from those that could be readily stored to those that could be most readily converted into energy in the form of alcohol, methane, dry fuel, etc.

Chart 3. Aboveground, Dry Biomass Yields of Selected Plant Species or Complexes.[34]

Species	Location	Yield (tons/acre/year)	Species	Location	Yield (tons/acre/year)
Annuals			*Perennials*		
Sunflower × Jerusalem Artichoke	Russia	13.5	*Cinnamomum camphora* (dominant species) and other species	Japan	6.8
Sunflower hybrids (seeds only)	California	1.5	*Fagus sylvatica*	Switzerland	4.3
Exotic forgae sorghum	Puerto Rico	30.6	*Larix decidua*	Switzerland	2.2
Forage sorghum (irrigated)	New Mexico	7–10	*Picea abies* (dominant species) and others	Japan	5.5
Forage sorghum (irrigated)	Kansas	12	*Picea omorika* (dominant species) and others	Japan	6.4
Sweet sorghum	Mississippi	7.5–9	*Picea densiflora* (dominant species) and others	Japan	6.1
Exotic corn (137-day season)	No. Carolina	7.5	*Castanopsis japonica* (dominant species) and others	Japan	8.3
Silage corn	Georgia	6–7	*Betula maximowicziniana* (dominant species) and others	Japan	3
Hybrid corn	Mississippi	6	*Populus davidiana* (dominant species) and others	Japan	5.5
Kenaf	Florida	20	Hybrid poplar (short-rotation)		
Kenaf	Georgia	8	Seedling crop (1 year old)	Pennsylvania	4
			Stubble crop (1 year old)	Pennsylvania	8
			Stubble crop (2 years old)	Pennsylvania	8
Perennials			Stubble crop (3 years old)	Pennsylvania	8.7
Water hyacinth	Florida	16	American sycamore (short-rotation)		
Sugarcane	Mississippi	20	Seedlings (2 years old)	Georgia	2.2
Sugarcane (state average)	Florida	17.5	Seedlings (2 years old)	Georgia	4.1
Sugarcane (best case)	Texas (south)	50	Coppice crop (2 years old)	Georgia	3.7
Sugarcane (10-year average)	Hawaii	26	Black cottonwood (2 years old)	Washington	4.5
Sugarcane (5-year average)	Louisiana	12.5	Red alder (1–14 years old)	Washington	10
Sugarcane (5-year average)	Puerto Rico	13.3	Eastern cottonwood (8 years old)		3
Sugarcane (6-year average)	Philippines	12.1	*Eucalyptus* sp.	California	13.4
Sugarcane (Experimental)	California	32	*Eucalyptus* sp.	California	24.1
Sugarcane (Experimental)	California	30.5	*Eucalyptus* sp.	Spain	8.9
Sudan grass	California	15–16	*Eucalyptus* sp.	India	17.4
Alfalfa (surface irrigated)	New Mexico	6.5	*Eucalyptus* sp.	Ethiopia	21.4
Alfalfa	New Mexico	8	*Eucalyptus* sp.	Kenya	8.7
Bamboo	S.E. Asia	5	*Eucalyptus* sp.	South Africa	12.5
Bamboo (4-year stand)	Alabama	7	*Eucalyptus* sp.	Portugal	17.9
Abies sacharinensis (dominant species) and other species	Japan	6			

These energy-crops would not be stored but converted into their respective forms of energy and sold—at cost to the food system for use in meeting its energy needs, and at higher than cost to others. Such crops as sugarcane and sorghum (see Chart 3) are excellent energy crops. If just half of the energy contained in the humanly inedible portions of cereal grains were recovered by fermentation into alcohol or methane the energy requirements of modern agriculture, including fertilizer production, could be fully met.[32] Agriculture has the unheralded potential of solving the world's energy needs as well as feeding everyone on Earth. The farmer becomes an energy producer as well as a food grower. The agricultural lands of the Earth can produce enough biomass not only to feed everyone but to supply all our energy needs as well. Such a transition from food production to energy production could be started on forage lands that are not suitable for any other crops. Woody perennials, so called "BTU bushes," could be grown on poor land and harvested any time of the year. Even reclaimed strip mined areas could be terraced and planted with energy crops. Farmers could begin growing and harvesting these crops on their non-productive lands now during the "off-season" from their usual farming duties. Fresh water crops could also be developed. The water hyacinth, for instance, can be used to clean waters spoiled by sewage while producing around 134 metric tons per hectare per year, depending on the quantity of sewage in the water, which would be

converted to about 658,000 cubic feet of methane gas. It would take about 6 million hectares of water hyacinths to produce all the natural gas currently used in the world.

Besides food and energy crops, the farmer has the option of growing fiber crops. As fossil fuel prices continue to rise, synthetic fibers will become more expensive and the natural cotton and flax fibers more attractive.

Besides present day ocean-going grain tankers to ship foodstuffs, other means would be investigated and developed. One such method, described in the previous section on Food Processing/Storage, is the large hydrogen-filled airship. Such vehicles could transport about as much and as fast as ocean going tankers. For transport of food to and from the Antarctic the large airship would be better than the ocean-going ship because of the lack of ports and rough Antarctic seas. Other advantages might also accrue because the food will be transported at lower temperatures because of the height at which it will be traveling. This would help keep the food from deteriorating. In regions where there is enough energy, food spoilage can be prevented by refrigeration; in areas where energy supply has not been developed, community or home refrigeration facilities powered by wind or solar energy could be used. Local food needs and supplies will be integrated with other locales as well as with regional needs and supplies. Regions will in turn be interconnected with other regions and with global supplies and needs. Food processing/ preservation systems will be developed wherever needed. The best of Western technology will be used to improve, rather than displace, traditional food processing techniques. Given the incredible amounts of food that are

lost each year—more than enough to feed the world's population—there is an enormous potential to reduce this waste. The potential for "conservation" is as large or larger in the world food system as it is in the energy system. The case has been made that the United States could get along on about half the energy consumption that it presently does and still maintain its high standard of living. The U.S. could also get along on less than half the amount of food that it consumes and wastes and still have a more nutritious diet than its present one. This section of the Global Food Service will seek to reduce these enormous food losses around the world.

Urban Food Production would deal with developing those techniques for producing food that are appropriate for the urban environment. Roof top gardens, back and front yard and vacant lot mini-farms, expressway divider orchards or farms, basement fish ponds, sewage-fed algae production plants, and urban greenhouses would be developed for use throughout the cities of the world. The major thrust would be to make the city environment as self-sufficient as possible. It might prove to be possible that certain cities in good climatic situations might even be exporters of some types of food, rather than importers. Most cities should be able to produce all their own fresh vegetables during a good part of the year without much trouble. Urban Food Production would deal with all aspects of the urban environment that could potentially be used for producing food. It would look upon the city as a series of distinct neighborhoods (e.g., downtown, residential, commercial, etc.), each with its own potentials for various kinds of food production. Every residential neighborhood would be looked upon as being potentially self-sufficient or as a possible exporter of basic foodstuffs through the combination of its vacant lots, backyards, roof-tops, and basements.

The Water Resources section of the Global Food Service would deal with developing and processing the water resources of the planet. An International Water Research Institute, modeled after the successful international rice and wheat institutes, would be set up at once to deal with the major water problems facing the world food system. Water Resources would develop irrigation projects wherever appropriate around the planet. One major long-term project would be the development of irrigation for the Ganges plain and flood control of the annual monsoon. This 25-year project would begin at once and would result in over 37×10^6 irrigated hectares, enough to produce more than 165×10^6 metric tons of additional food—enough to feed more than 600 million people.

The *Agricultural Training* section of the Global Food Service will develop and coordinate the training of agricultural field workers. Local field workers will be trained in all aspects of farm productivity and will be specially competent in new production, storage, and processing techniques. They will be able to help the farmer determine the profitability of the various choices he is confronted with and will be accountable to the local farmer. That is, the field worker should not only be from the local region but part of his wages should be either paid or determined by

the local farmers.[4] In addition, Agricultural Training, along with other divisions of the Global Food Service, participating countries and their agriculture colleges, will help to reorganize those colleges to more closely fit into a rapid development mode.[4] The agriculture colleges will be tied more closely into agriculture development plans—both in a training sense and in undertaking research to solve specific development problems.

The Energy/Food Interface section of the Global Food Service would be primarily concerned with the energy needs of the world food system. It would seek means of conserving energy use by the food system through research, development, and education. The innumerable energy-conserving techniques for producing, processing, and distributing food that are currently available would be implemented. Ways of utilizing the non-depletable energy sources for agriculture would be developed around the world. The Energy/Food Interface Section would be responsible for phasing the fossil fuels out of the food system, and phasing in the income energy sources. It would also develop the long-range energy-producing capabilities of the world food system and oversee the development and deployment of new machines.

"Appropriate technology" has sometimes been naively bandied about by rich developed country inhabitants as a sort of palliative for the poor and ignorant natives of developing regions. It is questionable if some of these same people from developed countries would have enough intelligence to survive under the conditions they often romanticize elsewhere. Appropriate technology does not mean back-breaking human toil; it does not mean the right tools to facilitate

machine-like and endless heavy labor; "labor intensive" does not mean slavery or mindless toil. What it does mean is tools and organizational structures adapted to fit the given environment that improve the condition of the laborer; it means the doing of more with *less* labor. The new appropriate tool should allow the farmer to do things he could not do before, or to reduce the time he was forced to spend on some task. "Appropriate" means an incremental step in development, it is not an end in itself. After the metal horse-drawn plow replaces the human-drawn wood plow, it *may* be time for the small mechanical tiller. (This progression does not imply that ultimately every farmer will be sitting upon the throne of a $50,000, 600-h.p. John Deere thresher; what is appropriate for the labor-short fields of Kansas is not going to be suitable to the hills of Bali.)

One of the long range purposes of agricultural development should be to relieve human drudgery; or in present-day economic terms, to reduce the importance of human labor as a factor in agricultural production.[21] This does not mean though that any human being should be displaced from the land due to his/her labor no longer being needed. Every new human labor-saving mechanical advantage should provide humanity with more options, not fewer. The need for back-breaking human toil should decrease and the need and worth of each individual as a thinking, planning, researching synergy of the food system should increase. Human drudgery is not relieved by forcing a farmer and his family into the ranks of the urban unemployed. Productivity can be increased and back-breaking human labor reduced without putting people out of work. New machinery or techniques should be phased into an area so as to cause the least disruption to the human worker. All new techniques and machinery should be part of a system of development, not an isolated step. Humans relieved of one form of drudgery by a new development should have numerous options for channeling their energy and creativity in other, preferred directions. New developments would be accompanied by educational packages that would detail its advantages, disadvantages, and alternatives so that the people affected by the developments could choose whether they wanted it or not.

The fourth section of the Global Food Service is the *Food Research Agency*. This Agency would coordinate all the food-related research that is going on in the world and allocate funds for basic and applied research in all areas of food production, processing, and distribution. The aim of all research would be to increase the supply of food on Earth, be it through increases in food production from new seeds, improved efficiency of photosynthesis, better fertilizer, irrigation or pest control; or through decreases in loss of food or nutritional value of food during harvesting, storage, processing, distribution, or consumption. Old production systems will be studied and improved and new production systems will be devised for every crop for every season for every region of every country.[4] Research into multiple, relay, and intercropping in irrigated and non-irrigated areas, three-dimensional cropping—for example, coconut, cocoa, and pepper planting—alternative cropping strategies for the tropics and subtropics to alleviate adverse weather impacts, mixed farming based on a blend of crops, fish, and farm animals, more effective kitchen gardening and backyard poultry raising, as well as more effective flood and erosion control,

remote sensing, and non-depletable energy source development would be undertaken in a major way.[35] Better systems for harvesting, storing, transporting, marketing, utilizing, and disposing of waste food will be devised. Communication/education systems will be developed that allow the farmer to learn what the newest advances are and to allow the researcher to learn from the experience of the farmer. The individual farm will be looked upon as the ultimate experimental unit in any region's research program.[4] Large-scale funding for research into improving existing food sources or production techniques such as hydroponics, plant and animal breeding, organic farming, pest control, etc., and preliminary funding for such things as the mass production of insects, sprouts, or leaf proteins will be started.

The Food Research Agency will also develop a genetic resource bank for all the world's plants, animals, trees, fungi, and bacteria that have agricultural importance—including current and past crops, weeds, etc. Research and development will be directed at increasing the genetic diversity of all crops. This will consist of coordinating emerging and already-existing gene banks and developing new banks that will not only catalogue and store these resources, but make them globally available.

Current centers for research, such as the agriculture colleges in the United States, will be encouraged to "adopt" different developing, food-short countries of the world and participate in solving their food problems. Such centers would train students from these developing countries for the real jobs that exist in these countries, not for jobs in North America. More importantly, the Global Food Service will assist developing regions to establish their own

regional food system colleges. ("Agricultural College" is too limited a description, as "agriculture" refers merely to the cultivation of crops, and the food system is much larger than this.) These colleges will train people in the necessary skills to develop and maintain their food system. Each area's research program will be coordinated with other areas so that all food problems don't have to be tackled by everyone individually, resulting in the solution of no problems. Instead, each region will focus on the problems that have the highest priority to that region's needs.

Funding for energy research and development is vast compared to food funding. The reason for the difference in funding levels between energy and food research and development is that food scarcity is a poor man's disease and energy supply is a rich man's problem. This is further illustrated by the large emphasis in the United States on amassing a large—billion barrel or more—oil reserve but little emphasis on amassing even a small food reserve. This situation is not right; food is more basic and important to more people than fuel. It is also not an either/or situation. Energy reserves make sense as do food reserves, but food should have a *higher* priority. Especially when one realizes that there are not trillions of tons of food stored in the Earth as there are coal, oil, and gas. The only food we have in any quantities is what we grew last year. Food research should receive as much research resources as energy.

Funds for applied and basic research, agricultural resources development, and for the rest of the Global Food Service could be obtained from the production of food, animal feed, or biomass for energy conversion in out-of-the-way places such as the oceans and deserts, and from direct subsidy from the richer developed countries. A 1% donation/tax on gross profits of all multinational corporations could help support the Global Food Service, as could a small fraction or similar 1% tax of the world's military budget. Such a military expenditure tax would provide about $4 billion annually for the Global Food Service. Assuming that military expenditures are rationally designed to foster security in the world, a strong argument can be made for spending a great deal of the military's budget on food development throughout the planet as the most security increasing thing we could do. Food development could be supported instead of current military "foreign aid" expenditures. The disarmament discussions that have been going on between the U.S.S.R. and the U.S. have so far just been focused on limits, on the negative, on what each side can give up: the cruise missile, strategic bomber, or 1500 missiles instead of 15,000. This is an obvious first step but there is another dimension that has not been tried yet, that is, the positive, or what the two superpowers could do together, instead of spending their resources on weapons. One such proposal would be for the U.S.S.R. and the U.S. to agree to spend a progressively increasing percentage of their respective military budgets (starting at 1%) on supporting the Global Food Service. As time went on, more and more resources would be devoted to feeding the world and fewer and fewer toward preparing for Armageddon. Other countries could be invited or pressured by world opinion to become involved.

One of the greatest threats humanity has ever faced is the combination of the precarious

"The agricultural capabilities of North America are vast; and if U.S. farm policy over the past half century can be thought of as having a theme, it has been to prevent this productivity from driving down prices to the point where income to farmers could be maintained only by a massive exodus from the land. From Soil Bank (paying farmers not to put acreage into production) to Public Law 480 (distributing surplus to the needy) to drowning baby pigs, little that might elevate prices has not been tried."[3]

position of its global food supply balancing on the tip of the fickle finger of weather and the explosive growth of world armaments. Every country is arming to the teeth. Every day the weather changes. The synergetic combination of these factors is not unlike the mixing of alcohol and barbiturates. Unless something is done to ensure a safe supply of food for everyone on Earth there will be no safe Earth or earth.

It would also be possible for one or two countries, such as the United States and/or Canada to stop all their foreign aid programs, and instead "feed the world." Instead of isolated programs around the globe—an Aswan dam here, a squadron of jets there, a flood relief program here—the intent and purpose of the aid program would be simply to see to it—guarantee it—that no one on Earth was malnourished. This guarantee would have to be universal between the U.S. and the people of the planet. Food assistance would have to be uncoupled from its previous use as a political weapon. If it were not universal, global, it would be mistrusted. But the guarantee would come with some conditions: aid would be in the form of food and food technology, education, etc. to the poor, not in the form of money that could be

siphoned off by corrupt officials. Conditions would be designed to eliminate corruption. One possible format would be for the U.S. to issue "food stamps" directly to the malnourished poor of the world. Similar to domestic U.S. food stamps, these would be redeemable in basic food staples, either supplied locally by the respective countries or by U.S. food aid if this were not possible. The former alternative is much preferable to the latter, which would only be used in an emergency. In return, the unemployed food stamp recipient would work on public works projects such as reforestation. The local farmer who supplied the food to the poor could redeem the food stamp payments he received for fertilizer and other production-increasing inputs.

The social, economic, political, and good-will pay-offs of such a foreign aid program would be vast. The country that led the world in this endeavor could be a powerful force for world peace; more powerful than any B-1 bomber or other weapons system, and cheaper also. Such an undertaking would silence all but the most diehard critics of "foreign" aid. One step in this would be for the United States—as long as there are hungry people in the world—to earmark all of its food exports for human consumption. There should be different prices for different needs. A tax structure on grain

"We cannot have a peaceful and prosperous world if a large part of the world's people are at or near the edge of hunger. The United States has a stake in helping to solve this problem ... We must look for ways to tap the talents and commitment of the American nation in an effective international effort."
—Jimmy Carter

exports that would make the hungry poor of the world able to compete financially with the rich land's animals would go a long way towards making sure no one went hungry. Ideally, if Bangladesh needs food and Russia needs feed, Bangladesh should get the United States' exports, no matter what price Russia can afford.

Another step would be to combine, revitalize, and expand the Peace Corps, AID, and VISTA into one organization that would act as a human resources pool and help with rural development throughout the world.

A more far-reaching alternative to this would be to institute a Planetary Service System that would allow *all* youths of the world to participate in "making the world work." It would be a universal draft of all people between the ages of 18 and 22 and would allow the young women and men of the planet to learn to help in regions of the world that needed and requested such assistance. Secondary school could be looked upon as preparation/training for such an activity. Given present-day nation-states and their unfortunate fixations on armaments and armies, one option in the Planetary Service System might have to be in a particular country's army or else in a global peace-keeping force. One way of starting such a Planetary Service System would be for the U.S. (and preferably one or more other countries) to unilaterally institute it and then allow the youth of other countries to join.

Another tactic would be to develop tax structures that would encourage U.S.-based transnational corporations to participate in non-exploitative development in regions needing assistance. For example, New York advertising agencies could be encouraged to develop ad campaigns for nutritious foods in developing countries. The amount of the tax-writeoff should be determined by the success of the effort—the number of people who begin using the more nutritious foods—than by the amount of money spent.

Some critics of the idea of the U.S. guaranteeing the world freedom from hunger may claim that such an undertaking is impossible. Even accepting this false premise, the strategy should still be pursued to test this statement, for the benefit of those it can help, and for the American people, who would greatly benefit from having a specific, explicit national goal that they could feel proud of. One of the ways the Chinese achieved their vast social cohesiveness and high morale was through the battling against a common enemy: hunger and underdevelopment (later, when these problems were "licked" and no longer pressing, they developed a new, perhaps more symbolic enemy—Soviet "hegemony"). The U.S. (and the rest of the developed world) does not have the "benefit" of pressing survival-related issues such as widespread famine and under-development to cohere our purpose or enkindle national spirit or morale. The developed world has already "made-it" on the level of material well-being. We need a new "enemy," a new challenge. Feeding the world is such a challenge. World-wide respect and honor do not come from having the biggest gun and doing what is expedient, easy, and economic, but the courage to do what is "right." And in the face of hunger, not many people have difficulty in deciding what is right or wrong. North America, because of its fortuitous agricultural resources, has the possibility, and hence the responsibility, to make the difference between mass famine and food for everyone. If anyone doubts this capacity of North America, they should envision a world where North America was totally isolated, where her 112 million tons of exports in 1976 ($23 billion worth) didn't leave the country, but stayed within her borders. Eighty-six per cent of the world's surplus food is produced by the United States.[20] The grain exports alone of North America could feed the 600 million people of India.[36]

Even on the strictly economic side, a strong case can be made for such a policy. As mentioned earlier, the U.S. has severe economic difficulties in dealing with its bountiful agricultural surplus. The U.S. farmer's total income, in terms of what it can buy, is at the level it was during the 1930's Depression. Net income per farm in 1973 was $11,700; in 1977 it was $7200.[37] Farmers' debt has soared to over $100 billion in 1977.[38] When confronted by these harsh realities, it comes with little surprise that 2000 farmers go out of business each week and thousands more demonstrate for months in the capital of the U.S. and threaten to strike. To get the U.S. farmer out of the economic depression that he is trapped in (and to avoid depression for the rest of the economy[39]) more than palliative band-aid measures are needed. Guaranteeing the world freedom from hunger would rescue the American farmer from near bankruptcy, and the productive genius of the farmer would be justly rewarded, not schizophrenically punished. Surplus would not be the dreaded product of an agricultural system too good for its own good, but a just reward for hard work. When global surpluses reached safe levels the continuing excess farm production could be utilized for energy production. Balance of payments would be helped doubly by agricultural production: first by revenues from all exported crops and second by the decreased demand for imported oil that producing alcohol or methane with our agricultural products could bring about.

Another method of obtaining income for the Global Food Service is the previously mentioned series of taxes on all human foodstuffs that are consumed by animals, especially grains. In this way, poorer areas that do not have the money to compete with the animal producers in the richer areas would be advantaged, eating lower on the food chain would be encouraged, and an income would be generated for the Global Food Service.

As mentioned at the very beginning of this section, a plan to solve the world's food problems needs to deal successfully with the critical short term emergencies, with means for reducing or stabilizing food demand and loss of limited resources, and with long term measures to make sure the problem does not recur.

The one major area not yet covered is means for reducing or stabilizing food demand. Currently, demand for food is increasing because population is increasing and increasing numbers of people are eating higher on the food chain. This rising demand for food can be slowed, stopped, reduced, and even eliminated through a number of methods. Famine, war, and plague are history's more popular techniques. Modern science has added to these the alternatives of birth control, mass education, leaving the planet for colonies in space, and, with recent advances in genetic engineering, perhaps producing smaller people with smaller appetites. And, of course, modern contributions to the art and science of war-making have increased the guarantees offered by our ancestors for reducing demand for food

production through this alternative. Among these recent options of modern science, the first two are the more readily available and acceptable. Educating people to eat lower on the food chain could greatly reduce the demand for foods, but, as pointed out innumerable times, unless population eventually stabilizes, food demand will continue to rise.

Many simplistic analyses of the world's food situation blame the increase in the world's population for all its problems. To solve the world food problem then becomes the task of controlling population. As Buckminster Fuller has long pointed out, populations tend to stabilize as industrialization increases. As a region's life-support capabilities go up, the need for more people goes down. As the external metabolic system increases, the need for more and more internal metabolic systems decreases. The following charts help to illustrate these phenomena; as energy consumption goes up, birth rates come down.

If the current trends towards population stabilization in all the developed regions of the world continue, and if those just beginning in other regions (such as China) and others are started or elaborated upon with massive commitments in developing regions (South America, Africa, India), the world could achieve a stable population of 6 billion people by the year 2015.[36]

To adequately deal with the world's population problem demands that we deal with all the other problems facing humanity—food, shelter, health care, education, employment, social security, etc. By solving these problems the population levels off of its own accord. Any but the most superficial analysis of any world problem will disclose the same thing that the

population problem discloses: that to comprehensively solve the problem, all problems must be tackled as well. Whatever window one views development through, the scenery is all interconnected.

Having said this, it can then be pointed out that there are many things that can be done within this context to accelerate the decline in birth rates and the stabilization of the world's population. The global food strategy would accelerate population stabilization by establishing a global population agency that would coordinate world-wide population control efforts. Goals for population levels would be set by each country and for the world. Population control plans would be drawn up by each country and region. Massive family planning educational efforts would be implemented along with the widespread availability, where culturally appropriate, of free contraceptives, and sterilization. A major emphasis would be on progressively eliminating the severe health hazard caused by the estimated 40 million abortions per year in the world[34] through effective and available contraceptives. Breast feeding would be strongly encouraged for its beneficial nutritional and anti-infective effects on children, its contraceptive effect on nursing mothers, and economic benefits to the family. An extensive network of local health care centers in villages and rural areas would be established throughout the poor or developing regions. They would provide basic health services for a large percentage of a region's population. Staffed by local paramedics (modeled after the Chinese "barefoot doctor") and midwives, they would emphasize preventative medicine, disseminate family planning information and birth control devices,

The Birthrate and Energy Production

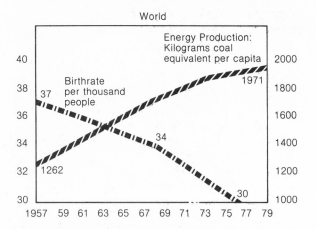

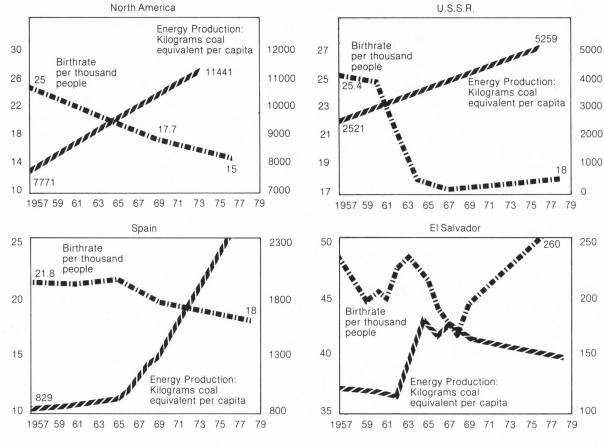

and focus on high-risk segments of the population—such as children under age five and child-bearing women. "The majority of common illnesses can be successfully treated by health auxiliaries with simple equipment and a quite limited range of medicines."[40] These health care centers would control infectious disease and improve nutrition as well as make family planning services available. They would give immunizations, direct local public health measures, provide maternal and child-health services, and administer simple nutrition programs. Eliminating blindness due to vitamin A deficiency, goiter and cretinism due to iodine deficiency, and anemia due to iron or folate deficiency, within ten years would be one of the goals of these centers. Economic incentives such as tax deductions for small families would be established or enlarged, and social securities increased. Also, increased economic and educational opportunities for women outside the home and family, child care facilities, pregnancy

leaves of absence from work, and other tactics would facilitate the transition from woman as only a child bearer to a more fully participating member of society and help to stabilize world population at 6 billion or below.

The most effective way, some would say the only way, of stabilizing population is to raise the standard of living.

Blueprints for Cornucopia

The following section outlines various individual tactics or strategies that comprise the overall global food development plan. The first part is just a linear listing of major "moves" or strategies, while the second is a more detailed explication of specific tactics done graphically in terms of "first-things-first," and "what-happens-where." These later "critical-path" charts and the strategies and tactics they help to illustrate are preceded by three other charts and graphs which illustrate the major strategic moves at different levels of aggregation. All the moves are to be viewed as one developmental plan; they outline or blueprint what needs to be done to reach the preferred global food systems that the book describes. The parts should be viewed as a synergetic sum; they have full meaning only in their relation to the whole. Each chart deals with one aspect of the overall food system development plan over two time periods—short term (five years), and long term (twenty-five years)—as well as on four distinct levels of use, organization, or production: home, community, region, and global.

Amass Large Food Reserves: Local storages of up to a twelve month supply, primarily in chronic food short regions and a multiple year global grain storage in Antarctica as a back-up to local storages would effectively function to maintain world stability in the face of possible severe climate disruptions and local weather anomalies.

Increase Conventional Agricultural Intensity: Increasing chemical fertilizer and pesticide production, high yield seeds, irrigation, small-scale appropriate machinery, double cropping, inter-cropping, and farmer education, primarily in the developing world, would dramatically increase crop yields.

Increase Land under Cultivation: Increasing cultivated land and growing or grazing locally appropriate crops and/or animals in all areas, but especially in South America and Africa where the largest reserves of arable land are, would greatly increase these areas' food production. Primarily a back-up, this strategy may be unnecessary if other strategies work out quickly enough.

Institute a Global Food Service: A non-profit, non-political, consumer-oriented world food organization coordinating food tactics and strategies; buying surplus grain from around the world to amass large food reserves; monitoring global food trends and problems; delivering food aid to avert famine; assisting local self-sufficiency development; funding food system research into unconventional food sources, storages, etc.; developing food system education; and setting up a world clearinghouse for food related information would effectively function to bring all the various components of the world food development plan together and also to do all those things that profit-motivated corporations or nation-centered states will not do.

Decentralize Food System: Producing, processing, consuming, and recycling food locally saves energy, materials, nutritional loss, and transportation costs, and dramatically lowers food costs because the middleman between food producer and consumer is reduced or eliminated. More food should be grown on small farms as they are more productive per acre than large farms.

Develop Regenerative Aboriginal Agriculture Methods: Increasing productivity and decreasing environmental impact with new and appropriate education, tools, and techniques would stabilize or reverse soil erosion and make these damaged regions largely self-sufficient once again.

Institute World Water Institute: A world water institute would greatly aid in solving the water supply and use problems of the planet.

Design and Build Energy, Food, and Water Harvesting Homes and Communities: Designing new and retrofitting old houses, high rises, and communities to be food, energy, and water producers, not just consumers, would decrease the demand for food, help decentralize the food system, and decrease the amount of food processing needed. Every household building should be able to produce all or most of its fresh vegetable food needs, thereby drastically cutting urban food requirements.

Develop Income and Conservation Energy Sources: Increasing the amount of non-depletable energy the global food system uses, implementing energy conserving technologies in the food system, and growing energy producing crops on marginal lands will decrease the food system's reliance on the depleting, rising in cost, polluting, and centralized fossil fuels. Small-scale income energies for the agricultural system will assist in decentralizing those parts of the food system that would benefit from such a move.

Reduce Infant Mortality Rates: By reducing infant mortality, population growth rates drop. By dropping population growth rate, population can stabilize. Stabilizing world population, especially in the quickest growing and food short developing regions, would take the tremendous pressure and tension off the world food system and allow for quicker growth of all facets of global human development.

Disseminate Nutrition Information: Disseminating information about complementary proteins, the advantages of breast feeding, the disadvantages of eating high on the food chain, and the dangers of fats, junk foods, etc. would make the food that is available go much further. Malnutrition in many parts of the world could be eliminated with education, thereby decreasing the pressure on the food system to produce more food.

Develop Organic Fertilizers: Recycling organic wastes of both city and farm to supply plant nutrients would decrease the need for chemical fertilizer and energy, stop soil erosion, and provide a useful outlet for organic waste.

Regulate Transnational Food Corporations: Global guidelines, regulations, incentives, and taxes for global corporations would stop abuses of the present system and bring the vast resources and talents of these corporations to bear on feeding people. Economic environments would be produced that would encourage transnational corporations to adapt and develop appropriate technologies for developing regions.

Regulate Exploitation of the Ocean's Food Resources: By having all the world's oceans from twelve miles offshore on out essentially in trusteeship to the Global Food Service, and all fishing licensed and regulated by the Global Food Service, the ocean fish stocks would be preserved and a sustained yield could be harvested.

Develop Soil Conservation: A world soil conservation and reclamation corps would stop soil erosion, control floods, and reclaim deserts, thereby providing more productive land and employment for urban and rural unemployed.

Develop Unconventional Food Sources: Developing single cell proteins—algae, bacteria, and yeasts—leaf proteins, sprouts, insects, synthetic nutrients, and other new foods for human and animal consumption would greatly increase the available foodstuffs in the world, relieve some of the pressure from possible changing weather or climate by providing humanity with food sources that are largely independent of the weather, and also provide new employment opportunities.

Develop Hydroponics: Growing plants in light weight soil-less controlled environments on urban rooftops and on coastal deserts and other appropriate locations would greatly increase urban food self-sufficiency and global food production.

Develop Aquaculture: Raising fish in ponds or tanks wherever appropriate would increase the amount of available protein in the world.

Develop Ecological Pest Control: Managing pests with their own predators, companion plantings, sterile pest insects, and other methods would decrease the amount of dangerous and harmful chemical pesticides in use.

Develop Non-Grain Animal Feeds: Weaning livestock from human food would vastly increase the amount of food available to the world.

Circumvent/Improve Food Processing: Reducing the amount of processing by growing food more locally as well as processing food so as to maintain or improve nutritional quality, rather than taste or shelf-life, would increase the amount of real food available in the world without having to produce any more.

North America to "Feed the World": Similar in scope to the Apollo Moon Project, the "Feeding the World" project would tap North America's unique gifts of natural resources, agricultural productivity, and technological know-how to provide food aid and assistance in achieving self-sufficiency wherever needed in the world so as to guarantee that every child, woman, and man on Earth is not hungry; it could provide a positive national goal, direction, identity, and spirit as well as vitalize a large segment of the North American economy. Building on North America's strength, it could do one of the things that North America does better than any other part of the planet. This strategy is not necessary for any of the other strategies to work but it would accelerate all aspects of the global food development plan.

Small Farm Loans and Crop Insurance: Primarily for the poor farmer in developing regions of the planet, this insurance—financed by a 1% tax on multinational food corporations—would protect the farmer from bankruptcy or dispossession by the rich or large landowner in times of crop failure due to bad weather and provide capital for purchasing the necessary agricultural implements to improve farm output.

Food Conservation: Reducing world-wide food losses, especially in developing countries, would increase food supply without having to increase production.

Develop Long Range Alternatives Today: Automated growth domes, ocean floating food production units, etc. developed now and used to produce biomass for conversion to alcohol and methane would provide fuel to relieve oil shortages, be non-competing with conventional agriculture, but provide a back-up system in case of climate disruptions. Related to unconventional food sources.

Centralize Food Production, Processing, and Storage Wherever Appropriate: Large scale and highly automated facilities in areas and for processes that this would be appropriate for would increase or maintain food production without the need for coerced (i.e., little or no choice involved) human labor.

Establish Global Energy Utility: The establishment of a global energy utility similar in scope and intent to the Global Food Service—a part of which would work on developing and coordinating income energy sources for the food system—would greatly facilitate all the energy-requiring parts of the food systems.

Issue Global Food Stamps: A global food stamp program for anyone, anywhere on Earth, who needed it, and redeemable in basic food staples, would help guarantee that everyone had economic access to food.

Land Reform: A realignment of land ownership in regions where there are large numbers of landless laborers and tenant farmers would increase rural stability, help increase farm productivity, and raise the standards of living in the regions involved by allowing the tillers of the farm to be the ones who were rewarded for improvements to the farm.

Decentralized Health Care: Establishing village-based health care facilities in rural regions would greatly increase the general well-being of the rural poor by helping to decrease infant and child mortality, disseminating nutrition, family planning, and health care information, developing and administrating village public health programs, and helping to eliminate the food lost to internal body parasites, thereby decreasing demand for food, helping to stabilize population, and raising the general quality of life.

Planetary Service System: Instituting a Planetary Service System where the 18–22 year old youths of the world could participate in "making the world work" in regions where assistance was requested, would aid the recipient country, provide invaluable experience for the participant, provide direction for secondary education (as preparation for this Service), and foster a global awareness and fellowship among the youth of the planet.

Goal Formulation: Formulating local, regional, and national goals for agricultural development would help focus attention on the problems of development, involve more people in the decision making process, and help bring about the changes needed to reach those goals.

Establish Emergency Relief Agency: Establishing a Global Emergency Relief Agency to prepare for and to deal with local and regional natural disasters (including famine) would help avert and ameliorate the tragedies and hardships which accompany such disasters.

World Inventory of Agricultural Technology: Inventorying all the agriculture technology that humanity has developed in all parts of the world and making this available to agricultural field workers, researchers, etc. would help the diffusion of technology and facilitate a decentralized interaction of the world's farmers.

Global Computerized Agriculture Information Network: By computerizing agricultural information—such as the World Inventory of Agricultural Technology; FAO statistics; seed, fertilizer, pesticide use, application, etc.—and then making this available (via low-cost solar-cell-powered computer terminals, satellite relay to data storages, etc.) to a global network of agricultural field workers, researchers, colleges, etc. the access to vital information for increasing yields, decreasing losses, decentralizing decision-making, etc. would be made much more widely available.

Global Agriculture Training Institute: Setting up a global agriculture training network to train agricultural extension workers in all aspects of new and old agricultural systems would greatly aid in diffusing the most productive techniques into the rural areas of the world.

World Food Game: Developing a "World Food Game" computer simulation that would allow food system decision-makers, policy-makers, researchers, and the general public to develop new strategies and to test out their present development strategies, would help educate policy-makers, etc. to the complexities of the world food system and help in the development of new strategies.

Grain Tax: By instituting a tax on non-human grain consumption, the poor of the planet will be able to compete economically with the animals of the developed world, thereby increasing their access to food.

Energy from Crops: By developing the energy potential of biomass in the various regions of the planet where large agricultural surpluses may result in the next twenty-five years would create a market for these surpluses, thereby keeping the farmer economically viable and reducing the dependence on imported energy supplies.

Eliminate Human Drudgery/Increase Reinvestable Time: When technological, social, and economic development can reduce mechanical, dull, or demeaning coerced human labor in all or any part of the food system, people will be more free to pursue their own educational, cultural, or spiritual interests, and this would lead to greater diversity, stability, and evolution.

Develop Extensive and Humane Life Support and Educational Systems throughout the World: If the world's clean technological systems continue to produce more life support with fewer resources, and if the world's population stabilizes as it is tending to, food production and procurement will cease to be the major preoccupation of the majority of humanity. The more options and choices that the billions of people have to grow into, the greater will be humanity's next step(s) in evolutionary development.

Strategy Outline—Level 1

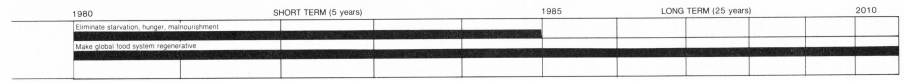

Strategy Outline—Level 2

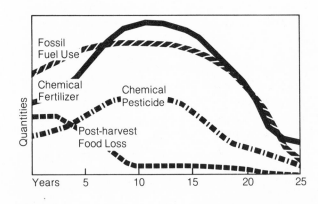

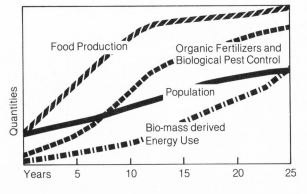

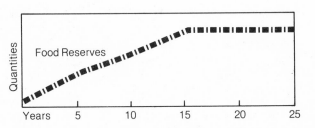

Strategy Outline—Level 3

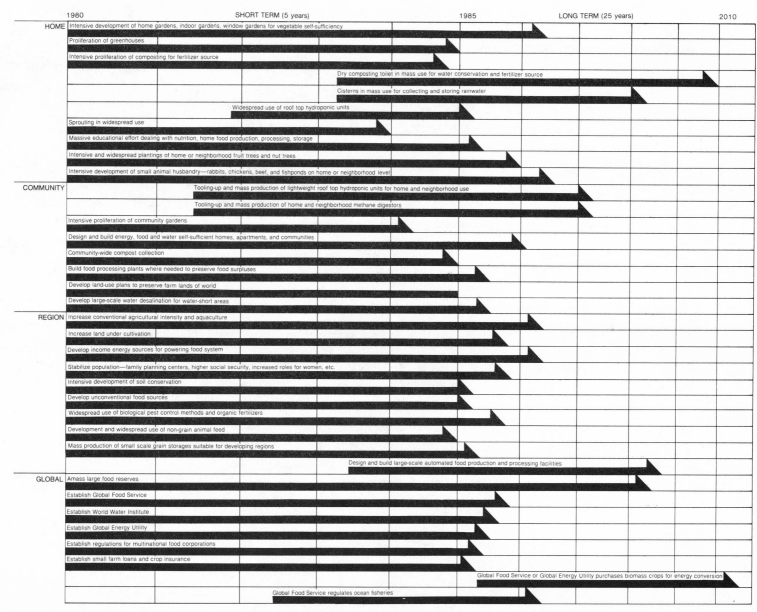

	1980		SHORT TERM (5 years)		1985		LONG TERM (25 years)		2010

HOME
- Intensive development of home gardens, indoor gardens, window gardens for vegetable self-sufficiency
- Proliferation of greenhouses
- Intensive proliferation of composting for fertilizer source
- Dry composting toilet in mass use for water conservation and fertilizer source
- Cisterns in mass use for collecting and storing rainwater
- Widespread use of roof top hydroponic units
- Sprouting in widespread use
- Massive educational effort dealing with nutrition, home food production, processing, storage
- Intensive and widespread plantings of home or neighborhood fruit trees and nut trees
- Intensive development of small animal husbandry—rabbits, chickens, beef, and fishponds on home or neighborhood level

COMMUNITY
- Tooling-up and mass production of lightweight roof top hydroponic units for home and neighborhood use
- Tooling-up and mass production of home and neighborhood methane digestors
- Intensive proliferation of community gardens
- Design and build energy, food and water self-sufficient homes, apartments, and communities
- Community-wide compost collection
- Build food processing plants where needed to preserve food surpluses
- Develop land-use plans to preserve farm lands of world
- Develop large-scale water desalination for water-short areas

REGION
- Increase conventional agricultural intensity and aquaculture
- Increase land under cultivation
- Develop income energy sources for powering food system
- Stabilize population—family planning centers, higher social security, increased roles for women, etc.
- Intensive development of soil conservation
- Develop unconventional food sources
- Widespread use of biological pest control methods and organic fertilizers
- Development and widespread use of non-grain animal feed
- Mass production of small scale grain storages suitable for developing regions
- Design and build large-scale automated food production and processing facilities

GLOBAL
- Amass large food reserves
- Establish Global Food Service
- Establish World Water Institute
- Establish Global Energy Utility
- Establish regulations for multinational food corporations
- Establish small farm loans and crop insurance
- Global Food Service or Global Energy Utility purchases biomass crops for energy conversion
- Global Food Service regulates ocean fisheries

Strategy Outline—Level 4   Global Food Service

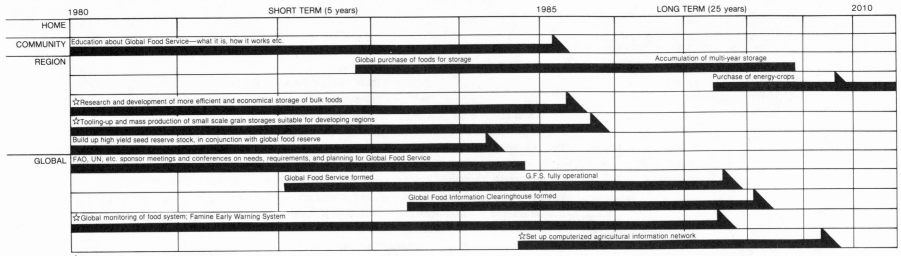

	1980	SHORT TERM (5 years)			1985	LONG TERM (25 years)		2010
HOME								
COMMUNITY	Education about Global Food Service—what it is, how it works etc.							
REGION			Global purchase of foods for storage				Accumulation of multi-year storage	
							Purchase of energy-crops	
	☆Research and development of more efficient and economical storage of bulk foods							
	☆Tooling-up and mass production of small scale grain storages suitable for developing regions							
	Build up high yield seed reserve stock, in conjunction with global food reserve							
GLOBAL	FAO, UN, etc. sponsor meetings and conferences on needs, requirements, and planning for Global Food Service							
			Global Food Service formed			G.F.S. fully operational		
					Global Food Information Clearinghouse formed			
	☆Global monitoring of food system; Famine Early Warning System							
					☆Set up computerized agricultural information network			

☆ Physical Artifact

Aboriginal Agriculture

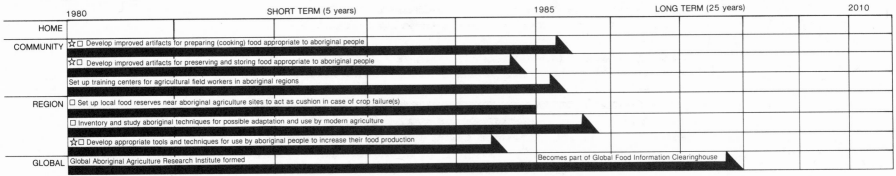

	1980	SHORT TERM (5 years)			1985	LONG TERM (25 years)		2010
HOME								
COMMUNITY	☆☐ Develop improved artifacts for preparing (cooking) food appropriate to aboriginal people							
	☆☐ Develop improved artifacts for preserving and storing food appropriate to aboriginal people							
	Set up training centers for agricultural field workers in aboriginal regions							
REGION	☐ Set up local food reserves near aboriginal agriculture sites to act as cushion in case of crop failure(s)							
	☐ Inventory and study aboriginal techniques for possible adaptation and use by modern agriculture							
	☆☐ Develop appropriate tools and techniques for use by aboriginal people to increase their food production							
GLOBAL	Global Aboriginal Agriculture Research Institute formed					Becomes part of Global Food Information Clearinghouse		

☐ Developing Regions   ☆ Physical Artifact

Energy Use

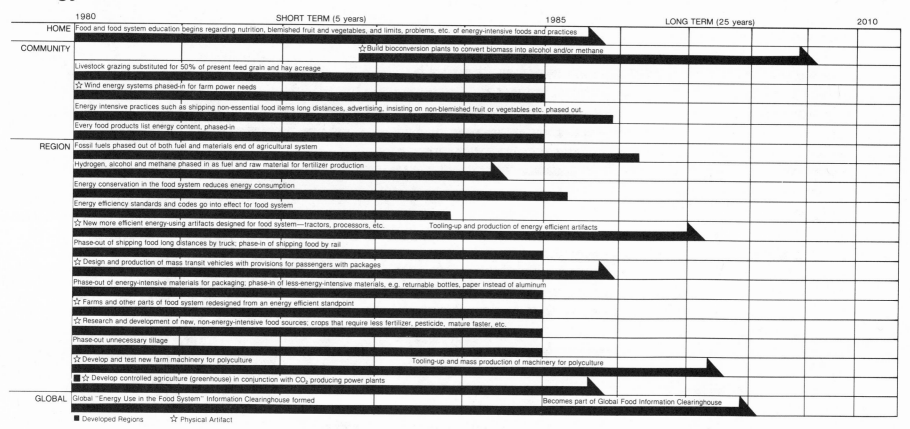

	1980	SHORT TERM (5 years)		1985	LONG TERM (25 years)		2010
HOME	Food and food system education begins regarding nutrition, blemished fruit and vegetables, and limits, problems, etc. of energy-intensive foods and practices						
COMMUNITY			☆ Build bioconversion plants to convert biomass into alcohol and/or methane				
	Livestock grazing substituted for 50% of present feed grain and hay acreage						
	☆ Wind energy systems phased-in for farm power needs						
	Energy intensive practices such as shipping non-essential food items long distances, advertising, insisting on non-blemished fruit or vegetables etc. phased out.						
	Every food products list energy content, phased-in						
REGION	Fossil fuels phased out of both fuel and materials end of agricultural system						
	Hydrogen, alcohol and methane phased in as fuel and raw material for fertilizer production						
	Energy conservation in the food system reduces energy consumption						
	Energy efficiency standards and codes go into effect for food system						
	☆ New more efficient energy-using artifacts designed for food system—tractors, processors, etc.		Tooling-up and production of energy efficient artifacts				
	Phase-out of shipping food long distances by truck; phase-in of shipping food by rail						
	☆ Design and production of mass transit vehicles with provisions for passengers with packages						
	Phase-out of energy-intensive materials for packaging; phase-in of less-energy-intensive materials, e.g. returnable bottles, paper instead of aluminum						
	☆ Farms and other parts of food system redesigned from an energy efficient standpoint						
	☆ Research and development of new, non-energy-intensive food sources; crops that require less fertilizer, pesticide, mature faster, etc.						
	Phase-out unnecessary tillage						
	☆ Develop and test new farm machinery for polyculture		Tooling-up and mass production of machinery for polyculture				
	■ ☆ Develop controlled agriculture (greenhouse) in conjunction with CO_2 producing power plants						
GLOBAL	Global "Energy Use in the Food System" Information Clearinghouse formed				Becomes part of Global Food Information Clearinghouse		

■ Developed Regions   ☆ Physical Artifact

237

Agribusiness

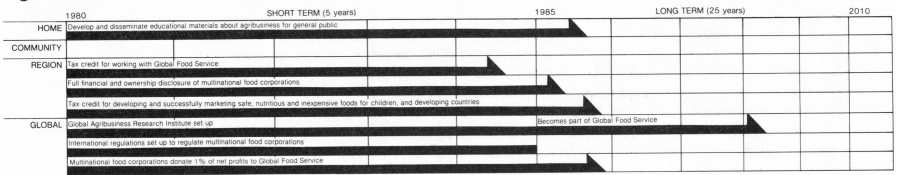

	1980	SHORT TERM (5 years)	1985	LONG TERM (25 years)	2010
HOME	Develop and disseminate educational materials about agribusiness for general public				
COMMUNITY					
REGION	Tax credit for working with Global Food Service				
	Full financial and ownership disclosure of multinational food corporations				
	Tax credit for developing and successfully marketing safe, nutritious and inexpensive foods for children, and developing countries				
GLOBAL	Global Agribusiness Research Institute set up		Becomes part of Global Food Service		
	International regulations set up to regulate multinational food corporations				
	Multinational food corporations donate 1% of net profits to Global Food Service				

Water Supply/Irrigation/Drainage

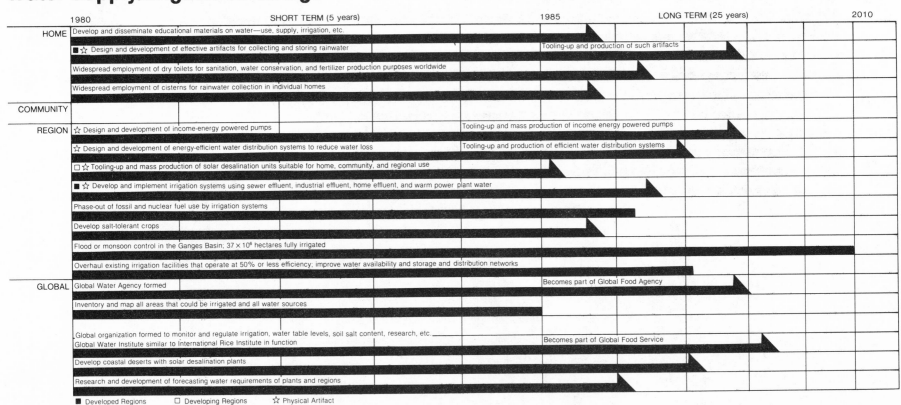

	1980	SHORT TERM (5 years)	1985	LONG TERM (25 years)	2010
HOME	Develop and disseminate educational materials on water—use, supply, irrigation, etc.				
	■ ☆ Design and development of effective artifacts for collecting and storing rainwater		Tooling-up and production of such artifacts		
	Widespread employment of dry toilets for sanitation, water conservation, and fertilizer production purposes worldwide				
	Widespread employment of cisterns for rainwater collection in individual homes				
COMMUNITY					
REGION	☆ Design and development of income-energy powered pumps		Tooling-up and mass production of income energy powered pumps		
	☆ Design and development of energy-efficient water distribution systems to reduce water loss		Tooling-up and production of efficient water distribution systems		
	□ ☆ Tooling-up and mass production of solar desalination units suitable for home, community, and regional use				
	■ ☆ Develop and implement irrigation systems using sewer effluent, industrial effluent, home effluent, and warm power plant water				
	Phase-out of fossil and nuclear fuel use by irrigation systems				
	Develop salt-tolerant crops				
	Flood or monsoon control in the Ganges Basin; 37×10^6 hectares fully irrigated				
	Overhaul existing irrigation facilities that operate at 50% or less efficiency; improve water availability and storage and distribution networks				
GLOBAL	Global Water Agency formed		Becomes part of Global Food Agency		
	Inventory and map all areas that could be irrigated and all water sources				
	Global organization formed to monitor and regulate irrigation, water table levels, soil salt content, research, etc. Global Water Institute similar to International Rice Institute in function		Becomes part of Global Food Service		
	Develop coastal deserts with solar desalination plants				
	Research and development of forecasting water requirements of plants and regions				

■ Developed Regions   □ Developing Regions   ☆ Physical Artifact

Fertilizer

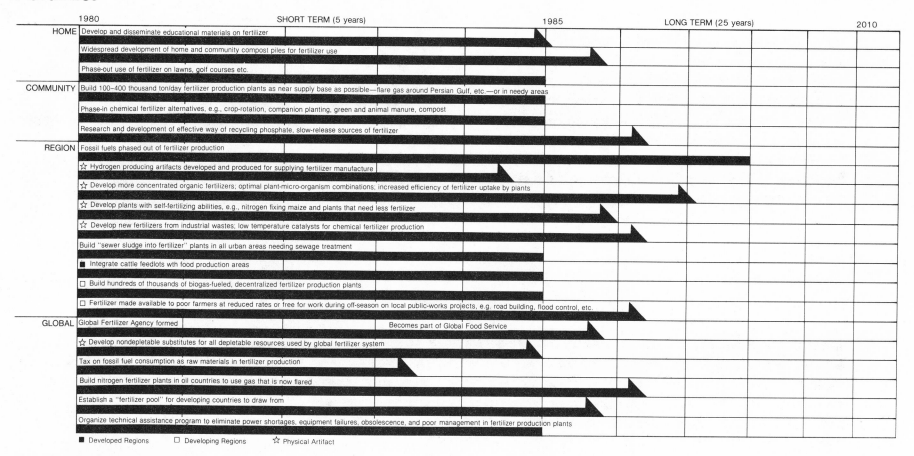

	1980	SHORT TERM (5 years)			1985	LONG TERM (25 years)			2010
HOME	Develop and disseminate educational materials on fertilizer								
	Widespread development of home and community compost piles for fertilizer use								
	Phase-out use of fertilizer on lawns, golf courses etc.								
COMMUNITY	Build 100–400 thousand ton/day fertilizer production plants as near supply base as possible—flare gas around Persian Gulf, etc.—or in needy areas								
	Phase-in chemical fertilizer alternatives, e.g., crop-rotation, companion planting, green and animal manure, compost								
	Research and development of effective way of recycling phosphate, slow-release sources of fertilizer								
REGION	Fossil fuels phased out of fertilizer production								
	☆ Hydrogen producing artifacts developed and produced for supplying fertilizer manufacture								
	☆ Develop more concentrated organic fertilizers; optimal plant-micro-organism combinations; increased efficiency of fertilizer uptake by plants								
	☆ Develop plants with self-fertilizing abilities, e.g., nitrogen fixing maize and plants that need less fertilizer								
	☆ Develop new fertilizers from industrial wastes; low temperature catalysts for chemical fertilizer production								
	Build "sewer sludge into fertilizer" plants in all urban areas needing sewage treatment								
	■ Integrate cattle feedlots wth food production areas								
	☐ Build hundreds of thousands of biogas-fueled, decentralized fertilizer production plants								
	☐ Fertilizer made available to poor farmers at reduced rates or free for work during off-season on local public-works projects, e.g. road building, flood control, etc.								
GLOBAL	Global Fertilizer Agency formed				Becomes part of Global Food Service				
	☆ Develop nondepletable substitutes for all depletable resources used by global fertilizer system								
	Tax on fossil fuel consumption as raw materials in fertilizer production								
	Build nitrogen fertilizer plants in oil countries to use gas that is now flared								
	Establish a "fertilizer pool" for developing countries to draw from								
	Organize technical assistance program to eliminate power shortages, equipment failures, obsolescence, and poor management in fertilizer production plants								

■ Developed Regions   ☐ Developing Regions   ☆ Physical Artifact

Seed Development

	1980	SHORT TERM (5 years)			1985	LONG TERM (25 years)			2010
HOME	Educational program for plant breeding, seed development, etc.								
COMMUNITY	Local contests for better crop/plant varieties								
REGION	Establish regional seed farms to produce high yield seeds appropriate to local and regional climates								
GLOBAL	Establish World Seed Development Institute to help produce high yield variety seeds								

239

Land Use

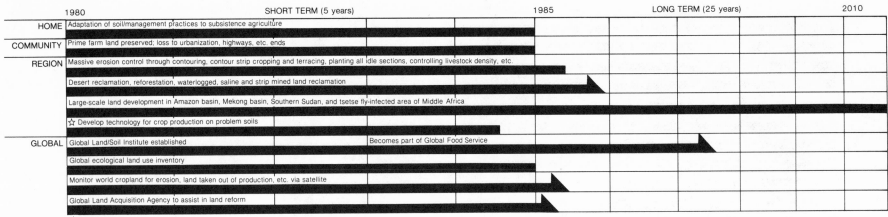

	1980	SHORT TERM (5 years)		1985	LONG TERM (25 years)		2010
HOME	Adaptation of soil/management practices to subsistence agriculture						
COMMUNITY	Prime farm land preserved; loss to urbanization, highways, etc. ends						
REGION	Massive erosion control through contouring, contour strip cropping and terracing, planting all idle sections, controlling livestock density, etc.						
	Desert reclamation, reforestation, waterlogged, saline and strip mined land reclamation						
	Large-scale land development in Amazon basin, Mekong basin, Southern Sudan, and tsetse fly-infected area of Middle Africa						
	☆ Develop technology for crop production on problem soils						
GLOBAL	Global Land/Soil Institute established		Becomes part of Global Food Service				
	Global ecological land use inventory						
	Monitor world cropland for erosion, land taken out of production, etc. via satellite						
	Global Land Acquisition Agency to assist in land reform						

☆ Physical Artifact

Pesticides

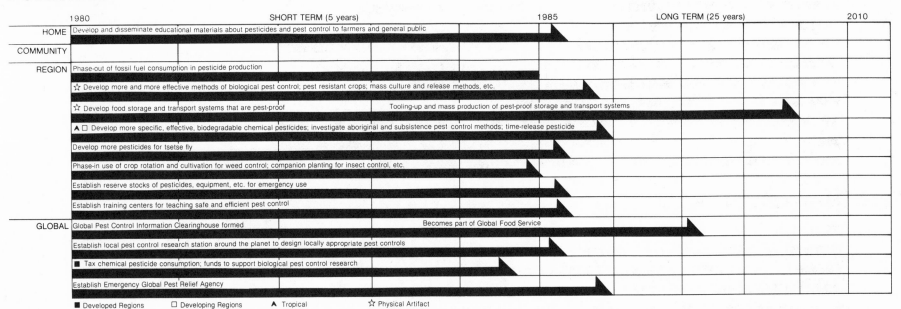

	1980	SHORT TERM (5 years)		1985	LONG TERM (25 years)		2010
HOME	Develop and disseminate educational materials about pesticides and pest control to farmers and general public						
COMMUNITY							
REGION	Phase-out of fossil fuel consumption in pesticide production						
	☆ Develop more and more effective methods of biological pest control; pest resistant crops; mass culture and release methods, etc.						
	☆ Develop food storage and transport systems that are pest-proof		Tooling-up and mass production of pest-proof storage and transport systems				
	▲ ☐ Develop more specific, effective, biodegradable chemical pesticides; investigate aboriginal and subsistence pest control methods; time-release pesticide						
	Develop more pesticides for tsetse fly						
	Phase-in use of crop rotation and cultivation for weed control; companion planting for insect control, etc.						
	Establish reserve stocks of pesticides, equipment, etc. for emergency use						
	Establish training centers for teaching safe and efficient pest control						
GLOBAL	Global Pest Control Information Clearinghouse formed		Becomes part of Global Food Service				
	Establish local pest control research station around the planet to design locally appropriate pest controls						
	■ Tax chemical pesticide consumption; funds to support biological pest control research						
	Establish Emergency Global Pest Relief Agency						

■ Developed Regions ☐ Developing Regions ▲ Tropical ☆ Physical Artifact

Animal Husbandry

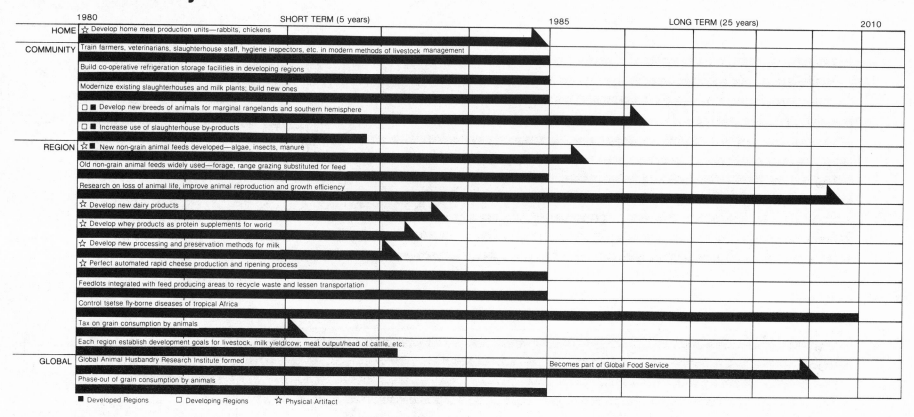

	1980	SHORT TERM (5 years)				1985	LONG TERM (25 years)			2010	
HOME	☆ Develop home meat production units—rabbits, chickens										
COMMUNITY	Train farmers, veterinarians, slaughterhouse staff, hygiene inspectors, etc. in modern methods of livestock management										
	Build co-operative refrigeration storage facilities in developing regions										
	Modernize existing slaughterhouses and milk plants; build new ones										
	☐ ■ Develop new breeds of animals for marginal rangelands and southern hemisphere										
	☐ ■ Increase use of slaughterhouse by-products										
REGION	☆ ■ New non-grain animal feeds developed—algae, insects, manure										
	Old non-grain animal feeds widely used—forage, range grazing substituted for feed										
	Research on loss of animal life, improve animal reproduction and growth efficiency										
	☆ Develop new dairy products										
	☆ Develop whey products as protein supplements for world										
	☆ Develop new processing and preservation methods for milk										
	☆ Perfect automated rapid cheese production and ripening process										
	Feedlots integrated with feed producing areas to recycle waste and lessen transportation										
	Control tsetse fly-borne diseases of tropical Africa										
	Tax on grain consumption by animals										
	Each region establish development goals for livestock, milk yield/cow; meat output/head of cattle, etc.										
GLOBAL	Global Animal Husbandry Research Institute formed						Becomes part of Global Food Service				
	Phase-out of grain consumption by animals										

■ Developed Regions   ☐ Developing Regions   ☆ Physical Artifact

Hydroponics

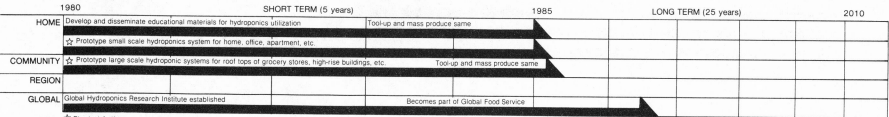

	1980	SHORT TERM (5 years)			1985	LONG TERM (25 years)			2010	
HOME	Develop and disseminate educational materials for hydroponics utilization			Tool-up and mass produce same						
	☆ Prototype small scale hydroponics system for home, office, apartment, etc.									
COMMUNITY	☆ Prototype large scale hydroponic systems for roof tops of grocery stores, high-rise buildings, etc.			Tool-up and mass produce same						
REGION										
GLOBAL	Global Hydroponics Research Institute established			Becomes part of Global Food Service						

☆ Physical Artifact

Fishing

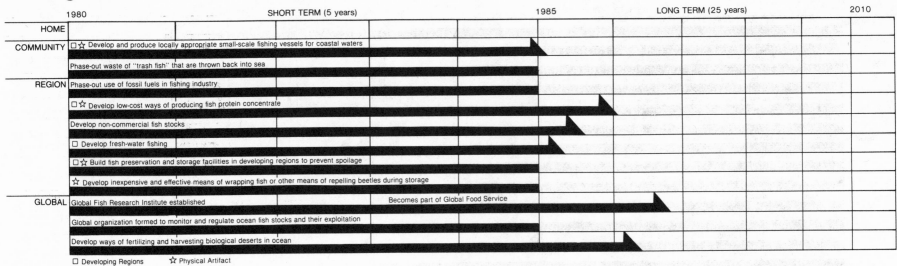

	1980	SHORT TERM (5 years)			1985	LONG TERM (25 years)		2010

HOME

COMMUNITY
- □ ☆ Develop and produce locally appropriate small-scale fishing vessels for coastal waters
- Phase-out waste of "trash fish" that are thrown back into sea

REGION
- Phase-out use of fossil fuels in fishing industry
- □ ☆ Develop low-cost ways of producing fish protein concentrate
- Develop non-commercial fish stocks
- □ Develop fresh-water fishing
- □ ☆ Build fish preservation and storage facilities in developing regions to prevent spoilage
- ☆ Develop inexpensive and effective means of wrapping fish or other means of repelling beetles during storage

GLOBAL
- Global Fish Research Institute established — Becomes part of Global Food Service
- Global organization formed to monitor and regulate ocean fish stocks and their exploitation
- Develop ways of fertilizing and harvesting biological deserts in ocean

□ Developing Regions   ☆ Physical Artifact

Greenhouses

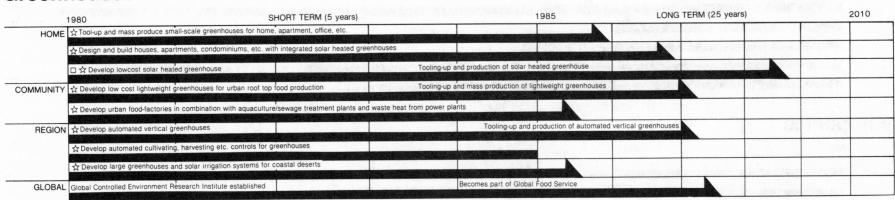

	1980	SHORT TERM (5 years)			1985	LONG TERM (25 years)		2010

HOME
- ☆ Tool-up and mass produce small-scale greenhouses for home, apartment, office, etc.
- ☆ Design and build houses, apartments, condominiums, etc. with integrated solar heated greenhouses
- □ ☆ Develop lowcost solar heated greenhouse — Tooling-up and production of solar heated greenhouse

COMMUNITY
- ☆ Develop low cost lightweight greenhouses for urban roof top food production — Tooling-up and mass production of lightweight greenhouses
- ☆ Develop urban food-factories in combination with aquaculture/sewage treatment plants and waste heat from power plants

REGION
- ☆ Develop automated vertical greenhouses — Tooling-up and production of automated vertical greenhouses
- ☆ Develop automated cultivating, harvesting etc. controls for greenhouses
- ☆ Develop large greenhouses and solar irrigation systems for coastal deserts

GLOBAL
- Global Controlled Environment Research Institute established — Becomes part of Global Food Service

□ Developing Regions   ☆ Physical Artifact

Aquaculture

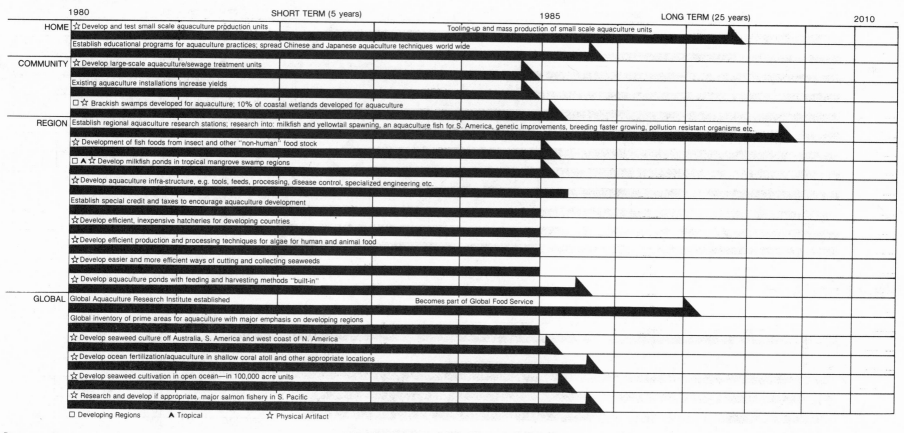

	1980	SHORT TERM (5 years)		1985	LONG TERM (25 years)		2010
HOME	☆ Develop and test small scale aquaculture production units		Tooling-up and mass production of small scale aquaculture units				
	Establish educational programs for aquaculture practices; spread Chinese and Japanese aquaculture techniques world wide						
COMMUNITY	☆ Develop large-scale aquaculture/sewage treatment units						
	Existing aquaculture installations increase yields						
	□ ☆ Brackish swamps developed for aquaculture; 10% of coastal wetlands developed for aquaculture						
REGION	Establish regional aquaculture research stations; research into: milkfish and yellowtail spawning, an aquaculture fish for S. America, genetic improvements, breeding faster growing, pollution resistant organisms etc.						
	☆ Development of fish foods from insect and other "non-human" food stock						
	□ ▲ ☆ Develop milkfish ponds in tropical mangrove swamp regions						
	☆ Develop aquaculture infra-structure, e.g. tools, feeds, processing, disease control, specialized engineering etc.						
	Establish special credit and taxes to encourage aquaculture development						
	☆ Develop efficient, inexpensive hatcheries for developing countries						
	☆ Develop efficient production and processing techniques for algae for human and animal food						
	☆ Develop easier and more efficient ways of cutting and collecting seaweeds						
	☆ Develop aquaculture ponds with feeding and harvesting methods "built-in"						
GLOBAL	Global Aquaculture Research Institute established		Becomes part of Global Food Service				
	Global inventory of prime areas for aquaculture with major emphasis on developing regions						
	☆ Develop seaweed culture off Australia, S. America and west coast of N. America						
	☆ Develop ocean fertilization/aquaculture in shallow coral atoll and other appropriate locations						
	☆ Develop seaweed cultivation in open ocean—in 100,000 acre units						
	☆ Research and develop if appropriate, major salmon fishery in S. Pacific						

□ Developing Regions   ▲ Tropical   ☆ Physical Artifact

Insects

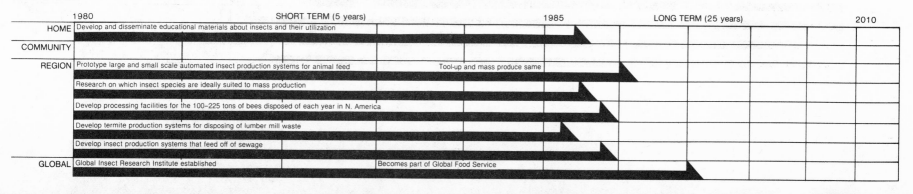

	1980	SHORT TERM (5 years)		1985	LONG TERM (25 years)		2010
HOME	Develop and disseminate educational materials about insects and their utilization						
COMMUNITY							
REGION	Prototype large and small scale automated insect production systems for animal feed		Tool-up and mass produce same				
	Research on which insect species are ideally suited to mass production						
	Develop processing facilities for the 100–225 tons of bees disposed of each year in N. America						
	Develop termite production systems for disposing of lumber mill waste						
	Develop insect production systems that feed off of sewage						
GLOBAL	Global Insect Research Institute established		Becomes part of Global Food Service				

Leaf Protein, Sprouting, Single-Cell Protein

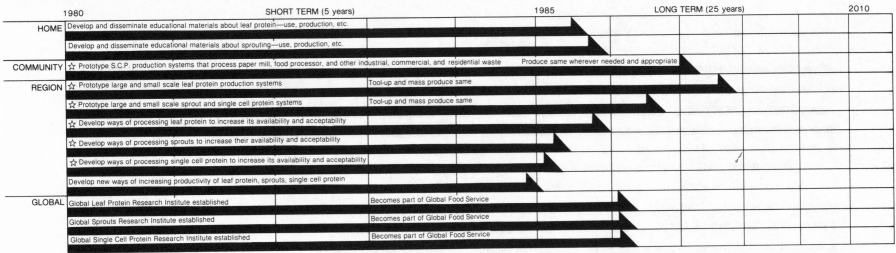

	1980	SHORT TERM (5 years)	1985	LONG TERM (25 years)	2010
HOME	Develop and disseminate educational materials about leaf protein—use, production, etc.				
	Develop and disseminate educational materials about sprouting—use, production, etc.				
COMMUNITY	☆ Prototype S.C.P. production systems that process paper mill, food processor, and other industrial, commercial, and residential waste		Produce same wherever needed and appropriate		
REGION	☆ Prototype large and small scale leaf protein production systems	Tool-up and mass produce same			
	☆ Prototype large and small scale sprout and single cell protein systems	Tool-up and mass produce same			
	☆ Develop ways of processing leaf protein to increase its availability and acceptability				
	☆ Develop ways of processing sprouts to increase their availability and acceptability				
	☆ Develop ways of processing single cell protein to increase its availability and acceptability				
	Develop new ways of increasing productivity of leaf protein, sprouts, single cell protein				
GLOBAL	Global Leaf Protein Research Institute established	Becomes part of Global Food Service			
	Global Sprouts Research Institute established	Becomes part of Global Food Service			
	Global Single Cell Protein Research Institute established	Becomes part of Global Food Service			

☆ Physical Artifact

New Foods

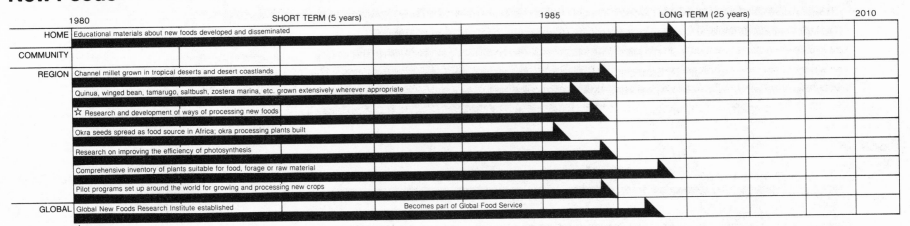

	1980	SHORT TERM (5 years)	1985	LONG TERM (25 years)	2010
HOME	Educational materials about new foods developed and disseminated				
COMMUNITY					
REGION	Channel millet grown in tropical deserts and desert coastlands				
	Quinua, winged bean, tamarugo, saltbush, zostera marina, etc. grown extensively wherever appropriate				
	☆ Research and development of ways of processing new foods				
	Okra seeds spread as food source in Africa; okra processing plants built				
	Research on improving the efficiency of photosynthesis				
	Comprehensive inventory of plants suitable for food, forage or raw material				
	Pilot programs set up around the world for growing and processing new crops				
GLOBAL	Global New Foods Research Institute established	Becomes part of Global Food Service			

☆ Physical Artifact

Exotic, Synthetic Nutriments

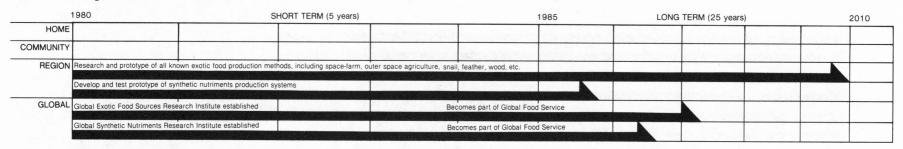

	1980	SHORT TERM (5 years)	1985	LONG TERM (25 years)	2010
HOME					
COMMUNITY					
REGION	Research and prototype of all known exotic food production methods, including space-farm, outer space agriculture, snail, feather, wood, etc.				
	Develop and test prototype of synthetic nutriments production systems				
GLOBAL	Global Exotic Food Sources Research Institute established		Becomes part of Global Food Service		
	Global Synthetic Nutriments Research Institute established		Becomes part of Global Food Service		

Decentralized Food Production

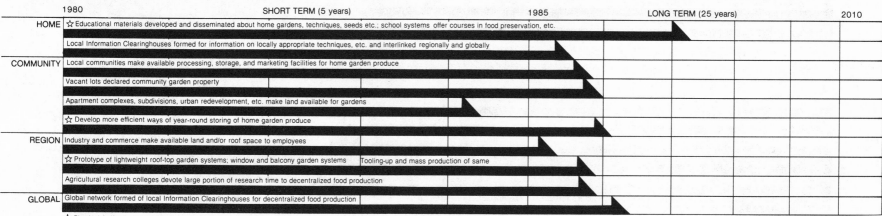

	1980	SHORT TERM (5 years)	1985	LONG TERM (25 years)	2010
HOME	☆ Educational materials developed and disseminated about home gardens, techniques, seeds etc.; school systems offer courses in food preservation, etc.				
	Local Information Clearinghouses formed for information on locally appropriate techniques, etc. and interlinked regionally and globally				
COMMUNITY	Local communities make available processing, storage, and marketing facilities for home garden produce				
	Vacant lots declared community garden property				
	Apartment complexes, subdivisions, urban redevelopment, etc. make land available for gardens				
	☆ Develop more efficient ways of year-round storing of home garden produce				
REGION	Industry and commerce make available land and/or roof space to employees				
	☆ Prototype of lightweight roof-top garden systems; window and balcony garden systems	Tooling-up and mass production of same			
	Agricultural research colleges devote large portion of research time to decentralized food production				
GLOBAL	Global network formed of local Information Clearinghouses for decentralized food production				

☆ Physical Artifact

245

Nutrition

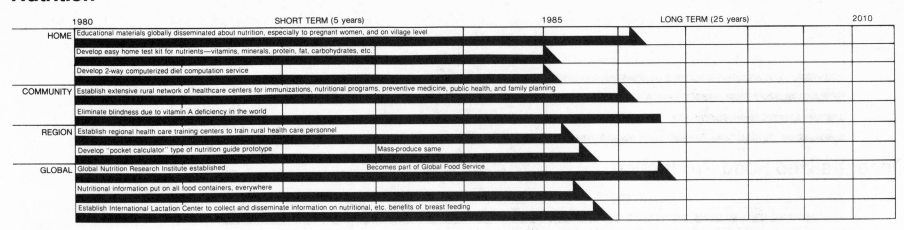

	1980	SHORT TERM (5 years)		1985	LONG TERM (25 years)	2010
HOME	Educational materials globally disseminated about nutrition, especially to pregnant women, and on village level					
	Develop easy home test kit for nutrients—vitamins, minerals, protein, fat, carbohydrates, etc.					
	Develop 2-way computerized diet computation service					
COMMUNITY	Establish extensive rural network of healthcare centers for immunizations, nutritional programs, preventive medicine, public health, and family planning					
	Eliminate blindness due to vitamin A deficiency in the world					
REGION	Establish regional health care training centers to train rural health care personnel					
	Develop "pocket calculator" type of nutrition guide prototype		Mass-produce same			
GLOBAL	Global Nutrition Research Institute established		Becomes part of Global Food Service			
	Nutritional information put on all food containers, everywhere					
	Establish International Lactation Center to collect and disseminate information on nutritional, etc. benefits of breast feeding					

Population

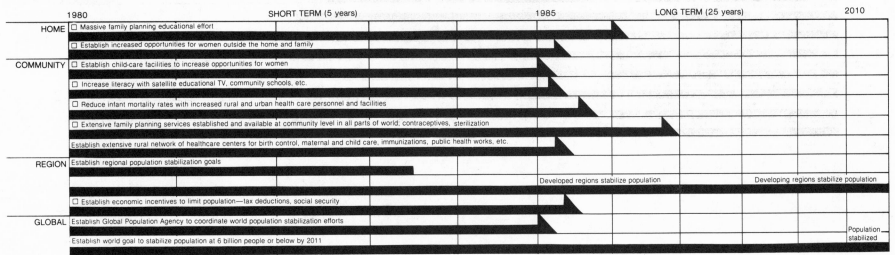

	1980	SHORT TERM (5 years)		1985	LONG TERM (25 years)	2010
HOME	☐ Massive family planning educational effort					
	☐ Establish increased opportunities for women outside the home and family					
COMMUNITY	☐ Establish child-care facilities to increase opportunities for women					
	☐ Increase literacy with satellite educational TV, community schools, etc.					
	☐ Reduce infant mortality rates with increased rural and urban health care personnel and facilities					
	☐ Extensive family planning services established and available at community level in all parts of world; contraceptives, sterilization					
	Establish extensive rural network of healthcare centers for birth control, maternal and child care, immunizations, public health works, etc.					
REGION	Establish regional population stabilization goals					
				Developed regions stabilize population		Developing regions stabilize population
	☐ Establish economic incentives to limit population—tax deductions, social security					
GLOBAL	Establish Global Population Agency to coordinate world population stabilization efforts					
	Establish world goal to stabilize population at 6 billion people or below by 2011					Population stabilized

☐ Developing Regions

Africa

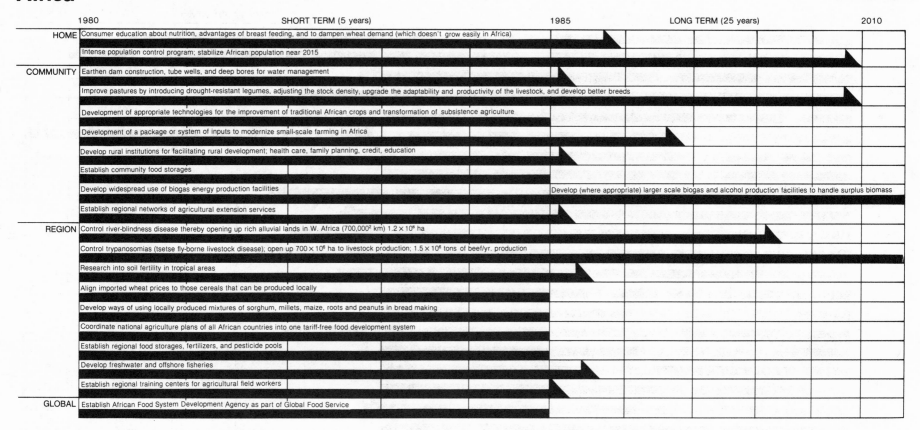

		1980 — SHORT TERM (5 years) — 1985	LONG TERM (25 years) — 2010
HOME	Consumer education about nutrition, advantages of breast feeding, and to dampen wheat demand (which doesn't grow easily in Africa)		
	Intense population control program; stabilize African population near 2015		
COMMUNITY	Earthen dam construction, tube wells, and deep bores for water management		
	Improve pastures by introducing drought-resistant legumes, adjusting the stock density, upgrade the adaptability and productivity of the livestock, and develop better breeds		
	Development of appropriate technologies for the improvement of traditional African crops and transformation of subsistence agriculture		
	Development of a package or system of inputs to modernize small-scale farming in Africa		
	Develop rural institutions for facilitating rural development; health care, family planning, credit, education		
	Establish community food storages		
	Develop widespread use of biogas energy production facilities		Develop (where appropriate) larger scale biogas and alcohol production facilities to handle surplus biomass
	Establish regional networks of agricultural extension services		
REGION	Control river-blindness disease thereby opening up rich alluvial lands in W. Africa (700,000^2 km) 1.2×10^6 ha		
	Control trypanosomias (tsetse fly-borne livestock disease); open up 700×10^6 ha to livestock production; 1.5×10^6 tons of beef/yr. production		
	Research into soil fertility in tropical areas		
	Align imported wheat prices to those cereals that can be produced locally		
	Develop ways of using locally produced mixtures of sorghum, millets, maize, roots and peanuts in bread making		
	Coordinate national agriculture plans of all African countries into one tariff-free food development system		
	Establish regional food storages, fertilizers, and pesticide pools		
	Develop freshwater and offshore fisheries		
	Establish regional training centers for agricultural field workers		
GLOBAL	Establish African Food System Development Agency as part of Global Food Service		

Far East

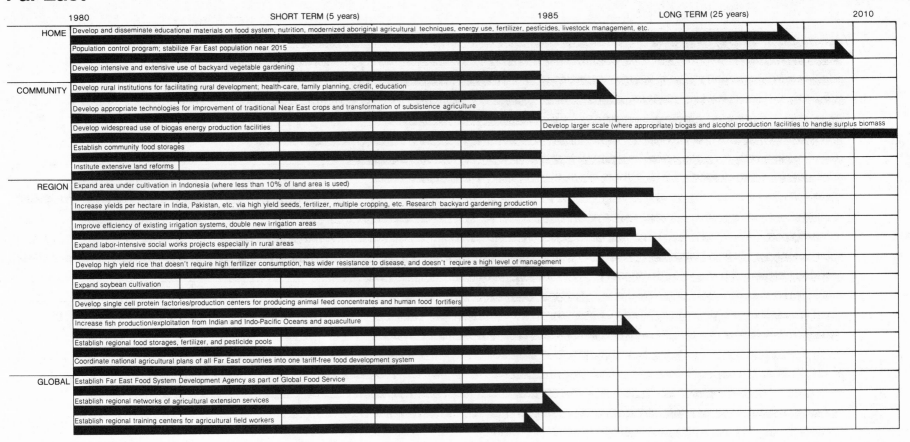

	1980	SHORT TERM (5 years)			1985	LONG TERM (25 years)			2010
HOME	Develop and disseminate educational materials on food system, nutrition, modernized aboriginal agricultural techniques, energy use, fertilizer, pesticides, livestock management, etc.								
	Population control program; stabilize Far East population near 2015								
	Develop intensive and extensive use of backyard vegetable gardening								
COMMUNITY	Develop rural institutions for facilitating rural development; health-care, family planning, credit, education								
	Develop appropriate technologies for improvement of traditional Near East crops and transformation of subsistence agriculture								
	Develop widespread use of biogas energy production facilities					Develop larger scale (where appropriate) biogas and alcohol production facilities to handle surplus biomass			
	Establish community food storages								
	Institute extensive land reforms								
REGION	Expand area under cultivation in Indonesia (where less than 10% of land area is used)								
	Increase yields per hectare in India, Pakistan, etc. via high yield seeds, fertilizer, multiple cropping, etc. Research backyard gardening production								
	Improve efficiency of existing irrigation systems, double new irrigation areas								
	Expand labor-intensive social works projects especially in rural areas								
	Develop high yield rice that doesn't require high fertilizer consumption, has wider resistance to disease, and doesn't require a high level of management								
	Expand soybean cultivation								
	Develop single cell protein factories/production centers for producing animal feed concentrates and human food fortifiers								
	Increase fish production/exploitation from Indian and Indo-Pacific Oceans and aquaculture								
	Establish regional food storages, fertilizer, and pesticide pools								
	Coordinate national agricultural plans of all Far East countries into one tariff-free food development system								
GLOBAL	Establish Far East Food System Development Agency as part of Global Food Service								
	Establish regional networks of agricultural extension services								
	Establish regional training centers for agricultural field workers								

Near East

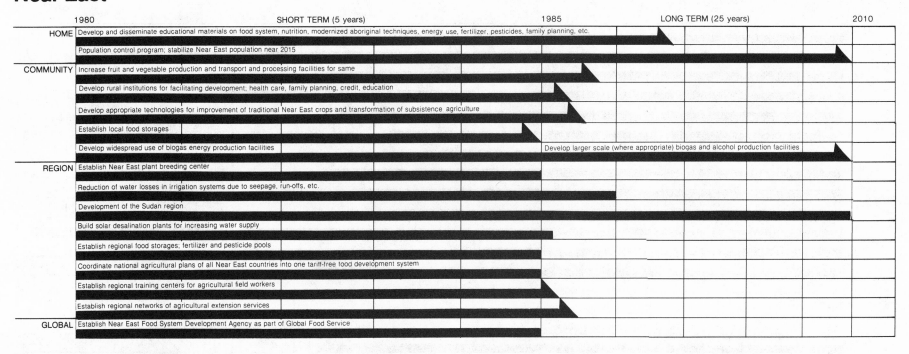

	1980	SHORT TERM (5 years)			1985	LONG TERM (25 years)			2010
HOME	Develop and disseminate educational materials on food system, nutrition, modernized aboriginal techniques, energy use, fertilizer, pesticides, family planning, etc.								
	Population control program; stabilize Near East population near 2015								
COMMUNITY	Increase fruit and vegetable production and transport and processing facilities for same								
	Develop rural institutions for facilitating development; health care, family planning, credit, education								
	Develop appropriate technologies for improvement of traditional Near East crops and transformation of subsistence agriculture								
	Establish local food storages								
	Develop widespread use of biogas energy production facilities					Develop larger scale (where appropriate) biogas and alcohol production facilities			
REGION	Establish Near East plant breeding center								
	Reduction of water losses in irrigation systems due to seepage, run-offs, etc.								
	Development of the Sudan region								
	Build solar desalination plants for increasing water supply								
	Establish regional food storages; fertilizer and pesticide pools								
	Coordinate national agricultural plans of all Near East countries into one tariff-free food development system								
	Establish regional training centers for agricultural field workers								
	Establish regional networks of agricultural extension services								
GLOBAL	Establish Near East Food System Development Agency as part of Global Food Service								

Europe and USSR

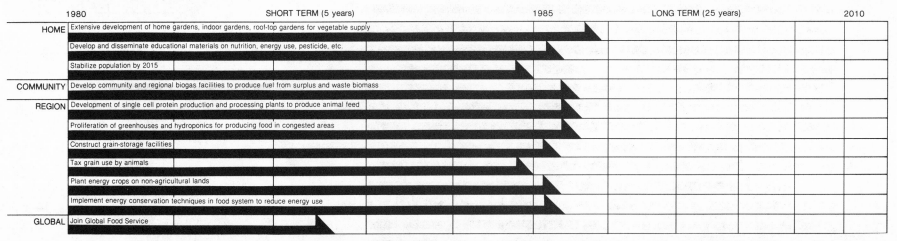

	1980	SHORT TERM (5 years)			1985	LONG TERM (25 years)			2010
HOME	Extensive development of home gardens, indoor gardens, roof-top gardens for vegetable supply								
	Develop and disseminate educational materials on nutrition, energy use, pesticide, etc.								
	Stabilize population by 2015								
COMMUNITY	Develop community and regional biogas facilities to produce fuel from surplus and waste biomass								
REGION	Development of single cell protein production and processing plants to produce animal feed								
	Proliferation of greenhouses and hydroponics for producing food in congested areas								
	Construct grain-storage facilities								
	Tax grain use by animals								
	Plant energy crops on non-agricultural lands								
	Implement energy conservation techniques in food system to reduce energy use								
GLOBAL	Join Global Food Service								

249

North America

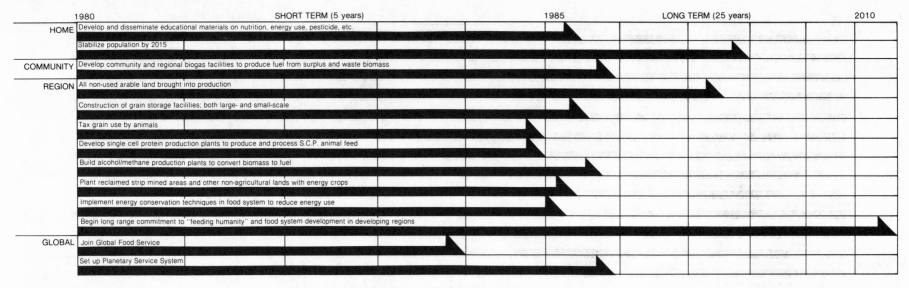

	1980	SHORT TERM (5 years)	1985	LONG TERM (25 years)	2010
HOME	Develop and disseminate educational materials on nutrition, energy use, pesticide, etc.				
	Stabilize population by 2015				
COMMUNITY	Develop community and regional biogas facilities to produce fuel from surplus and waste biomass				
REGION	All non-used arable land brought into production				
	Construction of grain storage facilities; both large- and small-scale				
	Tax grain use by animals				
	Develop single cell protein production plants to produce and process S.C.P. animal feed				
	Build alcohol/methane production plants to convert biomass to fuel				
	Plant reclaimed strip mined areas and other non-agricultural lands with energy crops				
	Implement energy conservation techniques in food system to reduce energy use				
	Begin long range commitment to "feeding humanity" and food system development in developing regions				
GLOBAL	Join Global Food Service				
	Set up Planetary Service System				

Latin America

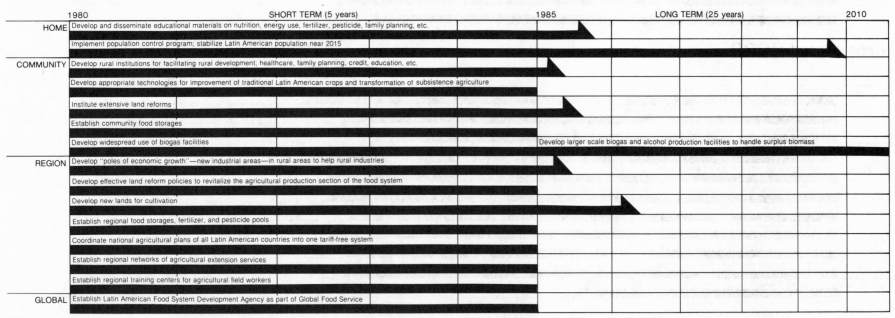

	1980	SHORT TERM (5 years)	1985	LONG TERM (25 years)	2010
HOME	Develop and disseminate educational materials on nutrition, energy use, fertilizer, pesticide, family planning, etc.				
	Implement population control program; stabilize Latin American population near 2015				
COMMUNITY	Develop rural institutions for facilitating rural development; healthcare, family planning, credit, education, etc.				
	Develop appropriate technologies for improvement of traditional Latin American crops and transformation of subsistence agriculture				
	Institute extensive land reforms				
	Establish community food storages				
	Develop widespread use of biogas facilities			Develop larger scale biogas and alcohol production facilities to handle surplus biomass	
REGION	Develop "poles of economic growth"—new industrial areas—in rural areas to help rural industries				
	Develop effective land reform policies to revitalize the agricultural production section of the food system				
	Develop new lands for cultivation				
	Establish regional food storages, fertilizer, and pesticide pools				
	Coordinate national agricultural plans of all Latin American countries into one tariff-free system				
	Establish regional networks of agricultural extension services				
	Establish regional training centers for agricultural field workers				
GLOBAL	Establish Latin American Food System Development Agency as part of Global Food Service				

The Long Ranger

Human beings are, among other things, biological systems. As such, they are designed to maximize survival. If biological systems, no matter how exquisite, were not so designed, they would no longer be around. A species' perceptual system is designed to perceive those bandwidths or frequencies of sight, sound, smell, taste, and touch that favor or maximize its survival. Out of the vast universe, each species is tuned into those specific sights and sounds that favor its continuing existence. A species' perceptual system forms the basis for its value system. You do not value what you do not know exists. A system values what it has learned leads to survival.

Just as "measurement" is an objective form of perception, an "accounting" system is an objectified form of a value system. An economic accounting system is a value system. One counts what one values. As humanity evolved new means of perceiving—x-ray, radio, television, infra-red, ultra-violet, etc. "sight"—it learned to value more and more, but its accounting system did not grow similarly.

As science developed new techniques of perceiving and measuring, it developed new units of measurement—light years, angstroms, ergs, etc. As humanity developed new insight into the workings of the universe it learned to value things and processes it did not know even existed before. But economics evolves slower than the "hard" sciences and has not yet incorporated the realities of the twentieth century (some would say even nineteenth century) into their measurements. Buckminster Fuller points out that pure science paces applied science and applied science paces technology and technology paces economics.[41] That is to say, an Einstein comes before a Fermi, Fermi comes before the first operating nuclear electric power plant, and that plant comes before its economic feasibility.

A science can be known by what it measures and what it measures with. Economics is in the unfortunate positon of trying to measure a twentieth century world with nineteenth century or earlier measuring devices. It is analogous to trying to measure an angstrom* with a yardstick. Economic measurements, economic accounting, need to become in tune with what we now reliably know about the entire universe. This calls for a tremendous transformation of our present accounting systems.

One of the things that needs to be incorporated into our economic accounting system is the astrophysical and astronomical perspective that we are an infinitessimal part of an incredibly large system; that the Earth rotates around the sun, the sun, one of a billion stars in our galaxy, rotates within the Milky Way, and that the Milky Way is one of a billion galaxies. Our economic accounting needs to be in tune with the largest system of which we are

*An angstrom is one ten billionth of a meter.

a part, not the smallest. Current accounting perspective operates as if it were on a stagecoach rather than a spaceship or part of a galaxy or part of a system of galaxies. We need a cosmic accounting system, not a backyard ledger. An example of what is meant by this is again Buckminster Fuller's point about the worth of each gallon of gasoline. From a more cosmic perspective, that is, asking what it took Nature to produce a gallon of oil—in terms of the work she performed in growing the plants that were then geologically covered and held under enormous pressures for eons of time, not just what it cost us humans to pump it out of the ground and refine it into gasoline—we would find that each gallon costs about one million dollars. Including the work performed by Nature in our economic ledgers (physics has known at least since the law of the conservation of energy that nothing is free) would make us a little more up to date. As we obviously value the work performed by Nature, we should count it.

Such a cosmic accounting system should include the work done for us by present-day ecology, meteorology, hydrology, etc. as well as ancient geology. As mentioned earlier in the book, water is carried here and there by Nature through its processes of evaporation (300 cubic miles of water are evaporated each day) and atmospheric circulation without charge in current economic perspective to the user. Rainfall onto the planet's land areas involves the steady expenditure of 160 billion h.p. for just the work done against gravity, ignoring completely the energy used in evaporation and transporting the water from the ocean to land areas.[42] At today's residential electrical rates this would cost about $260 trillion per year. Or put another way, the world's total annual oil production would "operate" the world's rainfall system for about thirty-five hours. Nature also fixes $35 billion worth of nitrogen each year. One way of seeing the worth of water or any other material or process provided by Nature is to determine what it would cost to replace it ourselves. What would it cost to pipe water in and desalinate it? What would it cost to replace the whale?

The proposed colonies in space will give us some indication of the costs of developing our own primitive ecosystem. What we learn from this will greatly aid in the work being done on Earth. Work on the supra-system always sheds light on the sub-system. That is one reason why our problem-solving perspective has to be, minimally, global in its scope. The best way of understanding and solving the local problem is to understand the larger system that it fits into.

Besides the insights of twentieth century astronomy, physics, biology, ecology, etc., our accounting system needs to include within its frame of reference what anthropology and psychology now know about the value of cultural and individual diversity and stability; what did it cost in terms of human-hours (at minimum wage) to evolve any particular culture? What would it cost to replace the Sioux Indians? Obviously, we can't replace them, but we can ask—how much did it cost for them to get their unique culture to where it is, or was?—to put a *minimum* non-synergetic dollar value on their "worth." What is the value of human growth and happiness?

Present day economics is on a yearly accounting schedule. Profits are measured by the year. This naturally came about because our accounting system grew out of agriculture. What we counted were bushels of wheat and corn and their production was on a yearly schedule. Agriculture is 10,000 years old and many things have happened in the meantime—like the industrial revolution—but we are still largely on a yearly accounting schedule. Industrial processes do not necessarily, and perhaps never, have the same production rates as agriculture. Everything has its own gestation rate; a human being takes nine months, a pig four months, a wheatfield three to six months, an automobile one to five years, and a global food problem maybe twenty years to be born. Different times than that arbitrarily imposed by our yearly agricultural accounting are needed to make a production change in modern industry or to bring a new product into mass production or to solve a worldwide problem. This is not to say that yearly accounting is no good, it's just pointing out that it is somewhat arbitrary, and for some processes, not well suited.

The long range view would put our economic accounting more in tune with what we now know and value about our universe. The management of our resources would shift from attempting to maximize short-term productivity and profits to the optimizing of long term sustainable yields. The way this transformation

will come about is through know-how. The substitution of know-how (and know what and where) for brute strength and massive amounts of materials will get us ever closer to Nature. To design with Nature takes a lot more know-how than to design against her. To control agricultural pests biologically or to fertilize with newly bred plants that fix their own nitrogen or with companion plantings, takes an enormously larger amount of know-how than to use pesticides or chemical fertilizers. The farmer has to be an ecologist, meteorologist, hydrologist, agronomist, limnologist, geologist, etc. (and poet would help too) instead of a machine operator or power baron.[43]

Design Initiative and What Needs to be Done

A major focus in this book has been on long range global processes and strategies. There are many things implicit throughout this approach that are directly applicable to short range local problems. Without a decentralized populist involvement in the problems of the world, this world is sunk. There isn't anything in the world food problem situation that prohibits any individual from plugging in their time, energy, and intellect and helping to solve it. Enthusiasm that is willing to learn by doing, thereby transforming itself into competent, knowledgeable enthusiasm, can change the world. Anger, concern, and compassion that is willing to discipline itself into being thorough and to see all sides to our problems, thereby transforming itself into effective action, can change the world. Many of the items pointed out in the "What Needs to be Done" parts of the various chapters on Food Sources/Production Techniques could be developed by an individual or group willing to inform him/her/itself about the item in question. We don't need to wait for someone else to do it. We don't *have* to wait for major government or foundation support to undertake the development of a solution to an aspect of the world food problem that our own experience tells us needs to be dealt with and which we see is not being dealt with. All long range, large scale strategies have to both start and finish on the short range and small scale. Every world food strategy sooner or later begins with something the individual can do in his/her backyard and ends in the stomach of someone who needs food.

Besides the numerous artifacts that need to be developed that are listed in Critical Paths, there are other things that an individual, a high school or college class, or any group concerned about the world and the local food situation can do, both to educate themselves and to contribute to solving the local and world food problems. These projects include 1) researching, prototyping, and testing those needed artifacts; 2) doing for the local or regional "neighborhood" what this book does for the world, that is, comprehensive analysis and planning for the locality; this would involve developing an inventory of the items for your town and region listed under No. 1 below and the synthesis of these items into what is listed in Nos. 2 to 6 below.

1. a) where the food comes from;
    b) what types come from where;
    c) how much is grown and stored locally;
    d) how much could be grown locally with the various sources and production techniques;
    e) what are the wastes from the food system or other systems that could be used in the food system;
    f) who needs food or nutritional information;
    g) what techniques are available for making food or nutritional information accessible to those who need it;
    h) how much energy is consumed by the local food system and how could this be reduced;
    i) what income energy sources are available to power the local food system;
    j) what can the local food system do for the region and the world;
    k) what are the unique economic, ecological, technological, cultural, and political restraints and possibilities regarding the food system in the region;
    l) how much food is needed locally at present and in the future;
    m) who are all the local human resources regarding food development.

The above information needs to be synthesized into local developmental plans and activities by:

2. formulating a preferred state for your region and locality which includes specific and measurable quantitative goals; and
3. formulating strategies and tactics for achieving this preferred state, in incremental steps, from the present-day situation (as well as inventorying all those that don't work); and
4. demonstrating the technological, ecological, economical, political, and cultural benefits/costs of doing/not doing the strategy; and
5. involving (after you've done your homework, i.e., the above) more and more people, institutions, decision- and policy-makers, etc.; in other words, getting the strategy, or a refined, better version of it, implemented; and
6. growing your own food; and,
    a) performing experiments with backyard, rooftop, and greenhouse gardens;

References

b) dealing with growing different varieties of food, testing different fertilizers, controlling pests, and storing food;

c) keeping a log to record experiments and results; new experiments should be tried each growing season;

d) contacting local information media—newspapers, radio, etc.—with results.

Any decision maker makes decisions by choosing among alternatives. With new alternatives, new options, the decision maker can improve the performance of the system he/she is deciding for. In the above, numbers 1–5 are primarily designed to furnish the policy maker with new options, and number 6, the individual. Both categories can be done by an individual who is willing to take the initiative. As with most of the most important things that need to be done on Earth, no one will pay you to do them. All you need is your time, energy, mind, and initiative.

1. *Food Needs of Developing Countries: Projections of Production and Consumption to 1990,* Research Report No. 3, The International Food Policy Research Institute, Dec. 1977.

2. Erb, G. F., Kallab, V., eds., *Beyond Dependency: The Developing World Speaks Out,* Overseas Development Council, Washington, D.C., 1975.

3. Thomas, T. T., "World Food: A Perspective," *Science,* Vol. 188, 5-9-75, pp. 510–18.

4. Wortman, S., Cummings, R. W., *To Feed This World: The Challenge and The Strategy,* Johns Hopkins Univ. Press, 1978.

5. Adapted from McHale, J., McHale, M. C., *Basic Human Needs: A Framework for Action,* Transaction Books, 1978; Burki, S. J., Voorhoeve, J. J. C., World Bank paper, reported in *Christian Science Monitor,* 10-3-77; "1978 World Population Data Sheet," Population Reference Bureau, Inc., Washington, D.C.

6. FAO, *1977 Production Yearbook,* Vol. 31, FAO/UN, Rome, Italy, 1978.

7. Sprague, G. F., "Agriculture in China," *Science,* Vol. 188, 5-9-75, p. 552.

8. Kuo-Feng, Hua, "Let the Whole Party Mobilize for a Vast Effort to Develop Agriculture and Build Tachai-type Counties throughout the Country," summing-up report at the National Conference on Learning from Tachai in Agriculture, Foreign Language Press, Peking, Peoples' Republic of China, 1975.

9. The World Food Conference: Selected Materials for the Use of the U.S. Congressional Delegation to the World Food Conference, Rome, Italy, 11-5-74; Compiled for the Subcommittee on Foreign Agricultural Policy of the Committee on Agriculture and Forestry, U.S. Senate, p. 98.

10. Loomis, R. S., "Agricultural Systems," *Scientific American,* Sept. 1976, p. 105.

11. Pimentel, D., "Land Degradation: Effects on Food and Energy Resources," *Science,* Vol. 194, 10-8-76, pp. 149–55.

12. United Nations, *Total Population Estimates for World, Regions, and Countries,* Each Year 1950–1985, Population Division Working Paper No. 34, Oct. 1970.

13. FAO, *Energy and Protein Requirements,* Report of a Joint FAO/WHO Expert Group, FAO, Rome, Italy, 1972.

14. Sanderson, F. H., "The Great Food Fumble," *Science.* Vol. 188, No. 4188, 5-9-75, pp. 503–09.

15. The global strategy presented here identifies many functions that need to be performed and the type of organizations that need to perform them to reach the preferred state. Because the stated methodology is one of starting with the whole and working back, we have purposely chosen to identify organizations as they would exist and operate in this future preferred state rather than identifying those already existing food, agriculture, and development organizations that presently perform some of the functions necessary for the operation of the global preferred state. Even though the existing United Nations Development Program, U.N. Food and Agriculture Organization, the World Food Council, International Fund for Agricultural Development, World Bank, U.S. Department of Agriculture, Agency for International Development, etc. all engage in varying degrees in one or more of the activities described in this strategy, new names are used to describe the organization that would perform the necessary functions to bring about, maintain, and evolve the preferred state. One reason for this includes the fact that every organization has some inertia and resistance to change. The somewhat drastic changes called for in parts of this strategy could run against this. Rather than starting from the position of seeking to bring about ad hoc changes in present-day organizational structures to more adequately deal with present-day crises, the focus is instead on the design and functioning of the ideal organization, starting from scratch with what we now know about the dimensions of the world food problem and, more importantly, the goal the new organization is seeking to reach. Starting fresh from the future and working back to the present-day, we can then identify those existing organizations that are doing parts of the strategy and see what else needs to be done that that organization could undertake. The reverse process—that is, starting with present-day organizations and seeking to change them in incremental ways—usually ends up resisted and doomed to at best a "band-aid" measure for a systemic disorder.

16. Mayer, J., "Management of Famine Relief," *Science,* Vol. 188, 5-9-75.

17. This is based on Howard Brown's idea for a "National Energy Game" for the United States. H. Brown, Earth Metabolic Design, Box 2016, Yale Station, New Haven, CT 06520.

18. Wellhausen, E. J., "The Agriculture of Mexico," *Scientific American,* Sept. 1976, p. 143.

19. Hopper, W. D., "The Development of Agriculture in Developing Countries," *Scientific American,* Sept. 1976, p. 203.

20. Wittwer, S. H., "Food Production: Technology and the Resource Base," *Science,* Vol. 188, 5-9-75, pp. 579–84.

21. Loomis, R. S., "Agricultural Systems," *Scientific American,* Sept. 1976, p. 172.

22. Merrill, R., "Toward a Self-Sustaining Agriculture," *Radical Agriculture,* Harper & Row, 1976.

23. Todd, J., "A Modest Proposal: Science for the People," in *Radical Agriculture,* ed. Merrill, R., Harper & Row, 1976, pp. 259–83.

24. Prosterman, R. L., "Land Reform as Foreign Aid," *Foreign Policy,* No. 6, 1972, pp. 128–41.

25. Fuller, R. B., "Universal Requirements for a Dwelling Advantage," in *No More Second-Hand God,* Southern Illinois Univ. Press, 1964.

26. U.S. Secretary of Agriculture Robert Bergland, quoted in *The Christian Science Monitor.*

27. Bryson, R. A., Murray, T. J., *Climates of Hunger,* Univ. of Wisconsin Press, 1977; Gribbin, J., *Forecasts, Famines, and Freezes: The World's Climate and Man's Future,* Walker & Co., New York, 1976; Broecker, J., "Climatic Change: Are We on the Brink of a Pronounced Global Warming?" *Science,* Vol. 189, No. 4201, Aug. 1975; Collis, R., "Weather and World Food," *American Meteorological Society Bulletin,* Oct. 1975; Duckham, A. G., "Climate, Weather, and Human Food Systems: A World View," *Weather,* Vol. 29, 1972; Gasser, W. R., "World Climatic Change and Agriculture: The Issues," Paper presented at Symposium on Living with Climatic Change, Phase II, Reston, VA, Nov. 1976; McBoyle, G., *Climate in Review,* Houghton Mifflin Co., Boston, MA, 1973; McQuigg, J. D., "Climatic Constraints on Food Grain Production," World Food Conference, June 27–July 1, 1976, Ames, IA; Newman, J., "World Climates and Food Supply Variations," *Science,* Vol. 186, No. 4167, 12-6-74; Thompson, L., "Weather Variability, Climatic Change, and Grain Production," *Science,* Vol. 188, No. 4188, 5-9-75.

28. Hare, F. K., "A Change in the Wind," *Development Forum,* Nov.–Dec. 1978, Center for Economic and Social Information, UNICEF, p. 16.

29. *Alternative Futures for World Food in 1985,* U.S. Department of Agriculture, Economics, Statistics, and Cooperative Service, Foreign Agricultural Economic Report No. 146, 1978.

30. Enzer, S., Drobnick, R., Alter, S., "World Food Prospects: The Next 20 Years," *The Futurist,* Oct. 1978, p. 286.

31. Brown, L., "The Politics and Responsibilities of the North American 'Breadbasket,' " *World Watch Paper No. 2,* Oct. 1975.

32. Revelle, R., "The Resources Available for Agriculture," *Scientific American,* Sept. 1976, pp. 168–70.

33. *Food Update,* GAO, Community & Economic Development Division, June 1977, Washington, D.C.

34. *Capturing the Sun through Bioconversion,* Proceedings of a Conference, 3-12-76, Washington, D.C.; Conference Coordination, Washington Center for Metropolitan Studies, 1717 Massachusetts Ave. N.W., Washington, D.C. 20036.

35. Mahajan, B., "TCDC," *Ceres,* FAO Review of Agriculture and Development, FAO, Rome, Italy, May–June 1978, pp. 15–18.

36. Brown, L., "Population Strategy for a Finite Planet," Overseas Development Council Communique No. 26.

37. U.S. Secretary of Agriculture Robert Bergland, Letters to the Editor, *New York Times,* 12-7-77, p. 38.

38. Robbins, W., "Farmers Total Income at Depression Level," *New York Times,* 9-23-77, p. 1.

39. R. Buckminster Fuller's analysis of the 1930's U.S. Depression attributes the general "crash" to a previous crash of the agriculture sector brought on by poor producing seasons and bank foreclosures that happened because the farmer could not keep up the payments on the new farm machinery he had recently purchased. Farm foreclosure was so widespread that there was no market for the now bank-owned farms. The rural banks were left with semi-worthless (because no one could buy them) properties. When the larger city banks were forced to call in their loans, the smaller banks could not pay and were closed. Roosevelt's rushed inauguration and subsequent "bank moratorium" saved the biggest banks from going under.

40. Latham, M. C., "Nutrition and Infection in National Development," *Science,* Vol. 188 5-9-75, p. 564.

41. Fuller, R. B., *Nine Chains to the Moon,* Lippincott, Philadelphia, 1936.

42. *Technology Review,* M.I.T., June 1972, p. 59.

43. For a more thorough discussion of these concepts, see Gabel, M., *Energy, Earth and Everyone,* Doubleday, New York, 1979.

Appendix

U.S. Organizations Involved in Food Issues[1,2]

Anti-Hunger Organizations

	Research/Function	Coverage	Founded
American Freedom from Hunger Foundation 1028 Connecticut Ave., N.W. Washington, DC 20036	Citizen support lobby for UN/FAO through fund-raising, testimony before Congress, conferences	U.S.	1961
Children's Foundation 1028 Connecticut Ave., N.W. Suite 614 Washington, DC 20036	Federal food assistance funds and program information	U.S.	1969
Community Nutrition Institute 1910 K St., N.W. Washington, DC 20006	Federal/state legislation	U.S.	1970
Food Advocates 2288 Fulton St., Suite 200 Berkeley, CA 94710			
Food Research and Action Center 25 W. 43rd St. New York, NY 10036	Public interest law firm for federal food assistance	U.S.	1970
National Child Nutrition Project 303 George St. New Brunswick, NJ 08901	Technical advice on federal food programs	U.S.	1972
Consumer Federation of America 1012 14th St., N.W. Washington, DC 20005	Consumer action/legislation/education on product quality, food cost, natural resources	U.S.	1967
Consumers' Union 256 Washington St. Mount Vernon, NY 10550	Food information and testing	U.S.	

	Research/Function	Coverage	Founded
The Hunger Project P.O. Box 789 San Francisco, CA 94101	Global education to end hunger	World	1976
National Consumers' League 1785 Massachusetts Ave., N.W. Washington, DC 20036	Labor standards, consumer protection, federal legislation	U.S.	1899
World Hunger Year, Inc. P.O. Box 1975 Garden City, NY 11530	Education through broadcast media	World	1975

Agriculture/Agribusiness Organizations

	Research/Function	Coverage	Founded
Agribusiness Accountability Project 1000 Wisconsin Ave., N.W. Washington, DC 20007	Analyzes policies and actions of agribusiness firms	U.S.	1970
Center for Rural Affairs P.O. Box 405 Walthill, NB 68067			
Corporate Information Center 475 Riverside Dr., Rm 566 New York, NY 10027	Investigative reporting for Interfaith Center on Corporate Responsibility	World	1971
The Elements—Institute for Policy Studies 1520 New Hampshire Ave., N.W. Washington, DC 20009	Research	World	1963
Gardens for All, Inc. 180 Flynn Ave. Burlington, VT 05401	Promotes community gardens	U.S.	1972
Kansas Farm Project Box 3527 Lawrence, KS 66044			

	Research/Function	Coverage	Founded
National Catholic Rural Life Conference 3801 Grand Ave. Des Moines, IA 50132	Education/consultation on land, food, community development, rural ministry	U.S.	1923
National Farmers' Organization 485 L'Enfant Plaza, S.W. Washington, DC 20024	Marketing problems of owner-operator farmers' products	U.S.	1955
National Farmers' Union 1012 14th St., N.W. Washington, DC 20006	Promotes welfare of owner-operator farms	U.S.	1902
National Sharecroppers Fund 1145 19th St., N.W. Washington, DC 20036	Lobby for legislation benefitting small farmers and agricultural workers	U.S.	1933
Northern Plains Resources Council 421 Stapleton Bldg. Billings, MT 59101	Agricultural research and lobbying	U.S. and regional	1972
Rodale Press Emmaus, PA 18049	Publishes material on organic farming, environment, health	U.S.	1932
Small Towns Institute P.O. Box 517 Ellensberg, WA 98926	Research data on small town revitalization programs	U.S.	1969

World Food and Development Research and Analysis Organizations

	Research/Function	Coverage	Founded
American Friends Service Committee 160 N. 15th St. Philadelphia, PA 19102	Anti-hunger research, education, political action	World	1920
Bread for the World 602 E. 9th St. New York, NY 10009	Christian education/direct action on hunger and poverty	World	1973
Center for the Study of Power and Peace 110 Maryland Ave. Washington, DC 20002			
Center for War/Peace Studies 218 E. 18th St. New York, NY 10003	In-depth research on global problems	World	1966
Center of Concern 3700 13th St., N.E. Washington, DC 20017	International action/policy research on behalf of poor and powerless, founded by Jesuits	World	1971

	Research/Function	Coverage	Founded
Earth Metabolic Design, Inc. Box 2016, Yale Station New Haven, CT 06520	Anticipatory design science approach to global problems	World	1972
Friends Committee on National Legislation 245 Second St., N.E. Washington, DC 20002	Quaker-sponsored lobby on humanitarian concerns	U.S.	1943
Institute for World Order, Inc. 11 W. 42nd St. New York, NY 10036	Education/research on developing new institutions with human values	World	1961
National Council of Churches Task Force on World Hunger 475 Riverside Dr. New York, NY 10027	Education/research/action on domestic and international food problems	World	1974
Overseas Development Council 1717 Massachusetts Ave., N.W. Washington, DC 20036	Reports on economic and social problems of developing countries	Developing countries	1969
Task Force on World Hunger Presbyterian Church in the U.S. 341 Ponce de Leon Ave. Atlanta, GA 30308		World	
Transnational Institute Institute for Policy Studies 1901 Q St., N.W. Washington, DC 20009	Studies and develops programs to deal with poverty	World	1973
United Nations Association U.S.A. 410 E. Capitol St., N.E. Washington, DC 20002	Foreign policy issues	World	1963
Washington Interreligious Staff Council/Hunger Task Force 110 Maryland Ave., N.E. Washington, DC 20002			
World Bank 1818 H Street, N.W. Washington, DC 20433	Loans, especially for comprehensive rural development programs aimed at small farmers	World	1944
World Council of Churches Commission on the Churches' Participation in Development 150, rue de Ferney 1211 Geneva 20, Switzerland	Education/policy analysis	World	1970
World Federalist Association—Action for World Community 1424 16th St. Washington, DC 20036	Promotes world law system for social, political, economic justice, including problems of food and famine	World	1947

	Research/Function	Coverage	Founded

Worldwatch Institute
1776 Massachusetts Ave., N.W.
Washington, DC 20036 — Research anticipating global problems — World — 1974

International Development Projects

Organization	Research/Function	Coverage	Founded
Africare 1424 16th St., N.W. Washington, DC 20036	Operates and helps fund rural development programs	Sahelian region of West Africa	1972
Agricultural Cooperative Development 1430 K St., N.W. Washington, DC 20005	Technical assistance programs	World	1968
Community Development Foundation 48 Wilton Rd. Westport, CT 06880	Family-oriented self-help and disaster-relief	World	1959
Heifer Projects, Inc. P.O. Box 808 Worthen Building Little Rock, AR 72203	Livestock improvement assistance for Indian reservations, rural Blacks, also international projects	World	1944
International Voluntary Services 1555 Connecticut Ave., N.W. Washington, DC 20036	UNESCO-affiliated self-help work camps and projects	World	1920
Maryknoll Fathers 123 E. 39th St. New York, NY 10016			
Operation Bootstrap 1817 North 11th St. Moorhead, MN 56560	Assistance in self-help construction and development projects	Tanzania	1964
Unitarian Universalist Service Committee 78 Beacon St. Boston, MA 02108	Non-sectarian service with nutrition, education, rural health care programs	World	1958
Volunteers in Technical Assistance 3706 Rhode Island Ave. Mt. Vernon, MD 20822	Free technical assistance publications	World	1959
World Neighbors 5116 N. Portland Oklahoma City, OK 73112	Community self-help	World	1952

Relief Agencies

Organization	Research/Function	Coverage	Founded
American Jewish Joint Distribution Committee 60 E. 42nd St. New York, NY 10017	Education, cooperatives, and medical aid to needy Jews	Europe	1914
Baptist World Relief, Baptist World Alliance 1628 16th St., N.W. Washington, DC 20009	Relief, refugee, development programs	World	1946
CARE, Inc. Tri-State Regional Office 660 First Ave. New York, NY 10016	Food and self-help aid	World	1945
Catholic Relief Services 350 Fifth Ave. New York, NY 10001	Crisis relief, also technical assistance for pilot agricultural projects/ training programs/improved food storage facilities	World	1943
Christian Reformed World Relief Committee 2850 Kalamazoo Ave., S.E. Grand Rapids, MI 49508	Some agricultural food programs	World	1962
Church World Service 475 Riverside Dr. New York, NY 10027	Crisis relief; extensive agriculture, land conservation, livestock projects	Asia, Latin America, Africa	1946
CROP Box 968 Elkhart, IN 46514	Free loan of films on hunger, fund-raising for education projects	U.S.	1947
International Red Cross 150 Amsterdam Ave. New York, NY 10023	Emergency relief and extensive social/health services	World	1919
International Rescue Committee 386 Park Ave. South New York, NY 10016	Assists refugees	Europe	1933
Lutheran World Relief 315 Park Ave. South New York, NY 10010	Emergency and long-term material/financial assistance for needy as well as land reclamation, new seed varieties, experimental agricultural projects	World	1945
Meals for Millions Foundation P.O. Box 680 Santa Monica, CA 90006	Develops self-help projects in area of food-nutrition	World	1946
Mennonite Central Committee 21 S. 12th St. Akron, PA 17501	Relief and service with agriculture and development programs	World	1920
Oxfam-America 302 Columbus Ave. Boston, MA 02116	Famine and disaster relief	World	1970

	Research/Function	Coverage	Founded
Project Hope 2233 Wisconsin Ave., N.W. Washington, DC 20007	Promotes health programs	World	1958
Right Sharing of World Resources Program Friends World Committee, American Section and Fellowship Council 152-A N. 15th St. Philadelphia, PA 19102	Funds small grass-roots development projects	Africa and Latin America	1967
Salvation Army 120 West 14th St. New York, NY 10011	Social/religious welfare projects, clinics, emergency feeding and shelter	U.S.	1880
Seventh-Day Adventist Welfare Service 6840 Eastern Ave., N.W. Washington, DC 20012	Volunteer relief agency	Developing countries	
United States Committee for UNICEF 331 East 38th St. New York, NY 10016	Educational/fund-raising for children	World	1920
World University Service Lehman College Bedford Park Blvd. Bronx, NY 10468	Student-to-student self-help activities and education	World	1920
World Vision International 919 W. Huntington Dr. Monrovia, CA 91016	Missionary childrens' aid service	World	1950

Environmental Organizations

	Research/Function	Coverage	Founded
Concern, Inc. 2233 Wisconsin Ave., N.W. Washington, DC 20007	Consumer-oriented environmental protection; education	U.S.	1970
Conservation Foundation 1717 Massachusetts Ave., N.W. Washington, DC 20036	Workshops/policy research	World	1948
Environmental Action, Inc. 1346 Connecticut Ave., N.W. Washington, DC 20036	Lobbies Congress on issues such as air, water quality, pesticides	U.S.	1970
Environmental Defense Fund 1525 18th St., N.W. Washington, DC 20036	Litigation/education	U.S.	1967
Environmental Policy Center 324 C St., S.E. Washington, DC 20003	Litigation-lobbying for state and national conservation groups	U.S.	1972

	Research/Function	Coverage	Founded
Foresta Institute for Ocean and Mountain Studies 6205 Franktown Rd. Carson City, NV 89701	Research, training, consultation on fauna/flora protection		
Friends of the Earth 529 Commercial St. San Francisco, CA 94111	Conservation lobbying, litigation, publication, organization	World	1969
National Audubon Society 1130 Fifth Ave. New York, NY 10028	Promotes wildlife conservation through research/education	U.S.	1905
Natural Resources Defense Council 1710 N St., N.W. Washignton, DC 20036			
Sierra Club—Population Division 1050 Mills' Tower San Francisco, CA 94104	Policy research and legislation/lobbying/education/organization	U.S.	1892
Public Citizen, Inc. (Ralph Nader) DuPont Circle Building Washington, DC 20036	Research/investigation/public interest suits, including consumer action for improved foods	U.S.	1971

Population

	Research/Function	Coverage	Founded
Planned Parenthood—World Population 810 7th Ave. New York, NY 10019	Research/education/training on family planning	World	1961
Population Council 245 Park Ave. New York, NY 10017	Research and research funding	World	1952
The Population Institute 110 Maryland Ave., N.E. Washington, DC 20002	Education on population trend and related problems	World	1969
Population Reference Bureau, Inc. 1755 Massachusetts Ave., N.W. Washington, DC 20036	Research/education	World	1929
Zero Population Growth, Inc. 1346 Connecticut Ave., N.W. Washington, DC 20036	Research, action, education, lobbying	U.S.	1968

Nutrition

	Research/Function	Coverage	Founded
American Institute of Nutrition 9650 Rockville Pike Bethesda, MD 20014	Professional society of experimental nutrition scientists	U.S.	1928
Society for Nutrition Education 2140 Shattuck Ave., Suite 1110 Berkeley, CA 94704	Education through publications, bibliographies	U.S.	1970

U.S. Government Agencies Involved in Food Issues[2]

Government Agency	Research/Function
Department of Agriculture	
Department of Agriculture 14th St. and Independence Ave., S.W. Washington, DC 20250	Information, publications, reference service
Economic Research Service (Foreign Development Division)	Free publications, financial/technical aid to developing countries
Extension Service	Teaches farming, gardening, food preservation, nutrition on state/county levels, also 4-H Clubs
Food and Nutrition Service	Information/publications on food stamps, child nutrition, etc.
Foreign Agriculture Service	Administers Food for Peace Program and agricultural grants; research on world commodities production
National Agricultural Library 10301 Baltimore Boulevard Beltsville, MD 20705	Public reference service on food/nutrition
Department of State	
Department of State Agency for International Development (AID) 320 21st St., N.W. Washington, DC 20523	Coordinates programs in developing countries
Bureau of Population and Humanitarian Assistance	Grants/training/foreign assistance programs for disaster relief and family planning
Bureau of Technical Assistance	Pest management, post-harvest food losses, crops, soil, water, livestock research and development
Office of Food for Peace	Distributes U.S. agriculture commodities to developing countries
The White House	
The President's Commission on World Hunger Washington, DC 20506	Advisory group on global food problems
U.S. Congress	
General Accounting Office (GAO) 441 G St., N.W. Washington, DC 20548	Investigating arm of Congress
Senate Select Committee on Nutrition and Human Needs Senate Annex 119 D St., N.E. Washington, DC 20510	Free publications/reports on food stamps, nutrition, national and international food policy and pricing
House Agriculture Committee 1301 Longworth House Office Building Washington, DC 20515	Advisory on family farms, livestock, grains, etc.
Senate Agriculture and Forestry Committee 322 Russell Senate Office Building Washington, DC 20510	Agriculture production and marketing policy, also foreign

Federal Agencies Affecting National Food Policy

Department of Agriculture
Department of Labor
Department of State
Department of the Interior
Department of Commerce
Department of Army, Corps of Engineers
Department of Health, Education and Welfare
Department of Transportation
Federal Energy Administration
Treasury Department
Farm Credit Administration
Central Intelligence Agency
Environmental Protection Agency
Federal Trade Commission
Federal Maritime Commission
Federal Reserve Board
Commodity Futures Trading Commission
Internation Trade Commission
Office of Management and Budget
Domestic Council
Council of Economic Advisors
Council on Wage and Price Stabilization
Office of Special Representative for Trade Negotiations
National Security Council
Council on International Economic Policy
President's Economic Policy Board
President's Commission on World Hunger

United Nations Organizations Involved in Food Issues[2]

Organization	Research/Function	Founded
Consultative Group on Food Production and Investment (CGFPI) c/o World Bank 1818 H St., N.W. Washington, DC 20433	Helps developing countries establish national food plans	1975
Consultative Group on International Agricultural Research (CGIAR) c/o World Bank 1818 H St., N.W. Washington, DC 20433	Funding for research/publications	1971
Food and Agriculture Organization (FAO) 1776 F St., N.W. Washington, DC 20437	Applied research, consultation; administers U.N. World Food Programme; coordinates Freedom From Hunger Campaign, etc.	1945
International Bank for Reconstruction and Development (IBRD) (World Bank) 1818 H St., N.W. Washington, DC 20433	Loans aimed at smaller farmers	1944
International Development Association (IDA) 1818 H St., N.W. Washington, DC 20433	Special need, no-interest World Bank loans to developing countries	1960
International Fund for Agricultural Development (IFAD) (see World Food Council)	Stimulate food production, improve nutrition in neediest groups in developing countries	1976
Protein/Calorie Advisory Group (PAG) 1 U.N. Plaza, Room 866 New York, NY 10017	Scientists' advisory group on global malnutrition	1955
United Nations Childrens Fund (UNICEF) U.N. New York, NY 10017	Action and training to improve children's food and nutrition in developing countries	1946
United Nations Development Program (UNDP) U.N. New York, NY 10017	Coordinates technical services and development projects; free publications	1965
United Nations Fund for Population Activities (UNFPA) 485 Lexington Ave. New York, NY 10017	Projects/publications; largest multi-lateral population agency	1969
World Food Council Via delle Terme di Caracalla Rome 00100 Italy	Implements resolutions of World Food Conference for General Assembly	1974
World Food Programme (WFP) Via delle Terme di Caracalla Rome 00100 Italy	Development and relief aid	1963
World Health Organization (WHO) 20 Avenue Appia 1211 Geneva, Switzerland	Experimentation; education in food supplements, nutrition, identifies famines and malnutrition	1948
International Monetary Fund (IMF) 700 19th St., N.W. Washington, DC 20431	Free publications	1945
United Nations Conference on Trade and Development (UNCTAD) Palais des Nations 1211 Geneva 10, Switzerland	Coordinates economic/social development of low-income countries	1964

International Food Organizations[3]

Organization	Research/Function	Coverage	Founded
African Development Bank P.O. Box 1387 Abidjan Republic of the Ivory Coast West Africa	Technical assistance/ concessional loans, half of them agricultural	Africa	1964
Asian Development Bank P.O. Box 789 Manila, Philippines	Development loans	Afghanistan to Western Samoa, Nepal to Indonesia, not including India	1966
Commonwealth Agricultural Bureaux Farnham House, Farnham Royal Slough SL2 3BN, Bucks., England	Exchange of information for researchers	World	1929
Dairy Society International 30 F Street, N.W. Washington, DC 20001 USA	Extension of dairy enter-prise internationally	World	1946
European Confederation of Agriculture C.p. 87, 5200 Brugg Aargau, Switzerland	Technical, economic, and social problems of European agriculture	Europe	1889
Inter-American Development Bank (IDB) 808 17th St., N.W. Washington, DC 20557 USA	Financial/technical assistance, one-quarter to agriculture; free publications	Latin America	1959

Organization	Purpose	Region	Year
Inter-American Institute of Agricultural Sciences Secretariat Apdo. 10281 San Jose, Costa Rica	Plant and animal products	Americas	1944
International Association of Agricultural Economists 600 South Michigan Avenue Chicago, IL 60605 USA	Economic investigation of agricultural processes	World	1929
International Association of Horticultural Producers Stadhoudersplantsoen 12-18 POB 361 The Hague, Netherlands	Represent common interests of horticulturists	W. Europe/ U.S.A.	1948
International Centre for Advanced Mediterranean Agronomic Studies Secretariat 21 rue Octave Feuillet Paris, 16e, France	Post-graduate study in international problems of agricultural development	Mediterranean Countries	1962
International Commission of Agricultural Engineering 10-12 rue de Capitaine Menard Paris, 15e, France		Europe	1930
International Commission of Agricultural and Food Industries 18 avenue de Villars Paris, 7e, France	Coordinate activities that concern food industry	Europe/USA	1934
International Committee on Veterinary Animal Nomenclature Linke Bahngasse 11 Vienna 1030, Austria			1957
International Confederation of Technical Agriculturalists Beethovenstrasse 24 8002 Zurich, Switzerland	Promote and develop relations between agricultural technicians	Europe	1930
International Dairy Federation Square Vergote 41 1040 Brussels, Belgium	Represent dairy organizations	Europe	1903
International Federation of Agricultural Producers Room 401, Barr Building 910 17th Street, N.W. Washington, DC 20006 USA	Represent farmers' organizations	Europe/ North America	1946
International Food Policy Research Institute 1776 Massachusetts Avenue, N.W. Washington, DC 20036 USA	Policy problems of food production, consumption, availability, distribution	World	1975
International Seed Testing Institute POB 68 1432 Vollebekk Norway	Testing and judgment of seeds	Europe	1924
International Organization for Biological Control of Noxious Animals and Plants Department of Entomology Swiss Federal Institute of Technology Universitatstrasse 2 8006 Zurich, Switzerland	Coordinate research	Europe/ Mideast	1955
International Society of Soil Science c/o Royal Tropical Institute 63 Mauritskade Amsterdam, Netherlands	Soil	World	1924
International Standing Committee on Physiology and Pathology of Animal Reproduction and of Artificial Insemination Royal Veterinary College Boltons Park Hawkshead Road Potters Bar Hertfordshire, England		Europe	1964
International Union of Forestry Research Organizations Forest Service U.S. Department of Agriculture Washington, DC 20250 USA	Forestry	World	1891
International Veterinary Association for Animal Production c/o Sociedad Veterinaria de Zootécnica Facultad de Veterinaria Ciudad Univ. Madrid 3, Spain		Europe	1951
International Wheat Council Haymarket House Haymarket London SW1, United Kingdom			1947
Organization of American States (OAS) 19th and Constitution Aves., N.W. Washington, DC 20006 USA	Initiates and funds development projects as regional organization of U.N.	North, Central and South America	1890
Organization for Economic Cooperation and Development (OECD) 2 Rue Andre Pascal 75775 Paris 16 France (Publications: 1750 Pennsylvania Ave., N.W. Washington, DC 20006 USA)	Promotes international trade through research and publications	Industrialized nations with market economies	1960
U.S. Department of Agriculture 14th Street & Independence Ave., S.W. Washington, DC 20250 USA	U.S. agriculture	USA	1862

International Agricultural Research Organizations[4]

Center	Location	Research	Coverage	Date of Initiation	Proposed budget for 1975 ($000)
IRRI International Rice Research Institute	Los Banos, Philippines	Rice under irrigation; multiple cropping systems; upland rice	Worldwide, special emphasis in Asia	1959	8,520
CIMMYT International Center for the Improvement of Maize and Wheat	El Batan, Mexico	Wheat (also triticale, barley); maize	Worldwide	1964	6,834
CIAT International Center for Tropical Agricultura	Palmira, Colombia	Beef: cassava; field beans; farming systems; swine (minor); maize and rice (regional relay stations to CIMMYT and IRRI)	Worldwide in lowland tropics, special emphasis in Latin America	1968	5,828
IITA International Institute of Tropical Agriculture	Ibadan, Nigeria	Farming systems; cereals (rice and maize as regional relay stations for IRRI and CIMMYT); grain legume (cowpeas, soybeans, lima beans, pigeon peas); root and tuber crops (cassava, sweet potatoes, yams)	Worldwide in lowland tropics, special emphasis in Africa	1965	7,746
CIP (International Potato Center)	Lima, Peru	Potatoes (for both tropics and temperate regions)	Worldwide including linkages with developed countries	1972	2,403
ICRISAT International Crops Research Institute for the Semi-Arid Tropics	Hyderabad, India	Sorghum; pearl millet; pigeon peas; chick-peas; farming systems; groundnuts	Worldwide, special emphasis on dry semi-arid tropics, nonirrigated farming. Special relay stations in Africa under negotiation	1972	10,250
ILRAD International Laboratory for Research on Animal Diseases	Nairobi, Kenya	Trypanosomiasis; theileriasis (mainly east coast fever)	Africa	1974	2,170
ILCA International Livestock Center for Africa	Addis Ababa, Ethiopia	Livestock production systems	Major ecological regions in tropical zones of Africa	1974	1,885
IBPGR International Board for Plant Genetic Resources	FAO, Rome, Italy	Conservation of plant genetic material with special reference to cereals	Worldwide	1973	555
WARDA West African Rice Development Association	Monrovia, Liberia	Regional cooperative effort in adaptive rice research among 13 nations with IITA and IRRI support	West Africa	1971	575
ICARDA International Center for Agricultural Research in Dry Areas	Lebanon	Probably a center or centers for crop and mixed farming systems research, with a focus on sheep, barley, wheat, and lentils	Worldwide, emphasis on the semi-arid winter rainfall zone		

The Largest U.S. Corporations with Major Food Product Lines[5]

(in order by sales 1977)

Company	Headquarters	Major Food Product Line	Sales ($000)	Net Income ($000)
Beatrice Foods	Chicago, IL	Dairy Products	5,288,278	182,566
Esmark	Chicago, IL	Meat Packing	5,280,160	66,970
Kraft	Glenview, IL	Dairy Products	5,238,807	154,115
General Foods	White Plains, NY	Processed Foods	4,909,737	177,338
Ralston Purina	St. Louis, MO	Processed Foods	3,756,300	142,700
Borden	New York, NY	Dairy Products	3,481,300	126,870
General Mills	Minneapolis, MN	Processed Foods	2,909,404	117,034
Consolidated Foods	Chicago, IL	Processed Foods	2,891,927	88,069
CPC International	Englewood Cliffs, NJ	Processed Foods	2,869,800	132,900
United Brands	New York, NY	Meat Packing	2,421,941	7,548
Carnation	Los Angeles, CA	Dairy Products	2,334,660	109,124
Central Soya	Fort Wayne, IN	Commodity Processing	2,177,385	12,372
Standard Brands	New York, NY	Processed Foods	2,124,311	68,554
Nabisco	East Hanover, NJ	Baking and Milling	2,117,574	78,016
Archer-Daniels-Midland	Decatur, IL	Commodity Processing	2,114,168	61,404
Iowa Beef Processors	Dakota City, NE	Meat Packing	2,023,765	29,965
H. J. Heinz	Pittsburgh, PA	Canned Foods	1,868,820	83,816
Campbell Soups	Camden, NJ	Canned Foods	1,769,132	107,103
Norton Simon	New York, NY	Processed Foods	1,756,982	101,773
Assoc. Milk Producers	San Antonio, TX	Dairy Products	1,640,736	N.A.
Quaker Oats	Chicago, IL	Processed Foods	1,551,348	67,574
Kellogg	Battle Creek, MI	Processed Foods	1,533,400	138,200
Del Monte	San Francisco, CA	Canned Foods	1,483,809	50,936
Pillsbury	Minneapolis, MN	Processed Foods	1,460,826	57,856
Land O'Lakes	Minneapolis, MN	Dairy Products	1,407,558	N.A.
Oscar Mayer	Madison, WI	Meat Packing	1,188,429	35,023
R. E. Staley Mfg.	Decatur, IL	Commodity Processing	1,116,641	24,480
George A. Hormel	Austin, MN	Meat Packing	1,106,274	21,951
Castle & Cooke	Honolulu, HI	Canned Foods	1,018,764	45,050
MBPXL	Wichita, KS	Meat Packing	986,509	5,278
Amstar	New York, NY	Cane Sugar Refiner	950,374	28,091
Kane-Miller	Tarrytown, NY	Meat Packing	916,669	2,359
Internat'l Multifoods	Minneapolis, MN	Baking and Milling	847,030	19,960
Campbell Taggart	Dallas, TX	Baking and Milling	787,420	25,940
Hershey Foods	Hershey, PA	Confectionary Products	671,227	41,331
General Host	Stamford, CT	Meat Packing	666,993	−912
Fairmont Foods	Houston, TX	Dairy Products	533,176	5,838
Con Agra	Omaha, NE	Baking and Milling	532,218	12,831
Peavey	Minneapolis, MN	Baking and Milling	494,306	9,310
Green Giant	Chaska, MN	Canned Foods	479,008	7,877
American Bakeries	Chicago, IL	Canned Foods	478,735	5,822
Stokeley-Van Camp	Indianapolis, IN	Canned Foods	456,516	7,141
Ward Foods	New York, NY	Confectionary Products	443,667	7,741
Bluebird	Philadelphia, PA	Meat Packing	411,502	5,557
Gerber Products	Fremont, MI	Processed Foods	404,598	22,334
Wm Wrigley, Jr.	Chicago, IL	Confectionary Products	397,941	29,313
Rath Packing	Waterloo, IA	Meat Packing	365,197	−1,018

Sources: *Fortune*, "The 500 Largest Industrial Corporations, 1977. Standard and Poors: *Statistical Position of Common Stocks in the Food Processing Industry*.

Listing of the Largest Corporations Outside the U.S. with Food Products as a Major Business Line[6]

(in order by sales 1977)

Company	Country	Industry	Sales ($000)	Net Income ($000)
Unilever	Britain-Netherlands	Food Products, Soap	15,965,116	456,789
Nestlé	Switzerland	Food Products	8,392,275	346,633
Taiyo Fishery	Japan	Food Products	3,572,194	8,666
George Weston Holdings	Britain	Food Products	2,626,328	43,689
BSM-Gervals Danone	France	Food Products	2,621,671	2,818
Tate and Lyle	Britain	Food Products	2,143,116	47,171
Ranks Hovis McDougall	Britain	Food Products	1,885,631	25,847
Canada Packers	Canada	Food Products	1,711,253	20,262
Cadbury-Schweppes	Britain	Food Products, Beverages	1,542,297	50,095
Unigate	Britain	Food Products	1,496,163	23,568
J. Lyons	Britain	Food Products	1,333,423	−9,206
Koor Industries	Israel	Food, Electronics, Chemicals, Metal Products	1,310,108	15,490
Snow Brand Milk Products	Japan	Food Products	1,268,284	9,869
Beecham Group	Britain	Food, Beverages, Pharmaceuticals	1,249,846	119,471
Ajinomoto	Japan	Food Products	1,177,595	18,318
Spillers	Britain	Food Products	1,104,802	9,392
United Biscuits (Holdings)	Britain	Food Products	1,099,995	30,345
Union Laitière Normande	France	Food Products	1,007,589	2,911
Nippon Suisan	Japan	Food Products	995,564	16,279
Recketh and Colman	Britain	Food Products, Beverages, Soap	972,227	57,339
Mjölkentralen Arla	Sweden	Food Products	927,427	2,369
KoninklijkeWessanen	Netherlands	Food Products	900,837	6,766
Jacobs	Switzerland	Food Products	889,552	N.A.
Béghin-Day	France	Food Products, Paper Products	884,741	−25,902

Company	Country	Industry	Sales ($000)	Net Income ($000)
Nisshin Flour Milling	Japan	Food Products	867,507	9,172
Glano Holdings	Britain	Food Products, Pharmaceuticals	835,587	71,213
Meigi Milk Products	Japan	Food Products	825,253	5,125
Burns Foods	Canada	Food Products	824,849	3,861
Rowntree Mackintosh	Britain	Food Products	818,995	31,340
Hanson Trust	Britain	Food Products	813,824	24,889
John Labatt	Canada	Food Products, Beverages	770,689	28,079
Morinaga Milk Industry	Japan	Food Products	737,132	1,888
Nippon Meat Packers	Japan	Food Products	720,088	14,925
Imasco	Canada	Food Products, Tobacco	719,541	35,426
SAMBRA	Brazil	Food Products	707,296	22,162
Douwe Egberts	Netherlands	Food Products, Tobacco	704,934	17,200
Indústrias Reunidas F Matarazzo	Brazil	Food Products, Textiles, Chemicals	675,252	36,842
Ito Ham Provisions	Japan	Food Products	660,279	14,993
FMC	Britain	Food Products	649,055	3,666
Financière Lesieur	France	Food Products	634,886	11,323
Nichiro Gyogyo	Japan	Food Products	626,225	4,956
Nihon Nosan Kogyo	Japan	Food Products	622,202	2,702
Meiji Seika	Japan	Food Products, Pharmaceuticals	558,852	10,923
Olida and Caby	France	Food Products	547,328	3,201
Maple Leaf Mills	Canada	Food Products	541,208	13,360
Dansk Landbrugs Grovvareselskab	Denmark	Food Products, Fertilizers	530,104	11,559
Borregaard	Norway	Food, Paper, and Wood Products	527,964	− 3,481
Tiger Oats and National Milling	South Africa	Food Products	501,994	25,457
Meneba	Netherlands	Food Products	492,916	− 3,511
Interfood	Switzerland	Food Products	474,871	4,379
Yamazaki Baking	Japan	Food Products	466,420	15,726

References

1. Adapted from Lerza, C., Jacobson, M., eds., *Food for People, Not for Profit*, Ballantine Books, 1975

2. Kriesberg, M., *International Organizations and Agricultural Development*, Economic Research Service, U.S. Dept. of Agriculture Foreign Agricultural Economic Report No. 131.

3. *Encyclopedia of Associations*, 13th Edition, Gale Research Co., Detroit 1979.

4. Wade, N., "International Agricultural Research," *Science*, 5-9-75.

5. *Fortune*, "The 500 Largest Industrial Corporations," 1977; Standard & Poors: Statistical Position of Common Stocks in the Food Processing Industry.

6. *Fortune*, "The 500 Largest Industrial Corporations Outside the U.S.," 1977.

Weights, Measures, and Conversion Factors

Weights and Measures

Commodity	Unit[1]	U.S. (Pounds)	Metric (Kilograms)
Alfalfa seed	Bushel	60	27.2
Apples	do	48	21.8
	Northwest box[2]	44	20.0
	Fiberboard box, cell pack	37–44	16.8–20.0
Apricots	Lug (Brentwood)[3]	24	10.9
Western	4-basket crate[3]	26	11.8
Artichokes:			
Globe	1/2-box	20	9.1
Jerusalem	Bushel	50	22.7
Asparagus	Crate	30	13.6
Avocados	Lug[5]	12–15	5.4–6.8
Bananas	Fiber folding box[6]	40	18.1
Barley	Bushel	48	21.8
Beans:			
Lima, dry	do	56	25.4
Other, dry	do	60	27.2
	Sack	100	45.4
Lima, unshelled	Bushel	28–32	12.7–14.5
Snap	do	28–32	12.7–14.5
Beets:			
Without tops	do	50	22.7
Bunched	Wirebound crate	45	20.4
Berries, frozen pack:			
Without sugar	50-gal. barrel	380	172
3 + 1 pack	do	425	193
2 + 1 pack	do	450	204
Blackberries	24-qt. crate	36	16.3
Bluegrass seed	Bushel	14–30	6.4–13.6
Broccoli	Wirebound crate	20–25	9.1–11.3

Commodity	Unit[1]	U.S. (Pounds)	Metric (Kilograms)
Broomcorn (6 bales per ton	Bale	333	151
Broomcorn seed	Bushel	44–50	20.0–22.7
Brussels sprouts	Drums	25	11.3
Buckwheat	Bushel	48	21.8
Butter	Box	64	29.0
Cabbage	Open mesh bag	50	22.7
	Wirebound crate[7]	50	22.7
	Western crate[8]	80	36.3
Cantaloupes	Jumbo crate[9]	83	37.6
Carrots:			
Without tops	Bushel	50	22.7
	Open mesh bag	50	22.7
Castor beans	Bushel	41	18.6
Castor oil	Gallon	[10]8	3.6
Cauliflower	W.G.A. crate	50–60	22.7–27.2
	Fiberboard box, wrapper leaves removed, film-wrapped, 2 layers	23–50	10.4–15.9
Celery	Crate[11]	60	27.2
Cherries	Lug (Campbell)[12]	16	7.3
	Lug	20	9.1
Clover seed	Bushel	60	27.2
Corn:			
Ear, husked	Bushel	[13]70	31.8
Shelled	do	56	25.4
Meal	do	50	22.7
Oil	Gallon	[10]7.7	3.5
Syrup	do	11.72	5.3

Commodity	Unit[1]	U.S. (Pounds)	Metric (Kilograms)
Sweet	Mesh or paper bag	45–50	20.4–22.7
	Wirebound crate	40–60	18.1–27.2
Cotton	Bale, gross	[14]500	227
	Bale, net	[14]480	218
Cottonseed	Bushel	[15]32	14.5
Cottonseed oil	Gallon	[10]7.7	3.5
Cowpeas	Bushel	60	27.2
Cranberries	Barrel	100	45.4
	1/4-bbl. box[16]	25	11.3
Cream, 40-percent butterfat	Gallon	8.38	3.80
Cucumbers	Bushel	48	21.8
Dewberries	24-qt. crate	36	16.3
Eggplant	Bushel	33	15.0
Eggs, average size	Case, 30 dozen	47.0	21.3
Escarole	Bushel	25	11.3
Figs, fresh	Box, single layer[17]	6	2.7
Flaxseed	Bushel	56	25.4
Flour, various	Bag	100	45.4
Grapefruit:			
Florida and Texas	1/2-box mesh bag	40	18.1
Florida	1 3/5 bu. box	85	38.6
Texas	1 2/5 bu. box	80	36.3
California Desert Valleys and Arizona	Box[18]	[19]64	29.0
	Carton[20]	32	14.5
California other than Desert Valleys	Box[18]	67	30.4
	Carton[20]	33 1/2	15.2

Weights and Measures

Commodity	Unit[1]	Approximate net weight U.S. (Pounds)	Approximate net weight Metric (Kilograms)
Grapes:			
Eastern	4-qt. climax basket	6	2.7
	12-qt. basket	18–20	8.2–9.1
	Lug[21]	28	12.7
Western	4-basket crate[22]	20	9.1
Hempseed	Bushel	44	20.0
Hickory nuts	do	50	22.7
Honey	Gallon	11.84	5.4
Honeydew melons	Jumbo crate[23]	44	20.0
Hops	Bale, gross	200	90.7
Horseradish roots	Bushel	35	15.9
	Barrel	100	45.4
Hungarian millet seed	Bushel	48 and 50	21.8–22.7
Kale	do	18	8.2
Kapok seed	do	35–40	15.9–18.1
Lard	Tierce	375	170
Lemons:			
California and Arizona	Box[24]	[19]76	34.5
	Carton[20]	38	17.2
Lentils	Bushel	60	27.2
Lettuce	Fiberboard box, carton	38–55	17.2–24.9
Lettuce hothouse	24-qt. basket	10	4.5
Limes (Florida)	Box	80	36.3
Linseed oil	Gallon	[10]7.7	3.5
Malt	Bushel	34	15.4
Maple syrup	Gallon	11.03	5.00
Meadow fescue seed	Bushel	24	10.9
Milk	Gallon	8.6	3.90
Millet	Bushel	48–50	21.8–22.7
Molasses, edible	Gallon	11.72	5.3
Molasses, inedible	do	11.74	5.3
Mustard seed	Bushel	58–60	26.3–27.2

Commodity	Unit[1]	Approximate net weight U.S. (Pounds)	Approximate net weight Metric (Kilograms)
Oats	do	32	14.5
Olives	Lug[21]	25–30	11.3–13.6
Olive oil	Gallon	[10]7.6	3.5
Onions, dry	Sack	50	22.7
Onions, green bunched	Crate	60–65	27.2–29.5
Onion sets	Bushel	28–32	12.7–14.5
Oranges:			
Florida and Texas	1/2-box mesh bag	45	20.4
	Box[25]	90	40.8
California and Arizona	Box[18]	[19]75	34.0
	Carton[20]	37 1/2	17.0
Orchardgrass seed	Bushel	14	6.4
Palm oil	Gallon	[10]7.7	3.5
Parsnips	Bushel	50	22.7
Peaches	do	48	21.8
	Lug box[21]	20	9.1
California fruit box		[26]18	8.2
Peanut oil	Gallon	[10]7.7	3.5
Peanuts, unshelled:			
Virginia type	Bushel	17	7.7
Runners, southeastern	do	21	9.5
Spanish: southeastern	do	25	11.3
southwestern	do	25	11.3
Timothy seed	Bushel	45	20.4
Tobacco:			
Maryland	Hogshead	775	352
Flue-cured	do	960	431
Burley	do	975	442
Dark air-cured	do	1,150	522

Commodity	Unit[1]	Approximate net weight U.S. (Pounds)	Approximate net weight Metric (Kilograms)
Virginia fire-cured	do	1,350	612
Kentucky and Tennessee fire-cured	do	1,500	680
Cigar-leaf	Case	250–365	113–166
	Bale	150–175	68.0–79.4
Tomatoes	Crate	60	27.2
	Lug box[21]	32	14.5
	2-layer flat	21	9.5
Tomatoes, hothouse	12-qt. basket	20	9.1
Pears:			
California	Bushel	48	21.8
Other	do	50	22.7
Western	Box[27]	46	20.9
Peas:			
Green, unshelled	Bushel	28–30	12.7–13.6
Dry	do	60	27.2
Pepper, green	do	25–30	11.3–13.6
	Fiberboard carton	30–34	13.6–15.4
Perilla seed	Bushel	37–40	16.8–18.1
Pineapples	Crate[28]	70	31.8
Plums and prunes:			
California	4-basket crate[29]	28–34	12.7–15.4
Other	1/2-bu. basket	28	12.7
Popcorn:			
On ear	Bushel	[13]70	31.8
Shelled	do	56	25.4
Poppy seed	do	46	20.9
Potatoes	Bushel	60	27.2
	Barrel	165	74.8
	Bag	50	22.7
	do	100	45.4
Quinces	Bushel	48	21.8
Rapeseed	do	50 and 60	22.7–27.2
Raspberries	24-qt. crate	36	16.3
Redtop seed	Bushel	50 and 60	22.7–27.2
Refiners' syrup	Gallon	11.45	5.2

Weights and Measures

Commodity	Unit[1]	Approximate net weight U.S.	Approximate net weight Metric
		Pounds	Kilograms
Rice:			
Rough	Bushel	45	2.04
	Bag	100	45.4
	Barrel	162	73.5
Milled	Pocket or bag	100	45.4
Rosin	Drum, net	520	236
Rutabagas	Bushel	56	25.4
Rye	do	56	25.4
Sesame seed	do	46	20.9
Shallots	Crate (4–7 doz. bunches)	20–35	9.1–15.9
Sorgo:			
Seed	Bushel	50	22.7
Syrup	Gallon	11.55	5.2
Sorghum grain[30]	Bushel	56	25.4
Soybeans	do	60	27.2
Soybean oil	Gallon	[10]7.7	3.5
Spelt	Bushel	40	18.1
Spinach	do	18–20	8.2–9.1
Strawberries	24-qt. crate	36	16.3
	12-pt. crate	9–11	4.1–5.0
Sudangrass seed	Bushel	40	18.1
Sugarcane syrup (sulfured or unsulfured)	Gallon	11.45	5.2
Sunflower seed	Bushel	24 and 32	10.9–14.5
Sweetpotatoes	do	[31]55	24.9
	Crate	50	22.7
Tangerines, Florida	4/5-bu. box	47 1/2	21.5
Tung oil	Gallon	[10]7.8	3.5
Turnips:			
Without tops	Mesh sack	50	22.7
Bunched	Crate[8]	70–80	31.8–36.3
Turpentine	Gallon	7.23	3.3
Velvetbeans (hulled)	Bushel	60	27.2
Vetch	do	60	27.2
Walnuts	do	50	22.7

Commodity	Unit[1]	Approximate net weight U.S.	Approximate net weight Metric
		Pounds	Kilograms
Water 60° F	Gallon	8.33	3.8
Watermelons	Melons of average or medium size	25	11.3
Wheat	Bushel	60	27.2
Various commodities	Short ton	2,000	907
	Long ton	2,240	1,016

To Convert from Avoirdupois Pounds

To	Multiply by
Kilograms	0.45359237
Quintals	0.0045359237
Metric tons	0.00045359237

Conversion Factors

Commodity	Unit	Approximate equivalent
Apples	1 pound dried	7 pounds fresh; beginning 1943, 8 pounds fresh
Do	1 pound chops	5 pounds fresh
Do	1 case canned [32]	1.4 bushels fresh
Applesauce	do [32]	1.2 bushels fresh
Apricots	1 pound dried	6 pounds fresh
Barley flour	100 pounds	4.59 bushels barley
Beans, lima	1 pound shelled	2 pounds unshelled
Beans, snap or wax	1 case canned [33]	0.008 ton fresh
Buckwheat flour	100 pounds	3.47 bushels buckwheat
Calves	1 pound live weight	0.557 pound dressed weight (1954–63 average)
Cattle	do	0.561 pound dressed weight (1954–63 average)
Cane syrup	1 gallon	5 pounds sugar
Cherries, tart	1 case canned [32]	0.023 ton fresh
Chickens	1 pound live weight	0.72 pound ready-to-cook weight
Corn, shelled	1 bushel (56 lbs.)	2 bushels (70 pounds of husked ear corn
Corn, sweet	1 case canned [33]	0.030 ton fresh
Cornmeal:		
Degermed	100 pounds	3.16 bushels corn, beginning 1946
Nondegermed	do	2 bushels corn, beginning 1946
Cotton	1 pound ginned	3.26 pounds seed cotton, including trash [34]
Cottonseed meal	1 pound	2.10 pounds cottonseed
Cottonseed oil	do	5.88 pounds cottonseed
Dairy products:		
Butter	do	21.1 pounds milk
Cheese	do	10 pounds milk
Condensed milk, whole	do	2.3 pounds milk
Dry cream	do	19 pounds milk
Dry milk, whole	do	7.6 pounds milk
Evaporated milk, whole	do	2.14 pounds milk
Malted milk	do	2.6 pounds milk
Nonfat dry milk	do	11 pounds liquid skim milk
Ice cream [35]	1 gallon	15 pounds milk
Ice cream [35] (eliminating fat from butter and concentrated milk)	do	12 pounds milk
Eggs	1 case	47 pounds
Eggs, shell	do	39.5 pounds frozen or liquid whole eggs
Do	do	10.3 pounds dried whole eggs
Figs	1 pound dried	3 pounds fresh in California; 4 pounds fresh elsewhere
Flaxseed	1 bushel	About 2½ gallons oil
Grapefruit, Florida	1 case canned juice [33]	0.64 box fresh fruit
Hogs	1 pound live weight	0.579 pound dressed weight, excluding lard (1954–63 average
Linseed meal	1 pound	1.51 pounds flaxseed
Linseed oil	do	2.77 pounds flaxseed
Malt	1 bushel (34 lbs.)	1 bushel barley (48 lbs.)
Maple sirup	1 gallon	8 pounds maple sugar
Nuts:		
Almonds imported	1 pound shelled	3⅓ pounds unshelled
Almonds, California	do	2.22 pounds unshelled through 1949; 2 pounds thereafter
Brazil	do	2 pounds unshelled
Cashews	do	4.55 pounds unshelled
Chestnuts	do	1.19 pounds unshelled
Filberts	do	2.22 pounds unshelled through 1949; 2.5 pounds thereafter
Pecans:		
Seedling	do	2.78 pounds unshelled
Improved	do	2.50 pounds unshelled
Pignolias	do	1.3 pounds unshelled
Pistachios	do	2 pounds unshelled
Walnuts:		
Black	do	5.88 pounds unshelled
Persian (English)	do	2.67 pounds unshelled
Oatmeal	100 pounds	7.6 bushels oats, beginning 1943
Oranges, Florida	1 case canned juice [33]	0.53 box fresh
Peaches, California, freestone	1 pound dried	5⅛ pounds fresh through 1918; 6 pounds fresh for 1919–28; and 6½ pounds fresh from 1929 to date
Peaches, California, clingstone	do	7½ pounds fresh
Peaches, clingstone	1 case canned [32]	1 bushel fresh
Do	do	0.0230 ton fresh
Peanuts	1 pound shelled	1½ pounds unshelled
Pears	1 pound dried	6½ pounds fresh
Pears, Bartlett	1 case canned [32]	1.1 bushels fresh
Do	do	0.026 ton fresh
Peas, green	1 pound shelled	2½ pounds unshelled
Do	1 case canned [33]	0.009 ton fresh (shelled)

Conversion Factors

Commodity	Unit	Approximate equivalent
Prunes	1 pound dried	2.7 pounds fresh in California; 3 to 4 pounds fresh elsewhere
Raisins	1 pound	4.3 pounds fresh grapes
Rice, milled (excluding brewers)	100 pounds	152 pounds rough or unhulled rice
Rye flour	do	2.23 bushels rye, beginning 1947
Sheep and lambs	1 pound live weight	0.482 pound dressed weight (1954–63 average)
Soybean meal	1 pound	1.27 pounds soybeans
Soybean oil	do	5.49 pounds soybeans
Sugar	1 ton raw	0.9346 ton refined
Tobacco	1 pound farm-sales weight	Various weights of stemmed and unstemmed, according to aging and the type of tobacco. (See circular 435, U.S. Dept. of Agr.)
Tomatoes	1 case canned[33]	0.018 ton fresh
Turkeys	1 pound live weight	0.80 pound ready-to-cook weight
Wheat flour	100 pounds	2.30 bushels wheat[36]
Wool, domestic apparel shorn	1 pound greasy	0.48 pound scoured
Wool, domestic apparel pulled	do	0.73 pound scoured

[1]Standard bushel used in the United States contains 2,150.42 cubic inches; the gallon, 231 cubic inches; the cranberry barrel, 5,826 cubic inches; and the standard fruit and vegetable barrel, 7,056 cubic inches. Such large-sized products as apples and potatoes sometimes are sold on the basis of a heaped bushel, which would exceed somewhat the 2,150.42 cubic inches of a bushel basket level full. This also applies to such products as sweet potatoes, peaches, green beans, green peas, spinach, etc.

[2]Approximate inside dimensions, $10\frac{1}{2}$ by $11\frac{1}{2}$ by 18 inches.

[3]Approximate inside dimensions, $4\frac{5}{8}$ by $12\frac{1}{2}$ by $16\frac{1}{8}$ inches.

[4]Approximate inside dimensions, $4\frac{1}{2}$ by 16 by $16\frac{1}{8}$ inches.

[5]Approximate dimensions, $4\frac{1}{2}$ by $13\frac{1}{2}$ by $16\frac{1}{8}$ inches.

[6]Approximate inside dimensions, 13 by 12 by 32 inches.

[7]Inside dimensions vary. Common sizes are 13 by 13 by $22\frac{1}{8}$ inches, and 13 by $15\frac{1}{8}$ by 23 inches.

[8]Approximate inside dimensions, 13 by 18 by $21\frac{5}{8}$ inches.

[9]Approximate inside dimensions, 13 by 13 by $22\frac{1}{8}$ inches.

[10]This is the weight commonly used in trade practices, the actual weight varying according to temperature conditions.

[11]Approximate inside dimensions, $9\frac{3}{4}$ by 16 by 20 inches.

[12]Approximate inside dimensions, $4\frac{1}{8}$ by $11\frac{1}{2}$ by 14 inches.

[13]The standard weight of 70 pounds is usually recognized as being about 2 measured bushels of corn, husked, on the ear, because it required 70 pounds to yield 1 bushel, or 56 pounds, of shelled corn.

[14]For statistical purposes the bale of cotton is 500 pounds or 480 pounds net weight. Prior to Aug. 1, 1946, the net weight was estimated at 478 pounds. Actual bale weights vary considerably, and the customary average weights of bales of foreign cotton differ from that of the American square bale.

[15]This is the average weight of cottonseed, although the legal weight in some States varies from this figure of 32 pounds.

[16]Approximate inside dimensions, $9\frac{1}{4}$ by $10\frac{1}{2}$ by 15 inches.

[17]Approximate inside dimensions, $1\frac{3}{4}$ by 11 by $16\frac{1}{8}$ inches.

[18]Approximate inside dimensions, $11\frac{1}{2}$ by $11\frac{1}{2}$ by 24 inches.

[19]In California and Arizona from 1942 through 1953, the net weights as used by this Department were 77 pounds for oranges, 79 pounds for lemons, and 65 pounds for Desert Valleys grapefruit. Grapefruit in California areas, other than the Desert Valleys, averaged 68 pounds. The new weights effective in 1954 reflect the shift from the "box" to the $\frac{1}{2}$-box carton as the container used.

[20]Approximate inside dimensions $10\frac{1}{4}$ by $10\frac{11}{16}$ by $16\frac{3}{8}$ inches for oranges or lemons, and $9\frac{3}{4}$ by $10\frac{11}{16}$ by $16\frac{3}{8}$ for grapefruit.

[21]Approximate inside dimensions, $5\frac{3}{4}$ by $13\frac{1}{2}$ by $16\frac{1}{8}$ inches.

[22]Approximate inside dimensions, $4\frac{3}{4}$ by 16 by $16\frac{1}{8}$ inches.

[23]Approximate inside dimensions, $7\frac{3}{4}$ by 16 by $21\frac{7}{8}$ inches.

[24]Approximate inside dimensions, $9\frac{7}{8}$ by 13 by 25 inches.

[25]Approximate inside dimensions 12 by 12 by 24 inches.

[26]Approximate inside dimensions vary. Common size is $4\frac{1}{2}$ by $11\frac{1}{2}$ by $16\frac{1}{8}$ inches.

[27]Approximate inside dimensions, $8\frac{1}{2}$ by $11\frac{1}{2}$ by 18 inches.

[28]Approximate inside dimensions, 12 by $10\frac{1}{2}$ by 33 inches.

[29]Inside dimensions vary. Ranges from 4 by 16 by $16\frac{1}{8}$ inches to 6 by 16 by $16\frac{1}{8}$ inches.

[30]Includes both sorghum grain (kafir, milo, hegari, etc.) and sweet sorghum varieties.

[31]This average of 55 pounds indicates the usual weight of sweet potatoes when harvested. Much weight is lost in curing or drying and the net weight when sold in terminal markets may be below 55 pounds.

[32]Case of 24 No. $2\frac{1}{2}$ cans.

[33]Case of 24 No. 303 cans.

[34]Varies widely by method of harvesting.

[35]The milk equivalent of ice cream per gallon is 15 pounds. Reports from plants indicate about 81 percent of the butterfat in ice cream is from milk and cream, the remainder being from butter and concentrated milk. Thus the milk equivalent of the milk and cream in a gallon of ice cream is about 12 pounds.

[36]This is equivalent to 4.51 bushels of wheat per barrel (196 pounds) of flour and has been used in conversions, beginning July 1, 1957. Because of changes in milling processes, the following factors per barrel of flour have been used for earlier periods: 1790–1879, 5 bushels; 1880–1908, 4.75 bushels; 1909–17, 4.7 bushels; 1918 and 1919, 4.5 bushels; 1920, 4.6 bushels; 1921–44, 4.7 bushels; July 1944–Feb. 1946, 4.57 bushels; March 1946–Oct. 1946, average was about 4.31 bushels; and Nov. 1946–June 1957, 4.57 bushels.

Afterword
A Personal Note

While writing this book I was living in the country on an eighteenth-century American colonial farm, secluded in the midst of a large state park. The house was completed in stages between 1705 and about 1836, and steadily improved or maintained until the late 1940's, when it began a rather downhill slide toward oblivion. This skid was stopped (or accelerated, depending on your point of view) by the present trustees of the property. Plumbing and electricity and heaters were removed; floors, window and door frames were ripped out, walls removed. New life was breathed into this skeleton by craftsmen who fleshed out the structure with eighteenth-century handiwork. In effect, the house was restored to the rugged "charms" of the 1780's. Even the animals and crops became colonial; longhorn Devons replaced Jerseys; flax, corn, potatoes, winter wheat, rye, and barley replaced the single crop of corn. A quarter-acre kitchen garden, a root cellar, springhouse, and carriage barn complete with blacksmith's forge all appeared out of ruins. To make the mirage complete, people appeared in colonial outfit and proceeded to plant, weed, harvest, bake, preserve, churn, and laugh. The farm became a living history museum on weekends. I was the twentieth-century watchperson living in a secluded section of the second and third floors. Most of the time, there was no one present at the farm except friends and the animals.

Some of the big questions that permeated my farm life were things like—will the cord of wood that I use in my wood heater last through the winter? (As it turned out, it was gone by the end of January because of the severe cold.) When will Oriander the cow have her calf? (Right in the middle of that same cold spell.) and Shall I go for a long or short walk over the creek and around the hill and will I see deer again? (Yes to both.)

During the days, I left the eighteenth century in the country and worked in the big city in what often seemed to me to be the twenty-first century. Because this book deals with the world's food problems and what we can do about them, it necessarily deals with the future; and the twenty-first century is as close to us as the Eisenhower and Kennedy eras, the breaking of the four-minute mile, Sputnik, the nuclear-powered submarine, and the development of the transistor. Here, the big questions were entirely different; larger in scope, more complex, and harder to ask and answer. The constant juxtaposition of the two extremes of time frames and environments continues to be a delightful and enlivening experience that helped enormously to put a context on all aspects of my work. Experiencing first-hand some of the energy-efficient colonial farming practices that were replaced by our energy-intensive agribusiness taught me a lot about how our present system of accounting became too specialized. Experiencing the incredibly hard work of plowing a field with a horse and an iron-tipped wood plow made me realize in ways I never could before the immense strides we've taken with modern machinery. The romance of "country life" disappears as quickly as sweat or a toothache appears, but the respect for and awe of Nature only increases. The romance of dealing with the "future" or tackling "global problems" disappears as quickly as the first information overload and contradicting statistics, but the wonder and excitement of getting to know your planet only increases. The ebb and flow of the creek as it swells with rain, of country living and city working, of eighteenth-century home and heart life and twenty-first-century mind life engendered many thoughts, feelings, astonishments, and respects.

This book, as is probably every book, was the effort of an environment in search of a consciousness; writing it was filled with questions, a humble respect for the vast complexity of our global problems, the rich past from which we all grew, and a love for the growing consciousness of our collective home, the Earth. I feel that once any project like this book is "finished," it can always be done better, and this book is, to say the least, no exception. My main hope, here on the last page, is that you will let me know about the mistakes that I have made; that at least one insight into the incredible complexity of our world's problems or at least one additional option someone didn't know we had has been demonstrated in the preceding pages; and that we have come a step closer to the time when the end of starvation and hunger on our planet is at hand.

Medard Gabel

Conversion Factors

Commodity	Unit	Approximate equivalent
Prunes	1 pound dried	2.7 pounds fresh in California; 3 to 4 pounds fresh elsewhere
Raisins	1 pound	4.3 pounds fresh grapes
Rice, milled (excluding brewers)	100 pounds	152 pounds rough or unhulled rice
Rye flour	do	2.23 bushels rye, beginning 1947
Sheep and lambs	1 pound live weight	0.482 pound dressed weight (1954–63 average)
Soybean meal	1 pound	1.27 pounds soybeans
Soybean oil	do	5.49 pounds soybeans
Sugar	1 ton raw	0.9346 ton refined
Tobacco	1 pound farm-sales weight	Various weights of stemmed and unstemmed, according to aging and the type of tobacco. (See circular 435, U.S. Dept. of Agr.)
Tomatoes	1 case canned[33]	0.018 ton fresh
Turkeys	1 pound live weight	0.80 pound ready-to-cook weight
Wheat flour	100 pounds	2.30 bushels wheat[36]
Wool, domestic apparel shorn	1 pound greasy	0.48 pound scoured
Wool, domestic apparel pulled	do	0.73 pound scoured

[1]Standard bushel used in the United States contains 2,150.42 cubic inches; the gallon, 231 cubic inches; the cranberry barrel, 5,826 cubic inches; and the standard fruit and vegetable barrel, 7,056 cubic inches. Such large-sized products as apples and potatoes sometimes are sold on the basis of a heaped bushel, which would exceed somewhat the 2,150.42 cubic inches of a bushel basket level full. This also applies to such products as sweet potatoes, peaches, green beans, green peas, spinach, etc.

[2]Approximate inside dimensions, 10 1/2 by 11 1/2 by 18 inches.

[3]Approximate inside dimensions, 4 5/8 by 12 1/2 by 16 1/8 inches.

[4]Approximate inside dimensions, 4 1/2 by 16 by 16 1/8 inches.

[5]Approximate dimensions, 4 1/2 by 13 1/2 by 16 1/8 inches.

[6]Approximate inside dimensions, 13 by 12 by 32 inches.

[7]Inside dimensions vary. Common sizes are 13 by 13 by 22 1/8 inches, and 13 by 15 1/8 by 23 inches.

[8]Approximate inside dimensions, 13 by 18 by 21 5/8 inches.

[9]Approximate inside dimensions, 13 by 13 by 22 1/8 inches.

[10]This is the weight commonly used in trade practices, the actual weight varying according to temperature conditions.

[11]Approximate inside dimensions, 9 3/4 by 16 by 20 inches.

[12]Approximate inside dimensions, 4 1/8 by 11 1/2 by 14 inches.

[13]The standard weight of 70 pounds is usually recognized as being about 2 measured bushels of corn, husked, on the ear, because it required 70 pounds to yield 1 bushel, or 56 pounds, of shelled corn.

[14]For statistical purposes the bale of cotton is 500 pounds or 480 pounds net weight. Prior to Aug. 1, 1946, the net weight was estimated at 478 pounds. Actual bale weights vary considerably, and the customary average weights of bales of foreign cotton differ from that of the American square bale.

[15]This is the average weight of cottonseed, although the legal weight in some States varies from this figure of 32 pounds.

[16]Approximate inside dimensions, 9 1/4 by 10 1/2 by 15 inches.

[17]Approximate inside dimensions, 1 3/4 by 11 by 16 1/8 inches.

[18]Approximate inside dimensions, 11 1/2 by 11 1/2 by 24 inches.

[19]In California and Arizona from 1942 through 1953, the net weights as used by this Department were 77 pounds for oranges, 79 pounds for lemons, and 65 pounds for Desert Valleys grapefruit. Grapefruit in California areas, other than the Desert Valleys, averaged 68 pounds. The new weights effective in 1954 reflect the shift from the "box" to the 1/2-box carton as the container used.

[20]Approximate inside dimensions 10 1/4 by 10 11/16 by 16 3/8 inches for oranges or lemons, and 9 3/4 by 10 11/16 by 16 3/8 for grapefruit.

[21]Approximate inside dimensions, 5 3/4 by 13 1/2 by 16 1/8 inches.

[22]Approximate inside dimensions, 4 3/4 by 16 by 16 1/8 inches.

[23]Approximate inside dimensions, 7 3/4 by 16 by 21 7/8 inches.

[24]Approximate inside dimensions, 9 7/8 by 13 by 25 inches.

[25]Approximate inside dimensions 12 by 12 by 24 inches.

[26]Approximate inside dimensions vary. Common size is 4 1/2 by 11 1/2 by 16 1/8 inches.

[27]Approximate inside dimensions, 8 1/2 by 11 1/2 by 18 inches.

[28]Approximate inside dimensions, 12 by 10 1/2 by 33 inches.

[29]Inside dimensions vary. Ranges from 4 by 16 by 16 1/8 inches to 6 by 16 by 16 1/8 inches.

[30]Includes both sorghum grain (kafir, milo, hegari, etc.) and sweet sorghum varieties.

[31]This average of 55 pounds indicates the usual weight of sweet potatoes when harvested. Much weight is lost in curing or drying and the net weight when sold in terminal markets may be below 55 pounds.

[32]Case of 24 No. 2 1/2 cans.

[33]Case of 24 No. 303 cans.

[34]Varies widely by method of harvesting.

[35]The milk equivalent of ice cream per gallon is 15 pounds. Reports from plants indicate about 81 percent of the butterfat in ice cream is from milk and cream, the remainder being from butter and concentrated milk. Thus the milk equivalent of the milk and cream in a gallon of ice cream is about 12 pounds.

[36]This is equivalent to 4.51 bushels of wheat per barrel (196 pounds) of flour and has been used in conversions, beginning July 1, 1957. Because of changes in milling processes, the following factors per barrel of flour have been used for earlier periods: 1790–1879, 5 bushels; 1880–1908, 4.75 bushels; 1909–17, 4.7 bushels; 1918 and 1919, 4.5 bushels; 1920, 4.6 bushels; 1921–44, 4.7 bushels; July 1944–Feb. 1946, 4.57 bushels; March 1946–Oct. 1946, average was about 4.31 bushels; and Nov. 1946–June 1957, 4.57 bushels.

Afterword
A Personal Note

While writing this book I was living in the country on an eighteenth-century American colonial farm, secluded in the midst of a large state park. The house was completed in stages between 1705 and about 1836, and steadily improved or maintained until the late 1940's, when it began a rather downhill slide toward oblivion. This skid was stopped (or accelerated, depending on your point of view) by the present trustees of the property. Plumbing and electricity and heaters were removed; floors, window and door frames were ripped out, walls removed. New life was breathed into this skeleton by craftsmen who fleshed out the structure with eighteenth-century handiwork. In effect, the house was restored to the rugged "charms" of the 1780's. Even the animals and crops became colonial; longhorn Devons replaced Jerseys; flax, corn, potatoes, winter wheat, rye, and barley replaced the single crop of corn. A quarter-acre kitchen garden, a root cellar, springhouse, and carriage barn complete with blacksmith's forge all appeared out of ruins. To make the mirage complete, people appeared in colonial outfit and proceeded to plant, weed, harvest, bake, preserve, churn, and laugh. The farm became a living history museum on weekends. I was the twentieth-century watchperson living in a secluded section of the second and third floors. Most of the time, there was no one present at the farm except friends and the animals.

Some of the big questions that permeated my farm life were things like—will the cord of wood that I use in my wood heater last through the winter? (As it turned out, it was gone by the end of January because of the severe cold.) When will Oriander the cow have her calf? (Right in the middle of that same cold spell.) and Shall I go for a long or short walk over the creek and around the hill and will I see deer again? (Yes to both.)

During the days, I left the eighteenth century in the country and worked in the big city in what often seemed to me to be the twenty-first century. Because this book deals with the world's food problems and what we can do about them, it necessarily deals with the future; and the twenty-first century is as close to us as the Eisenhower and Kennedy eras, the breaking of the four-minute mile, Sputnik, the nuclear-powered submarine, and the development of the transistor. Here, the big questions were entirely different; larger in scope, more complex, and harder to ask and answer. The constant juxtaposition of the two extremes of time frames and environments continues to be a delightful and enlivening experience that helped enormously to put a context on all aspects of my work. Experiencing first-hand some of the energy-efficient colonial farming practices that were replaced by our energy-intensive agribusiness taught me a lot about how our present system of accounting became too specialized. Experiencing the incredibly hard work of plowing a field with a horse and an iron-tipped wood plow made me realize in ways I never could before the immense strides we've taken with modern machinery. The romance of "country life" disappears as quickly as sweat or a toothache appears, but the respect for and awe of Nature only increases. The romance of dealing with the "future" or tackling "global problems" disappears as quickly as the first information overload and contradicting statistics, but the wonder and excitement of getting to know your planet only increases. The ebb and flow of the creek as it swells with rain, of country living and city working, of eighteenth-century home and heart life and twenty-first-century mind life engendered many thoughts, feelings, astonishments, and respects.

This book, as is probably every book, was the effort of an environment in search of a consciousness; writing it was filled with questions, a humble respect for the vast complexity of our global problems, the rich past from which we all grew, and a love for the growing consciousness of our collective home, the Earth. I feel that once any project like this book is "finished," it can always be done better, and this book is, to say the least, no exception. My main hope, here on the last page, is that you will let me know about the mistakes that I have made; that at least one insight into the incredible complexity of our world's problems or at least one additional option someone didn't know we had has been demonstrated in the preceding pages; and that we have come a step closer to the time when the end of starvation and hunger on our planet is at hand.

Medard Gabel